WHERE RIVERS
AND MOUNTAINS
SING

WHERE RIVERS AND MOUNTAINS SING

~

SOUND, MUSIC, AND NOMADISM
IN TUVA AND BEYOND

NEW EDITION

Theodore Levin

with Valentina Süzükei

INDIANA UNIVERSITY PRESS

This book is a publication of

Indiana University Press
Office of Scholarly Publishing
Herman B Wells Library 350
1320 East 10th Street
Bloomington, Indiana 47405 USA

iupress.indiana.edu

New edition 2019

The Library of Congress has cataloged the original edition as follows:

Levin, Theodore Craig.
   Where rivers and mountains sing : sound, music, and nomadism in
Tuva and beyond / Theodore Levin with Valentina Süzükei.
      p. cm.
   Includes bibliographical references and index.
   ISBN 0-253-34715-7 (cloth : alk. paper) 1. Folk music—Russia (Federation)—
Tuva—History and criticism. 2. Throat singing—Russia (Federation)—
Tuva—History and criticism. 3. Tuvinians—Rites and ceremonies. 4. Music,
Influence of. 5. Ethnomusicology. I. Süzükei, Valentina. II. Title.
   ML3680.7.T9L48 2006
781.62'94330575—d   2005022438

ISBN 978-0-253-04471-6 (New ed.)

1 2 3 4 5   24 23 22 21 20 19

TO NAT

CONTENTS

PREFACE

The word "civilization" is charged with moral and ethical
overtones, the accumulated inheritance of our own self-esteem.
We contrast it with barbarism, savagery, and even bestiality,
whereas it means nothing more than "living in cities."

—Bruce Chatwin,
"The Nomadic Alternative"

In recent years, nomads have taken their place among the subversive heroes of modernity. For the burgeoning percentage of humans yoked to computers, cellphones, and mechanized transport, pastoral nomadism may have come to symbolize the last vestige of a lost innocence—a freedom and intuitive closeness to the natural world from which our technology-laden lives have distanced us. Ironically, this collective nostalgia is nourished by a highly sophisticated "vanishing cultures" industry that is itself very much a product of technology. Nomad-centered coffee-table books, photojournalist essays, television documentaries, and the occasional cult film or travelogue by turn elicit admiration, guilt, sympathy, and horror.[1] The nomadic heroes of travelogues and coffee-table books, however, are silent nomads, and the wondrous sound world to which their expressive culture is so intimately linked has had little airing, even in media ideally configured to represent it.

This work strives to represent the voices of musicians and sound artists whose remarkable art and craft are rooted in Inner Asian nomadism. The book's central focus is the relationship between nomadic music and sound-making and the natural and social environments that have shaped them. I distinguish sound from music at the outset because many of the sound-making practices discussed in the book are not considered to be music by those who practice them. Moreover, none of the Turkic and Mongolian languages and dialects in Inner Asia has a word that encompasses the diverse practices and concepts covered by the English word "music." Rather, particular categories and techniques of sound-making each have their own names. These names, categories, and techniques bring into focus the finely honed acuity of the nomadic sensorium and the deep respect for the natural world that imbues nomadic sound-making with a sacred quality.

Offerings to spirits, blessings, praise-songs, and rituals of healing and purification are core elements of nomadic expressive culture. All of them exemplify what I call "sound mimesis"—the use of sound to represent and interact with the natural environment and the living creatures that inhabit it. This mimetic impulse also appears in a variety of narrative forms. Epic tales as long as thirty times the length of Homer's *Iliad*, and instrumental pieces whose wordless melodies and rhythms relate beloved stories, all reflect a nomadic spirituality. In passing from one generation to the next, this spirituality has been actively reshaped and reanimated wherever nomadism, or the cultural memory of nomadism, is alive.

Existing studies of music in Inner Asia typically use contemporary national identities or political boundaries as templates for documenting musical styles and repertories, for example, *Tuvan Folk Music, Kyrgyz Folk Musical Art,* and *Mongolian Music, Dance, and Oral Narrative.*[2] Yet as I learned during more than a decade of music research in Uzbekistan and Tajikistan, such templates tend to be either too large or too small to represent the musical richness of a region both united and divided by its complex history of ethnic migration and intermingling.[3] The featured actors of *Where Rivers and Mountains Sing* come from different nations, speak different languages, and represent the worldviews of different generations. Their musical practices illustrate continuities as well as ruptures of repertory, style, and sensibility that are incongruent with present-day political boundaries. My aim has been to cross these boundaries—literally and figuratively—to look at Inner Asia from a broader perspective that illuminates links among ethnohistory, physical environment, and sound-making.

My own interest in nomads—or "mobile pastoralists," as they have recently been renamed by scholars in search of a more rigorous nomenclature[4]—arose not as a result of any epiphany, but gradually, and by accident. As a musician, and later, a musical ethnographer, I was educated in the musical and pedagogic traditions of sedentary societies, first in the West and later in Central Asia. After studying piano and European music history, I traveled east in the 1970s and became immersed in the art music traditions of the Islamic world. As I read learned treatises by medieval Muslim scholars amid the urban bustle of Tashkent, Uzbekistan and stood awestruck before the great architectural monuments of Samarkand and Bukhara, the nomadic world seemed far beyond the horizon—and indeed, it was. The distance was not only geographic, but conceptual. For my urbane colleagues schooled in Central Asia's stormy history, the devastating thirteenth-century Mongol conquests seemed all too fresh, and nomads remained unrepentant barbarians. As for nomadic music, a typical view was expressed by an acquaintance, a virtuoso performer of Persian classical music, who said, "Nomads have no civilization; they have no music."

It was in Tuva (or Tyva), an isolated swath of south Siberian grasslands, mountains, and boreal forest far northeast of Central Asia, where I had my first encounter with the world of pastoral nomads—or what was left of them after decades of Soviet social engineering that favored and often forced a sedentary life on nomadic groups.[5] In 1987 I had wangled an assignment from *National Geographic* magazine to travel to Tuva with a photographer and produce an article about the miraculous vocal technique whose Tuvan name, *xöömei*, is usually translated into English as "throat-singing" (the *Geographic* never published the article). In throat-singing, a single vocalist can simultaneously produce two distinct pitches by selectively amplifying harmonics naturally present in the voice.

In the mid-1980s throat-singing was all but unknown in the West, and Tuva, an autonomous republic within the Soviet Union, was a destination diplomatically off-limits to Americans.[6] I knew little about throat-singing other than that it was a musical and physiological wonder and that I wanted to meet people who were able to do it.[7] What I did not expect to discover in Tuva was that throat-singing was only the most visible—or rather, audible—point of entry into a vast realm where music, music-making, and music cognition were attuned to a nomadic understanding of sound and its place in the world. This understanding was nowhere written down, nowhere codified as a theory. But it wasn't secret or esoteric. On the contrary, it was embodied in knowledge and experience so utterly ordinary among the pastoralists that it was difficult for them to talk about—like explaining how to tie shoes. Only by deeply sharing their life could one begin to fathom the motivating principles and ideas that lay behind their music. But that wasn't easy.

My first explorations of music in Tuva in 1987 were treated by the local government as a challenge to create a Potemkin village that would conceal much of what I was searching for behind the facade of official performing troupes and choreographed presentations. Working with Moscow-based folklorist Eduard Alekseyev, chairman of the U.S.S.R.'s All-Union Folklore Commission, and Tuvan musicologist Zoya Kyrgys, of the Tuvan Institute for History, Language, and Literature, I was able to collect enough material during two month-long expeditions to release a recording in 1990 that provided an initial glimpse into the Tuvan sound world.[8] Beginning in 1995, I returned almost annually to Tuva and later traveled to other parts of the south Siberian Altai region—western Mongolia, Xakasia, the Altai Republic—and to Kyrgyzstan and Kazakhstan, where nomadic heritage is being newly celebrated as a focal point of national identity (see maps pp. xxvi–xxvii).

Throughout my Inner Asian travels, Tuva has remained a core focus of interest for reasons both personal and professional. My visit to Tuva in 1987 marked the first time that a researcher from the West had been given permission to study Tuvan music in situ. Since then, my affection and respect for the place, its people, and its music has continued to grow, and with each visit, I have ventured more deeply into the music and the social and natural environment that has nourished it. At the same time, the remarkable worldwide circulation of Tuvan music over the past fifteen years has become a story in itself. Almost from the beginning of my visits, Tuvan music has been traveling far beyond the borders of the Altai. Music from Tuva and, increasingly, from other parts of nomadic Inner Asia has taken on a globalized life of its own, and to write an ethnography of this music that ignores its worldly adventures would be to leave out an essential part of the story.

These days if you are traveling to Tuva to study music, you're likely to find that Tuva's famous throat-singers are all away on tour. Folk music has become Tuva's best-known export product, and possibly its most lucrative. The savvy ethnographer will have telephoned or e-mailed his musical friends far in advance to ensure that they are back in Tuva awaiting his arrival, and that they stay put long enough to run through a few songs and tunes before flying off to their next engagement in Los Angeles, London, or Athens. Or alternatively, one can simply tag along with the musicians. The field, as I have learned, is wherever the music is.

The urban nomadism represented by the travels of musicians from Tuva and other parts of Inner Asia is not simply a postmodern calque of ancient cultural patterns of migration, emigration, or diaspora. Rather, globe-trotting Tuvan musicians—and they are of course only a tiny subset of Tuvans generally—represent a new form of cultural equipoise in which they simultaneously inhabit two worlds. Like middle-class Americans, these musicians drive cars, own cellphones, and have passports. They are knowledgeable about Western music—from Mozart to Miles Davis—and they're interested in exploring the potential meeting points of Western traditions with their own. But they are not on a linear trajectory that is carrying them from a traditional way of life to a postmodern one. On the contrary, their working lives take them constantly back and forth. Many were trained on Western musical instruments and gradually worked their way backward toward their own cultural roots, making them what one could call "neotraditionalists."

These days, shamans in Tuva read Carlos Castaneda and present workshops in Mill Valley, California. In a remote region of western Mongolia, a throat-singing master awaits a helicopter full of Japanese tourists. Yesterday's "informants" are today's Internet mavens. How could I have imagined upon first alighting in Tuva that, a decade-and-a-half later, I'd be e-mailing with one of the shy musicians who was trotted out in his colorful silk robe and pointed hat to demonstrate throat-singing for an errant American? Being a world music performer these days demands extraordinary inner strength as well as flexibility—musical, emotional, and psychological. It is only a little more than a decade since Tuvan music came to the West, yet there are already too many tragic stories of talented young singers who couldn't play the Janus-like game that being a Tuvan musician now demands—young musicians who left this earth at the height of their powers.

For an outsider coming to learn about music in the Altai region—not only in Tuva but also in neighboring western Mongolia, Xakasia, and the Altai Republic—the conditions I have described create a field fraught with sensitivities. What right does an outsider have to come from far away with the intention of exporting and exploiting—even in the best sense of the word—an individual's or group's intellectual property, as contemporary jurisprudence would now define what used to be called "traditional knowledge"? What is the exchange value of such knowledge? And what about locally based professional colleagues who serve as culture brokers, providing access to musicians, putting their own credibility on the line, offering invaluable explanations, interpretations, translations? What obligations does an outsider assume to help insider colleagues join the global economy of scholarship: travel to conferences, opportunities for research stipends, access to English-language publishing?

The only sensible way to do ethnographic research is collaboratively, and I have had the greatest of fortune to work with a fellow ethnographer from Tuva, Valentina Süzükei, who is at once an outstanding intellect, intrepid fieldworker, and delightful traveling companion (see plate 1). My outsider perspective is balanced by her insider knowledge and experience, and her important contribution merited recognition in the authorship of this work. Though I have written *Where Rivers and Mountains Sing* in its entirety, the ideas presented in the first section of chapter 3, "Timbre-Centered Music," are almost entirely Valentina Süzükei's, and these ideas resonate in other parts of the book as well (though the conversations recorded in the text were in Russian, Valentina reads English well and approved the final version of all textual accounts of these conversations).[9]

The kaleidoscopic musical world that is everyday fare for musicians from Tuva begs for a form of ethnographic description that can adequately represent it. How to convey the creative tensions that both inspire and bedevil those who move back and forth between their own communities and the West, between a sense of place and the jarring effect of displacement? Rather than generalize, my solution has been to particularize—to build the text of *Where Rivers and Mountains Sing* around a select group of these musical road warriors. Beginning in the early 1990s, I hitched myself to Huun-Huur-Tu, the four-man ensemble from Tuva whose picaresque travels have carried Tuvan music around the world in forms both traditional and contemporary—and, at times, futuristic. These are the travels depicted in the ethnographic snapshots that open the book, illustrating the sometimes bizarre effects of radical cultural decontextualization.

For a glimpse of Huun-Huur-Tu in the United States, see the video files online, track 1, "Huun-Huur-Tu on the Road."

Back in Tuva, the text zooms in on members of Huun-Huur-Tu on their own turf, and then arcs backward to the Soviet era, when Tuvan music succumbed to the Procrustean schemes of Soviet cultural policies aimed at modernizing and Russifying the expressive traditions of Asian peoples. Picking up in the early post-Soviet years, the text follows Huun-Huur-Tu and other musicians as they illustrate the multiple ways in which Inner Asian pastoralists have used sound and music—prominent among them, throat-singing—to represent and interact with the physical, biological, and spiritual habitat of the Altai region. The middle part of the book surveys various forms of sound mimesis and looks at the central role of animals in the nomadic soundscape. Completing the circle, the last chapter consists of a series of personal encounters with tradition-bearers that depict the tensions between renascent forms of expressive culture, which are rooted in beliefs about animistic spirituality, and the forces of the cultural marketplace that are dominated by Western tastes and capital.

Throughout the book, musicians speak in their own voices and address readers directly. Authors, of course, maintain editorial control over the voices in their texts, and in representing these voices, I have made every attempt to ensure the accuracy of quotations. Most of what is quoted was transcribed from audio recordings or written down directly in notebooks or on a laptop computer, and subsequently translated into English. Though I am a neophyte videographer, wherever possible I have included online access to video clips in order to share with readers the extraordinary visual interest of nomadic performance traditions, in particular, those involving gesture, narration, and movement. I hope that the inherent value of the material will compensate for its technical shortcomings.

As drafts of this work have been written and rewritten, read and reread, I have been asked by readers—and often asked myself—in what tense I mean to be writing. Do the forms of nomadic knowledge and traditions described by the book's actors belong to the present, the past, or both? Providing an answer is complicated because the actors themselves are frequently inconsistent or vague about whether certain practices exist, have disappeared, or exist more in cultural memory than in reality. In the end, though, notwithstanding the ubiquitous discourse of "endangerment" that surrounds present-day representations of nomads, I have emerged from this project a musical optimist. Wherever I traveled, I met musicians who have contributed generously to the resilience of the nomadic spirit amid grave social, economic, and environmental challenges. Moreover, the nomadic imagination's ingenious transformation of landscape and soundscape into music can surely inspire not only pastoralists. For the rest of us, such music may provide a moment of clarity that connects us to our collective past—and if we listen carefully enough, to a future more in harmony with the environment that sustains our planet's fragile experiment with human life.

ACKNOWLEDGMENTS

The travels, research, and conversations that became this book cover nearly two decades, and during that time I have accumulated many debts of gratitude both to organizations and individuals. It is a pleasure to acknowledge them here, not only to express appreciation for generous help and support but also to illustrate the highly collaborative nature of this project.

Most of all, I am indebted to the many musicians whose names appear in the following pages for so graciously sharing their knowledge, talent, and ideas. I feel privileged and blessed to have been entrusted to represent their voices.

My first visits to Tuva in 1987 and 1988 were made possible by an assignment from *National Geographic* magazine. Smithsonian Folkways released the recordings gathered during those visits and supported a second Tuvan recording project in 1998. Twelve of those recordings appear in the audio and video files online, and I thank Smithsonian Folkways for licensing them back to me.

For support of field research and writing, I am grateful to the following organizations: the John Sloane Dickey Center for International Understanding at Dartmouth College, the Ford Foundation, and, in particular, Ken Wilson; the International Research and Exchanges Board (IREX), the National Endowment for the Humanities, the National Geographic Committee for Research and Exploration, the Silk Road Project, the Trust for Mutual Understanding, and the Jasper and Marion Whiting Foundation. Valentina Süzükei and I both thank the Rockefeller Foundation's Bellagio Study and Conference Center, which provided the opportunity to work collaboratively in its idyllic facilities, and also Dartmouth's Dickey Center for the opportunity to work collaboratively at Dartmouth. Field research in Kyrgyzstan and Kazakhstan was seamlessly interwoven with my work as a consultant to the Aga Khan Music Initiative in Central Asia, a program of the Aga Khan Trust for Culture. I thank the Music Initiative and in particular, its director, Fairouz Nishanova, for enthusiastic help and support.

This project connected me to many wonderful colleagues and friends who joined my own nomadic peregrinations to study and document music. For all that they so generously gave to our collective work, I thank Eduard Alekseyev, Sayan Bapa, Erdenechimig, Bill Gaspirini, Joel Gordon, David Harrison, Stefan Kamola, Anatoli Kuular, Zoya Kyrgys, Peter Marsh, Nurlanbek Nyshanov, Liesbet Nyssen, Sansargereltech, Aleksei Saryglar, Karen Sherlock, Raziya Syrdybaeva, Mark van Tongeren, and Kaigal-ool Xovalyg. I also thank Ross Daly for warm hospitality on Crete while I accompanied Huun-Huur-Tu on their Grecian travels, and Alexander Cheparukhin and Raisa Cheparukhina for untiring assistance with travel and logistics.

For memorable conversations about music, nomads, and much else that helped improve the book, I thank Eduard Alekseyev, Dina Amirova, André Bernold, Win Carus, Marianna and Katya Devlet, Jean During, Mongush B. Kenin-Lopsan, Alma Kunanbay, and Yo-Yo Ma. I also thank Michael Edgerton, my coauthor for an article on throat-singing published in *Scientific American,* and George Musser, who edited the article, for helping me grasp some of the intricacies of the human vocal tract. Long before my first visit to Tuva, I learned about "harmonic singing" from David Hykes, who encouraged me to join his ensemble, the Harmonic Choir, and become a singer myself. That experience cultivated a curiosity about not only how, but also why, people sing with reinforced harmonics, which I have been trying to answer ever since.

Drafts of the book manuscript were read by Eduard Alekseyev, Marjorie Balzer, Katheryn Doran, Joel Gordon, Lenore Grenoble, David Harrison, Molly Levin, David Peterson, Mark Slobin, and Kathryn Woodard, and I thank all of them for suggesting improvements. Marjorie Balzer went far beyond the call of readerly duty in pointing me toward work by other scholars that has enriched my own. I also thank the Dickey Center at Dartmouth College for supporting a seminar that brought three of the above-named readers together for discussion and critique of a first draft of the manuscript.

Postproduction support for the audio-video files and subvention of licensing fees was generously provided by Dartmouth College through the Dean of Faculty office, where I am particularly grateful to Lenore Grenoble, Associate Dean of Faculty for the Humanities.

The two maps were created by geographer-cartographer Sebastien Cacquard, and the audio-video files were designed and engineered by Yuri Spitsyn, working in Dartmouth's Bregman Electro-Acoustic Music Studio. To both of them, I express thanks for their expertise and patience. I am also grateful to Raziya Syrdybaeva and Janyl Chytyrbaeva, who helped me translate the excerpt of the Kyrgyz epic *Manas* included here, and to Vyacheslav

Kuchenov and Liesbet Nyssen for their help with the translation of Kuchenov's Xakas-language epic "Siber Chyltys." Kathryn Greenwood assembled much of the bibliography, and I thank her for her careful work. Thanks also to Molly Levin for preparing the index.

For permission to use photos, I thank Karen Sherlock, who accompanied me to Tuva in 1987 and 1988 on assignment from *National Geographic;* Cloé Drieu; Clark Quin; Coriolana Simon; and the Metropolitan Museum of Art (photos not identified by a credit are my own). Thanks also to Joan Morris for helping me organize and prepare the photos.

Permission to include "Ancestors," a track from a recording by the Tuvan fusion group Malerija, was kindly granted by the group's manager, Alexander Cheparukhin. I am most grateful to Manos Andriotis and Lily Polydorou of Kino TV & Movie Productions S.A. for arranging permission to include a television advertisement produced by Kino with music by Huun-Huur-Tu, and to Alexander Cheparukhin and Greenwave Music for licensing the music rights. Mark van Tongeren gave permission to include video footage of Altai singer Raisa Modorova. A television advertisement with music by Huun-Huur-Tu that was directed and produced by Traktor is included by courtesy of Traktor.

Finally, I express my profound gratitude to Valentina Süzükei for all she has contributed to our collaborative work, and for making it so rewarding and enjoyable along the way.

ON LANGUAGE AND PRONUNCIATION

Field research for this study took place among native speakers of seven distinct languages: Tuvan, Xakas (Khakas), Altai, Mongolian, Kazakh, Kyrgyz, and Russian. All except Mongolian and Russian are Turkic languages that share many features of syntax, morphology, and phonology. Mongolian does not belong to the Turkic group, but centuries of cultural intermingling between Turkic and Mongol peoples has led to a significant number of shared words, particularly in contemporary Tuvan and Mongolian. Examples include *xögjüm,* the word that corresponds most closely to "music" in both languages, and *xöömei* (Tuvan) or *höömii* (Mongolian), the general term for "throat-singing."

With one or two exceptions, all of the musicians and scholars who figure in this work spoke Russian in addition to their native language, and in some cases, Russian *was* their native language. During the Soviet era, official language policy favored the adoption of Russian by the "small peoples" of Siberia, and many of these groups, among them the Xakas and Altai, experienced severe language loss. Fortunately, Tuvans managed to preserve their language—the 1989 U.S.S.R. census showed that 99.2 percent of Tuvans consider Tuvan their mother tongue, while around 60 percent of Tuvans also know Russian.[10]

Notwithstanding the dark side of Soviet language policies, the ubiquity of Russian as a language of scholarship in the former U.S.S.R. has made it an indispensable research tool for musical ethnography. In my own case, it has also served as a lingua franca for musical fieldwork: the conversations with musicians quoted in the text were almost all in Russian (in Mongolia, I also benefited from the Mongolian-Russian translations of Mongolian colleagues Erdenechimig and Sansargereltech). Bilingual speakers of Russian and a Turkic language helped me elucidate the meaning of local musical terms, while my own earlier work with Turkic languages (Uzbek and Turkish) provided a grounding that facilitated the translation of song and poetic texts in collaboration with native speakers (see Acknowledgments). In these texts, which appear in the original language as well as in English translation, transcriptions from Turkic languages and Mongolian into the Latin alphabet follow international conventions adopted by present-day scholars. The pronunciation of most letters will be intuitive to English-speakers, but the following pronunciation guide is provided for sounds not found in English, as well as for a few letters with more than one possible English pronunciation:

Transcription	Sound	Example
x	"ch" as in Scottish "loch"	*xöömei* (throat-singing)
j	"j" as in jewel	jaxsy (good)
ö	"u" as in "put"	*kök* (blue, green)
ü	"u" as in "tutor"	*xün* (sun)
q	"c" as in "cot" (a hard "c" formed in the back of the throat)	*qil qiyak* (two-stringed fiddle)
y	"i" as in "lit"	*sygyt* (style of throat-singing)

During the Soviet era, spellings of many toponyms and ethnonyms in indigenous languages were Russified, and in the post-Soviet era, these have tended to revert to their pre-Soviet forms. For this study, the most significant of these transformations concerns "Tuva" itself, for Tuva is a Russification of what in Tuvan is pronounced "Tyva" (written in Cyrillic as Тыва). The widespread use of "Tuva," however, offers a persuasive reason to adopt it in this work.

DRAMATIS PERSONAE
(in order of appearance)

Huun-Huur-Tu	Four-person musical group from Tuva, whose members include: Sayan Bapa Anatoli (Tolya) Kuular* Kaigal-ool Xovalyg Alexei Saryglar
Alexander Cheparukhin	Huun-Huur-Tu's manager
Eduard Alekseyev	Russian-Sakha specialist in Siberian music who participated in 1987–1988 Tuva expeditions
Zoya Kyrgys	Tuvan folklorist and expert on *xöömei* (throat-singing) who participated in 1987–1988 Tuva expeditions
Idamchap Xomushtu	Tuvan stringed instrument and jew's harp player; important informant of Valentina Süzükei
Alexander Bapa	Former member of Huun-Huur-Tu; brother of Sayan Bapa
Anya Xovalyg	Kaigal-ool's wife
Sengedorj	Mongolian musician and outstanding throat-singer from Hovd City
Tserendavaa	Mongolian musician from Chandman Sum, Hovd Aimag
Tumat Kara-ool	Throat-singer recorded for Smithsonian Folkways release later licensed for television commercial

*replaced in 2003 by Andrei Mongush

Joel Gordon	Recording engineer and radio producer from Boston who participated in Tuvan and Mongolian field research
David Harrison	Linguist and advocate for preservation of endangered languages; specialist in Tuvan language and culture
Sarymai Orchimaev	*Kai* singer and multi-instrumentalist from the Altai Republic
Sat Maar-ool	Throat-singer and teacher from Teeli, in western Tuva
Narantsogt	Elderly *tsuur* (reed flute) player in Hovd Aimag, western Mongolia
Gombojav	*Tsuur* player from Hovd City, son of Narantsogt
Albert Saspyk-ool	Expert mimic of animal sounds from Chyraa-Bajy, Tuva
Alexander Tülüsh	Hunter who imitated sound and movement of wolves and other animals
Aldyn-ool Sevek	Throat-singer and school teacher from Kyzyl-Xaya, in western Tuva
Grigori Mongush	Tuvan musician who transforms visual land-scapes into whistled sound sketches
Evgeni Ulugbashev	Xakas singer who performs on the *chatxan* (zither) and composes songs
Nurlanbek Nyshanov	Kyrgyz multi-instrumentalist, leader of Ensemble Tengir-Too
Abdulhamit Raimbergenov	Kazakh *dombra* (long-necked lute) player and music educator
Ruslan Jumabaev	Kyrgyz *komuz* (long-necked lute) virtuoso
Namazbek Uraliev	Kyrgyz *komuz* virtuoso
Deleg Bayansair	Tuvan singer in Tsengel Sum, western Mongolia
Mongush Kenin-Lopsan	Tuvan scholar of shamanism, writer, and cultural revivalist
Dari Bandi	Mongolian singer and herder, expert at using sound to manage herd animals

Vyacheslav Kuchenov	Xakas musician and epic composer, member of ensemble Sabjilar
Sergei Charkhov	Xakas musician and instrument builder, member of ensemble Sabjilar
Anya Burnakova	Xakas musician, member of ensemble Sabjilar
Lazo Mongush	Tuvan shaman
Kara-ool Dopchuur	Tuvan shaman
Ai-Churek Oyun	Tuvan shamaness
Rysbek Jumabaev	Kyrgyz *manaschi* (epic singer)
Tyva Kyzy	Female throat-singing group from Tuva whose members include: Choduraa Tumat Ailangmaa Damyrang Ailang Ondar Shoraana Kuular
Raisa Modorova	Altai singer-songwriter and performer of *kai* (guttural) vocal style
Kongar-ool Ondar	Tuvan throat-singer and informal cultural ambassador
Svetlana Bapa	Wife of Huun-Huur-Tu member Sayan Bapa
Ross Daly	Irish musician and world music impresario who resides on Crete
Manos Andriotis	Greek music producer and world music fan
Jamchid Chemirani	Iranian percussionist who performed with Huun-Huur-Tu in Greece

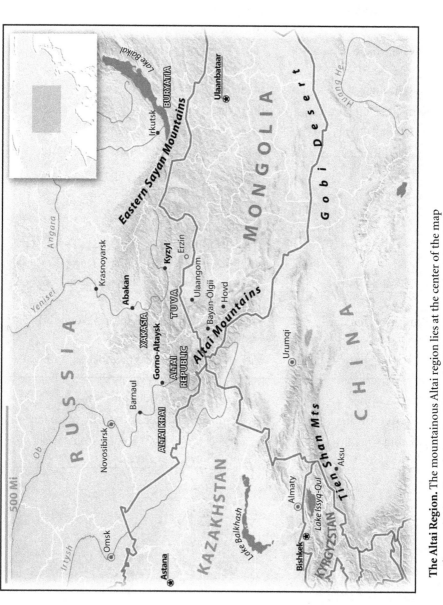

The Altai Region. The mountainous Altai region lies at the center of the map and comprises territory belonging to Russia, China, Mongolia, and Kazakhstan.

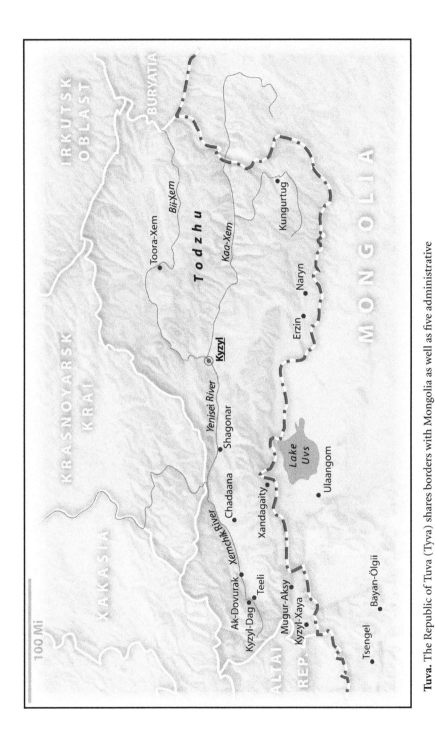

Tuva. The Republic of Tuva (Tyva) shares borders with Mongolia as well as five administrative units of the Russian Federation: Altai Republic, Republic of Xakasia (Khakasia), Krasnoyarsk Krai, Irkutsk Oblast, and the Republic of Buryatia.

WHERE RIVERS
AND MOUNTAINS
SING

1

FINDING THE FIELD

ROAD WARRIORS

SANTA FE, NEW MEXICO: FEBRUARY 1999

Santa Fe's well-burnished charm has eluded the Days Inn on Cerrillos Road, just off Interstate 25 near the southern edge of town. It's classic Strip Motel. If you check in after 9:00 PM, the front lobby is locked, and you slip your credit card to the night clerk through a slot under the bulletproof window punched in the adobe. Around back, the doors to the guest rooms hang a little crooked in their frames. Daybreak illumines ghostly, naked vines that grip a chainlink fence surrounding a swimming pool filled with stagnant brown water. This is the sort of roadside joint whose rock-bottom rates perfectly suit the four members of Huun-Huur-Tu, the music ensemble from Tuva that has been throat-singing its way around the world since 1994 and has now come to Santa Fe to croon Tuvan melodies in a night spot called the Paramount. I am along for the ride in the loosely defined role of group ethnographer, compact-disc flogger, and tour manager emeritus, having happily ceded active duty to my friend and former assistant, Alexander Cheparukhin, who oversees Huun-Huur-Tu's extensive tour schedule from an office in Moscow.

The Paramount has been open only a short time and the Santa Fe promoter has worked valiantly to publicize Huun-Huur-Tu's appearance. But as the concert begins, there are empty rows of folding chairs in the back of the room. The Tuvans, though, are not the evening's main attraction. The star of the show is a local diva named Laura Rodriguez, who has just released a new compact disc. Rodriguez is going to follow Huun-Huur-Tu, and halfway through the Tuvans' first set, her fans begin to show up and noisily wait for the strange music from Siberia to end. A commotion around the buzz-shorn, handcuff-equipped security men standing watch at the front door announces

Rodriguez's arrival in a white stretch limousine. Dressed in seamless hip-to-toe leather and a gold top, she kisses and hugs everyone at the door as she sweeps into the club. Rodriguez appears not to notice the four musicians in exotic silk robes onstage, who make unearthly sounds with their mouths and play instruments such as the *igil,* the *doshpuluur,* and the *xapchyk,* a rattle made from sheep's knee bones sewn inside a bull's scrotum.

The sound engineer, a young man named Alex with a shaved, perfectly ovoid head, is puzzled and a little frightened by Tuvan music. What is it supposed to sound like and how should it be programmed on his big mixing console? To make matters worse, one of the microphones is on the fritz, and Huun-Huur-Tu threatens to stop the concert in the middle of a song. Abrupt gestures and anxious faces transcend the language barrier. Several songs later, the microphone problem is fixed. At intermission, Tuvan music fans near the front clap loudly as the musicians slip away to their dressing room, which doubles as the club's kitchen. Sayan Bapa, who speaks a little English and is Huun-Huur-Tu's liaison to the English-speaking world, hysterically curses the sound engineer in Russian. "If that guy doesn't stop fucking our brains with the sound, there's not going to be a second set. Go and do something about it!" he orders me sternly.

As 10:00 PM approaches, the house manager paces nervously. Laura Rodriguez's fans fill the entrance foyer, line the front bar, and stream down the long corridor to the back bar. The club is reaching capacity, and in order to let more people in, the audience listening to Huun-Huur-Tu has to be moved out.

The house manager confronts me. "When are they going to finish?" he barks.

"Two more songs," I reply.

"Are they long?"

"One is, one isn't."

The last song ends, but the Tuvan music fans offer so much applause that Huun-Huur-Tu returns for an encore. The house manager clenches his teeth and narrows his eyes. Then it's finally over. Stage equipment is hastily rearranged for Rodriguez's set, and the Paramount is once again its usual self. The evanescent sounds from Siberia have touched some listeners and passed through others without leaving a trace. A few fans approach the members of Huun-Huur-Tu for autographs. "Hope you'll come back to Santa Fe soon!" chirps a young, ponytailed well-wisher as the Tuvans sign her newly purchased CD.

"Sure," says Sayan. "We hope so, too."

Xapchyk, a Tuvan percussion instrument consisting of sheep knee bones inside a bull scrotum.

LOS ANGELES, CALIFORNIA: MARCH 1999

We rent a Jeep Cherokee at the airport, and Tolya Kuular takes the wheel, even though he's not allowed to be an official driver because he doesn't have a credit card. Jeep Cherokees have a lot of cachet in Tuva, partly because jeeps are ideally suited for Tuva's rough roads but also because of their infamous role as a favored vehicle of the Russian Mafiosi. In the boom years of the new Russia, Mafia tycoons were typically followed in their Mercedes or BMWs by bodyguards driving Jeep Cherokees with smoked windows.

Tolya has tractor-trailer and bus driving licenses, and he worked as a professional driver in Tuva before he became a fulltime musician. Los Angeles freeways don't faze him. He is one of the most competent drivers I've ever met, and he navigates the complex traffic patterns with complete assurance, somehow assimilating the welter of highway signs written in an alphabet he can barely read and invariably responding correctly.

We are headed to Valencia, where Huun-Huur-Tu has a two-day residency at the California Institute of the Arts. An afternoon workshop has been arranged with student composers to explore how Tuvan throat-singing might serve as a resource for cutting-edge electroacoustic music. Two students are preparing to demonstrate a computer-based program for sound processing that they have developed for the occasion. The Tuvans' singing triggers filtering mechanisms run by the computers that create reverberant sound loops and metallic-sounding drones. These loops and drones are fused with the source sounds, and the whole clamorous cacophony is amplified through speakers. One of the student composers explains to the Tuvans what's going to happen. "We have two computers and one of them is going to take vocal sounds from the microphone and the other will take instrumental sounds. We'll take your input as it comes into the computer and run it through some filters, and we'll also be recording ten-second snippets of sound and repeatedly playing them. So there'll be kind of a sequence thing going on, where there's some continuous processing and also some repetition."

At the end, we assess the results. "We didn't really feel anything," Sayan says. "We heard some strange sounds, but we don't understand how they were related to what we're doing, or what the point is." The students are not discouraged. It was just a first attempt, they acknowledge, and it would have been more interesting if it had been more interactive.

Following the workshop, some members of the audience linger to ask questions. A rumpled older gentleman stands up and poses a question: "I've read that there are old Chinese documents attesting to the fact that in ancient China, music was used as a way of cleansing the inner organs. Are there documents about these kinds of practices in Tuva?"

"The Tuvan language wasn't written down until 1930," Sayan replies. "In any case, we don't need documents to tell us about our music. What we do comes naturally to us."

Later, Sayan remarked that it had been a good workshop. "They were normal people. They didn't want to touch us, feel up our chests, look down our throats. They just enjoyed the music and tried to appreciate what we're doing. Why is it that people always want to sing like us?"

SEATTLE, WASHINGTON: FEBRUARY 1999

The members of Huun-Huur-Tu are the last to board the flight to Denver. The ticket agent asks whether my traveling companions understand English, and when I shake my head, she says apologetically that they must be asked the two security questions in their native language. I volunteer to translate, but the agent looks insulted. "Sir, if I allow you to ask those questions, I could lose my job. I'll have to request an authorized interpreter. What is their native language?" I tell her that their native language is Tuvan. Showing no reaction, she dials a phone number.

"I need a Tuvan-speaking interpreter to do a security check," she says.

There is a pause, and then she asks me, "Sir, what language is Tuvan similar to?"

"Xakas and Altai. It belongs to the Oghuz branch of Eastern Turkic." Another pause.

"Sir, do they speak any other language?"

"Russian." The ticket agent remains expressionless, but evidently there is action on the other end of the line. A few moments later, an émigré named Volodya is chattering with the members of Huun-Huur-Tu, and somewhere in the conversation he throws in the questions about whether they packed their own bags and whether anyone has given them items to carry. When it's over, I ask the ticket agent what would have happened if my companions had not been bilingual in Russian.

"They wouldn't have been allowed to board," she replies curtly. Trying to put a human face on the matter, she adds, "If there had been enough time, we could have used other means to get the answers."

On board, a young man in the aisle seat in front of me turns around and asks whether my companions are from Tuva. "I've been to Tuva," he says. "In 1993, I rode a bicycle through the west of Tuva with a couple of friends from California. Awesome trip."

MOSCOW: AUGUST 2003

For centuries, the principal trade routes from Tuva pointed southeast, toward Mongolia, and beyond to China. These days, however, Tuva's links to the world beyond the Altai-Sayan Mountains run north and west—to Abakan, Krasnoyarsk, and Novosibirsk. It's difficult to go far without transiting through Moscow, and Huun-Huur-Tu has logged a lot of time there. I have arranged to arrive in Moscow on the same day that they are flying in from a concert in Copenhagen, and we agree to meet near Red Square for a leisurely stroll in the damp evening air.

In front of the TASS Building, a policeman carrying a semiautomatic weapon steps out of the shadows and blocks our path. Saluting, he commands crisply, "Your documents, please!" The Tuvans calmly extract Moscow residence permits from their wallets and hand them to the policeman. He scrutinizes their faces, then the papers, and then looks at their faces again before returning the papers without comment. I hand the policeman my passport and immigration form, which on the reverse side had the hotel registration stamp I received earlier in the day.

"Your registration is invalid," says the policeman. "It has to be issued not by the hotel, but by the Office of Visa Registration. You'll have to come with me to the police station and pay a fine. I have the right to hold you for up to three hours."

The policeman's scam triggers an instant response from Sayan. "Perhaps the American could pay the fine on the spot, and avoid having to go the police station," he says in a conciliatory tone.

"I'm not allowed to accept payment of fines," the policeman replies, stony-faced, serving notice that he is not going to be a pushover. He knows precisely how much it is worth to an American not to spend three hours in a Moscow police station. Sayan does not know that number, but he takes a guess.

"We're talking about five hundred rubles."

The policeman shakes his head. "I'll explain to your friends where the station is, so they can come down later and pick you up," he tells me firmly. I look at Sayan and jerk my head and eyes ever so slightly upward.

"How about a thousand rubles," Sayan says softly.

The policeman hands back my passport. "Put a thousand rubles inside the passport and give it to me," he orders.

It is over quickly. As I stow the passport in its secure pouch while the policeman disappears back into the shadows of the TASS Building, Sayan jabs me in the ribs. "Now you know what it's like to be an *uryuk.*"

Uryuk means "dried apricot," but in Russian army slang, it's a crude descriptive for soldiers from Uzbekistan, the land of apricots, or just about anywhere else east of the Urals. Huun-Huur-Tu may be well known in the world music emporia of London and Los Angeles, but on the streets of Moscow, where an undeclared war is being fought against Chechen militants, they're just four more faces from the nebulous hinterlands of Russian Asia. Even with their Moscow residence permits, the members of Huun-Huur-Tu mostly stay indoors during their transits to avoid police checks and confrontations with the local skinheads. "It's the capital of our country," Sayan laments, "but we feel like foreigners here. It was almost eight hundred years ago that Russia fell to the Mongols, and some people are still trying to even the score."

PORTLAND, OREGON: FEBRUARY 1997

The Aladdin Theater, on Portland's East Side, is a renovated movie hall, and there's no barrier to the backstage area. You just plunge through a velvet curtain, walk up a flight of stairs, and you're in the dressing rooms. After Huun-Huur-Tu's concert, some local overtone-singing luminaries invite themselves backstage to share tradecraft with the Tuvans. Ed and Gloria (not their real names) are both large and bespectacled, and as they approach the Tuvans, their expression is one of reverence mixed with awe. "Thank you for your wonderful music," says Ed, pressing palms and fingers together in a votive bow.

"You're welcome," replies Sayan.

"We also do throat-singing," adds Gloria. "Would you like to hear us sing?" The syntax of Gloria's sentences overloads Sayan's command of English, which was still tenuous in 1997, and I am asked to translate. Without waiting for an answer, Ed and Gloria join hands, screw their eyes shut, and, breathing deeply, emit a nasal, undulating harmonic whine above a fundamental tone that sounds like a buzz saw. The noisy undulations continue for what seems a long time. At the end, Ed and Gloria open their eyes.

"Harmonics have healing powers," Gloria says blankly. "They can harmonize the body at the cellular level. Did you feel anything from our singing?"

"It's fine, what you do," answers Sayan, with studied diplomacy. "But it's not the same as what we do. If you can heal with harmonics, so much the better, but that's not what we do. We don't know how to heal anyone. We're just musicians."

VALENCIA, CALIFORNIA: MARCH 1999

We are five weeks into Huun-Huur-Tu's North American tour, and the Tuvans are showing signs of weariness. Only a week remains before they are to take a plane from Los Angeles to Moscow and then fly on to Tuva. They'll have a break of around two months before their musical nomadizing starts again in mid-May. During a brief lull in the residency activities at California Institute of the Arts, Tolya Kuular announces that he'd like to go shopping for some gifts he wants to bring to his family. At the neighborhood Wal-Mart, Tolya, Alexei, and Sayan go off in search of binoculars, flashlights, and underwear. Kaigal-ool stays with me in the jeep. We are silent, but I sense that he wants to talk. Kaigal-ool has a sentimental side that occasionally overpowers his habitual reticence.

"Are you thinking about home?" I ask.

"I'm tired of traveling," Kaigal-ool says ruefully, "but I don't have any other profession. I don't know how to do anything except be an artist. I've been on the road for twenty years."

KYZYL

KYZYL, TUVA: MAY 1998

Kaigal-ool Xovalyg eases his well-worn Zhiguli sedan—the Russian version of a Fiat 124—into a parking spot in front of the gritty, puce, brick-and-concrete blockhouse where he lives with his wife, son, and daughter in a three-room apartment on the fifth floor. The climb up the barren stairwell belies the comfortable, if sparsely furnished space that awaits behind the triple-locked double doors. On the living room walls are Kaigal-ool's musical mementos: concert and publicity posters, a string of backstage passes from festivals around the world, and a letter signed by the president of Harvard University thanking him for his service as a visiting artist.

Kaigal-ool is small, round-faced, and mustachioed, with black hair combed down over his forehead and trimmed in neat bangs—a Tuvan Ringo Starr. The beginnings of a belly stand out on an otherwise taut frame. "It's America's fault," Kaigal-ool said with a hint of bitterness when I jokingly patted his stomach. "Too many McDonald's. It's all we can get when we're on the road."

Kaigal-ool doesn't look anything like the way I imagine a horse thief, but that's what his name, *kaigal,* connotes in Tuvan ("ool" means "boy" or "lad"). Kaigal-ool grew up among stockbreeders near the dusty town of Chadaana, whose reputation as a gangster haven long ago earned it the local nickname "Chicago." In fact, Kaigal-ool did steal a horse once, when he was seventeen, and he served time for it—two months in the local lock-up. After that, he reformed and became a musician. Now that he's a star, everyone has forgotten about the horse and the jail time.

"I didn't want to come to Kyzyl," Kaigal-ool told me one morning as we sat in his apartment. "I dropped out of school after eighth grade to help my parents with their animals. I loved horses, herding, and open land. My father tried to make me into an auto mechanic, but I hated cars and missed horses, so he sent me back to my settlement. I worked as a herder for two years, and people knew I had a talent for music. I was about eleven or twelve when I began to throat-sing. No one taught me. I heard it from grown-ups and on the radio, and began to try it myself. I sang on the steppe when I'd go to visit my parents on horseback, and the sound of my voice would echo off the cliffs. People heard that sound, and encouraged me. They said I should go to Kyzyl. My father brought me here almost by force. I was wild and free, and I didn't want to live any other way."

Kaigal-ool's music may feel as out of place in Kyzyl as it does in Los An-

Kaigal-ool Xovalyg playing the *igil,* a two-stringed horsehead fiddle, 1998.

geles or Santa Fe. Despite Kyzyl's proximity to the steppe—a fifteen-minute drive from the center of town will put you in open range land—it is hard to imagine a city less in harmony with its natural surroundings. The Tuvan chic that has been commodified and marketed around the world hasn't reached Kyzyl yet. Viewed from a distance as you descend from the hills on the north bank of the Yenisei River—or, as it is called in Tuvan, the Ulug Xem (Great River)—Kyzyl looks as if it had been designed and assembled elsewhere, then dropped into its present location. And in a sense, that is what happened. Kyzyl was conceived and built by the Russians, and its name means "red" in Tuvan and other Turkic languages. Tuva didn't have any cities before the Russians came. The oldest parts of Kyzyl date from just before World War I, when it was called *"Byelotsarsk"*—which means something like "White Czarville." Otto Mänchen-Helfen (1894–1969), the German Sinologist and historian who traveled to Tuva in 1929, wrote in his account of the trip that "the Mongols (and indeed all the Lamaists from the Tibetans to the Kalmyks

9

on the Volga) called the Russian czar *Tsagaan Baatar,* the 'White Ruler' or White Hero. They saw in him the incarnation of a deity, the white Tara. The name Byelotsarsk was chosen deliberately. It was to show the Tuvans that not a human but a god was the ruler of the land, that it was nothing short of religious duty to submit to him."[1] The city's symbolic color morphed from white to red via an interregnum period extending from 1918–1926, when it was called Xem-Beldiri, which in Tuvan means "river confluence," in this case referring to the confluence of the Bii-Xem and Kaa-Xem Rivers that merge languidly at Kyzyl to form the Yenisei.

If the apartment complex that is home to Kaigal-ool and his family were in an American city, you'd call it a housing project. In Kyzyl, it's just home. Everyone lives in a project, except for people still residing in the old Russian log-cabin barrios on Kyzyl's east side or in the densely settled quarter on the west side that locals call "Shanghai," where tin-roofed log-and-plank houses molder behind stockade fences lining narrow alleys. More than a third of Tuva's total population of around 300,000 now live in Kyzyl, and more than half of these urbanites are Russians or members of other non-Tuvan ethnic groups.[2] The center of town, known as Lenin Square during the Soviet era and renamed Nomad Square in 1992, is a purely Soviet creation. On one side is the whitewashed concrete Tuvan National Drama Theater, and on another side is the marble headquarters of the city administration and the Tuvan parliament (the parliament is called *"Xural,"* in a recent bow to the old Turkic word that means a gathering of clan chieftains). Between these buildings, a statue of Lenin still gazes down on pedestrians. Considerably more modest than Lenin, and situated far from the center of the square along a walkway on the perimeter, is a statue of Salchak Toka (1901–1973), the Tuvan Bolshevik who brought Stalinism to his homeland at the end of the 1920s, during the era of the Tanna-Tuva People's Republic, and who was the ranking Communist Party official in Tuva from 1932 until his death.[3]

The entire, dismal history of Soviet-era residential design unfolds as one travels the short distance from Nomad Square toward the city's periphery. There, jutting out of rubble-strewn construction sites, are the newest apartment complexes, whose prefabricated concrete slabs could just as well have been erected in Murmansk, Sayansk, or Kansk. Beyond the apartment projects, lining the two-lane road that transects Kyzyl east to west, are Tuva's hulking monuments to Soviet industrialization. A leviathan generating station pumps black smoke into the pristine Siberian sky; a rusting concrete plant crumbles even as it turns out building materials. In the small open markets adjacent to Tuvan Volunteers Street, which runs along one side of Nomad Square, vendors dispense the flotsam of goods that have washed up in this remote outpost of capitalism: "Zyaki-Zyaki" beef-flavored snack chips from South Korea, a global farrago of colas, beauty products from a dozen countries, lemon-scented "Barf" laundry detergent and chocolate-flavored condoms from Russia, Barbie dolls and their clones. Recently an upscale restaurant has opened to cater to the increasing number of Tuvan *nouveaux riches*, the local variant of the Russian parvenus who have transformed Moscow into a madcap center of glitz, sin, and conspicuous consumption.

The new Russia is putting the squeeze on an entire genre of travel writing—the venerable tradition of travelogue set in the former Soviet Union and its successor republics, whose principal ingredients are martyrdom at the hands of Aeroflot (the former Soviet airline monopoly), sadistic waiters, and inedible food—but not much else. These days, traveling to Tuva isn't all that different from going to Indianapolis. From Moscow, you can take Transaero's Boeing 767 redeye to Krasnoyarsk, and after a hearty breakfast in the natty airport VIP lounge, where any foreigner with five dollars in hard currency qualifies as a VIP, you board a small jet for the one-hour flight to Kyzyl. Once a week, more or less, there's even a direct flight from Moscow to Kyzyl offered by Yak Servis, a.k.a. Yak Airlines, whose name does not actually refer to yaks but is short for Yakovlev, the founder of an eponymous aircraft company that builds airplanes and also now flies them on commercial routes.

Tuva has not always been so easily accessible. During the Soviet era, the U.S.S.R. was separated from the West not only by the infamous Iron Curtain that Winston Churchill used as a metaphor for totalitarianism, but also by an "iron scrim" that lay behind the iron curtain, whose purpose was to keep foreigners, particularly Americans, out of "nominally closed" regions of the U.S.S.R. Until the dissolution of the Soviet Union, large regions of the U.S.S.R. were closed to foreigners from capitalist countries (Soviet diplomacy divided the world into three categories: socialist, capitalist, and nonaligned, with different travel and visa regulations for citizens from each group). Entire cities could be closed off because they were home to military industries or strategic installations. Border regions such as Tuva were typically "nominally closed," meaning that while they were not explicitly closed for military reasons, foreigners as a practice were not allowed to travel there. And certain areas seem to have been closed simply based on the Cold War principle of quid pro quo. At the same time that the Soviet Union closed sections of territory to Americans, the United States had analogous regulations for citizens of the U.S.S.R. Soviets, for example, were officially prohibited from traveling to the New York borough of Brooklyn lest they cast a furtive glance at the Brooklyn Naval Yard.

Even before Tuva "voluntarily" joined the Soviet Union in 1944, Mänchen-

Helfen described how he prepared for his trip to what was then the Tuvan People's Republic by running "to a thousand agencies and offices [where he] obtained certificates, stamps, signatures, and attestations and filled in hundreds of columns of questionnaires," which he said included the question, "'What did you do in the year 1917, and why?'"[4] More than sixty years later, Ralph Leighton's humorous book, *Tuva or Bust!*, chronicled the whimsical efforts of Tuva's most famous near-visitor, the Nobel Prize–winning physicist Richard Feynman, to get permission to go there. Sadly, Feynman died just a week before a letter of invitation arrived from Tuva.

My own efforts were far more prosaic. Beginning in 1985, at the dawn of Perestroika, I had become involved in U.S.-U.S.S.R. cultural exchange. One of the Soviet organizations with which I worked was the U.S.S.R. Union of Composers. Like other artistic guilds established at the beginning of the 1930s, its purpose was to serve as an ideological gatekeeper to the world of public artistic production and presentation. Within its dominion was the All-Union Folklore Commission headed by the Moscow folklorist and Siberian music expert, Eduard Alekseyev. After Alekseyev and I became friends, I asked a Russian acquaintance in the Union of Composers whether he could arrange permission for a small musical expedition to conduct research in Tuva under Alekseyev's supervision. While my urbane acquaintance could never understand the allure of what seemed to him a barbarically remote province of the Soviet empire, he obliged my request. He never told me how he arranged the permission, and I never asked.

KYZYL: SEPTEMBER 1987

There were four of us in the *National Geographic*–sponsored research group that we dubbed "the Joint Soviet–American Musical–Ethnographic Research Expedition," in a spoof on Soviet *haute* bureaucratese. As it turned out, we were not the first group of visiting outsiders to include Americans. We learned that a few botanists and geologists had come before us, but their goal had been to search for rare plants and rocks, not to come to Tuva per se. While we were in Kyzyl, another American scientist, a biologist, received permission to study the mating behavior of the Siberian dwarf hamster. Karen Sherlock, the photographer assigned by *National Geographic* to our expedition, and I seemed to be the first American visitors with a specific interest in the people of Tuva, their history, and their culture. Eduard Alekseyev had invited a young Tuvan folklorist named Zoya Kyrgys, who had written her graduate thesis on "throat-singing" to join us as Tuvan music specialist, local guide, and Tuvan-Russian interpreter.

A recording session in a yurt. Zoya Kyrgys writes in a logbook while Eduard Alekseyev watches and Ted Levin records. Photo by Karen Sherlock, 1987.

Alekseyev, fiftyish, was a tall, sturdy character whose bespectacled face appeared permanently set in an impish grin. From the age of eighteen, when he set out to tour his native region of East Central Siberia by motorcycle and make recordings of elderly musicians, Alekseyev had been a folklorist and fieldworker extraordinaire. Born to a Jewish mother and a Sakha mathematician father, he felt a loyalty to both cultures.[5] "I'll give Moscow another ten years," he told me in 1987, "then I'm going back to Yakutsk to die." (Alekseyev could hardly have guessed then that, fifteen years later, we would be sitting in his apartment outside of Boston, Massachusetts, where he emigrated with his wife and children in the mid-1990s to escape the chaos of post-Soviet Moscow and the implosion of the academic system that had been the center of his life.)

When I had proposed to Alekseyev the idea of a Tuvan expedition, he expressed cautious interest. "The trouble with folklore is that the best of it is always in places that you can't get to," he said. The obstacles he had in mind were not only physical and logistical but also bureaucratic and financial. With sponsorship from the Union of Composers and the *National Geographic*, we had overcome the latter two obstacles; however, the presence of Karen Sherlock's camera made even the normally phlegmatic Alekseyev uneasy.

13

On our first night in Kyzyl, he took me aside and asked whether I was sure that the *National Geographic* was the only organization in Washington for which Karen was working. I assured him that it was. "If the CIA wanted to learn about Tuva, they'd have much better ways," I told him confidently. "And anyway, why would they be interested in Tuva?" (A year later, I was questioned by FBI counter-intelligence agents in connection with the investigation of a suspected KGB informer who, it turned out, I knew. When I mentioned to one of the agents that I'd been working in Tuva, his face lit up. "Have you ever talked to the CIA?") As the first Americans to come in search of Tuvan folk music, we were welcomed with both solicitude and caution by the local authorities. In Kyzyl, we were accommodated in a comfortable hotel belonging to the Regional Party Committee, the reigning political authority in Tuva. Our fellow boarders were politicians and military men—a sure sign that we were living well in the Soviet Union. I was shown to a spacious three-room suite, and Karen had a room only slightly less ostentatious. Meals were served in a private dining room, on fine china from East Germany, and our waitress was an unfailingly cheerful young Russian woman—all in all, exactly the sort of isolation and special treatment that ethnographers try to avoid.

The morning after arriving in Kyzyl, we left for the west of Tuva, where the best throat-singers were said to live. Our mode of transport was a nine-passenger van commandeered from the Kyzyl taxi fleet. Our Russian driver had never ventured outside of Kyzyl, but he faced the prospect of a journey to the hinterlands with stoicism, if not alacrity. Our destination was Teeli, 250 miles from Kyzyl, at the westernmost extreme of paved road. From there we were to follow rutted tracks over the grasslands into hill country still farther west. Ranges of angular hills crisscrossed the steppe as we drove westward to Shagonar along the Yenisei River valley. Then we veered off to the southwest through rolling grassland and intersected the Xemchik River at Kyzyl-Majylyk. As we pulled into Teeli at dusk, a red fox pranced across the road in front of our van—by local reckoning, a sign of good luck.

Teeli is a regional center of 3,000 people (see plate 2). At first glance, it seemed barely to qualify as a frontier outpost, but we quickly learned that Teeli contained a hospital (from which a physician was dispatched to check on our condition after the drive from Kyzyl), a school, a House of Culture that served as the center of official cultural life in the town, administrative offices for the Regional Party Committee, and a hotel that was to be home during our stay. We drove along broad, unpaved streets in search of the hotel, which was located adjacent to a mangy park filled with oversized metal sculptures of animals (a Socialist calque of Tuva's venerable tradition of stone-carving animals). The hotel looked freshly painted, and later we learned that it was painted specially for our visit. It was clean and austere, and the double rooms cost a ruble a night. Facilities were commensurate with the price: a small pail suspended above a sink in the upstairs hallway was the extent of the indoor plumbing.

Our host in Teeli was the Regional Party Committee. Within the committee, the chairman of the local cultural directorate was responsible for our activities. She had arranged for us to set up our recording equipment in the House of Culture and had invited the best musicians from the region to meet us. The musicians arrived in costumes—ankle-length silk robes in solid colors, accessorized with embroidered belts and pointy wizard's hats (made in Czechoslovakia, it turned out, for silk was unavailable in Soviet Tuva)—and it quickly became apparent that they had come with the expectation of presenting a formal concert. Later we learned that the twenty-five or so musicians in the performing collective had been released from work with pay for a full week to rehearse for this event. The concert was carefully choreographed, with harmonized ensemble arrangements of Tuvan folksongs performed by a mixed chorus and consort of instrumental accompanists. They played struck zithers that looked like hammer dulcimers, plucked lutes similar to balalaikas, and two-stringed fiddles held upright like cellos.

Though we listened politely to the concert, I was frustrated. We had come to Tuva in search of music that represented a living connection to the past. I had imagined myself as a kind of latter-day Alan Lomax, squatting in yurts with herders as they chanted archaic melodies into my microphone. Yet here we were, guests of the Regional Party Committee, being treated to a variety show of bowdlerized folk music. After it was over, we asked whether we could take several of the singers and record them individually. The chairman of the cultural directorate nodded her head, and we retreated to a small room.

The musicians were nervous and did not know what was expected of them in front of foreigners. One singer, when asked to perform his favorite song, said that he wanted to sing "My Party." When we told him we would like to hear old, traditional songs, he insisted that "My Party" was the one he liked best. He launched into it before we could stop him, and we let our tape recorders idle. Another singer was curious about the land where Karen and I came from. "In America, are there many camels or few?" he asked. "Few," I replied. The men seemed inscrutable. I wondered, did the singer of "My Party" really like that song the best? Was the query about camels sincere, ironic, or a gag? I felt at a loss to read what they were thinking.

After a morning of recording in Teeli's House of Culture, our hosts proposed that we take several of the singers and drive to a beautiful spot in the mountains known for mineral springs that supposedly contained a small amount of radioactive radon. The spot was a favorite for rheumatics and childless women who wished to bear children. We invited two elderly men to accompany us who had promised to reenact a traditional ceremony of purification. Conducting such ceremonies is the province of specialists who serve as healers, diviners, and practitioners of domestic rituals. In Tuvan, such specialists are called *xam* (pl., *xamnar*), typically translated into English as "shaman." One of our traveling companions had been an assistant to a shaman in his youth, and he had often participated in purification ceremonies.[6] His name was Idamchap, and later I learned that he was one of the most respected musicians in Tuva (see plates 5 and 6).[7]

Like Buddhism, shamanism and spirit worship were officially liquidated in Tuva in the 1930s, labeled as reactionary and antimaterialist belief systems.[8] Shamans could not be exiled to Siberia, because they already lived there. But many were "repressed," as Russians say, meaning that they were shot. Others were jailed, committed to psychiatric hospitals, or terrified into acquiescence to Soviet atheism. Nonetheless, a belief in spirits and local deities persisted, and I was told sotto voce that shamans still existed deep in the mountains. Shamanism was a subject of great sensitivity to Tuvan cultural authorities, who were happy for us to record a shamanic ritual so long as we understood that it was simply a reconstruction of a bygone brand of folk superstition, long ago superseded by modern medicine, psychiatry, and dialectical materialism.

We drove for about twenty miles over the grasslands, slowly climbing higher into the hills along a rutted dirt track. At the radon spring, we set up a tape recorder and microphones at the base of a large tree covered with thousands of small strips of cloth (*chalama*) left by travelers and pilgrims as offerings to spirits. Idamchap and his assistant built a small fire and added twigs and pine needles to increase the amount of smoke. Both men donned silk robes and hats—fedoras of Soviet vintage, not the Siberian shaman's traditional feathered headdress. Idamchap stood over the fire, silhouetted against the mountains, and with his arms he sent smoke in different directions, chanting an incantation to exorcize evil spirits from the body of a sick person:[9]

> Eh, I'm hanging from the sky, oh
> The spirits are speaking to me, oh
> I'm flying among the clouds, oh
> The spirits are speaking to me, oh.
>
> Eh, I have been in the higher world, oh
> And in the lower world, oh
> Where only haven't I been, oh
> It seems that you've been in Ovyur [a place], oh.

Eh, you went hunting, oh
And in your trunk, oh
Lie the skins of a sable, oh
If you leave them in the ravine, oh.

Eh, all your sickness will go away, oh
Drive them away from their resting place, oh
Drive away all the bad spirits, oh
For heaven's sake, spare us, oh.

When the ceremony was over, we retreated downhill to a campsite, where a sheep had been freshly slaughtered for cooking. The Regional Party Committee from Teeli, anxious to ensure that its Western guests were not incapacitated by excessive culture shock, had trucked to the campsite folding chairs and tables, complete with white tablecloths and silverware. We sat at the little square tables, eating spiceless, saltless boiled sheep and drinking vodka and cognac (see plate 7). No part of the sheep was wasted. The intestines had been filled with blood and turned into blood sausage (*xan*). The organs—all of them—were arranged on a platter and placed in front of me, the guest of honor. The meal was accompanied by Tuvan tea, boiled with sheep milk and fat. We also ate *tirt xan,* a crock of fatty chopped meat, sealed tightly by a thin flour pancake stretched across the top and heated over the fire so that the liquid in the meat steamed the contents of the pot.

Trying to conjure up a way to escape from the choreographed performance activities, I came up with the idea of asking whether we might attend a wedding. It was the wedding season, and Zoya Kyrgys had assured us that many weddings would be taking place in the coming days and weeks. I explained to our host from the cultural directorate that I was particularly interested in music performed at weddings and that attending a wedding would also provide excellent visuals for Karen Sherlock's camera. She promised to procure us an invitation, but I could tell from the look on her face that the gesture was disingenuous. We left Teeli, with no further word about weddings. I repeated the request several days later in Chadaana, a town of 12,000 people that is the administrative center of Chöön-Xemchik Region. Of all the Regional Party Committees, the one in Chadaana seemed the most paranoid about our presence. Gracious, smiling, hospitable, the head of the committee's cultural directorate followed us around like a cat stalking its prey. When Karen momentarily escaped to try to snap a candid shot, he desperately tracked her, and when he caught up to her he sneaked up and pounced. Karen had never been prohibited from photographing anything. She was only discouraged from doing so by being made to seem foolish or crazy for wanting to take a certain shot. "Why would you want to shoot that old thing?" she was asked dozens of times.

To my surprise, however, the head of the cultural directorate responded positively to my request that we be allowed to attend a wedding. "There's one on Saturday," he said, "and we'll take you there." Karen cleaned her camera lenses in anticipation, and I rechecked my recording equipment. On Saturday morning, the head of the cultural directorate appeared in a dark suit with his jeep driver and told us to follow him to the site of the wedding. We drove a few miles out of town to a yurt set up on a scenic bluff. A few people were milling about. The head of the cultural directorate dismounted from his jeep and asked us to follow him so that he could introduce us to the bride and groom. Everyone was dressed in silk finery, and the bride was bedizened with gaudy lipstick and rouge. The head of the cultural directorate indicated to Karen where she should stand with her camera, and he helped me adjust my microphone stand (see plate 8).

"Okay, let's begin," he yelled to the bride and groom, and everyone took their places as the couple held hands and exchanged vows. But where were the guests? I did not want to appear ungrateful before our host, but I feared that we had been bamboozled. Eduard Alekseyev invited the head of the cultural directorate on a short walk and returned with a long face.

"The Party secretary was afraid that if we were invited to a real wedding, there might be drunkenness, and so they decided to stage a wedding specially for us," Eduard reported wryly. "The bride and groom were actually married last week, and agreed to reenact the ceremony."

The phony wedding was a fitting final touch to the Potemkin village that had been clumsily erected in an attempt to shield us from Tuvan reality. And yet all was not facade. The folklore ensemble that had posed for Karen's photo in front of a giant portrait of Lenin, though not what we were seeking, was only too real (see plate 4). Just as in Uzbekistan, where I had spent a year researching local music in the late 1970s, Soviet cultural policies had irreversibly altered the course of tradition.[10] As in Uzbekistan, "culture workers" trained in special institutes managed by the Soviet Ministry of Culture in distant Russian cities had returned with the mandate to establish amateur arts activities, called in Russian *samodeyatel'nost*. A charitable explanation of the Soviet amateur arts movement holds that its goals were partly educational and partly ideological: on the one hand, to encourage broad participation in the arts as a form of spiritual nourishment, and on the other, to exploit the arts as a tool of cultural politics. The latter included reifying politically approved group identities, using popular culture in sanitized forms to underscore Soviet cultural values, and advancing the Marxist-Leninist ideal of raising the cultural level of "primitive" Asian peoples within the Soviet Union to approach that of Russians and other Europeans.

The culture-building mission explained the treacly harmonizations and consortized arrangements of Tuvan folksongs, which in traditional practice are sung either as solos or, in the case of social songs, by small groups of responsorial singers. The amateur groups coached and choreographed by culture workers had become a tradition in their own right, replacing older performance traditions that evolved and changed slowly over centuries (see plate 3). By contrast, in the West, many great composers have arranged folk songs, but these arrangements were never intended as substitutions for the folk songs themselves.

How deep was Tuva's rupture with the past? Were there still remnants of what had existed before the Soviets—an understanding of music, and of sound itself, that was rooted not in the kinds of staged performances we had witnessed, but rather in the natural environment of grasslands, mountains, and taiga (the boreal, coniferous forests in which pastoralists had lived for millennia in south Siberia)? If only fragmentary elements existed, could one engage in a kind of musical archaeology whose goal would be to reunite the fragments and reassemble a coherent picture of the whole? These were the questions I pondered as our Moscow-bound Aeroflot flight lifted off from Kyzyl's ramshackle airport in the luminous morning sunlight. Looking down at the fields slipping away beneath, the earth seemed to sparkle with thousands of mirrors. "Broken vodka bottles," said my Tuvan seatmate with a look of disgust in response to my query. "That's what our 'brother' Russians bequeathed to this sacred land."[11]

REINVENTING TUVA

KYZYL: AUGUST 1995

By 1995 I had been away from Tuva for seven years. Teaching, writing, and child-rearing all kept me occupied elsewhere. Meanwhile, after sifting through the twenty-odd hours of field recordings collected during two hard and often frustrating months in 1987 and 1988, Eduard Alekseyev, Zoya Kyrgys, and I had managed to edit together thirty-eight minutes of music that became a Smithsonian Folkways recording called *Tuva: Voices from the Center of Asia.* Released in 1990, *Voices* was the first commercial recording of music from Tuva to appear in the West. At the time of its release, we had no expectation that our pastiche of throat-singing, reindeer-herding calls, jew's harp melodies, and animal domestication songs would travel beyond a small circle of connoisseurs of musical exotica. But to our surprise, the recording attracted attention not only in the West but also in Tuva, where it was not commercially available. The Tuvans' attention focused not so much on the recording itself as on the interest it had stimulated among Westerners. Pride that Tuvan music had achieved popularity in America was mixed with suspicion and anger. Why was the treasured musical heritage of a small people in Siberia being exported to countries far away and turned into a consumer item? What had happened to all the profits from sales of the recording? Zoya Kyrgys reported rumors in Kyzyl that I had become a millionaire after absconding with the musicians' royalties. An ugly article appeared in one of Kyzyl's newspapers.

The breakup of the Soviet Union at the end of 1991 stimulated the nascent free cultural marketplace that had begun to emerge during the Perestroika period in the late 1980s. Musicians, artists, writers, and film directors who had relied on the sponsorship of state organizations either chose or were forced to fend for themselves as government support for the arts shrank drastically. While the world's attention focused on the chaotic arrival of capitalism in Moscow and Saint Petersburg, artistic life all over the Russian Federation was disrupted and curtailed. In Tuva, the erstwhile Soviet Ministry of Culture had supported two professional song and dance troupes devoted to the propagation of Tuvan "national" music. In the new free-market conditions, these collectives, Ayan and Sayan, became cultural dinosaurs. The best musicians abandoned them and formed their own groups. The first such group to appear was the Tuva Ensemble, founded by Gennadi Tumat, a virtuoso throat-singer and vocalist from Xandagaity in southwestern Tuva, with help from folklorist Zoya Kyrgys.[12]

In 1991, Bernard Kleikamp, a Dutch record producer and world music impresario, brought the Tuva Ensemble to Amsterdam for concerts and a recording session. A year later, Ralph Leighton, America's premier Tuvan entrepreneur, invited Gennadi Tumat and two fellow members of the Tuva Ensemble, Kaigal-ool Xovalyg and Anatoli Kuular, to demonstrate their throat-singing skills while riding horseback in the Rose Bowl Parade in Pasadena, California, the hometown of both Leighton and the late Richard Feynman.[13] Hoping to expand the Tuvans' premiere in the United States beyond Pasadena and a few concert appearances he had arranged on the West Coast, Leighton phoned me to ask whether I might try to organize concerts on the East Coast as well. I agreed, and we went to work booking the ensemble as the "Throat-Singers of Tuva." There was only one hitch: Gennadi Tumat had a tough-talking Tuvan manager who was unmoved by Ralph Leighton's descriptions of how much fun Tumat would have riding horseback in the Rose Bowl Parade. The manager wanted cold cash—lots of it—and no amount of international friendship and cross-cultural understanding was going to palliate his demand. Little more than a week before the Rose Bowl Parade, Leighton was forced to come up with a last-minute substitute for Gennadi Tumat and he chose Kongar-ool Ondar, the man who would later become the Liberace of Tuvan music (see chapter 6, "The Ondar Phenomenon").

The impromptu concert tour of winter 1993 added considerably to the cachet of Tuvan music in the West. Frank Zappa invited the "Three Tuvans" home for a jam session with the Chieftains and Johnny Guitar Watson that was filmed by a BBC television crew. Mickey Hart, the drummer for the Grateful Dead, left a message on my answering machine asking whether the Tuvans would be willing to have their throat-singing digitally sampled for future use in his own music (the Tuvans had never heard of Hart or the Grateful Dead or digital sampling, but they were indeed willing). The Kronos Quartet invited the Tuvans to join a recording session at George Lucas's Skywalker Ranch, where Princeton University composer Steven Mackey quickly fashioned arrangements of two Tuvan songs for voice and punk string quartet.

As the Tuvans and I lumbered around the East Coast in my old station wagon en route from one concert to the next, Kaigal-ool popped a tape he had brought along into the cassette deck. It contained some of the most wonderful music I had ever heard. "Who's performing that music?" I asked after hearing it the first time.

"That's just me and some friends," said Kaigal-ool nonchalantly. "We were playing in Moscow last year, and a young guy from London came up after one of the concerts. He gave us his card and said that he was a sound engineer and had a studio, and if we ever came to London, he'd like to record us. A few months later, we borrowed some money, bought tickets to London, showed the card to a taxi driver, and turned up at his door. He wasn't expecting us, but we slept on the floor of his apartment for a week and recorded." Kaigal-ool fished the sound engineer's wrinkled business card out of his wallet, and soon I was on the phone with Trevor Goronwi.

The London recordings, supplemented by some made by Ralph Leighton following the Rose Bowl Parade, became *Sixty Horses in My Herd,* the first compact disc of the ensemble Huun-Huur-Tu, released in 1993 by Shanachie Records. The group of friends who had shown up at Trevor Goronwi's apartment was suddenly a band with a record contract. Kaigal-ool officially defected from the Tuva Ensemble, claiming that he wanted to take Tuvan music still one step further away from the folklorized performance style that had developed under the influence of Soviet-era culture policies. Kaigal-ool found kindred spirits in three other musicians: Albert Kuvezin and the Bapa brothers, Sasha and Sayan. Later, Anatoli Kuular also left the Tuva Ensemble to join Huun-Huur-Tu (Kuvezin would leave Huun-Huur-Tu to form his

The visual effect that Tuvans call *xün xürtü* (sun propeller): the vertical separation of light rays just after sunrise or before sunset. Central Tuva, 1995.

own ensemble, Yat-Kha, and Sasha Bapa would be replaced by Aleksei Sary-glar) (see plate 9).

Huun-Huur-Tu, or *xün xürtü* in standard transliteration, means "sun propeller" in Tuvan. Tuvans use the term metaphorically to describe the vertical separation of light rays— "Jesus rays" in American vernacular—often visible on the grasslands just after sunrise or just before sunset. As Sasha Bapa explained, "Tuvans call their open countryside *xün xürtü* because they are awed by the beauty of its light. Our ensemble used the name because the music we perform is rooted in that countryside and because the light rays on the steppe remind us of the separate lines of sound in throat-singing, except that in throat-singing, you're working not with light rays, but with sound rays."

Tuvan music had entered a new era. Not only was ethnographically recorded music from Tuva achieving commercial success in record stores, but Tuvan ensembles were performing in prestigious concert halls and collaborating with leading artists in the West. In Tuva, local cultural authorities had become alarmed. Zoya Kyrgys was furious about the defections from the Tuva Ensemble, and she blamed me for luring away Kaigal-ool by organizing tours and recordings for Huun-Huur-Tu. "Why should four musicians get all the work while fourteen musicians sit idle in Kyzyl?" she asked angrily in a burst of socialist logic.

Alarm about the exploitation of Tuvan music in the West spread to the top of the Tuvan government. The nominal president of Tuva, Oorzhak Sherig-ool, gave an interview to a group of visiting journalists in which he supported licensing throat-singers to perform abroad. "America does not send low-quality goods out to us," he reasoned with the journalists. "They don't supply the world with poor-quality merchandise. The same holds for bad actors and singers. They do not let them out of the country. Why should we? [Throat-singers] should be licensed. They should be tested so that only high-quality groups, real professionals not weak performers, travel abroad."[14] Meanwhile, Zoya Kyrgys nurtured a plan to patent throat-singing in the name of the Tuvan Ministry of Culture. If Tuva couldn't stop the worldwide spread of throat-singing, at least it could profit from throat-singing's popularity, she figured. In her scheme, the Ministry of Culture would collect a licensing fee from throat-singers—Tuvans or others—who earned hard currency income from their performances. She consulted with representatives of UNESCO and with several patent lawyers, who all advised her that trying to patent a musical style or technique was akin to trying to patent a language. It couldn't be done. Throat-singing was in the public domain.

Amid the clamor about commodification, exploitation, and ownership of Tuvan music, I returned to Tuva. My immediate goal was to disburse royalty income from the Smithsonian Folkways recording to the musicians who had sung into our microphones seven and eight years earlier, or, in the case of several who had died, to find family members to accept the money. But beyond this fiduciary responsibility, a larger issue was looming. After producing the Smithsonian recording and helping the ensemble Huun-Huur-Tu launch its career in the West, I had come to be regarded as a Tuvan music expert. The reality, however, was that I knew next to nothing about Tuvan music. Like all Westerners attracted to Tuva through its music, my point of entry had been throat-singing. Even after the two *National Geographic* expeditions, when we had recorded many different musical styles and genres, I had proposed limiting the Smithsonian release to throat-singing, arguing that it was all that would interest listeners in the West. Alekseyev had been wiser. "Throat-singing is only one part of a larger sound world," he had told me. "And you'll come to understand it only when you look at this sound world as a whole—at musical instruments like fiddles and jew's harps, at the articulatory features of language, at natural sounds and animal sounds—and not only in Tuva, but in surrounding parts of the Inner Asian nomadic world."

I hadn't forgotten those words, but amid the cult-like attention to throat-singing that followed the appearance of the compact discs and the concert tours, I had failed to take any action. Now I was back in Tuva to expand my tentative knowledge of its music in a direction that would lead not so much forward, into the world of commerce, digital sampling, artistic collaborations, and concert tours, as backward, into what remained of the traditional sound world of the Tuvan nomads. The members of Huun-Huur-Tu had agreed to be my guides and traveling companions. They understood that they would also benefit from this quest, for having come of age in the Soviet era, they had inherited a tradition that had been severely ruptured. Soviet cultural politics had promoted the creation of performing ensembles that could represent Tuva in the panoramic landscape of Soviet peoples and nationalities. But by doing so, they had cultivated a chimera whose relation to its Tuvan roots had become distorted.

Throat-singing, for example, had not been a performance art among the Tuvan herders. On the contrary, it was part of a highly personal dialogue between humans and the natural world. Putting throat-singing on a stage, where it was subjected to the demands of showmanship, represented a perversion of its original intent. But recovering what it had been before the Soviet era presented a challenge. The traditional worldview of the Tuvan pastoralists had been trammeled by the decades-long "struggle with the past" that was a centerpiece of Soviet cultural politics. During the 1930s, when Stalin's Terror bore down on the entire nation, Tuva had suffered even though it was not yet officially a part of the Soviet Union. The large Buddhist monastery at Chadaana was destroyed, the inhabitants were scattered, the senior lamas were shot.[15] Shamans were liquidated, and folk music was transformed into a tool of politics. Tuvans sang the Internationale and newly composed songs about building roads and the glories of collectivization—all in European bel canto style. Later had come the pallid socialist realist–infused folklore of the Khrushchev and Brezhnev eras. Soviet ethnographers such as A. N. Aksenov, whose anthology, *Tuvan Folk Music,* published in 1964, presented transcriptions of Tuvan folksongs collected from informants in the 1950s, helped to preserve in a passive form some of the richness of what had been.[16] But the tradition of performing this music had been marginalized in social life. Aksenov was able to conduct his ethnographic study of traditional music only because he was an outsider from Moscow, not a Tuvan, and local cultural authorities viewed his work as irrelevant to Tuvan culture itself.

Huun-Huur-Tu's Sasha Bapa was optimistic about the ability of Tuvan culture to regenerate itself. "Tuva is a small place," he said. "And fortunately, its resources are too limited to have attracted the worst of what the Soviet Union had to offer the 'small peoples' of Siberia: destruction of their natural habitat through industrialization, deforestation, and urbanization." Fortunately as well, Tuva's population of ethnic Tuvans—around 200,000 in the mid-1990s—had been large enough to avoid another of the ignominious fates of Siberian peoples: annihilation of their culture through language loss and assimilation.[17] Tuvan, which belongs to the Oghuz group of Eastern Turkic languages, was still very much alive in the countryside, and this fact bode well for our studies. The relationship between singing, language, poetics, and the sounds, topographies, and beings of the natural world would form a primary focus of our work. The animistic spirituality that nourished this relationship was also very much alive, even if it was not immediately apparent in the urban landscape of Kyzyl, where many of Tuva's best musicians resettled in order to pursue their careers.

At the end of my brief visit in 1995, I said goodbye to the members of Huun-Huur-Tu and promised to return the next year for a longer stay that would be the starting point for our journey backward toward the source of the music that had traveled from this tiny spot in Siberia all around the world.

2

THE WORLD IS ALIVE WITH THE MUSIC OF SOUND

MUSICAL OFFERINGS

Kaigal-ool optimistically threw another log on the fire as Tolya trolled the shallow waters of the Shemi River with his fishing rod. It was the middle of a sunny afternoon—too late for lunch and unfashionably early for dinner—yet when we'd approached the bridge over the Shemi on our drive westward from Kyzyl, Tolya had reflexively pulled the car over, and we'd unloaded a box of food and cooking utensils and created an instant campsite on a grassy knoll along the bank. We'd been traveling for two days, but had barely covered 150 miles, not due to car problems or bad roads, but because of constant stops like this one. There was no utilitarian purpose behind the stop; no one was hungry, needed to use the woods, or wanted to take a photo. The purpose was simply to pass some time by a river in the most natural of riparian activities: building a fire, cooling off in the fresh water, fishing, and, in the case of my Tuvan companions, singing. What they had in mind, however, was not your typical campfire songs.

Tolya was slouched on a rock perch, lazily casting his fishing line into the boulder-strewn river when I first heard him sing to the water. He was throat-singing in a style onomatopoetically called *borbangnadyr*—literally, "rolling." The soaring harmonics of his high, flute-like melody were seemingly amplified by the hissing and gurgling of the river water flowing, or rolling, over and around the rocks. I listened from a distance, afraid that if Tolya noticed I was paying attention, he might become self-conscious and stop.

"Spectacular!" I shouted when he had finished.

Tolya shrugged. "In the old days, herders used to sit by a stream in the evening and throat-sing," he said matter-of-factly. "The stream itself showed them how to sing. Listen." Tolya began again, trying several different initial pitches before finding one that satisfied him. Starting with a long drone note, he introduced rhythmic articulations with movements of his lips and tongue, shaping the drone into a pulsating, roiling tone that propelled itself forward with seemingly effortless ease. A piercing overtone melody rose out of the thick texture of the fundamental pitch, and the gyrating rhythm of the over-tones interlocked with rhythms created by the swiftly flowing water. Tolya sang a couple of breaths of melody at a time, pausing between breaths to listen to the river, like a jazz musician momentarily dropping out to listen to a fellow band member take a solo (see plate 11).

"People would pay big money in the States to hear throat-singing like that," I joked.

Tolya looked serious. "No one ever did this kind of singing for money," he replied. "It's not concert music. It's something I do for my own pleasure, and as an offering to spirits."

"Which spirits?"

"The local spirit, or master, of the river." When I asked Tolya to clarify what he meant in Tuvan—our conversation had been in Russian—he used the word *ee* (pronounced "ehhh") to translate the terms for "master" and "spirit."[2] The same word can mean "owner" or "host" when it refers to humans. When referring to spirits, it is often preceded by *cher*—"place" or "land"—thus *cher eezi* is most accurately translated as "local spirit-master" or "local spirit-host." For sake of consistency and brevity I will use the term "spirit-master," with the proviso that "local" is always implied. Among spirit-masters, those who preside over rivers (*xem eezi*) and water (*sug eezi*) are considered exceptionally powerful, for their benevolence affects not only the well-being of humans but also of fish, animals, and nature itself.[3]

"Every natural place has an *ee*—a master or guardian—who looks after it and protects all the beings that live there," Tolya continued. "Mountains, rivers, caves, springs—all are under the protection of a spirit-master. When you visit that place, you should show your respect to the master."

Tolya Kuular sings *borbangnadyr* with flowing water (Video File, track 3, "The Singing River"). Preceding Tolya's singing is a videographic soundscape of the Xündergei River, popularly known as the Yraajy-Xem, or Singing River. The video image focuses on a point in the river that Tolya considered to be particularly evocative of human singing and speech. Following the example of *borbangnadyr*, Tolya describes two onomatopoetic water sounds in a sequence filmed along a small tributary of the "Singing River."[1] (Subtitled text is printed in note 1.)

"How do you show respect to a spirit-master?" I asked.

"You leave an offering. The most common is to tie a piece of white cloth (*chalama*). But you can leave food, candy, cigarettes, money. And you can sing. Music is the best offering. Whether or not a person sings well, the spirit-master will be glad to hear the sound. The most important thing is not to upset the spirit—to calm the spirit."

"When does throat-singing calm the spirit-master?"

"If you are calm inside, your singing will calm the spirit. If you're angry or plotting against someone, it will arouse the spirit. A bad person shouldn't sing."

"How do you know what kind of singing will please the spirit-master?"

"The spirit-master likes to hear the sounds of the place or thing that it protects. If you want to please the spirit, you have to make those sounds. That's why people sing like a river, or like the wind on a mountain, or like a bird."

"So when you were just throat-singing, you were imitating the sound of the river's own singing?" I asked.

"Of course," said Tolya, looking surprised at my question. "The river is alive. Rivers sing."

Crouched amid the larch trees by the gushing water, I had just witnessed what some aficionados of neoprimitivism might have hailed as the reenchantment of the world, the reharmonization of man and nature, the reconsecration of the *anima mundi*. And yet there in the flesh, Tolya's display of vocal sorcery had seemed utterly ordinary, without the slightest pretense of heightened consciousness, elevated awareness, or any other privileged psycho-spiritual state. He had flipped his fishing line into the water and started to throat-sing, and that was that. Nonetheless, in this simple act, and in the brief explanation that followed, Tolya had proposed a way of understanding music and humankind's relation to nature that was possibly ancient, representing what one might call an animist view of the world. In quick strokes, he had sketched a theory of Tuvan musical aesthetics whose main line of reasoning went something like the following: Everything in nature is inhabited by spirit-masters (or spirit-mistresses; spirits can be female, although throat-singing has traditionally been confined to men; see chapter 6, "Women Are Not Supposed to Do This"). To coexist peacefully with these spirit-masters and gain access to the natural resources under their protection, humans have to make offerings, offer praise, and show respect. Sound and song provide a means of doing all three, albeit in different ways.

Praise-songs and chants, called *algysh,* and the rhythmically chanted poetic couplets that typically precede breaths of throat-singing, address spirit-masters with words. Throat-singing itself, that is, wordless vocalizations consisting of reinforced harmonics, imitates sounds produced by the places or beings in which the spirit-masters dwell. By reproducing their sound, the singer establishes contact with the spirit-master and enters into a conversation whose aim is supplication, an expression of gratitude, or an appeal for protection. The same imitative or mimetic interaction with the natural sound world may also be mediated through musical instruments. For example, performers use fiddles (*igil, byzaanchy*) and plucked lutes (*doshpuluur, chanzy*) to represent the sounds of horses, while the end-blown flute (*shoor* or *tsuur*) and jew's harp (*xomus*) can handily imitate a wide variety of animal and environmental sounds.

Tolya would have been the last to think of himself as a music theorist; indeed, he had never taken a music class. But within his own world, the conceptual underpinnings of animistic sound mimesis were perfectly apparent. To the question, "What is behind the human impulse to imitate?"—a question that has stirred the minds of Plato, Aristotle, Darwin, Freud (*Totem and Taboo*), and J. G. Frazer (*The Golden Bough*), to name only a few in the pantheon of Western thought—Tolya had a straightforward answer. "Imitation is a continuation of something. When you listen to the sounds of birds, they're very beautiful, so talented people try to imitate them. When you imitate something in nature, you remember it, and you put yourself there in that place."

Did Tolya, the intrepid Jeep Cherokee driver who sanguinely navigated Los Angeles freeways and crisscrossed the world in jet airplanes, really believe that the world was inhabited by spirits? "Absolutely," said Tolya when I put the question to him. "I'm proud to be an animist," he answered in response to my query. "Believing that there are many spirits makes more sense than believing in one god. There are a lot of rivers and mountains. How can one god watch over everything?"

For Tuvans who embrace a traditional worldview, the spirit world is hard to avoid.[4] For them, the world is thick with spirits. And it is not simply shamans and seers who have access to this world. Everyone can have such access. When you travel with Tuvans—just about any Tuvans—the proximity and ubiquity of the spirit world becomes clear. The spirits do not dwell in a distant Valhalla but are often easily accessible, particularly at points of spiritual power such as mountain passes, which typically feature a stone cairn (*ovaa;* Mongolian, *oboo*) where travelers leave offerings to the spirit-host of the pass, or at orifices in the earth's surface, such as springs and caves, that link the inner and outer worlds[5] (see plate 12).

For an example of an offering at an *ovaa,* see the video files online, track 2, "A Drive in the Mountains."

A ridge of hills near Chadaana known as "Tei" (meaning "crown," as in the crown of the head) may assume a human form for Tuvan viewers. Designations noted above were provided by Anatoli Kuular. 2003.

Sacred trees, often distinguished by great age, distinctive form, or anomalous location relative to their species, and draped with strips of cloth left as offerings, are also loci of spiritual power[6] (see plates 13 and 14). In a different sense, the spiritual animation of inanimate nature is expressed through the personification of landscape, in particular ridges of hills and mountains, in which Tuvans visualize the parts of a human figure. These figures seem to be imagined at once horizontally—laid out along the contour of a ridge, with a contiguous forehead, nose, neck, and shoulders—and vertically, rising from the bottom of an elevation to the top. In vertical configuration, the main features are the head, shoulders, liver (the principal planar surface of a hill or mountain), and, in the forested area at the bottom of the slope, the hemline of the figure's silk robe.[7]

IN A CAVE

Many legends speak about the power of music performed in caves. Valentina Süzükei recorded one such legend, about a young shepherd who was herding his animals in a place known by the toponym Eder-Kuilar ("Singing Caves"), whose name refers to the phenomenon of wind blowing across the mouth of a cave and creating ambient sound. In the legend, a shepherd wandered into the eponymous cave, where he encountered a man throat-singing to the accompaniment of an unknown and enchanting instrument. Begging the man to let him play the instrument, the shepherd picked it up and started to accompany his singing. He fell into a trance from the sound of his own music, and only many years later emerged from the cave to find all his loved ones long gone. Becoming an itinerant musician, he wandered the countryside, muttering, "Return, return, return to me, my loved ones" (*egider, egider*), and that's why the local people started to call his instrument *egil*.[8]

During a trip to the south of Tuva in the spring of 1996, I first heard spirit-calling music performed in the bone-chilling cold and dampness of a cave. The visit to the cave had been the idea of Kaigal-ool, who proposed including it in a project to record throat-singing and other types of Tuvan music in the natural acoustic environments in which, according to the members of Huun-Huur-Tu, they were meant to be performed.[9] Kaigal-ool had heard about a particular cave in the vicinity of Mören, a small settlement near Naryn, not far from the border with Mongolia, which was reputedly inhabited by spirits. Once, during a concert tour with his ensemble, Ayan, local people told Kaigal-ool that musicians made secret pilgrimages to the cave with the aim of leaving a musical offering to the spirit-master, and that stringed instruments such as the *igil* and *byzaanchy* were the favored medium for such offerings. Hidden in the steep face of a rocky hill known as *Ak-Xai-yrakan*, or "White Sacred Mountain," the cave was said to be difficult to find, and we were advised to take along a local guide. *Xaiyrakan* is a Tuvan word with a double meaning that illustrates the extent to which belief in spirits has infused language itself. In one sense, *xaiyrakan* is a pseudonym for a zoological term, *adyg*, which means "bear." Out of respect for their spiritual power, Tuvans colloquially refer to bears by means of a taboo terminology (taboo terminologies for bear-naming exist in Indo-European languages as well; for example, "bear" derives from Germanic *beran*, literally "the brown one"; the Russian word for bear, *medved'*, literally means "honey-eater"). By extension, *xairyakan* refers to a sacred place inhabited by a bear spirit.[10] A well-known *xairyakan* near Kyzyl is a hill shaped like the profile of a recumbent bear. Hunting and foraging are forbidden there, and even an approach to such a sacred site must be made with the greatest respect.

A few inquiries in Mören led to a rough-hewn shepherd, who assured us that he knew where the cave was located and that he would be willing to lead us there. As we set out, an elderly woman urged us not to photograph

A pass near Shagonar is venerated both in Buddhist and animist traditions. The Tibetan mantra *Om Mani Padme Hum* (Behold the Jewel in the Lotus) is written on the lower sign, while the upper one says "Tuva's Great *Ovaa*, Ten Kum." In the background is the rock *xaiyrakan,* or sacred mountain, in the form of a recumbent bear, 2000.

or record anything in the cave. "It's a sacred place and you shouldn't disturb the spirits," she admonished us. Kaigal-ool was respectful, but firm.

"Don't worry about us," he told her. "We're musicians. We know how to behave around spirits." Our guide directed the jeep driver to a rutted track, and we lurched over the steppe for several miles until the guide suddenly held up his hand in an indication to stop. A wispy trail transected the ruts, and the old herdsman pointed up the trail.

"The cave is that way," he said, climbing out of the jeep. We unloaded recording equipment and instruments—Kaigal-ool's *igil,* Tolya's *byzaanchy,* Sayan's *doshpuluur,* and Aleksei's big bass drum, packed in a cloth bag that hung awkwardly from a shoulder strap. Kaigal-ool's wife, Anya, had also come along. A businesswoman who manages a portion of Kyzyl's sprawling wholesale market, she relished the chance to get away from her office for a few days of hiking and camping.

It was midmorning, but the herdsman's breath smelled of alcohol. Even with a walking stick, he wobbled as he picked his way slowly along the rock-strewn path. Kaigal-ool was not much faster. He is a heavy smoker, and when fawning Westerners would ask how he was able to produce the raspy bass tones used in throat-singing, he'd reply with a straight face that the first step was to smoke a pack of Camels a day. As we hiked, he would frequently call a halt to catch his breath. At one rest stop, a scenic spot where the trail dropped over the striated face of a small cliff, Kaigal-ool took his *igil* out of the case and accompanied himself in an improvised fantasia of *sygyt* and *xöömei,* two styles of throat-singing. As he sang, tears welled in the eyes of our guide.

"Your singing moved our guide to tears," I commented to Kaigal-ool when he had finished. "The music must have affected him strongly."

Kaigal-ool looked at the old herder dismissively. "Hard to know whether it was the music, or whether he's just drunk and feeling sentimental. Anyway, it's normal for Tuvans to cry when they hear music."

"Except at funerals," Anya interjected. "If you weep at a funeral, people would take you away. I didn't cry at my father's funeral. We knew our father would be proud that we didn't cry—that we were strong."

Kaigal-ool went on, "Music makes listeners remember their own feelings—of childhood and family, and of being in a particular place. For example, when I played that piece, I was creating an image of a summer pasturing area where I'd herded as a child, and I put myself there."

"So one of the purposes of music is to create nostalgia?" I asked.

"The point is not simply to bring back memories, but actually to travel back to that place and experience it again so that it comes alive."

The impromptu performance and the nostalgia-filled moment it created on the rock face offered a temporary distraction from the besotted orienteering of our guide. As he hobbled along the trail followed by four increasingly disgruntled, instrument-bearing musicians, the old coot could not have inspired less confidence. Not more than ten minutes after our musical rest stop, he suddenly halted and feebly confessed that it had been a long time since he had visited the cave and wasn't sure he could find it. Or perhaps, he added slyly in an attempt to cover his ineptitude, we had angered the mountain spirits and they had temporarily closed or hidden the entrance to the cave. Such occurrences were well known, he reminded us. He offered to keep searching on his own while the rest of the group waited by the trail, but Kaigal-ool angrily declined his offer. We did an about-face and, cursing and singing, carried knapsacks and instruments back to the jeep where the guide was minimally compensated and curtly dismissed.

A chance encounter with a teenage boy walking along the road led us to our second guide. With renewed determination, we set off in the jeep, this time avoiding roads, tracks, and trails, and setting off straight across the stubbly steppe. Our young guide suggested that on the way we should stop at a natural spring that served as a local pilgrimage site. Leaving an offering at the spring would be auspicious, said our guide, for it would be a sign of respect for the spirit-master who controlled the land that provided access to the cave. The Tuvan word for spring, *arzhaan,* means more than a place where water bubbles up from the ground. An *arzhaan* is always a place that is considered sacred, a place whose mineral-rich waters have healing powers. We parked the jeep a respectful distance from the spring and approached it on foot.

The spring bubbled up from a small pool at the foot of a rock escarpment and trickled over one of the edges of the pool to form a pebbly streambed. To one side was a makeshift shrine where visitors had placed a variety of offerings on plates set on top of a flat rock. Slices of sausage, a pickle, cigarettes, bread, and a can of sardines had been deposited on the plates. Next to it were the charred remains of *artysh*—juniper twigs—ritually burned when the offerings were left. The smoky, coniferous aroma of the green twigs is thought to be pleasing to the spirit-masters and is commonly used by shamans as a purifying incense. The spring itself was marked by pieces of white cloth tied to an adjacent juniper bush, and by a small portrait of the Dalai Lama set in a self-standing picture frame. Such syncretic shrines are common in Tuva: Buddhist icons joined to animist offerings.[11] I knelt in front of the small pool and started to dip cupped hands into the cold water.

"Not so close!" Tolya shouted, pushing my hands away from the water. "When you drink from a spring, you never take water from the place where it actually comes out of the ground so that you don't disturb the spirit-master. Take the water from where it goes over the pebbles," he said, pointing to the trickle flowing over the lip of the pool. Or in other words, just the opposite of what is taught to every Boy Scout who ever took a drink in the woods: scoop spring water from as close to the source as possible to avoid contamination. Later I heard much more dire warnings on this subject from an elderly singer in Mongolia. "People die because they don't respect the spirit of a spring," he told me gravely. "They take water from the center of the spring instead of from the periphery, and without offering a prayer. And then, all of a sudden, something happens to them, and they're gone."[12]

Having paid our respects to the spirit-master of the spring, we drove onward toward the cave. This time, our guide knew exactly where to go. Parking the jeep in a field of desiccated grass, we unloaded knapsacks and instruments and set off along a well-marked trail that ascended through a series of switchbacks to a steep, scree-covered slope. The trail gave out at the bottom of the scree, and we were left to scramble over it by whatever route seemed least treacherous. At the top of the scree was a series of pale ledges that rose verti-

Offerings to the spirit-master of a spring left on a nearby
rock near Mören Cave, southern Tuva, 1996.

cally for perhaps another 200 feet to the jagged summit of the hill. Tucked
into one of those ledges was the entrance to the cave. Standing at the bottom
of the scree and gazing up at the ominous rock, Kaigal-ool confessed that
he was acrophobic. He would wait in the safety of the shrubbery while the
rest of us, including his wife, Anya, climbed to the cave. Aleksei, once again
carrying the large bass drum, and also an acrophobe, readily agreed to keep
Kaigal-ool company.

Each to his own phobia. Mine is claustrophobia. I dread going into caves,
and it took all my willpower to follow Sayan, Tolya, and Anya into the cold
and dark passageway, ducking beneath a flock of exiting birds that swooshed
past us like a missile. Several hundred feet inside the cave, in a chamber dense
with stalactites, I unpacked the tape recorder and microphones and with
gloved hands began to set up for a recording session. Tolya assured me there
was nothing to fear, for we were under the protection of the spirit-master
of the cave. Outside the entrance, we had added a strip of white cloth to the
collection left by previous visitors. In a perversion of the ritual offering, some
visitors had scrawled graffiti on the rock overhang at the cave's entrance.
Sayan swore at the perpetrators and lamented their transgression. "No real

Anya Xovalyg, Sayan Bapa, Tolya Kuular, guide, and jeep driver
standing before the entrance to the Mören Cave, 1996.

Tuvan would do something like that," he growled, as if trying to convince himself.[13]

Inside the chamber, Tolya took out his *byzaanchy* by the light of a kerosene lamp and tuned it up. I plugged microphone cables into the DAT recorder and listened through headphones to the room sound. Water dripped from the stalactites onto one of the microphones, creating a loud ping in the earphones. All in all, it seemed to me an unlikely setting for musical offerings to spirits, but Tolya and Sayan relished the amplified resonance of the *byzaanchy* and the sharply reinforced harmonics of the different throat-singing styles they tried. For them, making music for spirits in a cave was an entirely realistic scenario. "You can really feel the presence of the spirit-master here," said Tolya, his face beaming in the lantern light. We recorded more music, but neither Tolya's ample physical stamina nor his stoicism could keep his fingers from freezing up. Signaling the end of the recording session by holding up his stiffened hand, he packed up his instrument while I put away the tape recorder and microphones, and we made our way back toward the entrance and the warm light of summer. An excerpt from the recording session inside the cave is available online (Audio File, track 5).

NATURAL REVERB

Tolya and Sayan had reveled in the strong reverberation of voices and instruments inside the cave, and they had connected the strong reverb with the ability of sound to reach spirits. But their love of reverb was not limited to caves. Any naturally reverberant acoustic space and the spirits that dwelled there could be animated by the physical stimulus of sound. Cliffs, valleys, forests, and mountains are all imbued with the power to resonate—indeed to sing—in response to sounds made by humans as well as wind, birds, and animals. One of the most dramatic examples of resonant reverberation is the vocal genre called in Tuvan *uzun yr* or in Mongolian *urtyn duu,* literally "long-song."[14] Long-songs are so called not because they are long, but because each syllable of text is extended for a long duration. Whatever a vocalist's range, long-songs are pitched near the top of it and sung at dynamic levels that extend from forte to fortissimo to earsplitting.

Theories about the origin of long-song abound in Mongolia and Tuva, and like most singers, Kaigal-ool had his own version.[15] "In the old days there weren't a lot of bridges, and it wasn't easy to cross rivers. People used to sing to one another across the banks of a river because song carries better than speech, and that kind of long-distance singing became long-song. Old people told me that." In Mongolia, I heard from a well-known singer that long-songs arose in the Gobi Desert because "it's difficult to be heard in the desert," so herders used their strong voices to shout and sing to their sheep. In another telling, people went to the mountains in times of drought and sang long-songs with the hope that their reverberation would please the spirits and bring rain. In other words, sound as a form of technology used to achieve a particular result had eventually become transformed into sound as art.

Long-songs are the fetish of connoisseurs of landscape acoustics. They elicit the distinctive sonic qualities of a favorite outdoor place, and long-song singers savor and recall these, perhaps like opera singers recounting the acoustical wonders of the world's great opera houses. Kaigal-ool is the first to admit that he is what pop musicians would call a "reverb freak." The difference is that he likes his reverb produced naturally, not digitally. He wanted me to hear and record the powerful effect of a long-song sung in the lee of a favorite riverine cliff, and one gloriously sunny day we drove east from Kyzyl along the macadam road that runs parallel to the Kaa-Xem, or Lesser Yenisei, to a spot about a half-hour from town, where a dirt track forks off toward the river and leads to a small beach popular with weekend picnickers and trysters. On the opposite bank of the river, not a hundred feet away, a sheer rock face loomed high above us. We built a small fire, and Kaigal-ool burned a few sprigs of *artysh* that he had brought for the occasion as an offering to the spirit-master of the river. Then he took up his position at the water's edge and, with a mighty intake of air, began to sing "Kyzyl-Taiga" (Red Taiga) in a plangent, open-throated voice. Each phrase of text ended on a loud, sustained pitch that Kaigal-ool cut off abruptly, leaving the echo from the cliff reverberating over the sound of water lapping against the stony beach. To my ears the effect was mesmerizing, but Kaigal-ool wasn't satisfied.

"The echo is muted," he complained. "It's the wrong time of day to be trying this. Reverb from cliffs sounds better in the evening or at night." Kaigal-ool's claim indeed can be empirically confirmed. Colder evening temperatures result in denser air, providing a less dissipative medium and a higher velocity of wave propagation, thus a crisper, louder sound. For optimum recording conditions, Kaigal-ool suggested that we return to the site at around 11:00 PM.

A video clip of Kyzyl-Taiga made during daylight hours in t he same location with sound dubbed from the late-night recording session appears in the online video files, track 23.

We did, but by that time, a wind had come up, a light rain had started to fall, and doing any more recording was out of the question. Repacking the equipment, we returned to Kyzyl. Bad weather or noisy late-night partygoers foiled our recording plans several times, but on one late-night foray, everything fell into place. The air was cold, the cliff reverberant, and Kaigal-ool was in fine form. After trying several different starting pitches, he found one that seemed just right for the reverberant space, and we got an excellent recording on the first take.

In using his voice to excite the reverberant qualities of the cliff, Kaigal-ool's aim was not simply to hear his own voice amplified, but rather to feel an interaction with the startlingly beautiful natural scenario in which he emplaced himself through singing. "I love to hear the voice of the cliff speaking back to me," he told me during one of our late-night recording sessions. "It's a kind of meditation—a conversation that I have with nature. After I've sung in a place, I can really feel that place as my own. And I feel like I belong to that place."

The spiritual quality of acoustically resonant landscapes can be evoked not only by human sound-makers but also by sounds originating in nature itself. It is exactly such acoustic phenomena—natural sound sources providing a sonic stimulus to an overtone-rich ambient environment—that are offered as examples of how people learned from nature to throat-sing. In Tuva, I heard one such story while hiking with Kaigal-ool, Tolya, and Sayan on a windy hilltop near the Mongolian border. Encountering ferocious gusts, I unpacked my microphone to capture the sound of wind. At that moment, Kaigal-ool remembered once hearing the sound of wind exciting the strings of a zither that a herder had placed on the roof of a yurt so that the gut strings could dry in the sun. The excitation of the strings had produced a soft wash of harmonics, as if the zither were an Aeolian harp, and these harmonic sounds had inspired humans to produce harmonics themselves—or so the story went, as Kaigal-ool remembered it.[16]

Kaigal-ool and Sayan, who happened to be carrying their instruments, quickly unpacked the *igil* and *doshpuluur,* held them up to the wind, and turned them until the wind passed over the strings at just the right angle to produce maximum harmonic output. The results of that impromptu recording session are reproduced in the audio files online (see track 2).

Musicians in the west of Mongolia recounted analogous stories to members of the Trans-Altai Musical-Ethnographic Expedition when we traveled there in summer 2000 to investigate similarities and differences between Tuvan and Mongolian music.[17] In Hovd Aimag, the region widely regarded in Mongolia as the birthplace of throat-singing, expert local opinion was unanimous: "*Höömii* is from the mountains," said Sengedorj (b. 1948), Hovd's foremost *höömiich,* or throat-singer, in a discussion during a recording session in the small auditorium of Hovd's theater. "*Höömii* is an imitation of wind," he added. "It's the sound of the mountain wind singing."

Sengedorj became even more specific. "People first learned to sing *höömii* in Chandman," he said. Chandman, a *sum,* or district of steppe bounded by mountains that abuts Hovd Aimag's largest lake, Har-Us, lies about sixty-five miles southeast of Hovd as the crow flies, although to drive there takes the better part of a full day since you have to skirt the mountains and the huge lake, and the route—not really a road—is pretty rough. "There's a mountain behind Chandman called Jargalant," said Sengedorj. "It's not part of a ridge, but sticks up all by itself. You can always tell when a storm is coming, because two or three hours before it arrives, you'll hear the wind blowing hard on the peak of Jargalant, and the whole mountain starts to hum and sing. When you hear the mountain sing, you know it's time to round up your animals. Those mountain sounds are like the sounds of the human voice. Listening to the mountain sing is how humans first got the idea to sing *höömii.*"[18]

Later we went to Chandman Sum, a dusty settlement of concrete block houses and yurt barrios, hoping to hear the singing mountain with our own ears. In open grazing land well beyond the town, we met Tserendavaa (b.

1955), a local musical notable as well as a prosperous herder who managed large numbers of sheep, goats, cows, horses, and a few camels. Tserendavaa and his family were preparing to break camp and move to new grazing grounds, but after the evening roundup was completed, he good-naturedly agreed to sit with us and share his knowledge of music (see Audio File, track 1) (see plate 15). Several of Tserendavaa's eight children joined the circle of listeners seated in front of him on a well-grazed lawn outside his yurt (or *ger,* the Mongolian word for yurt). Tserendavaa had toured the United States and Great Britain in the late 1980s, and his youngest daughter was wearing shoes with McDonald's golden arches, while New York Yankees and LA souvenir caps sprouted from the heads of the boys.[19]

Tserendavaa not only confirmed Sengedorj's story about Mount Jargalant but also added another story about how natural sounds inspired humans to sing *höömii.* "Around three hundred years ago, during the time of Galdan Khan (d. 1697), leader of the Oirats, the western Mongolian tribal confederation that controlled much of Central Asia until they were conquered by the Manchus in 1758, a famous teacher of *höömii* named Bazarsad lived in Chandman.[20] He used to walk near Lake Har-Us, where a lot of bamboo grew along the shore. He listened to the wind blowing off the lake and whistling through the bamboo, and began thinking about how it was possible to imitate that sound—how it was possible to sing and whistle at the same time. He tried imitating those sounds, and that's how he began to sing *höömii.* There's still bamboo down by the lake, and you can still hear the wind whistling through it."

Tserendavaa's stories about the origins of *höömii* flowed smoothly, and indeed, we were hardly the first outsiders to hear them. Tserendavaa's career and musical ideas are extensively described in Carole Pegg's *Mongolian Music, Dance, and Oral Narrative.* Another well-known singer in Chandman, Daavaajav, runs a virtual cottage industry that caters to the thriving international cult of throat-singing. On the day we visited, Daavaajav was less interested in talking about sound and nature than about the helicopter-load of Japanese tourists he was expecting later in the summer, and about the litany of foreign visitors who had come before us: German filmmakers, Yamaha sound engineers, and an advertising director from NHK, the Japanese television conglomerate. The singing mountain had reverberated around the world, but we never heard it during our brief and, alas, windless stay in Chandman.

INTERLUDE

A week after returning from Tuva, I was still going to sleep and waking up puritanically early as my body grudgingly adjusted to the twelve-hour time difference between southern Siberia and northern New England. Descending to my basement office at Dartmouth College just after sunrise on a crisp autumn morning, I saw that the answering machine had already recorded the first message of the day. The message was from Anthony ("Tony") Seeger, director of Smithsonian Folkways Recordings, who had supervised the release of *Tuva: Voices from the Center of Asia* five years earlier. Already at work in Folkways' Washington, D.C. headquarters, Tony had phoned to ask how Folkways should respond to a letter requesting permission to license a track from the *Tuva* compact disc. In the Folkways model of a socially responsible recording company, record producers are charged with representing the interests of musicians and communities involved in their projects. My advice about the license request would be crucial to Folkways' decision on how to handle it. Tony read the text of the letter into my answering machine:

"We are a production company in Sweden producing a commercial for a small Swedish snack company. We have created a story about a 'Cheese-tribe.' The inhabitants in the cheese village worship the cheese. But one day, a strange object falls down from the sky. It's the cheesier snack: the cheese doodles that are cheesier than cheese. The people in the village are very happy and a new era is born. I know it sounds crazy, but it would be even more crazy if we could use one of our favorite songs that we found on one of your records. The record is 'Tuva: Voices from the Center of Asia,' song no. 8. We would like to use thirty seconds. . . . We don't have much of a budget, but we could pay a thousand U.S. dollars."

Tumat Kara-ool accompanying throat-singing on a Russian *balalaika* for lack of a Tuvan *doshpuluur*. Photo by Karen Sherlock, 1987.

Tony ended his message with a question: "Is what is being proposed an appropriate use of the Tuvan music?"

Awash in impressions from my just-completed Tuvan travels, I considered the implications of Tony Seeger's question. I thought about the gratitude of musicians, and in some cases, their heirs, for receipt of the modest royalties from the Smithsonian Folkways recording—royalties that I had taken to Tuva to distribute. Several thousand dollars had been converted into tens of millions of rubles, and these rubles had been spread around the dusty settlements of the grasslands as Kaigal-ool, Sayan, and I knocked on the doors of yurts and tumbledown houses in search of the musicians who had performed for Eduard Alekseyev, Zoya Kyrgys, and me in 1987 and 1988. Recalling these encounters, I was sure that had the licensing request arrived before my trip to Tuva, and had I been able to consult with the musician who recorded "song no. 8," Tumat Kara-ool, he would have readily endorsed the sale of his music to the Swedes. The song was a *kojamyk*—a personal song not linked to a ritual context and devoid of explicitly spiritual content. The deal was honest, and Kara-ool needed the money. It was that simple.

But other concerns began to percolate. Did providing background music for a cheese-doodle commercial constitute "appropriate use of the music"? How, in any event, would one decide what was "appropriate," and who should make that decision? Suppose that one were able to find Kara-ool, who, as it turned out, was one of the musicians to whom we hadn't been able to disburse royalties; according to last reports, he had started to drink and often disappeared for days at a time. What would one ask him? Could Kara-ool, an aging herder and amateur musician from a tiny settlement, be expected to make informed decisions about the use of his music in a cultural milieu so utterly foreign? Finally, suppose it were decided that the use of Kara-ool's music was appropriate and that licensing permission ought to be granted. Was a thousand dollars a fair price for thirty seconds of such unique and extraordinary music? Or perhaps the ad agency's request to use the *kojamyk* for a cheese-doodle commercial ought to be considered a boon to Tuva and its music. Perhaps such requests represent exactly what is meant to happen in the free cultural marketplace to which many Tuvans aspire in their own land: that is, musicians in Tuva make a recording; a company in the United States releases it; a producer in Sweden hears it, and a new context is created for Tuvan music; its audience expands, its meaning evolves, and the music takes on a new life. Did I want to stand in the way of this process, which I had first set in motion and which would happen anyway sooner or later, regardless of the decision about the cheese-doodle ad?

Since the appearance of the Smithsonian recording in 1990, twenty-three compact discs of Tuvan music had been released around the world. Not a single one was commercially available in Tuva.[1] Rather, they were products that serviced the world music marketplace, recorded for the most part in studios in Europe, the United States, or Moscow by Tuvan ensembles recruited by Western producers. From the perspective of many Tuvans, the creation of these CDs exclusively for foreign markets appeared suspiciously like a colonialist enterprise: a local, natural (or in this case, cultural) resource is exported to the West, where value is added through the investment of labor, technology, and marketing expertise to create a product designed to generate profits, the bulk of which remain in the West. Moreover, such products seem invariably to nourish fear among the official cultural establishment about the tainting and cheapening of Tuvan music as a result of performers' efforts to blend local music with the latest trends in the West, or to cash in on throat-singing as a form of readily marketable musical exotica. Would the cheese-doodle ad be like pouring salt on a wound?

On the other hand, perhaps the concerns of the culture establishment about colonialist exploitation and loss of authenticity were paternalistic and condescending. While a few musicians may have suffered at the hands of un-scrupulous entrepreneurs, most of those who entered the free cultural marketplace seemed to be doing very well. And more than a few musicians were extremely cynical about the culture authorities' newly found solicitousness in defending their rights. "They never showed any interest in us until musicians started to earn money," one musician friend complained. "Musicians lived terribly—they were housed in dormitories, suffered from alcoholism, and were paid a pittance for making exhausting tours within Tuva, and if they were lucky, around other parts of Siberia. The government didn't give a damn about them during those times. Rather than support throat-singing, they tried to repress it. There were never more than a symbolic handful of throat-singing songs performed in festivals or concerts during Soviet times, because there had to be room for Soviet songs. Then, as soon as the rest of the world started to show some interest, all of a sudden, they wanted a piece of the action."

As to the issue of innovation contravening authenticity, I had never heard musicians or their immediate community of local listeners worry aloud about Tuvan music being tainted through contact with other musical traditions. On the contrary, bootleg cassettes of Tuvan music recorded in the West were greatly valued in Tuva, and many Tuvans spoke warmly of the success of groups such as Huun-Huur-Tu and Yat-Kha that brought Tuvan music to a worldwide audience in new forms accessible to a younger generation of listeners.

Thinking back to my recent trip, I was also reminded of the great sense of humor that is such an important part of Tuvan culture. With that in mind, I phoned Tony Seeger, took a deep breath, and told him, "Go ahead and license the *kojamyk* to the cheese-doodle people." Sometime later, I received a copy of the ad on a videocassette. Though to the best of my knowledge, Tumat Kara-ool has never seen it, other Tuvan musicians who did found it amusing and inoffensive, if rather silly.

The television commercial that resulted is included in the online video files, track 24.

3

LISTENING THE
TUVAN WAY

TIMBRE-CENTERED MUSIC

Valentina Süzükei did not set out to become Tuva's leading ethnomusicologist. As a student growing up in the 1960s and early 1970s, her passion was dance. Later, she studied conducting at the Moscow Institute of Culture, which trained arts specialists both to work in schools and to serve in the Soviet Union's sprawling network of community arts centers. These "houses of culture" or "palaces of culture" offered adult education classes and extracurricular activities for children with the goal of producing the emancipated and educated proletariat that was a cornerstone of early Soviet ideology. Working under Moscow conductor Alexei Kovalev, Valentina studied orchestration, composition, and music theory as well as conducting. After graduation, she returned to Tuva and became the conductor of the folk orchestra in Kyzyl's music high school.

The folk orchestra movement evolved from pre-Revolutionary balalaika orchestras, supported by wealthy patrons, which performed folk and popular music as well as arrangements of classical repertory *à la Russe*. As folklorist Eduard Alekseyev has pointed out, the original aim of these orchestras was a worthy one: to perform great music on Russian folk instruments to compensate for what, in the view of the orchestras' founders, was the limited scope of their traditional repertory. The orchestras featured not only standard-sized balalaikas but also, in the spirit of European string consorts, instruments of different sizes, including enormous bass balalaikas. During the Soviet era, these orchestras became a centerpiece of national culture policy, and they were reproduced all over the U.S.S.R., with Europeanized adaptations of indigenous instruments substituting for—or sometimes playing along-side—Russian instruments. It was the orchestra conductor's job to modify local instruments for use in the orchestra and to figure out which parts of an orchestral score should be assigned to particular instruments. "I loved Grieg and Tchaikovsky," Valentina recalled with amusement, "and I arranged their symphonic works for my orchestra, which included both Tuvan and Russian folk instruments."

While researching Tuvan instruments in order to alter them for use in the folk orchestra, Valentina began to understand, as she put it, "that the whole approach to working with these instruments was artificial and false." Treating the instruments simply as sources of exotic coloration for orchestral music did nothing to advance knowledge of indigenous Tuvan music.

In 1985, after eight years as a folk orchestra conductor, Valentina left the music high school and accepted a position at the Tuvan Research Institute of Language, Literature, and History. There she continued her work on musical instruments, but from the perspective of a folklorist-ethnographer rather than a conductor-arranger. "I began to search for what these instruments meant to the traditional players themselves and tried to understand the way musicians thought about their instruments and the sound they produced," Valentina told me during a series of conversations about Tuvan music that took place in 2003. The transformative event that led her toward a new understanding of the Tuvan sound world came in the late 1980s, just before she left Tuva to undertake advanced studies in folklore and ethnomusicology in Novosibirsk and Saint Petersburg.

"I was in Kyzyl-Dag recording an old man who played the *igil*," Valentina recounted. "His name was Salchak Shombul Ulaachy. When we were done, I said to him, 'Now don't play anything in particular, just bow the open strings so that I can record their pitches.' And he played both of the *igil*'s two strings together. I said, 'No, play them individually. I have to write down the tuning of the instrument.' And again he played them together. I must have asked him five times, and always there was the same response. Finally he got angry. 'You're a strange girl,' he said. 'Go drink some tea, and I'm going out to have a smoke,' and with that, he got up and left. As I sipped my cold tea, I was also angry. Why is he so stubborn, I wondered? All I was trying to do was figure out the pitch of each string. Is it that hard to play one string and then the other?

"It was only later that I understood the significance of this little episode. In my training as a folklorist, we were taught to record the range, register, and tuning of a musical instrument—for example, on a stringed instrument, that such-and-such a string is tuned to *sol*, another string is tuned to *do*, and so on. But what I learned from that *igil* player was that the absolute pitch of the strings meant nothing to him. All that was important was the relative pitch of the two strings one to another. That's why, when I asked to hear how the instrument was tuned, he played both strings in order to show me the interval between them. And more important, he didn't hear these strings as separate pitches, but as part of one total sound. In other words, discrimination of pitch height, the fundamental building block of melody and of melodic perception, didn't play a significant role in the way this musician perceived the sound of the *igil*. For him, pitch was subordinate to timbre—the specific quality of a tone determined by the presence, distribution, and relative amplitude of overtones. His way of listening represented an entirely different approach to the perception of sound than what you have in cultures where the focus is on melody. You could call this other kind of listening 'timbral listening.'

"The way I learned about timbral listening was indirect. The musicians I spent time with didn't use any special musical terms. Everything was explained through analogy and metaphor using examples drawn from nature and from other sounds, rather than from music itself.[1] In those years, I spent a lot of time with a *byzaanchy, igil,* and jew's harp player named Idamchap Xomushku (1917–1994)[2] (see plate 6). Often, I'd be with him, recording an interview or talking with him, and suddenly, in the middle of the conversation, he'd stop and cock his ear toward a radio playing in the background, and he'd say, 'That's good music.' When someone was playing music, I noticed how he sat and listened attentively, and sitting next to him, I also began to listen a little differently than the way I normally did. At a certain moment, I understood that he heard things and focused his attention on sounds that I didn't always hear. After that, I began to ask him to describe what he'd just heard—I was interested in the words he used and how he described sound.

"We'd be sitting outside and he'd say, 'Look over there at those mountains. Look at the shadows. There's a spot from the sun, shadows from the clouds, there are mountains that are closer, mountains that are farther away. They have different colors. Now it's changed. A shadow has suddenly appeared where only a second before, there was light.' Idamchap was trying to point to the way that visual images have depth and volume. And the analogy he wanted to make was with sound—that sound works the same way. When you play the *igil*, there are different layers of sound, and the resulting effect for the listener is what you could call volumetric.

"Another musician, Marjymal Ondar [1927–1996], used to draw a similar analogy to the different environmental sounds that people readily hear all at the same time—dogs barking, birds chirping, the whistling of wind, children's voices. His point was the same as Idamchap's—that our normal perception of

47

sound is multilayered. If you listen to instruments like the jew's harp or *igil*, they can completely fill a sonic space. But they don't do so through the use of melody, counterpoint, and harmony—the traditional tools of European music. Instead, each moment of sound is opened up and exposed to reveal a whole sonic universe within itself." To demonstrate her point, Valentina picked up a Japanese paper fan that she'd placed on the table in front of us with its accordion folds neatly collapsed between the narrow wooden slats that bound either end. With a quick flick of the wrist, she unfurled the fan, and the paper folds spread out into a broad "V" shape.

"It's easier to express graphically than in words," Valentina said. "When you make a sound on the *igil,* it's like spreading open the fan. Inside this one sound is a whole acoustic world created by the spray of overtones that results when you draw a bow across the instrument's horsehair strings." To ensure that I understood, Valentina came up with more visual analogies. "If you pick up snow, pack it into a snowball and throw it, it goes in a single direction and, depending on the force of your throw, it can go quite far. But if you scoop up some loose snow and toss it, no matter how much force you exert, the snow just scatters. Sound is like that. In European music, sound is packed compactly into discrete pitches, with the fundamental frequency and overtones all perceived as one. But Tuvan music is like loose snow, and overtones are like the snow spray."

Valentina plunged on with her explanation of timbral listening, turning next to a description of Tuvan instruments and how musicians produce sounds that lend themselves to such listening. She began with bowed instruments. "There's no Tuvan bowed instrument on which you press the string all the way to the neck. You touch the string lightly, and in the case of the *byzaanchy,* from underneath, using the fingernails. In European terminology it's called flageolet—touching a string lightly to produce a harmonic. But flageolet on the *igil* and *byzaanchy* is different than flageolet on Western bowed instruments like the violin, viola, or cello. On Tuvan instruments, flageolet tones are played everywhere, not just at the point of the harmonics, so the acoustical basis of sound production is different. Bowed instruments, like the bow itself, are strung with horsehair rather than metal or gut, and the resulting sound is rich in overtones although not very loud. In other words, volume and homogeneity of sound are sacrificed in favor of timbral richness.

"Bows and bowing techniques for the *igil* and *byzaanchy* are also different from what Western string players use. For example, on a violin bow, the tension is fixed before the musician starts playing. But an *igil* or *byzaanchy* player grips the bow from underneath the horsehair and constantly regulates the

Byzaanchy. The bow is locked between two strings and players use both upper and lower surfaces of the horsehair.

tension, making it now tighter, now weaker by tensing or relaxing the fingers. Changes in bow tension also affect the timbral characteristics of sound. The looser the bow, the more the 'spray' effect—just what Western string players don't want. They want a sound that's perfectly focused, consistent, unified.

"Jew's harps are also designed to maximize timbral complexity. If you look at the tongue of a jew's harp, it's cut in a 'V' shape so that the timbral profile of the material, whether metal or wood, is a little different at the narrow end than at the wide end. But the most important aspect of timbre-centered sound-making and listening among Inner Asian pastoralists concerns the relationship of drone and overtone. Idamchap used to say that you can't make sounds on a jew's harp whose tongue is broken. What he meant was that in order to produce the overtones, you first have to be able to produce the fundamental drone. Both come from the same source, unlike, for example, the bagpipes, where the drone is produced by one pipe and the melody notes by another; or the kind of drone that's used in many forms of vocal polyphony, where one singer or group of singers holds the drone while another sings the melody.

"Westerners who listen to drone-overtone instruments like the jew's harp, or to throat-singing, often ignore the drone and focus only on the melody. But for Tuvan listeners, drone and overtones form an inseparable whole, and the timbre of the drone is crucial to producing a harmonically rich sound that extends over a wide frequency range. When you are in this kind of sound space, you hear not only overtones but undertones—you can hear sound at all audible frequencies.[3] If you're the sound-maker, you can use these sonic resources to imitate or represent whatever kind of sound you want. All registers and pitch heights are theoretically available. The limits to what you can hear and reproduce are physical, not conceptual."

In the Inner Asian sound world, even where drone is not an inherent part of the acoustical mechanism of sound production, for example, on the end-blown flute variously known as *shoor, choor, tsuur, kurai,* and *sybyzghy,* it is added anyway. Mongolian *tsuur* player Gombojav explained that the breathy, vocal drone he produced while simultaneously blowing into the flute provided a way of making a melody "richer." What he evidently meant was that the combination of drone and melody produced a sound whose timbre was rich in overtones.

The evocation of timbral richness, however, could not account for all the diverse forms of music among the Inner Asian pastoralists. Melody-centered music also exists in many genres, both instrumental and vocal. When I pointed this out to Valentina, she nodded her head as if I had stated the obvious. "There are two sound systems in Tuvan music," she said. "There's the timbre-centered system, and there's a pitch-centered system, in which pitch height and melody are the predominant organizing principles, just as in Western music. You can find many Tuvan songs with catchy melodies that are played on instruments, set to words, and performed as throat-singing.

"When the Turks were all united in the nomadic state known as the Turkic Khaganate, which existed from the middle of the sixth century to the middle of the eighth century with its center in the Altai region, the timbre-centered system must already have been in place, because it's still present in the music of all the Turkic cultures of Inner Asia. It's present in the jew's harp playing of the Sakha, the *xai* and *kai* of the Xakas and the Altai, the mimetic instrumental music performed on the *qyl qiyak* of the Kyrgyz and the *qyl-qobyz* of the Kazakhs. And it's present among Turkic groups who moved away from the center of ancient Turkic culture in the Altai-Sayan region toward the periphery of Inner Asia, such as the Bashkirs, who now live in the Urals and preserve the timbre-centered system in the music of the end-blown flute *ku-*

rai. This system has held together for fourteen centuries. To survive this long, it has to be really solid, and backed by a musical logic, by a specific form of musical thinking. And where it doesn't survive as a living practice, it survives in cultural memory. For example, when Turkic peoples hear overtone singing, it arouses something in them. The aura of this kind of music nourishes them. I witnessed this in the days of the Soviet Union when there used to be big music festivals, and Uzbeks, Turkmen, Azeris, and others would come and listen to our Tuvan musicians."

"Are the two systems mutually exclusive?" I asked Valentina, "or can you find them mixed together in the same music?"

"These days it's not unusual to find them overlapping in one and the same musical style, or even in individual pieces. In their music-making and listening, Tuvans can go back and forth between one system and the other. But if you've been brought up listening exclusively to pitch-centered music, like most Westerners, it's very difficult to switch over to timbral listening.

"On the performing side, the difference between pitch-centered and timbre-centered music involves a physical dimension. In pitch-centered music, each sound has a separate source, and to get from one sound to the next requires a discernible physical movement. For example, string players change pitch by pressing their fingers down on the neck or fingerboard of an instrument. Wind and brass players change the length of a tube by depressing keys or moving valves. Even the smallest ornament is produced by a physical movement that changes the sound source. By contrast, in the timbre-centered system, a performer enters the zone of sound turbulence and just stays there with almost no movement. Listeners observing throat-singers for the first time are often puzzled about where the sound is coming from and how it's being modulated. 'The singers are not moving their mouths!' listeners exclaim. It's true—if you look at a throat-singer, you'll see only the most minimal movement of the facial muscles. The vocal cords are fixed, and only the most minute adjustments inside the mouth are needed to manipulate timbre. It's like jewelry work. The same is true of jew's harp players. Once the tongue of the jew's harp has been struck, the modulation of the sound takes place inside the player's mouth. The point is, when you're physically moving, chasing after the melody, you can't focus on what's happening in the timbre. It was the nomadic way of life and its focus on the timbral qualities of natural sounds that created this kind of musicality."

After our discussions about pitch-centered and timbre-centered music, I went back over recordings from the *National Geographic* expeditions of 1987 and 1988 with the aim of finding examples of the distinctions Valentina had made. In those years, I had little understanding of the concept of

Ex. 1. "Artyy-Saiyr"

The number above each note identifies the harmonic that produces it. By convention, the first harmonic (1) is the fundamental pitch; thus the second harmonic (2) is that which sounds an octave higher, and successive multiples of two produce harmonics at successively higher octaves above the fundamental.

timbre-centered music. On the contrary, I was attracted to throat-singers and jew's harp players who performed pitch-centered music—in particular, cheery songs and melodies such as "Artyy-Saiyr" (The Far Side of a Dry Riverbed), transcribed above in a performance by throat-singer Vasili Chazir (b. 1958). Using the throat as a precise type of band-pass filter that reinforces certain frequencies while attenuating others, Chazir isolates and reinforces a sequence of harmonics that corresponds to the successive pitches in the song (this technique is explained in more detail in the following section, "Throat-Singing: The Ideal Timbral Art"). In the transcription, the number above each note identifies the harmonic that produces it (see Audio File, track 3).

In music, harmonics are pitches that are integral multiples (1, 2, 3, etc.) of some fundamental pitch (by convention, the first harmonic ["1"] is the fundamental). To produce the melody of "Artyy-Saiyr," a singer reinforces harmonics that range between six and twelve times the frequency of the fundamental drone pitch—in other words, the segment of the harmonic series that extends from the sixth to the twelfth harmonic. These pitches form a pentatonic (five-pitch) scale: G-Bb-C-D-E-G, as shown in example 2. The nondiatonic eleventh harmonic, which falls halfway between E and G, is not part of this scale.

Ex. 2. First sixteen pitches of the harmonic series

Pitches typically used by Tuvan singers are indicated in black.

Note that the seventh harmonic, which produces a flatted seventh interval relative to the fundamental pitch (C–Bᵇ), does not figure in the melody of "Artyy-Saiyr" (nor does the nondiatonic eleventh harmonic). The absence of the seventh harmonic in all Tuvan and Mongolian throat-singing that I have ever heard suggests that the harmonic series is not used naturalistically, in its raw form, but selectively, within a tonal system rooted in cultural preferences. (The flatted seventh scale degree does turn up in Tuvan songs that are not performed with throat-singing, for example, the well-known "Orphan's Lament.") Moreover, the harmonic series is not reified among Tuvan throat-singers. For them, harmonics are "voices" (*ünner*) and, asked to produce an ascending sequence of such "voices" in the form of a scale, namely, the harmonic series, throat-singers look puzzled.

Other examples of throat-singing occupy a liminal area between pitch-centered and timbre-centered sound-making. For example, in the piece "Alash," named after a river in western Tuva, harmonics are used to articulate distinct pitches, yet the resulting pitch sequence, which leans heavily on repeated articulations of the ninth and twelfth harmonics, is banal from a melodic point of view. As Valentina put it, "If you listen from the perspective of melody, you'll begin to get bored and wonder why the singer doesn't change the pitch. So you have to listen in a different way, with more focus on how each reinforced overtone in succession opens the timbral qualities of a sound in a different way—as if you were holding a diamond up to the light and rotating it ever so slightly while observing the shifting prismatic effects of light passing through the crystals." "Alash" is transcribed in example 3 and reproduced in the audio files online, track 4.

The transcription is from a performance of "Alash" by throat-singer Mergen Mongush on the Smithsonian Folkways recording *Tuva: Voices from the Center of Asia*. When Eduard Alekseyev, Zoya Kyrgys, and I did the sound

Ex. 3. "Alash"

(aspirated exhalation)

editing for the Smithsonian CD, I suggested shortening and standardizing the long and irregular pauses between each segment of throat-singing in order to create a more coherent sense of a "piece" (some of the pauses were as long as thirty seconds). Only later did I realize my error. Throat-singers themselves do not attach importance to temporally linking separate phrases through measured silence. On the contrary, each phrase conveys an independent sonic image, and the long pauses provide singers with time to listen to the ambient sounds and to formulate a response—not to mention, of course, taking a breath.

Valentina pointed out that timbre-centered music and pitch-centered music work from different conceptions of time. "In pitch-centered music, sequences of pitches progress through a form that has a certain duration and that moves toward a prepared conclusion. But it doesn't make any sense to apply this conception of form to timbral logic. In timbre-centered music, the space dimension is different and the time dimension is different. Imagine being out in the steppe—nomads didn't have limitations on time. There were no boundaries. Performances could be extremely varied in length, from very short to very long, depending on the atmosphere and the mood of the performer. The *topshuur, igil, shoor*—people would play these instruments for a long time sitting around the campfire. Before the hunt, when they'd go out at dawn, they'd sing and play the whole night. The eternity of being was part of the herders' sense of time. It's no accident that oral epic had such a great development among nomads. It was only in the 1960s and 1970s that culture workers introduced the idea to performers that they shouldn't sing or play for too long."[4]

Valentina and I listened together to several other examples of the timbre-centered sound-making that for her constituted the quintessence of Tuvan music, and as we listened, she provided a running commentary. The first example illustrated the form of throat-singing known as *kargyraa* (see Audio File, track 6). "Here you have the feeling that the singer is just trying to open the sound," Valentina commented. "He's playing with it—making it now narrower, now wider, adding nasalization, letting it play in his mouth. He's not trying to perform anything in particular, or imitate anything. There's no particular context for what he's singing. It's like when you have a certain feeling and you just express it with some kind of sound. It's a spontaneous response to a mood."

A second example presented a brief *xöömei*, a form of throat-singing in which individual harmonics are clearly articulated and manipulated (see Audio File, track 7). "When you listen to the sequence of harmonics with ears accustomed to Western music," said Valentina, "it's difficult not to perceive the sequence as a melody. But the fact that one harmonic is higher and the next one is lower and that they're separated by precisely such-and-such an interval doesn't really matter. When I listen to this *xöömei*, I have a physical sensation of three different levels or planes of sound that you could call lower, middle, and higher. But the planes don't correspond to pitch height. It's like being weightless in space, where there's no up or down. You have to let go of your habitual tendency to hear the harmonics as forming a melody. Once you do that, you can float freely in the sound. You lose your bearings and swim around for a while, but then you begin to orient yourself and establish your balance. You understand that there's sound coming from everywhere and that it's not just one sound, but that it exists on different planes, in different dimensions.

"Try a little experiment," Valentina advised, returning to the musical example we had just listened to. "Try not to listen to the high notes and instead, hold your listening close to the bottom—to the drone. Then bring the middle into focus. It's like when there are a lot of people talking in a room and you're trying to focus on what one person is saying. The middle of the *xöömei* sound is thick—vibrations are everywhere, but this is the part that habitual listening filters out. If you can focus in on this middle part, you begin to feel the extent to which the sound space is filled up. And you hear things the way they really are, rather than through our customary filters."[5]

In an article titled "The Paradox of Timbre," published in the journal *Ethnomusicology*, African music specialist Cornelia Fales points out that the isolation of reinforced harmonics from a fundamental pitch that occurs in throat-singing can create a "profound if momentary disorientation" when harmonics break free from the "perceptual fusion of timbre" and are consequently less subject to the effects of "perceptualization" that customarily act on the signals we receive from the acoustic world.[6] In this condition, according to Fales, the perception of reinforced harmonics becomes "nearly identical to—or at least, directly dictated by—their character in the acoustical world." Another way, perhaps, of making Valentina Süzükei's point that timbral listening may provide access to hearing things "the way they really are" or, at the very least, hearing them differently.

Fales's article is based largely on a study of Burundi ritual song whose performers juxtapose isolated vocal harmonics with formant-rich, timbrally dense fundamental pitches in much the same way as do throat-singers (in the case of the Burundi ritual song, the harmonics and fundamental pitches are produced by different sources—the harmonics by high falsetto voices and the fundamentals by a plucked zither). In Fales's view, the weakened border between the acoustic and perceived worlds that results from the "redistribution of perceptualization" is precisely what may lead human listeners to the sense of "perceiving something normally imperceivable," such as the presence of spirits.[7] Her inclusion in the article of a range of musical examples from beyond Burundi suggests that her hypothesis is not exclusive to a single musical repertory and social group.

Indeed, Fales's work offers an attractive starting point for a psycho-physical explanation of the spiritual power attributed to throat-singing and jew's harp playing. Both forms of sound-making exploit what Fales terms "timbral manipulation" as a way of entering a different perceptual world. Fales's hypothesis may also explain why, for example, the end-blown flute (*shoor or tsuur*) commonly linked with access to spirits is always played with a vocal drone that increases the turbulence and timbral richness of the sound. This timbral richness is increased by still another order of magnitude when the instrument is played in a resonant acoustic environment or in consort with a natural sound source such as moving water or wind. Mongolian *tsuur* player Narantsogt acknowledged the effect of joining the sound of his flute to the wind, calling it "mountain *höömii*" (*uulyn höömii*).[8]

A third musical example from the 1987–1988 recordings provided the sort of transition between timbre-centered and pitch-centered sound-making that Valentina had suggested is common in present-day Tuvan music. In this example, Oleg Kuular performs a composite piece using throat-singing and jew's harp that begins with timbral "noodling," then switches to a melodic medley, and finally returns to pure play with timbre (see Audio File, track 8).

After we'd finished listening, Valentina said, "The beginning and end of that jew's harp piece are a perfect example of what Tuvans call *xomustung boduning ayalgalary* [lit., "jew's harp-in-itself motifs" (*ayalga* can mean "motif," "dialect," "accent," or "pronunciation," as well as "melody")]. Similarly, the *kargyraa* episode we just listened to [Audio File, track 6] illustrates *kargyraaning boduning ayalgalary* ["*kargyraa*-in-itself motifs"]." This "thing-in-itself" genre, attested not only for the jew's harp and *kargyraa* but also for other forms of throat-singing, as well as for instruments such as the *igil* and *shoor*, eschews melodic sequences and imitative gestures in favor of "pure timbral exploration of the sound source's sonic space," as Valentina put it.[9] She added that while not explicitly mimetic, such sounds typically evoke the sonic atmosphere and acoustic qualities of a particular kind of environment associated with herding or hunting. For example, an episode of *kargyraa* might represent the specific and quite different timbral environments of the steppe (*xovu kargyraazy*) or of a mountain (*kojagar kargyraazy*). Moreover, the noun *kojagar* does not refer to just any mountain but specifically to a steep-sided mountain with barren slopes. Both steppe and mountain *kargyraa* differ from taiga *kargyraa* (*arga-aryg kargyraazy*), which evokes the atmosphere of the forests where Tuvans hunt.

The boundary between the atmospheric timbral evocations of "things-in-themselves" and the imitation of specific sound sources—what Tuvans generically call "voices imitation" (*ünner öttündüreri*)—is still less distinct than the boundary between timbre-centered and pitch-centered sound-making. At what point does a sonic description or evocation of the steppe or taiga cross the line into an imitation of a particular sound phenomenon? In execution, the distinction may not always be immediately evident, but musicians have been clear that such a distinction exists. For example, Gombojav, the Mongolian *tsuur* player, made a point of distinguishing between praise-songs or pieces (*magtaal*) that create a general sound image of a site of spiritual power, such as a mountain or a river, and pieces that are explicitly imitative.

The sound world of the Inner Asian pastoralists extends along a continuum that ranges from abstract timbral evocations of "things-in-themselves" to rounded song forms with fixed melodies. Spanning the middle are various genres and styles of mimetic sound-making and pitch-centered music that may coalesce into hybrid forms. For example, long-song (Tuvan *uzun yr,* Mongolian *urtyn duu*) is a genre characterized by pentatonic melodies and fixed texts, yet the swooping leaps and virtuosic ornamentation of the long-song preserve vestiges of a purely timbral art, in which the voice plays with the acoustical properties of resonant spaces. An example of Mongolian long-song, "The River Herlen," appears in the audio files online (track 9). Similarly, episodes of throat-singing commonly begin with a text sung or chanted in a guttural voice on discrete pitches and then proceed to a timbre-centered section dominated by reinforced harmonics that may or may not comprise a melody. The same range of performance style characterizes the *igil,* used to accompany vocal songs, perform instrumental melodies, or simply evoke the quintessential timbre of the instrument in an episode of *igilding bodunung ayalgalary*—"*igil*-in-itself motifs."

For an ethnographer with an unslaked curiosity about the early history and prehistory of music, there is a temptation—admittedly a romantic one—to claim great antiquity for timbre-centered sound-making, to imagine that it represents a protomusical form that antedates the rise of melody (or more generally, fixed pitch-height) as a musical organizing principle.[10] But more sober reflection persuades me that no hard empirical evidence supports such a claim, and that the issue of relative antiquity is in any event moot. More important is to recognize that timbral listening is an ideal sonic mirror of the natural world. The timbral subtlety and variety of this world is a ubiquitous—and evidently, inspiring—presence for the herders who pass an entire lifetime of days and nights, dawns and dusks, the turning of seasons in intimate proximity to the primal sounds of nature.

"You have to have inside your head this stock of sounds that's built up over years of living on the grasslands," Valentina said, summing up the phenomenology of timbre-centered sound-making. "And you have to learn how to distinguish all the various sounds—for example, by going hunting with your father in the taiga forest, where the sounds are different than on the grasslands. All of these sounds filter into a child's sound world, and when they pick up an instrument and start to play it, or start to do throat-singing, they can easily reproduce those sounds. Moreover, you can't destroy the timbre-centered system, even if there is a lapse of a whole generation, because the sounds are lodged in the cultural memory of nomads. Timbral sound-making and timbral listening will survive as long as herders live in nature and listen to the sounds of the taiga and the steppe, birds and animals, water and wind."

THROAT-SINGING:
THE IDEAL TIMBRAL ART

It was the third week of May 1998, and Tolya Kuular led the way as we zigzagged across a thin crust of corn snow that stubbornly clung to the forested foothills of the Sayan Mountains, a half-hour drive north of Kyzyl. Tolya, sound engineer Joel Gordon, videographer Bill Gasperini, and I had driven up to the mountains with Kaigal-ool, Sayan Bapa, and Valentina Süzükei in search of flowing water. In particular, we were on the lookout for just the right stretch of river, stream, brook, creek, or rivulet—any kind of flowing water was fair game—to play a costarring role in an artistic collaboration with Tolya. After intermittent experimentation, including the episode in the Shemi River when Tolya spoke about spirit offerings (see chapter 2, "Musical Offerings"), he felt ready to make a definitive recording of *borbangnadyr* with water—or, as he preferred to think of it, of water with *borbangnadyr*. I had invited Joel Gordon to join me in Tuva with a four-microphone portable recording system that he assembled specially for our work, and now we were ready to put it to the test.

None of the Tuvans in our party had ever previously been to the larch-covered hillside, where we'd left our cars on the side of the road by a bridge and climbed down toward the streambed that transected the road. We'd picked this spot because it was the closest place to Kyzyl where there were steep slopes, and thus, we reasoned, swiftly flowing water. Fed by melting snow, the streams were running fast and full, and as we tromped through the woods, the hiss of churning water reached our ears long before we could see the source of the sound.

The first stream we considered as a recording site was the one we'd spotted from the road. Translucent wavelets rushed between ice-coated rocks with odd shapes and overhangs, forming a series of small reverberant pools and eddies. Sayan liked the "blup-blup" sounds of water being sucked into a whirlpool under a sheltering slab of stone. "Reminds me of a *tabla*," he said, referring to the paired drum used in North Indian classical music. But after standing back and listening to the composite sound of the stream, Tolya vetoed it.

"Not enough jazz," said Tolya. By that he meant that the sound was too homogenous, without the rhythmic detail and contrapuntal play of timbral colors that would make for a lively fusion with the rolling sounds of his *borbangnadyr*. Tolya had become the authoritative arbiter of taste in water sounds, and with his negative critique, we piled back into the cars and headed for higher elevations further north. As the road passed through a col between two ridges, a stream came into view, tumbling steeply between rocks on one of the ridge faces before swerving away from the road in a broad curve that descended into a forested glen.

"Too fast, too wide," said Tolya, barely getting out of the car. In other words, the sheer volume of water created so much sound that the subtle rhythms and timbral colors issuing from spots of turbulence were smothered by the overall white noise of the stream. Back into the cars, this time we headed downhill to flatter ground, where water might not be moving so quickly and loudly. We turned off the main Kyzyl-to-Abakan road onto a dirt track that led toward a clump of sheds in the distance. Along the track, cows grazed in pasturage that, warmed by direct sun, had shed the last of its snow and sprouted a thick carpet of velvety green grass. A narrow rivulet ran straight along the edge of the pasture. It wasn't much to look at—no craggy boulders or whirlpools with their gossamer of foam, no standing wave patterns clinging to the aft side of submerged rocks. But as we sat beside the brook and let our ears absorb the surrounding silence, the gentle music of flowing water came ever more sharply into the sonic foreground. Rounded stones created irregular popping and slurping sounds as the water slithered around them—just the sort of timbres that Tolya found seductive. For the recording, however, Sayan proposed increasing the amount of turbulence in the water and thus boosting the timbral complexity and dynamic range of the sound.

"Bring me stones," Sayan ordered. "We need to do some construction work." The rest of us fanned out along the length of the stream, collecting stones to bring back for Sayan's and Tolya's inspection. Sayan chose a few stones of different sizes, placing them strategically in the flow of the brook to create various sound effects, and in one spot he fashioned a small cascade. When he was done, we all listened attentively to the results of Sayan's craftsmanship.

"That's it!" said Tolya at last. "That's the sound Tuvans like. It's when you can hear sound coming from all directions at all levels—when sound maximally fills a space." Or something like what audiophiles would call "surround sound."

Joel quickly set up microphone stands, and our portable recording studio was ready for business. Tolya stood next to the brook, and began to sing *borbangnadyr* (Audio File, track 10). He intoned a phrase of text on a drone fundamental pitch that his ear told him corresponded to the fundamental pitch of the flowing brook, then began rhythmically modulating the fundamental to produce rippling sounds that merged with the rippling of the water. Next came a sequence of harmonics that led quickly to a sustained elaboration of the twelfth harmonic, three octaves and a fifth above the fundamental. Introducing a rhythmic shimmering made by subtle movements of his lips, Tolya propelled the harmonic forward, giving a sense of mass and velocity to what an instant before had been simply an inert pitch. The cycle repeated twice more, each time with intoned text, gurgling and rippling sounds on the fundamental, and the shimmering, pulsating twelfth harmonic. Each repetition presented new rhythmic and timbral effects, including a feather-light harmonic fantasia over the fundamental drone and a coda of soft, cloud-like harmonics at the end.

In Tolya's rendition, *borbangnadyr* became not only a representation of the turbulence of water as it roiled in a stone-studded stream bed but also a sonic collaboration with it. Tolya's stylization of the rippling water sounds did not, of course, sound exactly like the water itself. How could it? Talented mimics can imitate the sound of many birds and animals with great verisimilitude, and almost anyone can make a convincing wind sound simply by blowing and whistling at the same time. But the timbral complexity of flowing water defies the mimetic capacity of even the most supple human vocal apparatus. The artistry of representing this sound is precisely what makes it an object of interest to throat-singers—and to ethnographers who study throat-singers.[11]

Tolya's *borbangnadyr* exposes the inventive stylization represented by his transformation of water sounds to the apparatus of the human voice. But unlike, for example, the idylls, pastorales, and romantic song cycles of European composers, which represent water through musical conventions far removed from the actual sounds of water, Tolya's sonic stylizations strive to engage the sonic texture of flowing water directly and interactively through submersion, as it were, in the acoustical properties of water itself.[12] His collaboration starts from the supposition that rivers sing just as humans sing, and assumes the form of a sonic dialogue honed through control and manipulation of timbre, articulation, rhythm, pitch, tempo, and dynamics.

Tolya Kuular had not always sung *borbangnadyr* with water. Growing up in Chadaana, he had performed in an amateur music ensemble, and was one of the shy, costumed singers mobilized by the local culture authorities to demonstrate throat-singing during my 1987 visit. Tuvans of his generation—Tolya was born in 1965—grew up and were initiated into the world of throat-singing at a time when the tradition's center of gravity had already shifted from extemporized sound-making in natural conditions to formal performance by "artists." The sing-alongs with water came later, in the mid-1990s, after Tolya had joined the ensemble Huun-Huur-Tu and we had agreed to work together on re-emplacing Tuvan music and sound-making in the natural acoustical environments that had inspired it.[13] The topic of water had come up one evening while Tolya, Sayan, Kaigal-ool, and I were taking an after-dinner stroll along the bluffs overlooking the Yenisei River opposite Kyzyl. We were discussing the onomatopoetic meaning of the terms used for various kinds of throat-singing, and Tolya mentioned that *borbangnadyr* comes from the Tuvan verb *borbangnaar,* a causative verb form that means "to cause to roll," "revolve," "spin."

"What kind of rolling sound can it refer to?" I had asked. At that very moment, the trail we were walking along dipped down into a gulch to cross a shallow, stone-filled stream.

"For example, the sound of water rolling over rocks in a stream," Tolya answered, as we hopped across the stream.

"I heard from my grandfather that herders used to sit by a stream in the evening and throat-sing with the water," Kaigal-ool added. "It was a way of honoring the spirit-master of the stream."[14]

"Try it right here," I had coaxed Tolya. And that was the beginning of the trial-and-error experiments with *borbangnadyr* that led to the high-tech recording session by the cow pasture. In preparing for this session, Tolya worked not only on his vocal technique, but on his listening—on reengaging the mimetic faculty at the root of throat-singing. In doing so, he was striving to retrieve an older understanding of throat-singing that existed before it was transformed into a performance art centered around displays of vocal virtuosity.

Looking backward in throat-singing, however, is not like looking backward in the music of sedentary civilizations. There, particularly in traditions glossed as "classical," one can typically trace a chain of transmission from father to son or master to disciple through lineages that are sometimes centuries old. By contrast, in the culture of Inner Asian nomads, even though ancestors are venerated and oral genealogy is of vital importance, the concept of musical lineage among throat-singers is all but nonexistent. Throat-singing, like music performed on the jew's harp, *igil*, and other instruments, is absorbed through perceptual osmosis. As Valentina Süzükei had said, nature is the school of throat-singers. Even now, when actual schools of throat-singing have begun to appear in Tuva, older singers do not demonstrate to younger ones where to position the tongue to yield a certain overtone, how to move the lips to produce a certain rhythm, and so on. Rather, a teacher might ask a student to imagine a pastoral scene from his own experience and then illustrate it in sound.

Learning begins not from physical techniques, but from aural models; not from memorization of fixed sequences of sounds, but from a process of sonic self-exploration. It is not particular melodies and canonical performance styles that comprise the core of the throat-singer's art, but something more basic: a sound ideal that models the desired timbral quality of the voice. Once this basic model has been internalized, the shaping and sculpting of timbral, melodic, and rhythmic characteristics becomes a matter of personal sensibility and skill. Personal sensibility of course exists within boundaries of culturally determined style, taste, and technique. For example, in broad terms, one can contrast Mongolian throat-singing with Tuvan throat-singing or Xakas throat-singing. Yet within these broad realms, individual stylistic invention has flourished. Unbound by the constraints of collectivity imposed on ensemble-based music, throat-singers, the quintessential soloists, are free to experiment and indulge their artistic whimsy. The most revered among them have done precisely that.

To emulate the basic timbral sound model at the root of all throat-singing, singers manipulate their vocal tract—tongue, lips, jaw, soft palate—to shift the frequency of a formant, or resonant frequency, and align it with a harmonic naturally present in the voice, thus reinforcing the harmonic.[15] Although reinforced harmonics can be produced from a wide variety of fundamental drone timbres, with the exception of the rounded vowel sound "o" that issues from a pure sine wave, the timbral model for the fundamental drone sound ubiquitous in the Altai region emphasizes a raspy, tensed chest voice. This chest voice is often given additional power and depth through the use of double phonation—the production of a second vocal source pitched an octave below the fundamental frequency.[16]

The vocal tract contains many potential sources of double phonation, but the effect of all of them is to produce a deep, growling, harmonically dense, fundamental drone (the addition of the lower octave doubles the number of harmonics at play in the sound). Differences in the pressure and velocity of air delivered from the chest cavity through the vocal tract affect the timbre and amplitude of the drone pitch as well as the harmonics, and these differences are evident in the various styles of chanting and intoned recitative that draw on the double phonation technique. Controlled double phonation is the basis for many kinds of throat-singing, most notably, the basso profundo style that Tuvans call *kargyraa* and Mongolians call *harhiraa* (Audio File, track 6).

Mark van Tongeren, a Dutch student of throat-singing who wrote a lucid survey of overtone-centered music from the perspective of both a singer and an observer, noted that the density of harmonics in double phonation chanting "allows for an enormous variation of timbral nuances." Van Tongeren added that from his own experience as a singer, "there are more variables at stake in *kargyraa* than in any other type of throat—or overtone—singing."[17] One artifact of the double phonation technique is that it leaves the upper vocal tract free to articulate consonant and vowel sounds, and thus it may be used as a basis for intoning texts within a harmonically rich drone.

Among the Xakas and the Altai, two Turkic ethnolinguistic groups whose languages and cultural traditions link them closely to the Tuvans, double phonation drones are used as the sonic model for the recitation of oral poetry. The Xakas call this style of recitation *xai* and the Altai call it *kai* (for examples of *xai*, see Audio File, track 27, and Video File, track 16).[18] *Kai* is used to perform epic poems as well as shorter poetic texts. A superb illustration of the latter is the hymn (*alkysh*) transcribed below from the performance of Altai musician Sarymai Orchimaev (see Audio File, track 11).[19] Sarymai accompanies his singing on the *topshuur*—a long-necked lute similar to the Tuvan *doshpuluur*. "The *topshuur* gives an impulse," Sarymai explained. "It supports the voice, and I can't sing for long without it."

Starting from fir wood,	*Joigon agash bu tözineng*
I planed my *topshuur*.	*Jonup etken bu topshuurum*
Tightening the strings made from the	*Jorgo maldyng jarash kylynang*
Beautiful mane of a pacer horse, I sing.	*Kyldap, erep em oinogon*
Sing, sing, my *topshuur*,	*Oino, oino, topshuurum*
Let your strings not break,	*Kylyng sening üzülbezin*

Let those who hear your singing	*Oigor kalyk ugala*
Offer you praise.	*Alkysh-byianyn emdi aitsyn*
Starting from cedar wood,	*Emil agash bu tözineng*
My *topshuur* is made.	*Eptep etken bu topshuurum*
Tightening the strings made from the	*Erjine maldyng jarash kylyn*
Mane of a sacred horse, I sing.	*Kyldap, erep em oinogon*
Sing, sing, my *topshuur*,	*Oino, oino, topshuurum*
Let your strings not break.	*Kylyng sening üzülbezin*
Let those who hear your singing	*Oigor kalyk ugala*
Offer you praise.	*Alkysh-buian em jetirzin*
Starting from white birch wood,	*Ak kaiyngnyng bu tözineng*
My *topshuur* is made.	*Alkap etken bu topshuurum*
Tightening the strings made from the	*Argymak attyng bu kylynang*
Mane of a racing horse, I sing.	*Kyldai erep em oinogon*
Sing, sing, my *topshuur*,	*Oino, oino, topshuurum*
Let your strings not weep,	*Kylyng sening yilabazyn*
Let the words to my praise-song not know lies.	*Alkysh sözim jastyrbagyng.*

Double phonation drones and reinforced harmonics are also used in the liturgical chanting tradition of certain Tibetan Buddhist monasteries, where they serve as a vehicle for communal prayer. The Tibetan sound, which some researchers call "chant mode," yields overtones that are audible but not exceptionally loud, or "sensed without being explicitly heard," in the words of Huston Smith, the philosopher of religion whose 1967 reports on the biphonic chanting of Tibetan lamas in the Gyütö Monastery near Dalhousie, India provided the first glimpse of overtone-singing for many Westerners (including this writer).[20]

While to the uncultivated ear the various double phonation techniques sound broadly similar, singers and scholars often emphasize their differences rather than similarities. For example, Tuvan folklorist Zoya Kyrgys takes pains to distinguish Tuvan *kargyraa* from Tibetan-style double phonation chant, noting patriotically that *kargyraa* demands considerably more chest tension than the sound produced by Tibetan monks.[21] Mark van Tongeren also offers a comparison, remarking that "the secret of the esoteric [Tibetan] *yang* technique, though widely demonstrated in the West by lamas in recent years, is neither revealed nor imitated as 'easily' as *kargyraa*."[22]

In contrast to the extremely low-pitched fundamental drone characteristic of Tibetan Tantric chant, *kargyraa, harhiraa, kai,* and *xai,* another variant of the basic timbral model at the root of throat-singing uses as its starting point a fundamental pitch in the baritone range. This variant does not employ double phonation, but it depends on a large supply of air under strong pressure from abdominal and chest muscles. Simultaneous contractions of muscles in the neck constrict the trachea, further increasing pressure as air passes through the engorged vocal folds of the larynx into the upper vo-

Sarymai Orchimaev playing the *topshuur*. Near Ongudai, Altai Republic, 2000.

cal tract. The result is a husky, guttural fundamental drone with a rich harmonic spectrum. This sound model is the basis for diverse forms of throat-singing associated with Tuvan practitioners, most commonly *sygyt* and *xöömei*, as well as for the most widespread throat-singing style in Mongolia, generically called *höömii*. (For a good example of *sygyt*, see Audio File, track 4, "Alash.")

The timbre of the fundamental pitch is of cardinal importance in any type of overtone-singing. Neophyte overtone singers from the West often tend to focus on the seemingly magical sounds of harmonics, but among Tuvans and Mongolians, the timbral quality of the fundamental is considered the most important criteria for distinguishing authentic throat-singing from inauthentic, good from less good, powerful from flaccid. It is no accident that Zoya Kyrgys, who created a neologism for the overall phenomenon of Tuvan throat-singing in an apparent attempt to distinguish it from neighboring styles, in particular Mongolian *höömii*, chose the word *xörekteer*, from *xörek*, which means "chest"; thus "chest-singing." (Kyrgys may face an uphill battle in gaining acceptance for the term. As she admitted in her 2002 book, *Tuvan Throat-Singing*, "Not one Tuvan language dictionary treats the term '*xörekteer*' in relation to singing. It is usually used to mean 'raising one's voice at someone,' 'swearing.'")[23]

Scholars who have written about Tuvan music have typically described "styles" of throat-singing as representing normative categories—that is, as prescriptive models for performance. For example, in *Tuvan Folk Music*, published in 1964, A. N. Aksenov identified four melodic styles: *borbangnadyr, sygyt, ezenggileer,* and *kargyraa.* In *Tuvan Throat-Singing*, published almost forty years later, Zoya Kyrgys repeats Aksenov's four basic styles and adds a fifth: *xöömei.* She also includes a host of "substyles." Kyrgys notes, however, that "the understanding of 'style' includes diverse concepts. Among them are the individual features of different performers. . . . In this sense, [style] approaches the notion of a creative manner and method linked to particular techniques of solo polyphony."[24] In other words, style as personal self-expression rather than style as generalized convention.

Kyrgys is on the right track here. At root, stylistic classification of throat-singing comprises an open system, not a closed one with a finite number of fixed categories. It is open to expansion and evolution as a consequence of individual ingenuity and innovation. Conversely, stylistic diversity can contract as a result of homogenizing forces that work against innovation. While stylistic diversity is hard to measure, throat-singing in Tuva may indeed have become more stylistically homogenous in the decade-and-a-half since I first went there in the late 1980s. The cause seems clear. Increasingly distant from its origins as a spontaneous, expressive response to the sound world of the steppe and taiga, throat-singing as concert art is motivated by more practical concerns. What kind of singing will rouse an audience? What kind of singing works well with musical instruments, percussion, and other kinds of vocal music in the various hybrid and fusion forms that have become popular among musicians and audiences alike? Answers to these questions have led most concertizing throat-singers in the same direction: toward the well-established styles that Tuvans call *sygyt* and *kargyraa.*

When I first came to Tuva, elderly throat-singers performed *ezenggileer,* which means "stirrups" and imitates the rhythmic clacking of a horseback rider's boots, and *borbangnadyr,* whose pulsing harmonics Tolya Kuular used in his collaboration with flowing water. Well-known singers alive or recently deceased had lent their names to eponymous styles: Kombu *xöömei,* Oidupaa *kargyraazy.*[25] These so-called "styles" were in practice embodied in particular melodies that became identified with their creators, no matter who else performed them. And idiosyncratic styles such as *tespeng xöömei, kanzyp,* and *chylandyk*—the work of anonymous creators—circulated among an older generation but did not find a ready place in the repertory of younger concert throat-singers.

The full force of Soviet cultural politics that had waged the "struggle against the old" in Tuva may have had little effect on the underlying diver-

Plate 1. On the road to Kyzyl-Xaya, southwestern Tuva. Valentina Süzükei is third from left. Summer 2003.

Plate 2. Teeli, the regional center of Bai-Taiga Region, western Tuva. Photo by Karen Sherlock, 1987.

Plate 3. An ensemble of musical amateurs performs in the auditorium of the House of Culture in Chadaana. Photo by Karen Sherlock, 1987.

Plate 4. Performers in an amateur ensemble in Kyzyl-Majalyk, Baryyn-Xemchik Region, pose on the stage of the local House of Culture. The instrumentalists hold Russian *balalaikas*, a substitute for the Tuvan *doshpuluur*. Photo by Karen Sherlock, 1987.

Plate 5. Idamchap Xomushtu making an offering to the spirit-masters during a recording session near Teeli. Photo by Karen Sherlock, 1987.

Plate 6. Idamchap playing the *byzaanchy*. Photo by Karen Sherlock, 1987.

Plate 7. A catered luncheon of boiled mutton with milk tea and vodka following the recording session with Idamchap, 1987.

Plate 8. A fabricated wedding staged for our *National Geographic* expedition, near Chadaana. Photo by Karen Sherlock, 1987.

Plate 9. Huun-Huur-Tu, photographed on the outskirts of Kyzyl. From left, standing: Anatoli Kuular, Alexei Saryglar, Sayan Bapa. Seated: Kaigal-ool Xovalyg, 1996.

Plate 10. A herding family's home in western Tuva. Photo by Karen Sherlock, 1987.

Plate 11. Anatoli Kuular on the bank of the Xündergei, also known as Yraajy-Xem (Singing River), western Tuva, 2003.

Plate 12. Valentina Süzükei adding an offering to an *ovaa*. In the background is Mongun-Taiga, the highest point in Tuva. Summer 2000.

Plate 13. A site of spiritual power reflects Tuvans' syncretic animist-Buddhist beliefs and practices. A sacred tree (identified in Tuvan and Russian in the sign on right) is hung with strips of cloth left as offerings (*chalama*), while on the wooden platform is a Buddhist statue. The paper cups placed in front of the statue contain an offering of distilled sour milk (*araga*). Nearby, radioactive radon springs disgorge water believed to have healing properties. Shivilig, Bai-Taiga Region, western Tuva, 1996.

Plate 14. Travelers make offerings to the spirit-masters of the Xündergei-Arty Pass, near Xandagaity, in southwestern Tuva, by tying strips of cloth to a tree. The plates at lower left also contain offerings, 2000.

Plate 15. Tserendavaa's family dismantling a ger in front of Mount Jargalant, the singing mountain of Chandman Sum, western Mongolia, 2000.

Plate 16. The international border between Tuva and Mongolia is marked only by a cairn. Western Tuva, near Kyzyl-Xaya, 2003.

sity of the throat-singing tradition. Tuvan musicians, for example, could perform choral odes to industrialization on the stage of a House of Culture and also sing *xöömei* while riding horseback or sitting alone atop a hill. But the transformation of Tuvan music into a globalized cultural commodity was showing signs of winning the struggle that Soviet cultural politics had ultimately lost. In throat-singing, the old had begun to fade away, and the new, for all its technical polish and global chic, was less diverse, less eccentric, less rooted in its original inspiration. The self-regenerating power of Tuvan culture, which Sasha Bapa of Huun-Huur-Tu had lauded during my 1995 visit when we had first discussed the idea of trying to reanimate the musical past, was focused elsewhere—at least for the moment.

Tuvan musicians and scholars, however, remain proud of the breadth and depth of their throat-singing tradition. In *Tuvan Throat-Singing,* Zoya Kyrgys compares the plethora of documented Tuvan styles with what in her view are the more homogenous styles characteristic of neighboring regions—Mongolia, Xakasia, the Altai Republic—and concludes that Tuvan throat-singing is the oldest of them all. The longer throat-singing exists, Kyrgys reasoned, the more opportunity it has to evolve and develop in different directions, and thus greater stylistic diversity is evidence of greater antiquity.[26]

Tuvan throat-singing may indeed be very old, but Kyrgys's explanation is by no means the only way to account for its apparently greater stylistic diversity, and other explanations may be more persuasive. For example, throat-singing may have existed long ago in more diverse forms elsewhere, but it may have atrophied due to the loss of cultural "habitat" when pastoralists became sedentarized, as happened in Xakasia. Or old styles may have become fixed in canonical forms, as in Tibetan Buddhist chant. Or, as in Mongolian *höömii,* distinctive features of vocal production perceived as differences of style by local musicians and listeners may be imperceptible to outsiders. The example of Mongolian *höömii* offers a good illustration of the diverse ways in which throat-singing has been taxonomized and metaphorized in the Altai region.

While Tuvans describe styles of throat-singing by the sounds they are said to represent, for example, *sygyt* ("whistle"), *kargyraa* ("wheeze"), *ezenggileer* ("stirrup"), and *borbangnadyr* ("rolling"), some Mongolian singers have used taxa rooted in anatomy. Carole Pegg describes three such classification schemes in *Mongolian Music, Dance, and Oral Narrative,* all of which describe the anatomical locus of timbral resonance or manipulation.[27] The most sophisticated was provided by Tserendavaa, of Chandman Sum, who worked out his scheme with the help of Ulaanbaatar-based musicologist Badraa. Tserendavaa wrote an almost identical taxonomy in my field notebook during our visit to Chandman in the summer of 2000. It divides melodic *höömii* into seven categories: labial (*uruulyn*), palatal (*tagnain*), glottal (*bagalzuuryn*), nasal (*hamryn*), throat (*hooloin*), chest cavity (*tseejiin*), and, finally, a combination of all of the above (*hosmoljin*).[28] Tserendavaa distinguished these varieties of *höömii* from *harhiraa*, which in his view should be classified separately because it is not a melodic style.

Sengedorj, the throat-singer from Hovd, was skeptical about the proliferation of styles proposed by Tserendavaa. "Nose *höömii* doesn't really exist," Sengedorj told us. "It's just a variant of palatal *höömii*. And chest *höömii* shouldn't be a separate category. All breathing is from the chest." Sengedorj described his own classification scheme when we met in Hovd in summer 2000.[29] He divided Mongolian throat-singing into three broad categories: *hargaa*—a "light" form of *harhiraa* used in Buddhist temple rituals; *harhiraa*—good for accompanying the *tsuur* and also used by reciters of oral epic; and finally, "liquid *höömii*" (*shingen höömii*), which Sengedorj described as a "Mongol-Altai" style. This was the style for which he was renowned (at our first meeting, Sengedorj had ticked off his extensive performing credits, including nine visits to Japan and two to Germany and France; a year later he traveled to Washington, D.C., to participate in the Smithsonian Folklife Festival). The style's name provided an apt description of the loud and lubricious melodies Sengedorj produced with harmonics.

Liquid or solid, the sheer vocal power of Sengedorj's *höömii* was remarkable. Two examples of his singing are included in the audio files online (tracks 12 and 13). The first is a *höömii* version of a song melody called "Buyant Gol," the name of a river that flows through his homeland of Hovd. The second is a popular folksong called "Gooj Nanaa," the name of a young woman, who, according to Sengedorj, lived around a century ago.[30] Sengedorj sings the words and then reproduces the melody with *höömii*:

Young geese are honking outdoors	*Galuu shuvuuny degdeexei*
My beloved Gooj Nanaa is singing on and on	*Gadnaa garaad ganganaj baina*
Young swans are honking in the bamboo grove	*Golyn xairtai Gooj Nanaa*
Happy Gooj Nanaa is singing	*Galav yültel duulj suunaa Gooj*
in her native place.	*Nanaa xö.*

Sengedorj's poetically named "liquid *höömii*" represents a personal interpretation of the timbral *ur*-model at the root of all throat-singing, yet it closely resembles the performance style of other Mongolian *höömii* singers while differing noticeably from throat-singing typical among Tuvans. An acculturated listener can easily distinguish "Mongolian" *höömii* from "Tuvan" *xöömei* purely by the timbral and dynamic qualities of the sound and also by the tendency of Mongolian throat-singers to reproduce flowing pentatonic song melodies using harmonics. How and when did different personal ap-

Mongolian throat-singer Sengedorj performing at the Smithsonian Folklife Festival, "The Silk Road: Connecting Cultures, Creating Trust," on the National Mall, Washington, D.C. Photo by Coriolana Simon, summer 2002.

proaches to throat-singing coalesce into reified national styles? Comparison of these styles has become a burning issue among performers, scholars, and cultural authorities in both Tuva and Mongolia, who continue to spar over claims to the origins and purest form of the tradition.

Tserendavaa, for example, told us that sometimes he gets angry when he hears Tuvan claims that *höömii* comes originally from Tuva. This is impossible, Tserendavaa said, "because Mongolian people say it's from Chandman." Moreover, Tuvan *höömii*, in Tserendavaa's view, is not authentic *höömii*, but a simplified, reduced form produced in the throat rather than in the chest, lacking the physical power of Mongolian *höömii*.[31] Representing the opposite view, Zoya Kyrgys devotes large parts of her recent book, *Tuvan Throat-Singing*, to defending the claim that the origins and most sophisticated development of throat-singing are incontrovertibly Tuvan. But since scholarly ethnographic accounts of throat-singing date back only about a century, and the earliest usable recordings are from the 1930s and 1940s, claims about throat-singing's origins and prehistoric development are invariably reduced to conjecture based on circumstantial evidence.[32] What is beyond cavil is that in both Tuva and Mongolia the elevation of throat-singing to the status of a "national" music is a recent phenomenon that belies its proliferation among specific social groups living largely within a limited geographical region.

Among Tuvans, for example, the most tenacious practice of throat-singing has been documented in areas of central and western Tuva that comprise the traditional herding territory of around ten clans, and it is these clan names that turn up repeatedly in the pantheon of throat-singers: Ondar, Oorjak, Kuular, Kyrgys, Xovalyg, Dongak, Mongush, Tumat, Sat, Xomushku.[33] The correlation between throat-singing expertise and clan names is particularly striking in light of evidence that, as anthropologist Caroline Humphrey wrote, "The Tuvinian clans and lineages more or less disappeared in the Manchu period (mid-eighteenth to twentieth centuries) as functioning units in society."[34] In other words, the concentration of throat-singing talent among members of these nonfunctioning kinship units may provide one of their principal cultural legacies.

In other parts of Tuva, most notably the eastern region of Todzhu—where vast, thickly forested hills, bogs, and lakes provide the habitat for around 5,000 Todzhu-Tuvans, who form an ethnolinguistic subgroup among Tuvans—throat-singing is all but nonexistent.[35]

The case of Todzhu is an interesting one. Difficult to access, with rivers providing the main means of travel, Todzhu maintains an ethnolinguistic and cultural identity distinct from other parts of Tuva. The traditional economy of the Todzhu-Tuvans centers on hunting and reindeer herding rather than stockbreeding. The Todzhu dialect differs from Tuvan as it is spoken in the center and west of Tuva and is related to Tofa, the language of the Tofalars, a small Turkic group living southwest of Lake Baikal whose language is endangered.[36] During a visit to Todzhu in 1988, Eduard Alekseyev, Zoya Kyrgys, and I recorded a variety of material that included songs and intoned speech addressed to animals and spirits, melodies played on wooden jew's harps, and imitations of wild and domestic animal sounds. In its focus on sonic interaction with the natural environment and with the spirit world, this material overlapped broadly with what we recorded in other parts of Tuva, with one exception: in Todzhu, we found only minimal throat-singing, and none of it displayed the vitality and inventiveness of throat-singing in the west of Tuva.

Was the paucity of throat-singing among the Todzhu-Tuvans a result of differences in the topography and environmental conditions in which they lived? Or was it due to their focus on reindeer herding rather than steppe pastoralism or cattle- and horse-herding? Or did differences perhaps arise from social tradition that may have been only indirectly related to physical environment and occupation, for example, a taboo? Living just several hundred miles from the western grasslands and maintaining trading contacts with other parts of Tuva, Todzhu-Tuvans have certainly not lacked exposure to throat-singing. But in a landscape of densely forested hills, lakes, and bogs that lacks the magnificent open vistas and constant sonic stimulation of the windblown grasslands, it is possible that the practice of throat-singing is simply one that did not resonate with the Todzhu-Tuvans, literally or figuratively.[37]

Like Tuva, Mongolia also owes its tradition of throat-singing to a compact local geographic region. The relatively small size of this region becomes apparent when compared to the vastness of Mongolia as a whole, which is many times larger than Tuva. Sengedorj and Tserendavaa had told us that throat-singing came from the west of Mongolia, from Chandman, and they invoked as evidence the legendary figure of Bazarsad, who was inspired to throat-sing by the sound of wind whistling through bamboo on the shore of Lake Har-Us. But among a small population of Tuvans who have long inhabited Tsengel Sum, the westernmost district of Mongolia, we heard a different legend of origin, which was not set in Chandman but farther south, beyond the border of Mongolia, in what is now the Xinjiang Uyghur Autonomous Region of China. There, so the legend goes, flows a river called the Eev or Eevi, and it was the sound of its waters tumbling in reverberant waterfalls that first inspired humans to throat-sing. Curiously, although the Tsengel Tuvans venerate the Eevi, our fieldwork turned up no evidence that throat-singing has flourished in Tsengel in recent times, nor does it seem to have flourished among the separate community of Tuvans who live among the Oirats and Halha Mongolians of Hovd Aimag, farther to the east of Tsengel.[38]

The complex ethnogenesis and continual movements of Turkic and Mongolian groups in the Altai region suggest that, rather than pitting Tuvan and Mongolian throat-singers against one another in a pointless contest of antiquity and authenticity, it is surely more sensible to regard them as broadly sharing a common geocultural origin. The particular intersection of environment and culture—of topography, animistic beliefs, and musical practices—that provided the crucible of throat-singing was almost certainly the zone of mountains and high grasslands that extends from the center and west of present-day Tuva into western regions of present-day Mongolia and the northwest corner of what is now Chinese Xinjiang. There, herders from a variety of Turkic and Mongolian tribal and clan groups intermingled, intermarried, and shared techniques of representing the powerful forces of their natural environment in sound.

Even after the creation of the Tuvan People's Republic in 1921 and continuing after Tuva became part of the Soviet Union in 1944, herders crossed back and forth freely between Tuva and Mongolia (see plate 16). The characteristic performance styles that have come to define Mongolian throat-singing and Tuvan throat-singing may actually be of quite recent vintage. The origin of these styles may not lie in deeply rooted cultural distinctions but rather in the quirks of particular singers, whose influence became magnified in recent years through the cultivation of "national" musical styles.

Tserendavaa had explained how a few singers from the west of Mongolia brought throat-singing to Ulaanbaatar, and how throat-singing has come to play a central role in performances by national folk troupes, festivals, radio and television broadcasts, and recordings representing Mongolian music.[39] These days even a brief visit to Ulaanbaatar cannot help but confirm Tserendavaa's account. Throat-singing in Mongolia has become reterritorialized in Ulaanbaatar to such an extent that, during our month of field research in the west of the country in summer 2000, my colleagues and I documented far fewer *höömii* singers than we were able to document in several days in the capital city.

Ethnomusicologist Carole Pegg chronicled this transformation of throat-singing from a regional tradition in decline to a much-celebrated form of national art and cultural heritage. She also noted that the story has a political edge, for the musicians from Chandman who lay claim to the origins of the present throat-singing revival belong to the Halha group, which is the dominant force in Mongolian politics and, by extension, cultural politics.[40] The elevation of throat-singing to a national art is symbolically understood as the elevation of the Halhas, to the consternation of Oirats who see throat-singing as their own cultural legacy, or at least a shared one.

Conflicting claims to the cultural ownership of throat-singing are possible because of the elusiveness of its origins and evolution. But in the end, this "musical phenomenon born in the steppes," as the Russian ethnographer Sevyan Vainshtein termed throat-singing in the title of a scholarly article, merits a place in the annals of human musical diversity, not as the musical shibboleth of any particular group but as a jewel in the artistic legacy of an entire civilization that arose in the mountains and grasslands of Inner Asia.[41]

Throat-singing is but one element of a coherent musical world in which jew's harps, fiddles, plucked zithers, end-blown flutes, and raspy-voiced recitative all exploit the timbral dimension of sound as a way of representing sensory experience in broadly shared conventions of musical style and genre. While the accumulated history of centuries of migration, intermingling, hostilities, and empire-building, as well as the charismatic influence of individual musicians, has led to aesthetic divergences among different performance traditions, their similarities are far more striking than their differences, offering compelling evidence of a common past. Perhaps, like the proto–Indo-European language whose existence is conjectured by linguists, a proto-Turkic musical language once existed as a comprehensive whole among the Inner Asian nomads in the halcyon days of the Khaganate.

4

SOUND MIMESIS

MIMESIS AND THE POWER OF REPRESENTATION

They are excellent mimics: as often as we coughed or yawned or made any odd motion, they immediately imitated us. Some of our party began to squint and look awry; but one of the young Fuegians (whose whole face was painted black, excepting a white band across his eyes) succeeded in making far more hideous grimaces. . . . They could repeat with perfect correctness each word in any sentence we addressed them, and they remembered such words for some time. . . . All savages appear to possess to an uncommon degree this power of mimicry. . . . How can this faculty be explained? Is it a consequence of the more practised habits of perception and keener sense common to all men in a savage state as compared with those long civilized?

—Charles Darwin, describing the inhabitants of Tierra del Fuego, *Journal of Researches into the Natural History and Geology of the Countries Visited during the Voyage of H.M.S. Beagle Round the World*

Charles Darwin was twenty-three years old and a year into the *Beagle*'s four-year-long voyage of discovery when, in December 1832, he described the Fuegians and their wondrous mimetic prowess. Darwin did not respond to his own questions about the relationship of mimetic ability and culture, but the answers are implicit. Indeed, Darwin seems to suggest, mimetic ability is enhanced by sensory acuity, and sensory acuity is honed by the challenge of living in close proximity to the natural world.[1]

Darwin never made an explicit connection between mimesis and music. The little he wrote about music came almost forty years after the visit to Tierra del Fuego, when, in *The Descent of Man*, he suggested that musical ability was a biological adaptation linked to courtship behavior, drawing an analogy between the evolutionary role of human music-making and bird-song. Darwin's idea was essentially that the best musicians, whether birds or humans, would end up with the most desirable mates—or simply with the most mates.[2] (In a recent article that reexamines Darwin's hypothesis in light of present-day knowledge about both music and evolution, evolutionary psychologist Geoffrey Miller puts forward the example of rock guitarist Jimi Hendrix as an example of how Darwin's theory works in real life.[3]) Yet in his youthful musings about mimicry, Darwin may well have unwittingly pointed to a novel way of thinking about what I call "sound mimesis"—the use of sound to represent and interact with the natural environment and the living creatures that inhabit it, and more broadly, the exploration of representational and narrative dimensions of sound-making.

Darwin's unvarnished description of the Fuegians aside, mimetic ability in the broadest sense is unquestionably a universal attribute of *Homo sapiens*. Infants acquire language and become behaviorally socialized through processes of imitation. Many aspects of culture—games, athletics, rituals, expressive arts such as dance, drama, and music, and diverse forms of pedagogy such as in arts, crafts, and trades—are rooted in mimetic imitation.[4] The ubiquity of mimetically based learning, expression, and communication may be the vestige of an archaic stage of cognitive evolution among early hominids that predates the development of language. A hypothesis about exactly such an epoch of "mimetic culture" has been persuasively advanced by evolutionary psychologist Merlin Donald in *Origins of the Modern Mind: Three Stages in the Evolution of Culture and Cognition*.[5] Donald draws on evidence from primatology, psychology, linguistics, anthropology, and archaeology to link cognitive evolution to related stages in the development of culture, and he points to "representational strategy" as a key to understanding differences in the cognitive ability of hominids at these various stages.[6] A fundamental assumption of Donald's hypothesis is that each stage of cognitive and cultural evolution survives as a functional vestige in later stages, and that human consciousness weaves together different representational systems that to varying degrees may all be simultaneously active.[7]

Mimetic skill or mimesis, Donald says, "rests on the ability to produce conscious, self-initiated, representational acts that are intentional but not linguistic." Donald distinguishes among mimicry, imitation, and mimesis. These terms—"imitation" in particular—have multiple and overlapping usages that range through biology, psychology, sociology, and the arts. For the sake of consistency, I will use them here in the sense in which they are defined by Donald. Thus mimicry is "literal, an attempt to render as exact a duplicate as possible," and Donald notes that "many animals possess some capacity for mimicry." Imitation is less literal than mimicry in Donald's trichotomy and is common among monkeys and apes. Donald provides the example of offspring copying a parent's behavior, in which the copying involves imitation but not mimicry. Mimesis, by contrast, "adds a representational dimension to imitation. It usually incorporates both mimicry and imitation to a higher end, that of re-enacting and re-presenting an event or relationship," and thus it involves "the *invention* of intentional representations."

Donald's work offers a rationale for understanding the extent to which human mimetic faculties may be deeply engrained in the cognitive evolution of our species. Sound mimesis, whether exhibited by a hunter imitating the rutting calls of wild animals to lure game, a child mimicking the buzzing of a mosquito, or a comedian parodying a foreign accent, may represent one of our oldest and most abiding mental and physical capacities.[8]

In representing one sound by another, humans draw on a range of cognitive resources. Donald's point that mimesis "adds a representational dimension to imitation" is key. Symbol, metaphor, and other forms of trope are all central to sound mimesis, as examples from the previous chapters make clear.[9] When Tolya Kuular represents the sound of flowing water with *borbangnadyr*, the analogy he suggests between the sound of water and the sound of his voice makes sense because listeners understand it as a metaphor, not as a literal imitation. Moreover, the metaphor implicit in mimetic *borbangnadyr* is not just a figurative way of depicting flowing water but is imbued with a craft and sensibility open to aesthetic critique. Simply put, it is art—"a lie that tells the truth," in Picasso's famous formulation. The metaphoric basis of sound mimesis becomes still more complex when sound is used to represent not only other sounds but also sights, as in the composite mimetic representations of soundscape and landscape discussed later in this chapter (see "Sound Mimesis and Spiritual Landscape").

If the mimetic faculty constitutes such a central aspect of human nature, why is sound mimesis not a more prominent part of present-day musical languages? For example, to anyone whose ear has been shaped primarily by Euro-American musical traditions, whether classical, folk, jazz, pop, or some mixture of these, music based primarily on the mimetic representation of environmental sounds or images would stand out as an oddity. It is true that these days, many kinds of pop and New Age music incorporate sampled ambient sounds ranging from industrial noise to waterfalls, and avant-garde composers have created radically mimetic works in which "music" is defined by framing or sequencing sound events external to the artist. The best known of these is John Cage's *4'33"* (1952)—four minutes and thirty-three seconds of silence whose content (if the absence of content can be considered content) depends entirely on chance, that is, on the unintentional ambient sounds that listeners hear within and around themselves.[10]

Mainstream contemporary concert music may also be taking a turn toward the topical and programmatic, as, for example, in new work by the much-performed American composer John Adams: *Dharma at Big Sur*, a stylistic mélange that reflects the East-West crosscurrents of West Coast musical life; *On the Transmigration of Souls*, an elegy to the victims of the September 11th terrorist attack; and *My Father Knew Charles Ives*, a work that references compositions by Charles Ives, whose own musical references are to real-world places (for example, *Concord Sonata, Three Places in New England*).[11] But it is not yet clear whether these works are a harbinger of a more general turn—or return—to mimesis from abstract music.

At the more imitative end of the mimetic continuum, musical onomatopoeia is not entirely absent in the Western classical tradition. It turns up more commonly in Western folk traditions—for example, fiddlers and violinists imitate birdcalls, blues artists use the harmonica to imitate the sounds of a moving train or to "speak" words, and children's songs offer a rich repertory of barnyard sounds and other kinds of mimicry. Yet taken together, these instances of sound mimesis are relatively marginal within the musical traditions where they occur.

One need not accept Igor Stravinsky's unrepentantly formalist view that music is "powerless to *express* anything at all, whether a feeling, an attitude of mind, a psychological mood, a phenomenon of nature, etc."[12] to agree that whatever is expressed in the diverse music of Euro-American traditions is overwhelmingly contained within autonomous melodic, harmonic, and rhythmic systems devoid of direct reference to external sound models.[13] Yet the word "mimesis" is a loan word from Greek—indeed, from ancient Greek—where it can mean both "imitation" and "representation," and the term has a long history in Western philosophies of art. Plato discussed mimesis in *The Republic* as an element of the dramatic arts, pointing out that actors represent or impersonate characters in a play and, in so doing, render themselves vulnerable to absorbing the moral qualities of those characters. Mimesis thus acquires an ethical dimension in which imitation or representation can stimulate the development of either honorable or dishonorable behavior, depending on the qualities that are imitated or represented. "You must have noticed how the reproduction of another person's gestures or tones of voice or states of mind, if persisted in from youth up, grows into a habit which becomes second nature," Plato says to his foil, Adeimantus, in Book III of *The Republic*.[14]

Later Plato extends the purview of mimetic representation to poetry and music, thus launching a long tradition of theories of musical *Affekt* that posit systematic links between melodic modes, intervals, and harmonic structures and corresponding mental states or *ethoi* evoked in performers or listeners: sorrow, joy, courage, passivity, licentiousness, and so on. Explanations of affective connections in ancient philosophy served as the basis for elaborations of music's mimetic power among Renaissance humanists and medieval Islamic music theorists, who developed diverse schemas relating melodic modes and intervals to ethical qualities and bodily humors. In our own time, this mimetic tradition has morphed into a broad arena of beliefs about the power of music to heal, harmonize, and demonize, which are embraced by groups as varied as clinically trained music therapists, New Age "sound healers," and Christian fundamentalists railing against the diabolical effects of heavy metal.

A related belief about music's mimetic power of representation, also rooted in antiquity and still very much alive in contemporary esotericism, addresses the way that the musical harmony of chords and intervals may reflect a cosmic harmony embodied in laws of planetary motion.[15] Or, as it is sometimes gnomically expressed, "As above, so below." Harmonics and the perfectly tuned intervals derived from them—the physical manifestation of small, whole-number frequency ratios—exemplify the link between music and number, and they loom large in musical representations of cosmic order and harmony.

Overall, the mimetic tradition in Western art music focuses mainly on abstractions independent of time and place. With the exception of opera and explicitly programmatic works, specific places are rarely represented, while representations of affective states and human attributes (*pace* Stravinsky) typically do not invoke sonic models drawn from real life; rather, they rest on formal or expressive semantic conventions that have evolved within music itself.

While metaphors of planetary motion as cosmic music and harmonics as a source of human harmoniousness remain central in Western speculative traditions of musical mimesis, these metaphors are not embraced by Tuvan throat-singers. For them, harmonics represent not harmony, either cosmic or human, but, metaphorized as "voices," they are the sonic embodiment of landscapes, birds, and animals along with the spirits that inhabit them.

For the pastoralists, the mimetic impulse is stimulated by perceptual immediacy. A throat-singer overcome with an urge to sing while standing next to a river will likely represent the river, not the sound of a horseback rider's boots clacking in stirrups. It is not that singers lack imagination. On the contrary, legendary or imaginal beings are frequently represented in sound mimesis as if they really existed, and landscapes or soundscapes that have been experienced in the past may be recalled and mimetically evoked with great precision.[16] Even landscapes that have never been experienced may be mimetically represented (see chapter 4, "Mimesis as Cultural Memory").

Set against the form-driven, nonrepresentational impulse of so much Western music, the place-driven, mimetic reflex of human sound-making in the Inner Asian nomadic world becomes all the more striking. Or perhaps it is the reverse: that form-driven, abstract music is exceptional amid a profusion of place-driven, mimetic music arising from diverse cultural settings. Whatever the case, the distinction between the two must be rooted in culture and environment, not in biology, for presumably every human with normal cognitive and sensory abilities begins life with the same innate mimetic faculty. Individual genetic differences may of course produce mimetic aptitudes that are both unusual and specific, for example, among gifted actors, musicians, and artists. Such cases, however, cannot explain the systematic cultivation of mimetic behavior, whether manifested through oral, graphic, or gestural means in a cultural group at large. One is brought back to the questions the young Darwin recorded in his journal on the shores of Tierra del Fuego, but from the perspectives of cultural anthropology and ethnography rather than evolutionary biology: If the mimetic faculty is innate, what social and environmental factors lead some groups to cultivate mimetic behavior more than others? How and why do specific mimetic practices develop among particular groups? Is mimetic ability linked to enhanced perceptual acuity? If it is, might some mimetic practices, including sound mimesis, serve as a cultural metaphor for the value of sensory attentiveness and mental agility in an unforgiving environment?

Mimetic practices among the hunter-pastoralists of Inner Asia may suggest preliminary responses to these questions, as well as many more questions. In the following sections, I will characterize some of the ways in which human sound-makers mimetically represent their relationship to the natural beings and forces that surround them, both in real life and in the magical-realistic world of narrative performances, where the "voices" of musical instruments represent events in the lives of humans and animals. Forms and modalities of mimetic expression are diverse, and in their mixture of spiritual, ludic, aesthetic, and economic motivations, they reflect the multilayered complexity of the mimetic impulse.[17]

HUNTERS: THE EARLIEST
SOUND TECHNOLOGISTS?

Sat Maar-ool Ertin-oglu, or Maar-ool, as he was known to his friends, balanced himself on a rock midway up the steep incline of a barren hill near

Mar-ool Sat demonstrating the *amyrga*. Near Teeli, 1996.

the settlement of Teeli, where the sea-like flatness of the Tuvan grasslands col-
lides abruptly with the Altai Mountains, and pointed his long, conical *amyrga*
(hunting horn) towards the valley below. He tightened his lips around the
end of the wooden cone and inhaled (yes, inhaled!) mightily, drawing from
the instrument a bugle-like series of explosive overtones that ricocheted
against the opposite side of the valley (Audio File, track 14).

"Not bad for a schoolteacher," Sayan Bapa joked, after the sound had faded
and I had turned off the tape recorder.

"Teaching might be my profession," Maar-ool replied with feigned indig-
nation, "but don't forget that I've hunted practically since I was old enough
to walk. I know which end of an *amyrga* to put in my mouth."

Sat Maar-ool Ertin-oglu, who died in 2002 ("Sat" was the name of his clan,
"Maar-ool" was his given name, and "Ertin-oglu" meant "son of Ertin"), had
a broad knowledge of music and musical instruments, folklore and tradition, natural history, and the topography of the grasslands and mountains
that surround Teeli. His brief demonstration on the *amyrga* and riff about
the glory of hunting exemplified the traditionally intimate role of music and
sound-making among the nomadic pastoralists of western Tuva. The word
"nomad" derives from the Greek *nomein*, "to pasture," and pastoralism is

79

indeed at the heart of nomadic life. In Tuva and adjoining parts of southern Siberia, however, stockbreeding and hunting have been economically, socially, and spiritually intertwined for as long as nomads have roamed the Eurasian steppe. And compared to hunting, nomadism is a historical upstart in central Eurasia, where it seems to have emerged only toward the beginning of the first millennium BCE as an adaptation, possibly to climatic, political, and economic changes, among groups that had long practiced both agriculture and sedentary animal husbandry.[18] In Tuva's diverse ecological zones, herders—whether of sheep and goats, cattle, yaks, or reindeer—are also invariably hunters, and the lore of wild animals is an intimate part of their everyday lives. An entire musical instrumentarium is associated with hunting calls and the spirits of animals, and these instruments embody what may be the oldest forms of sound mimesis to remain part of a living, albeit now endangered, tradition in Tuva.

For an instrument of presumably great antiquity, the *amyrga* projects little of the mystic aura that surrounds similar ancestral inventions, such as the didjeridu and shaman's drum. It is a slightly tapered cone fashioned from two pieces of hollowed-out wood held together by ties made from animal sinew or willow bark, or by intestinal membrane wrapped snugly around the wood (the material from which the cone is made seems to matter little; during a field recording session when Tolya Kuular had forgotten his *amyrga*, he quickly fashioned one out of a roll of film, spiraling the film into overlapping helixes to form a cone). As an artifact of mimetic sound technology, the *amyrga* serves a highly specific function for hunters: to imitate the call of the male Siberian red deer during the fall mating season in order to lure rival males rearing for a territorial fight. When these males appear, the hunter puts away his *amyrga* and takes out his rifle. Listening to the *amyrga*, one imagines with some difficulty an animal that actually sounds like it, but the *amyrga* offers a remarkable facsimile of a deer call.[19]

Tuvans have their own term for iconic sound mimesis: *ang-meng, malmagan öttüneri*—literally, "imitation of wild and domestic animals." This broad category includes instruments such as the *amyrga* and the *ediski* (a small reed made from a folded piece of birch bark used to mimic wild goats or female musk deer), vocal techniques such as howling into cupped hands with the thumbs held together in front of the lips to lure wolves,[20] shamans' imitations of the sounds of animals and birds, and imitations both instrumental and vocal whose purpose is purely ludic—to provide entertainment or play.[21]

Instruments like the *amyrga* and *ediski* and vocal imitations of howling wolves are part of the tradecraft of hunting. But other forms of sound-making are associated with hunting's spiritual dimension, that is, with mediating the relationship between humans and the spirits of animals. Foremost among these is performance on the end-blown flute that Tuvans call *"shoor"* and Mongolians call *"tsuur."*[22]

The *shoor,* made from a hollowed-out willow or larch bough, is an instrument imbued with magical and healing powers that figures prominently in stories and legends throughout the Altai region, many of them connected to hunters. Valentina Süzükei recounts several such legends in her book on Tuvan musical instruments.[23] In one legend, a hunter makes himself a *shoor* following several days of unsuccessful hunting, and after dinner, he sits and plays a long, sad melody. Late at night, the hunter suddenly hears a voice coming from the *shoor.* "Tomorrow you'll find a large beast that's blind in one eye." The hunter becomes frightened and looks around, but he sees nothing except the campfire and the dark taiga forest. He decides that he has had a hallucination and goes back to sleep. Awakening early in the morning, he checks his snares, traps, and crossbows. The traps are all empty, but next to the farthest crossbow lies a large elk, and it has only one eye.

In another legend, two hunters are working together, one with great success and one with absolutely none. In the evening, the hunter who had caught nothing makes himself a *shoor,* and sitting by the fire, he begins to play it. The other hunter has the ability to see into the spirit world (Valentina Süzükei emphasizes that Tuvans believe such abilities are not limited to shamans and lamas). This hunter sees that the spirit-master of the taiga forest is sitting on the nose of the *shoor*-playing hunter, listening with pleasure to the music. Then, dozing off, the spirit-master slides from the hunter's nose onto the *shoor,* and from the *shoor,* he slips down onto the ground. This is so funny that his companion can't contain himself and, laughing loudly, tells the *shoor* player what he is laughing about. It is said that from this time forth, the spirit-master of the taiga took offense at the laughing hunter, and that he was never again able to hunt successfully.[24]

In a third legend, the female spirit-master of the taiga falls in love with a young *shoor* player because of the beauty of his music, and she steals his spirit away and takes it with her. After several days of searching, hunters find his body in a seated pose underneath a centuries-old larch tree with the *shoor* in his hands, snow covering him almost up to the shoulders. Each of these legends illustrates the power of the *shoor* to affect the spirit-masters of the taiga forest, who in turn act on the outcome of the hunt. But despite the power of the *shoor* illustrated in the legends, it has disappeared from active practice in Tuva, and survives among only a handful of players in the west of Mongolia. Two of them comprise the last two generations of a family lineage of *tsuur* players. The elder player, Narantsogt, born sometime between 1920–1922, was recorded and interviewed by Carole Pegg in 1989[25] and even earlier by Alain Desjacques.[26] When I met Narantsogt in his *ger* camp in a stunningly beautiful mountain pasturage during summer 2000, he could no longer summon the breath to make strong sounds on his instrument. But Narantsogt's son, Gombojav, spent many hours playing the *tsuur* and discussing the instrument and its powers (see plates 17, 18, 19).

Narantsogt had spent his life as a herder and hunter, and he spoke to us about playing the *tsuur,* not so much as a means of representing nature but as a way of praising it and conversing with the spirit-masters. "Playing the *tsuur* is like asking a question," he told us. "If I play for a long time, nature tells me what to do. I play for the mountains and the rivers, and the spirit-masters take pleasure from this." Narantsogt started playing the *tsuur* as a ten-year-old. Later, during the years of socialism when the *tsuur* was forbidden because of its connections with spirits, Narantsogt hid his instrument in the mountains and went alone to play it, afraid to speak to anyone about his music and his contact with the spirit world. Narantsogt had started to speak about these things, and was speaking to us, he said, because a spirit-master told him that his time on earth was approaching an end. Gombojav had no such premonitions, but as bad luck would have it, he died two years later, of cancer, at age thirty-five.

Gombojav grew up in the mountains, but he had come to Hovd City to attend school. He studied mathematics and economics, and when we met him in summer 2000, he was campaigning as a member of the Mongolian Green Party for a seat in Parliament. Gombojav was passionate about the *tsuur,* but living in a town, his music-making was less oriented toward pleasing spirits to ensure a successful hunt or to bring rain and more toward the healing power of the *tsuur* as a form of music therapy, for which he had a coterie of regular clients. In addition to his work as a music therapist, Gombojav enjoyed providing entertaining sonic caricatures of wild and domestic animals.

LUDIC MIMESIS

The varied uses of instruments such as the *shoor/tsuur, ediski,* and *igil,* and of vocal practices such as throat-singing, whistling, and animal imitations, all illustrate the extent to which sound-making in the traditional culture of the Altai region crosses back and forth between tradecraft and entertainment. Such crossing over may well be as old as the instruments and techniques themselves, and the practice of mimetic sound-making outside the context of tradecraft may mark the archaic moment at which sound technology began a new life as sound art. Removed from the need to duplicate precisely the sound of an animal call in order to bring home his next meal, a hunter would have become attuned to a different logic—the logic of sound for sound's sake, of the ludic element in sound production (from Latin *lûdere*, "to play").[27] Iconic mimesis would have become stylized, with the sound-maker transformed from a precision-oriented technologist to a performance artist open to the world of interpretation and innovation.

In the tiny room that functioned as living room/dining room/bedroom in his spartan apartment in Hovd, Gombojav unraveled for us a rich mimetic lexicon in which animals, humans, and aspects of landscape were depicted through miniaturized sound portraits. Working within the limited range and technical possibilities of the *tsuur*, Gombojav used melodic contour, rhythm, dynamics, and timbre to draw a sonic image of each subject. The point of the portraits was not so much to represent sounds themselves but rather, through sound metaphors, to convey the rhythm of physical movements and the appearance and psychological character of animals and humans. Five of these portraits appear in the audio files online (tracks 15–19):

1. Two lovers riding horseback. The relaxed gait of their horses is represented through the rolling syncopation of a repeated melodic pattern (track 15).
2. Running horse. Here the horse neither canters nor gallops, but literally runs, the rolling melodic pattern in the previous example replaced by a trilling rhythmic figure centered on a single pitch (track 16).
3. Wounded bear. A hunter wounds a desert bear (*mazaalai*), and the bear limps away. Melodic rhythm depicts the limp, while a strong air flow represents the bear's agitation and anger (track 17).
4. Young show-off. A young man rides horseback while drunk, swaying from side to side in the saddle. His woozy movements are depicted not so much through rhythm as by the wave-like shifts in dynamic level (track 18).
5. Camel gait. Camels walk with a lurching gait, onomatopoetically called *jonjoo* in Mongolian ("*jon-joo jon-joo jon-joo*"), which English might render, less onomatopoetically, as "clump, clump, clump." Gombojav's representation seems at first to be in regular 2/4 meter, but the subtle rhythmic asymmetry suggests an intimate familiarity with ambulatory camels (track 19).

After we had recorded a dozen or so of Gombojav's miniature sound portraits, he switched to a different sort of music—soothing, drawn-out melodies that by turns glided and meandered over the ever-present vocal

Gombojav playing the *tsuur* near his home in Hovd, western Mongolia, 2000.

drone. These were the melodies that Gombojav played in his role as music therapist for a growing local clientele. Asked to reveal the source of the *tsuur*'s healing powers, Gombojav's answer was straightforward: "It relaxes people and improves their mood." But it was not the sound of the *tsuur* in particular that mattered. "Any instrument can serve the purpose of healing," Gombojav told us. "What's important is the player—that the player should have mastery, and that the player should believe in the power of spirits. Am I playing the *tsuur*, or is the *tsuur* playing me? Both are happening," Gombojav concluded. He told us that not only sick people came to him to hear the *tsuur* but also businessmen who asked him to play to ensure good luck in their business affairs. In Gombojav's hands, the magical function of the *tsuur* had not disappeared; it had simply been updated.

Another major category of ludic mimesis involves children's sound-making. Among the diverse expressions of mimetic behavior in children, one of the most prominent is the imitation of animal sounds. Linguists are fond of pointing to the variety of ways that different languages represent one and the same animal sound, and they use such examples to illustrate how little of language is onomatopoetic, and how much—including onomatopoetic words—is arbitrary. For example, an English-speaking child learns early in life that ducks go "quack-quack," pigs, "oink-oink," and dogs, "woof-woof," while a Russian child learns that ducks go "kriyak-kriyak," pigs, "khryu-khryu," and dogs, "gaf-gaf."

In the United States, even children who grow up on farms are socialized very early into the representation of animal sounds through linguisticized onomatopoeia, for example, the "oink-oink" and "cluck-cluck" of children's songs such as "Old MacDonald Had a Farm." By contrast, in Tuva, the children of herders imitate animal sounds exclusively through iconic mimesis of the sounds themselves. According to Valentina Süzükei, only urbanized Tuvan children have adopted the Russian onomatopoetic animal sounds in recent decades. Iconic mimetic ability developed in childhood is maintained into adulthood, and the ability to imitate animal sounds with a high degree of verisimilitude is singled out for special praise. The term for such imitations, *ang-meng mal-magan öttüneri*, "imitation of wild and domestic animals," is widely used by herders.

During my travels in Tuva in the mid-1990s, I heard about a mimetic prodigy whose talent at *ang-meng mal-magan öttüneri* was said to be unparalleled. He lived in Chyraa-Bajy, a stockbreeding and agricultural settlement near Chadaana, where Kaigal-ool Xovalyg was born and raised, and one day, Kaigal-ool and I drove to Chyraa-Bajy to look for Albert Saspyk-ool. Albert, then twenty-one years old, suffered from epilepsy, and some of his admirers spoke of a connection between his mimetic talent and his illness, as if somehow his seizures provided a kind of mimetic clairvoyance.[28] Albert was happy to run through his repertory of imitations, which was not limited to animals, but also included police cars, ambulances, and motorcycles. I recorded Albert in a pasture, with the sounds of birds and crickets in the background. Later, Joel Gordon edited these recordings to create a sonic pastiche (leaving out the police cars et al. and adding additional bird sounds that we'd recorded elsewhere) (Audio File, track 20).

From early childhood, the daily routines of nomadic life nourish both aural acuity and oral inventiveness. "While children are out with herd animals, they're always playing with sound," Valentina Süzükei once told me. "You can't spend a whole day in silence, particularly at a young age, and kids are amazingly inventive in their sound-making. Researchers haven't studied this, because they haven't accompanied children while they're herding, and

Albert Saspyk-ool (*far right*) with Tolya, Kaigal-ool, Sayan,
and local friends, Chyraa-Bajy, near Chadaana, 1996.

children don't bring home the instruments they fashion from found objects
because these objects are literally all over the place. They just throw them
away when they're finished using them. But young children will blow into
horns shed by animals, or make an instrument called an *ediski* from a piece
of folded-over bark placed between the teeth that can imitate the sound of
a wild boar. They'll also whistle while using their fingers to modulate the
sound—there are dozens of ways to whistle. Sometimes they'll turn a hollow
stalk into a fipple flute. Or they imitate birds or play with echo. A common
children's toy is the *xirlee,* made from a wooden propeller or button that is
spun around on a piece of string to imitate the sound of wind. In European
music, people talk about performing 'schools' where students learn a particular technique, a particular approach to mastering their instrument. But
for herders, their 'school' is herding itself. Imitating sounds is for them the
equivalent of learning scales, arpeggios, and chords."

The ludic practice of imitating animal sounds does not fade as children
enter adulthood. On the contrary, *ang-meng mal-magan öttüneri* is widely
practiced by adults as well. My field recording tapes are full of animal imitations offered as a mimetic interlude by musicians who were mainly performing other repertory—throat-singing, instrumental music, or songs. Every

Alexander Chambal-oglu
Tülüsh imitating a wolf.
Near Shagonar, spring 1998.

imaginable bird, mammal, reptile, and insect with a recognizable sound print turned up sooner or later on my tapes. One of the most talented mimics was a herder, hunter, and trapper named Alexander Chambal-oglu Tülüsh, whose specialty was imitating wolves. When Joel Gordon and I met and recorded Tülüsh in 1998, he told us that he had trapped ninety-seven wolves and sold their skulls to shamans, for whom a wolf skull is as basic as a stethoscope is to a physician. Wolf skulls are used as *eerens*—physical objects that represent spirits—and may be attached to the back of a shaman's coat.[29] Tülüsh imitated not only the sounds of wolves but also their body movements. For our recording, Tülüsh composed a short medley of imitations, including the sounds of a camel, snake, duck, bull, and wild boar (Audio File, track 21).

While the ability to imitate animals is admired and enjoyed by children and adults alike, such imitations do not represent the highest, subtlest, or most meaningful form of mimetic achievement for Tuvan herders. As Valentina Süzükei put it, "When Tuvans hear naturalistic imitation, they'll smile with approval, the way you'd smile at a talented child who's just produced a clever drawing or improvised a little piece of music. But when you get to the level of serious sound-making, of someone who is a real master, what's central to their art is not just imitation. It's the ability to use timbre to create a perceptual association with a place—to emplace listeners in a landscape of great specificity. This is an example of the kind of sound-making Tuvans call *boidus churumaly*—a 'sketch of nature.'"

SOUND MIMESIS AND SPIRITUAL LANDSCAPE

It is true that the nomads have no history; they only have a geography.

—Gilles Deleuze and Félix Guattari,
"Treatise on Nomadology—The War
Machine," in *A Thousand Plateaus*

Sketches of nature, as the name would suggest, invoke minimal means to achieve their effect. The sound medium of the sketch may vary—throat-singing, jew's harp, *igil,* or even whistling—but in all cases, the core technique involves elaboration of the timbral dimension of sound. Among Tuvans, sketches of nature typically exemplify several conventional timbral motifs—steppe or grasslands, a steep-sided mountain, or taiga forest (these motifs were also discussed in the previous chapter as representatives of the "thing-in-itself" genre). Within these broad motifs, however, performers have in mind a specific area of steppe, for example, a *chailag,* or a summer pasture where they have camped, or a taiga forest where they have hunted.

When throat-singing is the sonic medium for the sketch, the most common style is *kargyraa,* of which there are several varieties: steppe *kargyraa* (*xovu kargyraazy*), steep-sided mountain *kargyraa* (*kojagar kargyraazy*), taiga *kargyraa* (*arga-aryg kargyraazy*), and so on. The specificity of the place may also be conveyed with a couplet of text chanted in a tensed, raspy voice before the purely timbral image. One of the masters of this *kargyraa* lexicon is Aldyn-ool Sevek, a throat-singer and schoolteacher from Kyzyl-Xaya, a remote settlement in Tuva's mountainous southwest. Aldyn-ool's powerful basso profundo was for a time a central feature of the Tuvan techno throat-singing band, Yat-Kha, led by Albert Kuvezin, but Aldyn-ool had tired of techno and touring. He returned to Kyzyl-Xaya, where I went with Valentina Süzükei, Tolya Kuular, Kaigal-ool Xovalyg, and Alexei Saryglar to record him in summer 2003.

Kyzyl-Xaya, a settlement created to sedentarize Tuvan nomads, 2003.

Telephone connections with Kyzyl-Xaya were sporadic, and Valentina was never able to speak with Aldyn-ool to alert him to our visit. "He'll be there when we arrive," Valentina assured me, as if by divination. "Kyzyl-Xaya is at the end of the road. He can't go anywhere." But after a 350-mile drive to Kyzyl-Xaya, we learned that Aldyn-ool was not at home. The previous day, he had traveled to a herding camp higher in the Altai range. Pursuing him there in a jeep aerobically driven by a good-natured Russian army veteran, we arrived at the camp to find that Aldyn-ool had vanished into the mountains that very morning to spend several days gathering wild onions. No one knew when he'd be back. With time running out before Kaigal-ool had to leave Tuva for a concert tour, we had no choice but to abort our mission.

Fortunately, however, Valentina and I were not the only ethnographers in Kyzyl-Xaya. By sheer coincidence, a young American student of Tuvan language and music, Stefan Kamola, had shown up there several days before our group. Stefan had also come to see Aldyn-ool, and he was determined to wait in the settlement until Aldyn-ool came down from the mountains. Stefan graciously offered to share with us the recordings he planned to make of Aldyn-ool, and excerpts from these recordings are included in the audio files online (see tracks 22–23).

Stefan, Valentina, and I were all interested in how Aldyn-ool distinguished steppe *kargyraa* from mountain *kargyraa*—a theme that Valentina had discussed with Aldyn-ool several months before during one of his infrequent visits to Kyzyl. "In mountain *kargyraa,* you have to represent the mountains very clearly, and a person who has lived in the mountains knows how to do this," Aldyn-ool had told her. He explained further that the physical height of mountains could be illustrated through its opposite, depth. That is, extremely low sounds produced with much chest resonance serve as a metaphor for towering heights. And just as Tolya Kuular had pointed out the subtle differences in the sound of streams at different points along their course, Aldyn-ool maintained that mountainous landscapes sound different at different elevations and also when perceived from higher and lower vantage points.

In discussing *kargyraa* with Stefan Kamola, Aldyn-ool introduced other ideas, explaining that mountain *kargyraa* acquired its name from the sound of mountain rivers. "The sound of a mountain river—its voice—is lively and full, and the structure of the melodies should also be like this large sound," Aldyn-ool said. "The melodies become like streams as they fall from high places. By contrast, the rivers of the steppe—of open places—are soft, and their melodies are soft and slow. There isn't such a large, thundering sound. Usually steppe *kargyraa* is sung on higher pitches than mountain *kargyraa*. Someone might hear the difference in these two *kargyraa*s only in that one is low and one is high. But to the performer, the shaping of the sound and the use of throat muscles are two different things. Mountain *kargyraa* uses the muscles of the lower throat, close to the chest. But steppe *kargyraa* comes up close to the glottis." Examples of Aldyn-ool Sevek's mountain *kargyraa* and steppe *kargyraa* appear in the audio files online (tracks 22 and 23, respectively).

Valentina Süzükei pointed out that distinctions between sonic sketches of different landscapes depend not only on performers but also on the experience of listeners—as, one might add, is the case with all music. "To you or me, steppe *kargyraa* and taiga *kargyraa* might sound identical," said Valentina. "If you haven't lived in a particular locale, you won't be able to make the association between sound and place. Listeners themselves make the music from what's performed. From all possible interpretations, they select the one to which their own experience gives priority. People who don't have experience of nomadism often think that this music is 'fantastic' or 'cosmic.' But for Tuvans it's just the opposite. It's utterly concrete. The only timbral symbol that's abstract, in the sense that it's common knowledge for more or less everyone, is echo. Everyone has an intuitive knowledge that echo is connected with mountains."[30]

One of the most remarkable examples of sonic sketching I came across in Tuva was during a brief trip in 1995, when Kaigal-ool, Sayan, and Tolya introduced me to their friend Grigori Mongush. Born in 1958 in the Chüün-Xemchik Region of central Tuva, Grigori had herded animals with his family and later went to work in the nearby town of Ak-Dovurak, where in the late 1950s, Soviet economic planners brought their campaign of industrialization and sedentarization to Tuva in the form of an asbestos plant built near the site of a mining operation. At its peak, the plant employed close to 2,000 people, and Grigori worked as a packer on a conveyor belt.

From the gentle pastoral soundscape of herd animals, wind, and birdsong that had surrounded him on the grasslands, Grigori was abruptly thrust into a sonic Walpurgisnacht that made him increasingly deaf.[31] Finally, he left the asbestos plant, but it was too late. Doctors told him that he suffered a ninety-five percent hearing loss, and when I met him, Grigori had been in such a state for ten years. Earlier in life he had been a musician. His one abiding connection to the world of music was whistling, whose vibrations Grigori could hear by putting his hand next to his ear. He loved to sit on a gentle hillside in the grasslands where he had roamed as a young man and, casting his eye across the landscape, whistle a sonic portrait of what he saw.

Grigori Mongush performs one of his whistling fantasias, filmed near his home in Chadaana (Video File, track 4).

Grigori's highly personal whistling style beautifully illustrates the protean quality of "sketches of nature" (*boidus churumaly*). Grigori told me, in response to a question (he speaks quite clearly, and can understand loud speech through a combination of lip-reading and physical audition), that he knows how to throat-sing, but prefers whistling. "Sheep and cows raise their heads and listen when I whistle," he said. Transforming the contours of hills, the outline of a distant yurt, and the silhouettes of grazing sheep into a sonic chiaroscuro of which his own hearing must provide only a faint simulacrum, Grigori's sound-making falls fully within the realm of synesthetic metaphor: one sense modality, vision, is represented in another, sound.

Any mimetic representation of landscape through music implies a transfer of properties of space and place to sonic parameters such as pitch, timbre, rhythm, and dynamics. Imagistic sketches of nature like steppe *kargyraa* and mountain *kargyraa* focus on timbre as the locus of the metaphorical transfer. Grigori's whistling seemed rooted in an even more abstract sense of metaphor relating to mood, atmosphere, and ambiance. But the mimetic process can also be more precise, drawing on one and the same dimension of measurement in both sound and space. An example of such "mapping" comes from Gombojav, who, among his sonic portraits, provided two that

Grigori Mongush (third from left) with Kaigal-ool Xovalyg,
Tolya Kuular, and Sayan Bapa, 1995.

depict contrasting landscapes. The first represents the Altai Mountains and
the second depicts the Hangai Mountains. In comparing the landscapes,
Gombojav's aim was to distinguish the sharper, steeper contours of the Altai
range from the more rounded peaks of the Hangai. He did so by changing
the rhythm and dynamic envelope of the melodic patterns he played on the
tsuur.

Physical qualities such as steepness, height, and roundedness have a clear
spatial reference, while in sound, the use of such terms is metaphorical. One
pitch is not literally "higher" than another. Rather, the actual physical referent
of pitch "height" is wave frequency: the higher a pitch, the larger the number
of wave cycles per unit of time. A "rounded" sound (again, a spatial metaphor)
is one whose dynamic contour reflects a gradual envelope of attack, duration,
and decay. Gombojav's mimesis of landscape relied on metaphorical common sense to transfer spatial contours to musical ones. His two examples
are reproduced in the audio files online (track 24, Altai Mountains; track 25,
Hangai Mountains).[32]

For Gombojav, the aim of these musical representations was more poetic
than eidetic. Speaking about one of his favorite melodies, "Altai Magtaal"

(Praise-song to the Altai Mountains), Gombojav had said, "When you play 'Altai Magtaal,' you can play it all night long, and as you play, you can imagine images of humans, animals, yurts, and even people you know—there's my uncle, there's my mother—and you see inside the whole Altai world. When you see all these images, you play with the main melody, and you embellish it."

Another example of a sound portrait of mountains was created by a talented young musician from Xakasia, Evgeni (Zhenya) Ulugbashev (b. 1969) (see plate 20). Like so many musicians of his generation throughout Inner Asia, Zhenya Ulugbashev moved from the small settlement where he was born and reared to a large city in order to build a career as a professional musician. Settling in Abakan, Xakasia's capital, Ulugbashev spent part of each summer in the countryside, taking long hikes in the mountains to draw inspiration from nature. He is an outstanding *xaiji,* or performer of Xakas oral poetry, as well as a master performer on the *chatxan,* the Xakas version of a plucked zither with movable bridges.[33] Analogous instruments are known in Tuva as *chadagan,* among nomadic Kazakhs as *jetigen,* and in the epic and court music traditions of the Mongols as *yatga.* Sitting with Zhenya Ulugbashev in his modest apartment in Abakan, I asked him to talk about how a *xaiji* uses sound to represent the natural world.

"In *xai,* you can imitate many different kinds of sounds, for example, birds, mountains, or wind," said Zhenya.

"So where the words mention birds, mountains, or wind, you make those kinds of sounds?" I asked.

"Yes. Every *xaiji* hears these sounds in his own way, and sings them in his own way. For example, I listen to the sound of the mountains, and I sing these sounds in my own way."

"What does the singing of the mountains sound like?" I asked. Zhenya paused for a long time, as if he were trying to access sonic reminiscences that did not come to him easily in his apartment in downtown Abakan. Finally, he took a deep breath and sang the three-minute piece that is excerpted in the audio files online (track 26). The piece is remarkable for the subtle harmonic pulsations that represent the sound of wind. When Zhenya was finished, I asked him whether the sound he had represented was of a particular mountain or more a general picture of mountains.

"The Ulugbashevs used to live in the Sayan Mountains," said Zhenya, "and when I go there in the summer, I climb up to the top of a mountain and look at the endless taiga. The part that's close to you looks green, and as you look into the distance it gets bluer and bluer. It's a feeling of endlessness, infinity. I'd stand on top of a summit, and when you cry out, the sound scatters in all directions. In my singing, I try to give the sound of echo. When you come to the mountains after being in the city, there's such a silence. You shout, and your voice goes and goes and then comes back."

Zhenya Ulugbashev not only sketched the sound of mountains, but had composed an entire song called "Mountain Voices" (Taghlar Ünneri). The song was inspired by different mountains than the Sayan range where he spent summers. "The mountains that inspired 'Mountain Voices' are closer to the Altai ridge," Zhenya explained. "The mountains there are completely different, and the taiga is different. In the Altai range, you have one kind of sensation, and in a different place, you have another kind of sensation. Even the smell is different, because there are different kinds of trees. It's wonderful when you capture that sensation of nature with your feelings. When you climb up on top of a ridge where you can see everything—the mountains, the distant forests—that's what gives rise to melodies, to words." The first two couplets of the song are included in the audio files online (track 27). The full text is transcribed and translated below. After singing the first couplet, Zhenya declaimed the text of the first and second couplets in the manner traditional for a *xaiji*, who continually interweaves singing and poetic declamation of what he is about to sing.

I will sing to you the voices	*Taghda isken ünnerni*
Heard on the mountain	*Sirerge köglep pirim*
I want to bring to the people	*Synda isken köglerni*
The melody heard at the summit.	*Chongha chitir pirim.*
Let the wind always blow	*Chikim turghan tasxyllarym*
On the high alpine summits	*Chilge küülep turghai*
Let clean water always flow from	*Kilkim tas chirlerden*
The great clumps of rock.	*Arygh sugh aghyp turghai.*
Let great trees shoot up	*Ibire ösken xorbylar*
Among the alpine bushes	*Aghas polyp turghai*
Let the birds soaring in the sky	*Tigirde uchuxxan xustar*
Return to my homeland.	*Chirime ailanyp turghai.*

Zhenya's song text is lovingly evocative, but it is not in any way specific with regard to topographic or toponymic features of landscape. Other songs, however, provide a much more specific immersion in a sense of place. When I first began listening to these songs and working with musicians to transcribe and translate their texts, I thought of the songs as maps that narrate a journey through a topographically and toponymically explicit landscape, like the famous "songlines" of the Australian Aborigines.[34] Later I concluded that the song texts offered not so much narrative maps leading singer and listeners sequentially through a particular topography but rather what one might regard metaphorically as a series of snapshots.

The meaning of the texts derives from the creation of a series of analogies between nature and culture that poignantly or piquantly juxtapose wide-angle images of landscape with close-up portraits of people. As with any good snapshot, their aim is to evoke a visceral sense that the image inside the frame is real and alive. Sonic "snapshots" accomplish this by emplacing both singer and listeners in the landscapes depicted. Here, for example, are the first three stanzas of "Bayan-Dugai," a song that Kaigal-ool Xovalyg loves to sing because it describes a ridge of hills near where he grew up and herded animals as a child and young man. In each stanza, the first couplet describes a natural landscape and the second couplet draws a parallel with human life. Thus an understanding of nature comes through analogy to culture, and vice-versa.

Kaigal-ool Xovalyg performs "Bayan-Dugai" while sitting in a field gazing at the eponymous ridge of hills (Video File, track 5).

Argarlyg and Koshkarlyg	*Astyng-kishting turlaa bolgan*
Became places where the ermine and sable live.	*Argarlygny Koshkarlygny.*
Bayan-Dugai is a place where forty or fifty herders	*Aldan-bezhen malchyn küzeesh*
Camp during the autumn and winter.	*Kyshtaglai beer Bayan-Dugai.*
The rear view of Bayan-Dugai is beautifully ornamented,	*Bayan-Dugai artyn kasstaan,*
And my Bayan-Mandaa is just as beautiful.	*Bayan-Mandaam taanda charash.*
The bridal head-ornament worn by Dugai's merry* daughter	*Bashtanggyzy xadyp orar*
Waves in the wind.	*Bashtak-kara Dugai kyzy.*
My Ezirlig and Byshkak	*Ezimneri edektelgem*
Whose forested slopes descend like a hem.	*Ezirlimnyi Byshkaktymny.*
Erge-Kara, that rascal	*Edekteri estep-orar*
Whose hem** waves in the wind.	*Erge-kara kulugurnu.*

* Lit., "joke-black," translated as "merry."
** "Hem" is a pun; the word also refers to "foothills" or "lower slopes."

In performing "Bayan-Dugai," Kaigal-ool creates a simulacrum of the place and its inhabitants that momentarily becomes real and transports listeners to this landscape with great verisimilitude. Argarlyg, Koshkarlyg, Ezirlig, and Byshkak are all hills in the vicinity of Bayan-Dugai whose names denote animals or animal parts: *argar* is a mountain sheep, *koshkar* is a ram, *ezir* is an eagle, and *byshkak* is skin from the paw of a roe deer used to make boots or shoes. Roe deer frequent the eponymous hill, and *byshkak* serves as

Ex. 4. "Bayan-Dugai"

As-tyng- kish-ting tur-laa_ bol-gan_____ Ar-gar-lyg-ny Kosh-kar-

lyg-ny_____ Al-dan_ bezh-en mal-chyn kü-zeesh

_ Kysh-tag-lai_ beer_ Ba-yan_ Du-gai_

a metonym that represents the animal itself. The *lyg/lig* suffix is a way of say-ing "has," for example, Koshkarlyg: "having rams," or "populated by rams"; Ezirlig: "having eagles"; and so on. Toponyms thus have an explicit double meaning: they refer to places and at the same time to the animals that live there. In this way, the animal world is mapped toponymically onto landscape. The same phenomenon exists vestigially in eastern North America, where toponyms were created by hunters, trappers, and farmers—or taken over from Native peoples—who depended for their livelihood on the land: Loon Lake, Moose Mountain, Deer Hill, Trout Pond, and so on.

In addition to the three verses of "Bayan-Dugai" transcribed above, Kai-gal-ool Xovalyg's rendition of the song includes three additional verses that he composed himself to commemorate the 1991 visit of His Holiness the Dalai Lama to Chadaana, a little west of Bayan-Dugai, where the Dalai Lama reconsecrated the remains of a Buddhist monastery destroyed in the 1930s and launched a campaign to rebuild it. Kaigal-ool's newly composed verses serve as a trope on the original three, not only depicting Bayan-Dugai as a place of natural beauty but also portraying neighboring Chadaana as a center of Buddhist religion:

Chadaana, our homeland, is a — *Shazhin-xuree tövüt bolgan*
Center of religion and [Buddhist] temple — *Chadaana dep churttuvuska*
My holy Dalai Lama came and blessed — *Dalai-Lama bashkym kelgesh*
My Upper-Temple [Üstüü-Xuree]. — *Dagyp bergen Üstüü-Xureem.*

It is my Dugai where the cuckoos fly — *Kedeeringe xekter xangash*
And often sing — *Kezek etken Dugaiymny*
And it is my Dugai that was blessed — *Kezer-Chinggis toorlap ertkesh*
By Kezer-Chinggis,* who passed — *Dagyp ertken Dugaiymny.*
  through here.

* Kezer-Chinggis is the hero of an eponymous epic tale.

It is my Dugai where all summer long	*Bora-xekter üjüp kelgesh*
The grey cuckoos sing	*Edip chailaar Dugaiymny*
And it is my Upper-Temple that was blessed	*Bogda-Kegeen bodu kelgesh*
By Bogda-Kegeen* who was himself here.	*Dagyp bergen üstüü-Xureem.*

*A high rank in the hierarchy of Buddhist lamas.

Songs that evoke nostalgia for other times and places are not of course limited to Tuvan herders. American folk music and minstrelsy is full of them—"Home on the Range," "Carry Me Back to Ol' Virginny," "Old Folks at Home," "On Top of Old Smoky," and so on ("old" is evidently a useful word for evoking nostalgia).[35] What distinguishes Tuvan songs, however, is the sheer density of toponymic and topographic detail in the texts. These references to landscape may be woven into a poem in such a way as to make understanding of its meaning dependent on intimate knowledge of topography. A good example is the following quatrain from a song about a hill near Bayan-Dugai whose name, Shanchyg, denotes a particular shape of protuberance. In this case, it refers to the angular shape of the hill's base, which resembles a bent forearm, and in particular, the angle made by the elbow. The word *konggurgai* at the end of each line is an onomatopoetic word that represents the sound of, for example, stones tumbling down a hillside. It also lends its name to the shaman's rattle (*kongguraa*) (Audio File, track 28).

If you dig a well before the grey Shanchyg, konggurgai,	*Küü-la Shanchyg baarynga, konggurgai*
Why wouldn't water appear, konggurgai?	*Kuduk kassa ünmes dep be, konggurgai?*
If you get engaged to one you love, konggurgai,	*Kuskun kara kulugurnu, konggurgai*
Why wouldn't [her parents] give her away, konggurgai?	*Kudalaza berbes dep be, konggurgai?*

As in the text of Bayan-Dugai, the quatrain breaks into two couplets that create a parallel between nature and culture. To understand the meaning of the verse, however, one has to understand that Shanchyg is a dry place where finding water would be all but impossible. Likewise, as the poem suggests, the likelihood that the girl's parents will allow her to marry is next to nil. The singer who composed the text—presumably inspired by his own predicament—put his knowledge of local landscape in the service of a poetic expression of irony. I, of course, did not understand the meaning at first, and Tolya Kuular, who had sung the song, had to explain it to me. After I had scribbled the words in my notebook, Tolya wanted to ensure that I understood the ingenuity of the poetry—namely, that the text had more than one possible interpretation. "You could also think of the poem as being about hopefulness—about accomplishing the impossible," said Tolya. "In other words, that if you dig and dig in front of Shanchyg, you'll eventually reach water, and in the same way, if the young guy who wants to get married asks once, twice, three times, perhaps he'll get what he wants."

Studying songs rich in evocations of topography and toponymy, and instrumental music that represents landscape and soundscape through sound symbolism, I found myself thinking often about the work of ethnomusicologist and anthropological linguist Steven Feld, who over the last two decades, has produced a distinguished body of scholarship based on field research in Papua New Guinea, among a small group who live in the tropical rainforest, the Kaluli. Feld's explorations of what he has called "acoustemology," which might be described as sound-centered epistemology, have become a locus classicus in ethnomusicology and in semiotic studies of music. Music-making among the inhabitants of a tropical rainforest might seem to have little in common with music-making among south Siberian pastoralists, but a comparison of Feld's findings with my own shows that both groups use surprisingly similar expressive techniques to emplace themselves in landscape and soundscape.

When Feld published his groundbreaking book, *Sound and Sentiment: Birds, Weeping, Poetics, and Song in Kaluli Expression,* the power of his work seemed to rest at least in part on the uniqueness of the Kaluli cultural practices he described. Yet Kaluli practices of "linking sensory experience of the rainforest to artistic processes in visual, verbal, musical, and choreographic media" may well be less a unique occurrence than a particular instance of a broader mimetic phenomenon.[36] At the same time, differences among the artistic processes and expressive techniques through which landscape and soundscape are represented are no less interesting than similarities.

Studying both differences and similarities can lead to a fuller understanding of the relationship between cultural and cognitive aspects of sound mimesis. For example, the "sonic snapshot" technique of emplacement that I discuss above might be contrasted with what Feld has called "poetic cartography," that is, songs that comprise toponymic and topographic maps or paths.[37] While more focused comparison would be necessary to pinpoint the differences between them, one could hope that they amount to more than merely a use of different metalinguistic metaphors. Likewise, Feld's description in *Sound and Sentiment* of music whose aim is to create nostalgia and evoke tears through song seems not unlike what occurs in Tuvan songs of place, yet the poetic strategies described by Feld are different from those used in Tuvan song texts. As more "acoustemological" field research becomes available from other parts of the world where people still live in an intimate relationship with nature, the field of comparison will grow richer, and researchers' inferences more persuasive.[38]

SOUND MIMESIS AS NARRATIVE

Songs and sonic sketches of nature like those discussed in the previous sections emplace performers and listeners in a natural landscape and convey a sense of being present through the aural equivalent of brushstrokes. Natural landscapes are depicted at a particular moment in time, as if frozen in a snapshot. The dynamism of these snapshots comes from their simultaneous expression of multiple sensory images that continually shift in and out of focus in an observer's perceptual field. Valentina Süzükei has used the term "sonic holography" to describe the three-dimensionality of sound-space in a specific acoustical environment. But episodic sound portraits, whatever the metaphor used to describe them, occupy only one end of a temporal continuum that extends at its other end to mimetic forms of extremely long duration. Spread out along this continuum are instrumental pieces, tales, legends interwoven with musical interludes, and vast epic poems, all of which share a narrative quality that is one of the hallmarks of nomadic expressive culture in Inner Asia.

At its simplest, narrative refers to the act of telling a story or providing an account of events and experiences. Narration with words, safe to say, is a universal attribute of humankind. Whatever their length, form, content, and thematic roots in the human psyche, stories, tales, and oral poetry, often supplemented by gesture, are culturally ubiquitous. In many cultures, oral literature is recited or performed to the accompaniment of music that may range from simple to elaborate—for example, from the two-stringed *dombra* strummed by a Kazakh bard to an entire Javanese gamelan orchestra accompanying a shadow puppet presentation of the ancient Ramayana epic. But the notion of telling stories exclusively through instrumental music itself without the aid of texts—what in the West would be called "program music"—is a more limited phenomenon.

In Western instrumental concert music, explicitly programmatic works such as Berlioz's *Symphonie Fantastique* and Musorgsky's *Pictures at an Exhibition* occupy limited territory within a musical realm that leans heavily toward the elaboration of abstract formal schemes to create compositions of long duration. Of course such compositions may also embody a narrative component, and narrative structures have been attributed to numerous works in the Western canon that are not explicitly programmatic. These claims, however, have often been contentious, and in any case they are typically based on a post factum interpretation of a work, rather than on overt evidence of what composers themselves meant their works to mean or express.[39]

In contrast to the limited role of explicit programs and the ambiguity that often surrounds the narrative dimension in Western art music, nomadic cultures in Inner Asia have shown a strong propensity for mimetic narrative in their music, and explicit programmatic content in instrumental music is widespread. In an inversion of Western norms, the narrative dimension of music is widely taken for granted by performers and audiences but little discussed by scholars, who have tended to focus their attention on text-based narrative forms, in particular, epic poetry, the Inner Asian narrative genre par excellence.[40]

The extent of popular beliefs about the power of music to convey specific images and ideas, and even to trump the power of language, is evident in many legends and stories. For example, in one story—an archetype that turns up in different versions in different parts of Inner Asia—a powerful khan has a favorite horse that suddenly takes sick and dies. It is well known that whoever brings the khan bad news will have his head cut off, and no one dares tell him about the death of his horse. Finally, a musician is summoned, and the task is explained to him. The musician requests an audience with the khan, and coming before him, plays a textless piece of music on his stringed instrument. Listening to the music, the khan understands that his beloved horse has died, and the musician's head is spared.[41]

Narrative instrumental music exists throughout the Inner Asian nomadic realm, but it has reached a particularly high level of professionalism south of the Altai region, among Kyrgyz and Kazakh performers, who play long-necked lutes called *komuz* (Kyrgyz) and *dombra* (Kazakh). Ever since their creation as Soviet republics in the early years of the U.S.S.R., Kyrgyzstan and Kazakhstan have been cast into the geopolitical realm of Central Asia, whose identity as a region is most commonly linked with the central role of Islam in shaping its history and culture.[42] These days, however, an increasing number of Kazakh and Kyrgyz musicians in search of their own historical and cultural roots look not south, toward Islamic Central Asia, but north, beyond the sphere of Islamic influence, to the pastoral Turkic cultures of the Altai region.

Indeed, the Kyrgyz have old links to the region that is now Xakasia and Tuva. Present-day Kyrgyz historiography has rallied around evidence that places the ancestors of the modern Kyrgyz in the vicinity of the upper Yenisei River, beginning as early as the sixth century. During the Soviet era, this view was suppressed in favor of the "autochthonic theory," which held that the Kyrgyz had always lived on the territory that under the Soviets became Kyrgyzia.[43] The ethnonym "Kyrgys" is still found in Tuva (as in the name of Tuvan music specialist Zoya Kyrgys), and for many contemporary Kyrgyz, particularly in the north of Kyrgyzstan, the historical link to the Yenisei explains both their feeling of kinship with the Altai pastoralists and the cultural distance they feel from the long-ago Islamized sedentary dwellers to the south and west, Uzbeks and Tajiks. From a musical point of view, it makes great sense to include Kyrgyz and Kazakh narrative instrumental genres in this study, as the material that follows ought to make clear.

A psychological watershed, however, divides the delicate and highly personal timbral atmospherics of "sketches of nature" from the extroverted listener-centered pieces that comprise narrative instrumental music. Sketches and their like might be described as music without performance. Their mimetic quality is motivated by a spiritual dimension, by sound-makers' urge to represent the beauty of a place and the feelings of exaltation that come from emplacing themselves in that beauty. In such conditions, displays of musical virtuosity seem gratuitous. No listeners wait to be impressed, no critics to be wowed. What matters is sincerity and modesty before the sole audience, the spirit-masters. But the same mimetic impulse that serves the spiritual in nomadic music can also be harnessed to the musical expression of another aspect of nomadic life: rivalry and competition. Respect for spirits in no way precludes competitive behavior toward other humans. Historical and ethnographic accounts of Inner Asian nomadism could not be clearer about the persistent rivalries and hostilities that have pitted people against people, clan against clan, brother against brother.

Not surprisingly, the martial and combative tradition in nomadic cultures has also found expression in the agonistic and the ludic—in sport, play, and arts.[44] Presented in the context of wrestling, horseracing, and a host of horsemanship games, such as polo played with the carcass of a goat, music and poetry are transformed into spectator sports with designated winners and losers. The notion of art as a spectator sport is exemplified in poetic and musical competitions known respectively as *aitys* and *tartys,* which once flourished among the Kazakh and Kyrgyz but are presently in a state of desuetude (both *aitys* and *tartys* have been objects of recent attempts at revivalism).[45]

An *aitys* may assume many forms and address a variety of themes, but at root it is a form of verbal combat, "usually a contest in the form of a dialogue between two or more poets or poet-singers," as Kazakh ethnomusicologist Alma Kunanbaeva notes in *The Garland Encyclopedia of World Music.*[46] The analogous *tartys* pits not poets, but instrumentalists, against one another.

Traditional rules of engagement illustrate the extent to which these latter-day versions of the ancient Greek *agones* are rooted in the social structure of the clan system. In her *Garland* article, Alma Kunanbaeva lists the following conventions: "1) Competition was forbidden between members of the same clan, and between clan members whose relation to the clan was through the father's lineage. 2) Every participant was obliged to praise his own clan and find fault with his opponent's clan. 3) During the competition, contestants were allowed to address their opponent in ways that violated normal etiquette."[47] *Aitys* and *tartys* thus represented not only competition among individuals, but among clans.

As a social stimulus for musical composition and performance, *tartys* had a predictable effect. Contestants vied to outdo one another in displays of technical virtuosity, musical humor, and mimetic ingenuity. The rewards for winning could be high—stories tell of victors taking away brides, camels, horses, and other bounties, while the vanquished could receive a mock punishment such as having to repeat from memory the winning player's composition. In the winner-take-all mentality of the nomadic *agones*, there were no second prizes.

This conception of art and music could not have been more different from that of the nomads' not-so-distant neighbors, the sedentary urbanites of Transoxania. In place of the city dwellers' contemplative, Sufi-inspired poetry and music, with its goal of inner illumination and mystic *gnosis*, the music and poetry of *aitys* and *tartys* comprised a bald declaration of strength, power, and endurance. Music served as a test of skill and will, cleverness and ingenuity—in short, traits that would serve a nomad handily in the harsh conditions of the steppe. Many stories tell of the stratagems adopted by performers to win a contest. And here, in contrast to the traditionally male world of throat-singing and epic performance that only recently has begun to open to women (see chapter 6, "Women Are Not Supposed to Do This"), female contestants in *aitys* and *tartys* are legendary.

One classic recounts a *tartys* in which a young man and a young woman, both virtuoso musicians, compete on the *dombra*, the two-stringed lute that is contestants' typical weapon of choice. As the competition heats up, the man removes the boot from his right foot, plants his heel against the bridge of his instrument, and plays the strings with his toes. In the protocol of the *tartys*, his opponent would have to try to best him by doing the same, with still better results. The laws of *shari'a*, however, forbade women from exposing their feet—a fact that the young man had shrewdly taken into account—and his female opponent was forced to forfeit the *tartys*.[48]

The culture of agonistic competition exemplified by *aitys* and *tartys* has left a legacy of brilliant musical pieces called *kui* (Kazakh) or *küü* (Kyrgyz)—both meaning "frame of mind" or "mood"—that have been transmitted orally down to our own time. Many are attributed to composer-performers who lived in the nineteenth century, and some are surely older. As performance art, they draw on a range of narrative devices to engage an audience. Before beginning to play, performers commonly provide a brief verbal summary of the story their music will tell. During a performance, they often supplement mimetic melodic, rhythmic, and articulatory figures with gestural movements of the hands and arms to illustrate aspects of the musical story and to add to the entertainment value of the performance. In Kyrgyz, these gestural movements are collectively known as *kol oinotuu,* "hand play."

The use of gesture is so engrained that performers themselves may not be consciously aware of what their gestures represent, or why they are using them. For example, during a videotaping session with Kyrgyz musician Nurlanbek Nyshanov, I asked him to perform a piece I had once heard him play on the metal jew's harp *(temir komuz)*. Nurlanbek played the short *küü,* gracefully twisting the wrist of his right hand and sweeping it to the side in stylized, arc-like movements after striking the instrument's protruding tongue. When he had finished, we had the following exchange:

> TL: "Tell me, what do those gestures mean?"
> NN: "Well, to be honest, they don't mean anything."
> TL: "Then why do you make them?"
> NN: "Because I feel like it."

Nurlanbek added, "For example, with dancers, their movements come from the soul, from the heart. All art—movement, playing, singing—should come from the heart. What I do is improvisation—a dance of the hand, so to speak. It's as simple as that."

> TL: "But why do those gestures play such an important role in this particular *küü*? What's the name of the *küü*?"
> NN: "Oh, it's called "The Swing" [*Selkinchek*]. It depicts the way girls and young women like to sit on a swing and go higher and higher."

Nurlanbek smiled sheepishly, twisting his index finger while pointing it at his head in the sign used universally in the former Soviet Union to signify lunacy or idiocy.

103

Nurlanbek Nyshanov and his wife, Gulbara Baigashkaeva.
Bishkek, Kyrgyzstan, 2003.

NN: "It never occurred to me that the gestures were an illustration of the *küü*," he said.[49]

In other examples of *kui* and *küü* that I recorded, performers readily explained how melody, rhythm, and gesture all combined to form a mimetic *gesamtkunstwerk*. One of the most memorable of these was a Kazakh *kui* called "I'm Ducking, I'm Ducking, I'm Ducking in a Ditch" (*Buqtym, buqtym, saida buqtym*). The performer was Abdulhamit Raimbergenov, a *dombra* player and music educator from Almaty, Kazakhstan whose fierce virtuosity leaps unexpectedly from his courtly, soft-spoken demeanor.

One evening, we sat in Abdulhamit's office at Kökil Music College, where he directs an innovative program to support the transmission of traditional music to future generations by training children not so much with the hope that they will become professional musicians, as loyal audience members. His students learn to play the *dombra* to build appreciation and respect for the achievements of musical tradition that they will carry with them throughout their lives. Abdulhamit was born into a family of musicians in Aktyubinsk Region, in western Kazakhstan. His great grandfather had been a famous *dombra* player, his grandfather, a mullah and Sufi, and his father,

Abdulhamit Raimbergenov, *dombra* player and visionary music educator. Almaty, Kazakhstan, 2003.

a professional musician who worked in a teacher's college and composed many *kuis* and songs. Abdulhamit had listened to the music and stories of musicians who gathered in the home of his grandfather, and he was filled with the lore of their exploits and adventures.

Among the greatest heroes of Kazakh music was Qurmanghazy Saghyrbaiuly (1823–1889).[50] "'Zhaldy Qurmanghazy,' they called him," said Abdulhamit, "'Qurmanghazy with a mane.' He was strong like a horse, and had hair running down the back of his neck. He was renowned for his cunning, courage, and skill on the *dombra,* and took part in many contests. Qurmanghazy lived at a time when czarist Russia had begun to exert a strong influence on the Kazakhs. He belonged to the Kyzyl Kurt tribe, and they all became followers of a revolutionary leader named Maxambed, who led a revolt against czarist colonization. There's a story that Maxambed was tricked into coming into a yurt as a guest—one always left one's weapons outside when entering a yurt—and someone sneaked up from behind and cut his head off. The story is that even as his head flew away, he grabbed a stick and swung it around, trying to hit the people who had decapitated him.

"After Maxambed was killed, the Russians tried to catch Qurmanghazy. He was accused of horse-stealing, and czarist soldiers were sent from Orenburg to arrest him. They came to his home, and not finding him there, took away his wife and baby son. That evening when Qurmanghazy returned, people told him what had happened, and Qurmanghazy mounted a horse and rode off to find his wife. In the dark of night, he spotted a fire burning in uninhabited steppe. Dismounting and scurrying closer, he saw his wife and son sleeping by the fire, and the soldiers asleep nearby. Silently, he crept up and removed the bullets from their rifles, took one rifle for himself, swept up his wife and baby, and ran away.

"Later Qurmanghazy composed a *kui* about the incident. The music illustrates the way he ducked down into gullies and crevices in the steppe to avoid detection as he crept up on the soldiers. At one point, he rolls down a hillock, and the music shows that with a portamento. The *dombra* also 'speaks' the words: *buqtym, buqtym, saida buqtym* (I'm ducking, I'm ducking, I'm ducking in a ditch). At the same time that the *dombra* speaks the words, it's clear from the musical representation how Qurmanghazy is moving, how he's ducking down and hiding." After Abdulhamit had finished playing, we transcribed the part of the *kui* in which the *dombra* "speaks" (see ex. 5).

Unlike other "talking" instruments such as jew's harps (discussed in the following section), whose performers manipulate a wide timbral palette to simulate speech sounds, the *dombra* presents limited possibilities for timbral variation. Abdulhamit ingeniously compensates for these limitations by alternately damping and strumming the strings to highlight speech rhythm and articulation. The *kui*'s loping rhythm and abrupt halts convincingly portray Kurmangaz's jerky movements as he sneaks up on the soldiers' campfire to save his wife and son.

Abdulhamit Raimbergenov performs "Buqtym, Buqtym" on the *dombra* (Video File, track 6).

In another *kui,* Abdulhamit demonstrated how the *dombra* can represent not only physical movements but also qualities of human character. The example he chose was an anonymous composition called "Karasai." On the basis of its style and subject matter, Abdulhamit guessed that it had been composed sometime in the nineteenth century. "Karasai was a *batyr,*" explained Abdulhamit. "The *batyrs* were fighters and epic singers, poets and composers. Karasai lived in the second half of the eighteenth century and the beginning of the nineteenth. In those times there were a lot of battles with the Jungars, with the Kalmyks. The *batyrs* were extraordinary people, and

Ex. 5. "Buqtym, Buqtym, Saida Buqtym"

buq-tym buq-tym sai-de buq-tym   jy-ra-de buq-tym   sai-de buq-tym

*×= damping string with a slight slap of the right hand

a famous group of them called the 'forty *batyrs*' became the subject of epic poems and instrumental *kuis*. The *kui* about Karasai portrays his great skill at riding, the power of his will, his determination, his fighting character."

The swift rhythmic pounding of horse's hooves is clearly audible in the robust strumming patterns, but it would oversimplify this miniature masterpiece to regard it simply as a literal representation of horseback riding. Rather, like the Tuvan "sketches of nature" that comprise a composite sensory impression of landscape and soundscape, "Karasai" evokes a composite image

Abdulhamit Raimbergenov performs "Karasai" on the *dombra* (Video File, track 7).

of the *batyr* and his horse: swiftness, strength, chivalry—"the feeling of someone who has been victorious, a winner in life," in Abdulhamit's words.

In both of Abdulhamit's *dombra* pieces, the mimetic element is conveyed by sound alone, without the assistance of gestural movements such as those used by Nurlanbek in his performance of "The Swing" on the jew's harp. Gesture, however, is a common element of playing stringed instruments among both Kazakhs and Kyrgyz. The stylized hand movements used by performers on the *dombra* and on the Kyrgyz *komuz*, a short long-necked lute with three strings, are not viewed as supplementary or optional. On the contrary, these movements are essential, and they are as integral to the performance of a piece as the music itself.

These days, Kyrgyz professional musicians, like their neighbors, the Kazakhs, perform a canonical repertory of instrumental pieces (*küü*) attributed to a pantheon of great composer-performers. Beginning in the 1920s, many of these pieces were systematically transcribed in European staff notation, recorded for radio programs, performed in concerts, and taught in the curricula of music schools and national conservatories.[51] Rooted in a living folk tradition, they have now become classicized, but, remarkably, they are not frozen into fixed performance versions. In the traditional spirit of competitiveness that still pervades the performance of narrative instrumental repertories, individual musicians develop their own variations of both music and gesture with the apparent goal of outdoing one another in displays of technical skill, musical daring, and ingenuity.

Two of the warhorses of the Kyrgyz *küü* repertory are "Ak-Tamak—Kök-Tamak" (White Neck—Blue Neck) and "Toguz Qairyq" (Nine Themes). Each illustrates a different aspect of the narrative principle in instrumental music. "Ak-Tamak—Kök-Tamak" was composed by Atai Ogonbaev (1900–1949), a *komuz* player from the region of Talas in the northwest of present-day Kyrgyzstan.[52] The program of the piece involves an argument between two birds, husband and wife, who disagree about whether to stay and nest where they are, or fly south in search of warmer weather. The wife, Ak-Tamak, who wants to fly south, proposes that they settle their disagreement by engaging in a singing contest. They do, and Ak-Tamak wins. Even though the story is known to every Kyrgyz music lover, it is always narrated by performers before they play the piece.

In the *küü,* the voices of the two birds are distinguished by different melodic patterns, contrasting registers, and contrasting types of articulation. For example, during the singing contest, one bird sings in pizzicato flageolet tones while the other is represented by repetitive melodic figures and clumps of strummed dichords at the lower end of the instrument's range. Dramatic gestures of the hands and arms are abstractly stylized to the point where their relation to events in the story is unclear, and left largely to individual interpretation.

Namazbek Uraliev performs "Ak-Tamak—Kök-Tamak on the *komuz* (Video File, track 8).[53]

"Toguz Qairyq" (Nine Themes), composed by Toktogul Satylganov (1864–1933), illustrates the versatility of the *komuz* and the eclecticism of the *küü* genre. The piece embodies not an explicit program, but the working out of a formal principle. Its structure suggests parallels with work by contemporary American composers such as Steve Reich and Terry Riley that critics (but usually not the composers themselves) have called "minimalist." That is, a melodic or rhythmic ostinato is repeated with minimal changes gradually introduced in successive repetitions. The effect is of a continuing wash of sound in which sinuous contours of pitch, rhythm, and timbre shift in and out of focus within the flow of the music. Even with no specific story to tell, "Toguz Qairyq" includes a dramatic gestural component. These gestures, like the music, exist at a level of formal abstraction devoid of explicit mimetic reference, yet remain an integral part of the performance. Like silent letters in English orthography, they are symbols that have lost their expressive meaning, yet remain a vestige of older conventions.

When I mentioned to Ruslan Jumabaev, the virtuosic performer of "Toguz Qairyq," my idea that the piece sounded like an example of contemporary

Namazbek Uraliev in his workshop holding an almost-finished *komuz*. Semenovka, Kyrgyzstan, 2003.

minimalism, he nodded his head. "Minimalism perfectly expresses the lifestyle of nomads," he said. "They have few things, and everything has to be compact and capable of being broken down into small pieces—like taking apart a yurt—so that it can be moved around. In some way, the music seems to reflect that."

Ruslan Jumabaev performs "Toguz Qairyq" on the *komuz* (Video File, track 9).

These days, no instrumental genres called *küü* or *kui* exist in Tuva and the Altai Region, but an analogue, *uzun xoyug* (*xoyug* is cognate with *küü* and *kui*), is in the process of revival. Like throat-singing, with its untidy distribution among different social groups and geographical territories, narrative instrumental music is represented to a greater or lesser degree, and on various instruments, in different Inner Asian cultures. In Tuvan music, where timbre is central to sound mimesis and melody plays a lesser role, it is natural that the narrative element should develop on instruments well suited to timbral manipulation, such as fiddles and jew's harps. The *igil* in particular has been the locus of a rich repertory of narrative pieces.

An interesting example of this tradition consists of narrative pieces that explain the origin of the musical instrument on which they are performed. Many of these pieces seem to share the mimetic principle of "enlivening." For example, playing a horsehead fiddle enlivens or animates the spirit of the horse, just as playing a shaman's drum enlivens the spirit of the animal whose skin was used to make it. Such pieces not only symbolically represent specific animal sounds, movements, and comportment but also offer a concrete representation of the mythology widely shared among the pastoralists that animals, particularly horses, have magical powers. Horses exist at the intersection of humankind, nature, and the supernatural. In some respects, the mythology of horses puts them on a par with humans, for example, through the power of language ascribed to talking equines. In other respects, horses represent a magical world apart from human life, as in the mythical archetype of the winged horse, called Tulpar in Inner Asian Turkic languages—an analogue to the Pegasus of Western antiquity.

Winged, talking horses turn up in many stories, legends, and narrative instrumental pieces throughout Inner Asia. One of the most beloved of these is the tale that recounts the origin of the fiddle. Fiddle players in Mongolia and Tuva invariably know the story, albeit in different versions, and perform it in different ways. A Tuvan version of the story that Valentina Süzükei learned from her mother, Süzükei Ondar (1927–2004), is translated below.[54]

"Long ago Ösküs-ool [a traditional hero of Tuvan folk tales] lived with his aging father. All they owned were three goats. The *noyon* [landowner] whom Ösküs-ool served had a skinny old mare. In the spring, she gave birth, but soon after, she died from exhaustion. The *noyon* ordered that her colt be taken to the steppe and left there for the wolves. He said he was not willing to pay for the colt's food. Ösküs-ool felt sorry for the colt. He took it home and fed it milk from his goats. The colt grew into a great gray stallion with a white star on his forehead. Ösküs-ool's horse started to beat all the *noyon*'s horses in races, and with each win, he became more famous throughout Tuva. The envious and evil *noyon* ordered his servants to kill Ösküs-ool's horse by pushing it over a sheer cliff.

"Ösküs-ool looked everywhere for his horse, and, unable to find it, fell asleep from exhaustion. Then, in a dream, he saw his horse speaking in a human voice: 'You'll find my remains under the sheer cliff. Hang my skull on an old larch tree, make a musical instrument from its wood, cover it with skin from my face, and make the strings from the hair of my tail. When you start to play this instrument, my double will come down from the upper world.'

"Ösküs-ool made the instrument the way the horse told him in the dream, and he began to play. He thought of his horse, remembering him as a tiny colt and how they played together, how they won all the races. He played and wept. And when he remembered that his beloved horse was no longer with him in this world, the instrument wept with him. Ösküs-ool grew angry remembering the evil *noyon,* and all the grief and anger found expression in his playing. They say that this is why the *igil* is such a complex and expressive instrument.

"Ösküs-ool played for a long time. As people listened, they laughed and wept with him. Suddenly, at the top of a high mountain, the clouds parted and down from the mountains came an exact copy of his horse—a strong gray stallion. And the stallion was not alone. With him came a whole herd of horses with black and white faces."

In Mongolian versions of the story, the name of the herder is Höhöö (Cuckoo) Namjil instead of Ösküs-ool, and in a common version, Höhöö Namjil is given a magical winged horse named Jonon Har (Black Jonon). Herding his sheep by day, he mounted his winged horse by night and flew to a distant place to meet his beloved. A woman became jealous of Höhöö Namjil and arranged for someone to cut off his horse's wings. Jonon Har fell and died, and from his bones and skin, the grieving herder created a fiddle on which he played songs about his horse.

According to Valentina Süzükei, performers always recite the story before playing a musical narration of it, even when performing for listeners who know the story well. "As the musician recites the text, he's also tuning himself, and getting in the mood to perform it," explained Valentina. Individual performance versions vary significantly from one player to the next, but as a rule, Mongolian performers ground their interpretation in the angular, rhythmic bowing style characteristic of *tatlaga,* the generic name in Mongolia for narrative instrumental music played on fiddles.

Tuvan players also represent a horse's gallop with rhythmic bowing, but the rhythmic pulse differs from the Mongolian *tatlaga.* In other words, instrumental interpretations of the story are filtered not only through the performance style of individual musicians but also through culture-specific stylistic preferences. A recording of "Jonon Har" performed on the Mongolian horsehead fiddle (*morin huur*) by Bat-Erdene, a talented young musician who grew up in the west of Mongolia and now lives in Ulaanbaatar, is included in the audio files online (track 29).

Other performances of "Jonon Har" that I heard during visits to Mongolia in 1999 and 2000 often included iconic imitations of the neigh of a horse. The first time I heard such a performance, I thought, "Oh, how lifelike! Surely this kind of iconic mimesis is evidence of great antiquity." But ethnomusicologist Peter Marsh—a specialist on Mongolian music and a strong advocate for its cultural traditions, who accompanied me on both trips—knew better. "The neighs and whinnies are for tourists," Marsh told me with a laugh. "A Mongolian listener wouldn't need the horse sounds in his face."[55] Valentina Süzükei made a similar comment about recent trends in Tuvan performances of narrative mimesis. "Tuvans can hear and imagine all of the action of the story through the play of different timbres and rhythms. The whole point of the artistry of this kind of performance is subtlety—representing the action and illustrating the characters with a light touch that draws on the imagination. In the end, people hear what they want to hear."[56]

Mongolian *tatlaga*, with its strong rhythmic pulse and minimal use of melody, is often used to accompany mimetic movements called *bie* or *biyelgee*. *Bie* (as I shall call it henceforth) occupies something of a middle ground between gesture and what would broadly be considered dance.[57] Performers use stylized movements of the hands, arms, and upper torso to represent scenes of work and play as well as to narrate the events of myths and legends. Some movements are transparently symbolic while the meaning of others is obscure even to the people who perform them. In Mongolia, *bie* is linked particularly closely with Oirat groups in the western Altai region, each group having somewhat different gestural styles and conventions. *Bie* must surely have once existed among Tuvans, but in contemporary Tuva, it has disappeared not only as a living practice but also as a living cultural memory.

An example of *bie* is performed by Hoton and Dörvöd Oirats in Uvs Aimag, western Mongolia (Video File, track 10).

The performers in the video are amateurs, members of a local ensemble, but the cheerful roughness of the bowed *tatlaga* rhythm played on the horsehead fiddle, the mixed ages of the dancers, and their clear enjoyment of the tradition they were demonstrating made this performance more vibrant than several I recorded in Ulaanbaatar, the emerging center of folklorized Mongolian music for export.

Tatlaga is one of the few genres of instrumental music played by pastoralists in which regular metrical rhythm is de rigueur. The old adage that straight lines do not occur in nature may have an analogue in sound: linear, or regular, meters do not occur in nature. Natural rhythms tend toward asymmetry—the syncopated "jazz" of fast-flowing water (as Tolya Kuular had characterized it), the jerky gait of a camel, the metrically irregular articulations of birdsong. Even the gallop of a horse, often considered the epitome of rhythmic regularity, turns out to be irregular on any terrain that is not

Girls performing *bie* dance. Uvs Aimag, Mongolia, 2000.

racetrack-flat, in particular, the rugged and finely contoured topography of the Inner Asian grasslands and steppe. It is hardly surprising, then, that music rooted in a mimesis of natural soundscapes would tend to favor rhythmic asymmetry over metrical rhythm.[58] Drumming is all but nonexistent among Inner Asian pastoralists, if one excludes the shaman's drum, whose specialized use in healing and spirit-calling represents more a technology of ritualized sound-making than an art. Moreover, it cannot be mere coincidence that the paucity of metered music correlates with a paucity of dance outside of ritual contexts.[59] Compare, for example, the abundant dance traditions of Central Asia's sedentary dwellers, among whom metrical drumming is a highly developed art.

Contrasting practices in the expressive culture of historically nomadic and sedentary peoples correlate with contrasts in their spiritual and material culture. To illustrate these correlations, French music scholar Jean During assembled a table of "Tendencies and Typology" that presents around two dozen contrasting attributes of *"musique nomade"* and *"musique sédentaire/ urbaine."*[60] These attributes represent not only music but also its broader social milieu. For example, During contrasts the preeminence of the solo bard and individual expression in nomadic music with the dominant role of ensembles and collective expression in sedentary cultures. Likewise, During contrasts nomadic music's focus on description and action expressed through narrative and epic with sedentary music's focus on the symbolic and contemplative expressed through lyrical genres.

In linking music to other aspects of culture and social life among nomadic and sedentary peoples, During drew on the writings of French philosopher Gilles Deleuze (1925–1995), and in particular, on the influential book, *Mille plateaux* (A thousand plateaus), which Deleuze coauthored with psychoanalyst and political activist Félix Guattari. In *Mille plateaux,* Deleuze and Guattari discuss nomadic perceptions of time and space as core elements of an alternative worldview—alternative, that is, to the foundations of Western philosophy and, as the authors argue, to philosophy's complicity with the State and its power structures.

Discussions of nomads and nomadism in *Mille plateaux*—most notably, in the chapter entitled "Treatise on Nomadology—The War Machine"—serve primarily as vehicles for Deleuze and Guattari's ideas about political philosophy, but Deleuze nurtured a personal fascination with nomadic music, and his ideas have resonated among music scholars. Particularly pertinent to the study of music is Deleuze and Guattari's opposition of "smooth" space and "striated" space and their correlation, respectively, to the domains of nomads and of sedentary dwellers.[61] Smooth space may be homogenous, amorphous, or nonformal, exemplified by the undifferentiated vastness of the steppe or by the continuous, compressed entanglement of animal fibers that produces felt. By contrast, striated space is heterogenous, measured and broken up, as in the walls, streets, and dwellings of cities and towns or the articulated warp and weft of a woven carpet.[62]

Music provides numerous models of smooth and striated space. For example, Jean During points to the contrast between the types of long-necked lutes used by nomadic and sedentary peoples. Lutes used by nomads tend to be unfretted, thus exemplifying "smooth" space in which musical intervals may be fluid and individualized, while lutes used by sedentary dwellers are fretted, making it easy for a group of performers to play one and the same interval—an example of striated space. During also uses the opposition of smooth and striated space to frame his discussion of asymmetrical and metrical rhythm, the starting point for this brief excursus into the nomadic aesthetics and metaphysics of Deleuze and Guattari.[63]

In conclusion, During underscores the flexibility of nomadic and sedentary tendencies in music, and he suggests that they be understood "not as designations, but, following the example of Deleuze and Guattari, as concepts, or, better, aesthetic categories." "These examples," During writes, "suggest that there is always a potential for 'nomadization' in artistic, institutionalized, academic, classical or 'imperial' musics. Inversely, an urban, political, or academic framework encourages 'nomad' musicians to gather together or crystallize their repertory in classical forms with all of their typical characteristics."[64]

THE MIMESIS OF MIMESIS

For how many centuries and millennia have nomads contributed their own personal discoveries to a communal mimetic knowledge of the sounding world? These discoveries have accrued not through any orderly sequence or scientific system but as a response to epiphany, invention, and spontaneous inspiration. A tiny shift in the chiaroscuro of sound and silence that washes over the grasslands provides ample resources for a nomadic sound artist.

The wealth of mimetic media at the nomads' disposal—linguistic onomatopoeia, texted song, throat-singing, whistling, instrumental music, gesture, and the whole panorama of vocally produced sound effects—is far too rich and intertwined to yield simple one-to-one correspondences between natural sounds and mimetic representations. All of these human-made sounds are assimilated into the acoustic environment to such an extent that they may themselves become the object of mimetic representation: thus, the mimesis of mimesis.

Vocal onomatopoeia, for example, may be used not only to imitate the metallic sound of stirrups jangling on a horse—*shinggir-shinggir* or *shunggur-shunggur*—but also to represent the sound of the *doshpuluur*, a long-necked lute whose strings are sometimes rhythmically plucked to imitate the sound of a trotting or cantering horse in a mimetic style called *dimble-dei: dimble-dei-dimble-dei, dimble-dimble-dimble-dei*. An onomatopoetic variant, *dingle-dei*, represents a hard strum across the strings. In Tuvan ethnophonetics, verbal onomatopoeia morphs into musical onomatopoeia.

Throat-singing, the ideal timbral sound art, may represent not only the sounds of nature but also other kinds of throat-singing. For example, Maarool Sat, the *amyrga* player of Teeli, explained that the style of throat-singing called *chylandyk*, which is the name of a species of songbird (*Caprimulgus europaeus*), is not actually a representation of the eponymous bird, but describes the sound of a young boy imitating his father's throat-singing, which reminded the style's anonymous creator of the sound of the *chylandyk*.

Valentina Süzükei devotes a section of her book on Tuvan musical instruments to "instrumental music without an instrument," in which she describes vocal imitations of the *shoor,* jew's harp, and *limbi*, a side-blown flute. The *shoor* imitation is executed by whistling with one thumb placed against the teeth while moving the lips to provide articulation. Thus a whistler may imitate a *shoor* player, who in turn is imitating the whistling of the wind. Elderly informants told Valentina that this form of music-making was once widely practiced in western Tuva.[65]

The broad timbral palette of throat-singing is well suited to imitating the sound of the jew's harp, whose own broad timbral palette is well suited to representing a wide range of natural and human-made sounds, including speech. In fact, a so-called talking jew's harp does not so much imitate speech as disguise or conceal it within the sound of the instrument. To make the jew's harp speak, the player articulates words without voicing them. These articulatory movements are amplified together with vibrations created by the tongue, or lamella, of the jew's harp as the player strikes it while manipulating the resonance characteristics of the mouth. The result is that normal speech timbres and intonation patterns are replaced by the acoustical qualities of the jew's harp itself—what acousticians call "resynthesis"—creating a flat, synthesized speech sound not unlike that produced by speakers who have undergone laryngectomy. Here the notion of "mimesis of mimesis" applies to a representation of the acoustic signature of spoken words themselves, with selective attention to frequency properties and removal of many articulatory features. The original words are, of course, not mimetic. The "talking" jew's harp phenomenon is analogous to the practice of Aboriginal didjeridu players who articulate unvoiced speech into their instrument while playing it.[66]

Sarymai Orchimaev, the epic singer and instrumentalist from the Altai Republic whose performance of *kai* is discussed in chapter 3, is also a masterful performer on the jew's harp. I recorded the following talking jew's harp text early one evening in summer 2000 in a field crackling with the sound of crickets. The recording appears in the audio files online (track 30).

There's the road where I walked	*Tolononyng tözinde*
Alongside the hawthorn bush	*Joldop salgan jolym bar*
There's the word which I gave	*Tostok köstü körkiige*
To my beloved with the big eyes.	*Aidyp salgan sözim bar.*
There's the road where I walked	*Kargananyng tözinde*
Alongside the acacia bush	*Joldop salgan jolym bar*
There's the word which I gave	*Kara köstü körkiige*
To my beloved with the black eyes.	*Aidyp salgan sözim bar.*
The red currant bushes grow	*Kyzylgattyng kyzyly*
In abundance along the cliffs	*Körym jerde özüp jat*
Beautiful girls	*Kys baldardyng jarajy*
Grow up on our lands.	*Bisting jerde jyryp jat.*

Wearing warm clothes, the Altai girl	*Tashtang tashka sekirgen*
Leaps from rock to rock	*Tere tondu altai kys*
Why aren't you smiling?	*Sen katkyrbas kaitkan kys?*
Indeed my heart is in love with you.	*Mening jüren sööi berdi.*
Wearing a yellow silk robe, the girl	*Saidang saiga sekirgen*
Leaps from one bunch of rushes to the next	*Sary-torko kiigen kys*
Why aren't you smiling?	*Sen katkyrbas kaitkan kys?*
Indeed my heart is in love with you.	*Mening küünim sööi berdi.*
Stars and stars	*Jyldystar, jyldystar*
Gather in the sky	*Tengeride jylyjat*
Boys fight with each other	*Deremnening kystary*
Over the country girls.	*Chuldar blaajyp sogujat.*

Among both the Altai and Tuvans, a typical social context for the resynthesis of speech sounds on the jew's harp involves courtship. For example, a young man approaches his girlfriend's yurt and, standing at some distance, but close enough for his jew's harp to be clearly heard, plays while articulating coded words to the effect of "meet me at the same place as yesterday," or "I'll wait for you on the far side of a sandy river." Other family members in the yurt will hear the sound, too, but they won't be paying particular attention. The girl who is expecting the signal will listen attentively, however, and hear the hidden words inside the jew's harp timbre.

Valentina Süzükei recalled that a mother and daughter sitting quietly together in their yurt might hear a suitor playing the jew's harp, and the mother might cock her ear and comment to her daughter, "You'd better not be thinking about going out again this evening!" Valentina also recalled humorous uses of talking jew's harp, for example, the following: "It was when I was conducting a folk orchestra, and our circle of musicians was sitting in a club rehearsing for a concert. A girl who worked in the club walked by, and one of the jew's harp players in my group played something. Immediately, his fellow jew's harp players all laughed. I stopped the rehearsal and asked what they were laughing at. The boys said, 'We were laughing at what our friend said about the girl.' Everyone who plays a jew's harp in Tuva has used it to hide speech at one time or another. It's also used by horse thieves to communicate with one another."

MIMESIS AS CULTURAL MEMORY

In so many words, musician after musician had recounted how the mimetic impulse to represent the aural, visual, and even olfactory environment is activated by sensory immediacy to the natural world. Gazing at the blueness of distant mountains, listening attentively to the syncopated rhythms of fast-flowing water—or as Merlin Donald described the basis of mimetic culture in *Origins of the Modern Mind,* "short-term responses to the environment"—is what inspires a mimetic response.

Narrative mimesis represents a step away from that immediacy. In place of direct sensory stimuli are mental images and constructed scenarios featuring people, places, and events that may or may not exist or ever have existed. Epic poetry reveals a world that seamlessly weaves together real places and beings with imaginal ones. Narrative instrumental pieces, freed from the constraints of indexical reference, dwell even more in the realm of the mythic, legendary, and supernatural. The borderline between the natural and the supernatural (or what some anthropologists now prefer to call "nonordinary reality") is not a distinct one for animists, and from a mimetic point of view, the gallop of Ösküs-ool's winged horse can be represented on the fiddle just as realistically as the gallop of the fiddle player's own steed.

Whether real, imagined, or a combination of both, musical narratives embody not so much mimetic response to an environment as the transmission of cultural memory. The tenacity of this memory must depend at least in part on the mimetic verisimilitude with which images, stories, and legends are transmitted. For example, it is possible that the strong mimetic imagination so central to Tuvan expressive culture has helped it prevail over the challenges of sedentarization, Russification, and the socialist "fight against the old" that consumed Tuva after it fell under the sphere of Soviet influence in 1921.

The mimetic power of memory and imagination is exemplified in the cultural symbolism of the legendary River Eev (or Eevi) among the Oirat and Tuvan populations of western Mongolia. Mentioned briefly in the previous chapter in connection with the origins of throat-singing, the Eev is said to be located south of Mongolia, among the tributaries that rush down from the Altai Mountains into the Black Irtysh River in what is now the Xinjiang Uyghur Autonomous Region of China, although no river in Xinjiang currently bears a name similar to the Eev.[67]

The region of the Black Irtysh was inhabited in the first half of the eighteenth century by Oirats (also known as Jungars), a confederation of western Mongol tribes that by turns fought and allied themselves with eastern Mongol groups under the leadership of Chingis Khan and his descendants. In 1758, the Oirats were routed by the increasingly powerful Manchu empire, and those Oirats who weren't exterminated fled northward into the mountains. The Manchu rulers repopulated the land vacated by the Oirats, and among the immigrants they invited to resettle the region of the Black

Irtysh were "Uriangqai or Soyot people of Tovinsk stock," as René Grousset, author of the magisterial *L'Empire des Steppes,* described them—in other words, Tuvans.[68]

A small Tuvan population still lives in the northwest corner of Xinjiang, and another small group lives across the Altai massif from the Black Irtysh in Tsengel Sum, the westernmost district of the westernmost region of Mongolia (Bayan-Ölgii Aimag).[69] The Tsengel Tuvans are presumed to have settled and resettled Tsengel over a period of centuries, with some of the inhabitants migrating from the region of the Black Irtysh and its tributary, the legendary Eev.[70] Tuvans, however, are not the only ones with feelings of nostalgia toward the Eevi Xem, as they call it. Carole Pegg notes that the Eev is the "dominant symbol that recurs in performance practices of all Oirat groups."[71] For contemporary Oirats, just as for Tuvans, the Eev—or Eevi—represents a link to their historical past, and to the long-ago migrations that brought them to their present lands in western Mongolia.

During the summer of 2000, my Trans-Altai musical-ethnographic research group recorded many performances of songs and tunes called "The River Eev" ("Eevi-Xem" in Tuvan, "Eeviin gol" in Mongolian). The first of these was by Gombojav, the Urianxai Oirat musician from Hovd, who evidently learned it from his father, Narantsogt.[72] Gombojav's sonic caricature represents the river through timbre and rhythm, using the reedy *tsuur* to evoke the sound of rippling water. But it was among the Tuvan herders encamped in the high pasturelands of Tsengel District that the River Eev came fully alive in song.

One of the main features of our visit to Tsengel was the participation of the four members of Huun-Huur-Tu. I had particularly wanted Sayan, Tolya, Kaigal-ool, and Aleksei to join us there to help canvass the local Tuvan population for songs and musical styles that might represent an older layer of tradition than that remaining in Tuva itself. Kaigal-ool had been to Tsengel on two previous occasions, and he had come away with what he regarded as musical treasures.

From a distance, the town of Tsengel, which serves as the district center, resembles a dark splotch amid the greens, duns, and ochres of the surrounding hills. Closer up, the splotch turns into a jumble of small wooden houses and yurts set on tiny plots walled off from the streets by stockade-like fences. In the one-block "downtown" area, paint peels from the sides of concrete buildings with boarded-up windows. Places like Tsengel cannot help but seem superfluous. They were built as the avant-garde of an ideological vision: to settle herders and create modern towns with the institutions of sedentary civilization—schools, a post office, a medical clinic, police. Streetlights still

Participants in the Trans-Altai Musical Ethnographic Research Group during its work in Mongolia. From left, standing: Sansargereltech, Sayan Bapa, Anatoli Kuular, Erdenechimig, Joel Gordon, Bill Gaspirini; Seated: Alexei Saryglar, Kaigal-ool Xovalyg, Ted Levin, Peter Marsh. David Harrison is not in the photo. Bayan-Ölgii, summer 2000.

hang high above the muddy avenues, but on a moonless night, the town is totally dark. The Tuvan principal of the local primary school, who generously offered hospitality in his house and *ger,* told us that since 1990, when Mongolia declared its independence from the Soviet orbit, Tsengel has had almost no electricity.

The population of Tsengel District includes around 1,000 Tuvans, 9,000 Kazakhs, and 20 Mongolians. The Kazakhs, who have herded there since the eighteenth century, as best as anyone can figure out, are slowly being repatriated to Kazakhstan (a poll conducted in the early 1990s showed that 85 percent wanted to leave Mongolia.)[73] The Mongolians leave for the summer and return to work in the town in the fall. The central government in Ulaanbaatar is not interested in spending Mongolia's money on resources for a region where so few Mongolians live and work.

The principal told us that when the last census was taken, Tuvans were listed as "*öske*"—"other" or "foreign"—and not counted. They have no status in Mongolia as an official minority. "We just know that we are an 'other,'" said the principal, "but we don't know who or what." From the perspective of Tsengel, Kyzyl is like a distant Rome. The principal's wife had attended a high school there, and an older musician we met had visited it once on a concert tour, but most younger Tsengel Tuvans have never been beyond the borders of Mongolia. Still, the Tsengel Tuvans preserve a sense of Tuvanness. Their own name for Tsengel Sum is "Ak-Sayan Kojuun"—"White Sayan District," referring to the Sayan mountain range that runs through the north of Tuva.

After a few days in the town center, we left to drive further south and west toward the grasslands where most of the Tsengel Tuvans were camping with their herds. It was among these Tuvans, not the sedentarized town dwellers, that we hoped to find vestiges of older music and performance styles. Our first stop was at a summer herding camp in a place called Chylannygh ("Snakey"), which took its name from the adjacent winding river. A Tuvan herder named Papizan welcomed us. Papizan played the *igil* and had performed in Kyzyl. He told us that there were others in his camp who played music, and he offered to invite them to trade songs with the members of Huun-Huur-Tu that evening. We readily agreed, but as we were preparing our recording equipment, an officious young Kazakh park warden drove up to the yurt to tell us that we were not allowed to be there. We had entered an area designated as national parkland without the required permit, and the warden said we would have to return to Bayan-Ölgii and apply for a permit. After Papizan slipped him some money in exchange for a promise to leave us alone, the warden grew more accommodating. All he requested was that we not take any photographs in the park. We satisfied him by saying that we were photographing only musicians, not nature.

That evening, thirty people jammed into Papizan's yurt. Mostly it was the members of Huun-Huur-Tu who performed. The music went on by candlelight until almost midnight, long past normal bedtime. After the music ended, two steel basins of freshly boiled mutton were brought. Eager fingers slithered through the greasy meat and organs. Thick slabs of fat—a special delicacy—were cut up and passed around. (For all of the animal fats consumed in Mongolians' overwhelmingly meat-and-dairy diet, we never saw anyone who looked overweight, let alone even chubby.)

In the morning, a horseback-riding visitor arrived early and spoke in a loud, aggressive voice. He told us that during the socialist era, he had been a policeman, but that he was also a shaman. He wanted us to accompany him to the top of a nearby hill so that he could demonstrate a shamanic séance—and presumably be paid for his performance. On Papizan's advice, we ignored him, but he was insistent. As we set off in our vehicles toward another camp at a higher altitude, the policeman-shaman mounted his horse and galloped alongside, threatening to punish us if we refused to follow him. "I'll let you live, but you won't make it back home in your car," he shouted menacingly at Kaigal-ool. Finally, he gave up, and with an angry stream of curses, rode off. It was at that moment that I leaned out the window of our jeep and snapped a photo of the policeman-shaman[74] (see plate 21).

Several days later, as Tolya Kuular drove Huun-Huur-Tu's four-wheel-drive van toward the Mongolian-Tuvan border on the return trip to Kyzyl, he misjudged the depth of a river-fording point, and the van quickly sank almost up to its roof. Tolya, Sayan, and Alexei were able to open the doors and escape, saving only their instruments and costumes, but Kaigal-ool, who does not know how to swim, nearly drowned, and he was stranded on the roof of the van. Hours later, a tractor winched the van out of the river. After the engine had dried for several days, Tolya managed to restart it. Kaigal-ool was certain that the accident had been the consequence of the shaman's curse.

Taking leave of the snarling shaman, we drove across high rock-strewn fields surrounded by snowy peaks, whose southern flanks looked toward China, not more than forty miles distant. At this altitude, fragile grass competed for space with stone and rock, creating a mottled pattern of green and grey that extended to the edge of the surrounding hills. We followed a shallow river into an expansive, bowl-shaped pasturage where hundreds of grazing animals dotted the landscape and several yurts held their own against a cold, gusty wind. We were in Kara-Adyr—"Black River Fork"—where Papizan said we could find singers and instrumentalists.

Huun-Huur-Tu set the stage for our work by performing an impromptu concert for the herders of Kara-Adyr under a tarpaulin that protected them from an intermittent rain. The audience huddled together to keep warm, but the cold drizzle fell on their mostly hatless heads as they listened to the music. After the concert, we invited anyone who wanted to sing or play to come to one of the yurts.

A seventy-year-old *shoor* player tried to perform for us, but he was unable to summon the strength to produce more than a wheezing, breathy tone in which the melody was barely audible over the vocal drone. He was the only *shoor* player in Tsengel, he said. He was followed by a fifty-two-year-old woman who played the *igil*, tuned not to the interval of a fifth, as is usual, but to a fourth, an older form of tuning. The woman played a rhythmic *tatlaga* that would have traditionally accompanied the gestural movements of *bie*. Sayan guessed that *bie* was formerly done in Tuva, but like the *shoor*, had disappeared. After several more singers and instrumentalists, seventy-two-

Huun-Huur-Tu gives an impromptu concert for herders in Tsengel Sum, Bayan-Ölgi Aimag, Mongolia, 2000.

year-old Deleg Bayansair squatted before our microphone. Dressed in a green *deel,* she radiated a quiet elegance. Her voice had a pellucid plainness whose warmth effortlessly pierced the cold air. I looked at Sayan. Tears welled in his eyes. "That's what Tuvan music is supposed to sound like," he said quietly after Deleg had finished. "That's the way Tuvans used to sing." The song was "Eevi Xem"—The River Eev (Audio File, track 31).

The seething, somersaulting River Eev	*Ergilip akkan Eevi Xem*
Rising up and connecting the Tuvans	*Edership ösken Tyvalar*
The River Eev, running very fast	*Xarxylyp akkan Xaraaty Xem*
Rising up and mixing together the Tuvans.	*Xadkyrjyp ösken Tyvalar.*
The seething white foam of the Altai's White River	*Agynnan akkan Ak-Xem Altai*
Rising up among the Tuvans who are visiting each other	*Aldajyp ösken Tyvalar*
Flowing along its entire length the Suundarak River	*Sunup akkan Suundarak-Xem*
Rising up and giving the Tuvans to each other.	*Sunchup ösken Tyvalar.*

I had gone to Tsengel with the hope of learning the truth about the River Eev, the Holy Grail of throat-singing, and in moments of fantasy I had dreamed about taking off into the mountains to search for it, perhaps even secretly crossing the border with China and descending down the far side of the Altai massif toward the Black Irtysh. In the end, I understood that whether or not the Eev really existed mattered little. What mattered was the power of music to bring it to life and evoke nostalgia for a place that perhaps no living person had seen, but that in the mimetic world of the imagination, was no less real for its lack of material existence.

5

MUSIC, SOUND,
AND ANIMALS

ANIMAL SPIRITS

"Our music all began from imitating the sounds of animals," pronounced Mongush Kenin-Lopsan, glaring at me sternly through eyes now all but sightless. "For Tuvans, the sounds of nature have been our school, our university."

I had come to see Kenin-Lopsan, the Nestor of Tuvan neoshamanism, on my first day in Kyzyl in summer 2000 in order not to repeat the mistake I'd made two years earlier, when I had waited until the fifth day to pay him a visit and he had spent an entire interview session reproaching me. My promptness, however, was not motivated by protocol alone. I had questions about the role of sound and music in calling animal spirits that I hoped Kenin-Lopsan could answer. Animal spirits have played a central role in the work of shamans, for whom they serve as spirit-helpers (*eerens*) in treating illness and addressing other human problems.[1] *Eeren*s occupy only a small part of the densely populated Tuvan spirit pantheon, which has been charted in a range of ethnographic studies extending back to the nineteenth century and still represents a core metaphysics for many, if not most, Tuvan herders.[2] For example, Tuvan friends and acquaintances had told me about *burxan*, the sky deity, and *albys*, a sly seductress who steals a man's heart and drives him mad.[3] I had heard about *azalar*, demonic spirits that inhabit the lower world; *buktar*, vengeful spirits that bring deathly illness; and *cher eeziler*, the spirit-masters described earlier in this work who protect rivers, mountains, springs, taiga forests, and other features of landscape.[4]

Kenin-Lopsan had written about how shamans imitate different kinds of animals in the course of their shamanic work. "The elder Chimba Lopsan said that if a shaman was cursing his enemy he imitated the raven; summoning rain, he imitated the crow; frightening people, he imitated the wolf or the eagle owl; uncovering a lie, he imitated the magpie; showing off his power, he imitated the bull; and expressing rapture, the bear." Another of his informants, Soruktu Kyrgys, told him, "The female shaman Shimit-Kyrgys also imitated various voices in the same séance. If it turned out that the patient was ill from 'meddling of the spirits' of water or earth, the female shaman imitated the voices of the raven, crow, wolf, Siberian stag, billy goat, marmot, and bear. Having decided that the patient was the victim of the anger of domestic animals, Shimit-Kyrgys imitated the voices of the nanny goat, sheep, camel, horse, and dog."[5]

In appealing to animal spirits through imitation of their sounds, shamans crystallize a skill that to a greater or lesser extent is available to all hunters and herders. And in any event, there is no shortage of shamans in Tuva. "One in five people is a shaman," Kenin-Lopsan told me once. "Every person's way of appealing to spirits is original, and that's the specific quality of Tuvan shamanism."

Valentina Süzükei confirmed Kenin-Lopsan's ideas. "Powerful shamans are those who can appeal to different kinds of spirits, for example birds who live in the sky, snakes who live in the earth, wolves and bears who live on the surface. But almost everyone has the power to call to some kind of animal spirits." With the hope of learning more about these spirits, and their role in shamanic ritual, I had come to see Mongush Kenin-Lopsan.

Kenin-Lopsan, seventy-five years old, maintained an office in a small wooden building in the back courtyard of Kyzyl's Aldan-Maadyr (Sixty Heroes) Regional Museum, where he was officially employed as a senior research associate. It was not his research position at the museum, however, that attracted a steady flow of visitors, but his widespread reputation as a practicing shaman, and his role as what one might call a shamanic entrepreneur.[6] To have an audience with Kenin-Lopsan, you're supposed to go through the museum and pay the regular entrance fee, plus an additional fee for your consultation. But when the museum is closed—or even when it isn't—you can save the museum admission by walking around the corner from the main entrance and entering Kenin-Lopsan's office through a small latch gate in the wooden fence that surrounds the courtyard, which is how the majority of visitors deliver themselves to his tiny waiting room. On most days, the single bench in the wood-planked foyer is lined with anxious-looking women, some holding young children, waiting to share their problems and questions with the master. Mounted on the back of the door to Kenin-Lopsan's office is a red

Mongush Kenin-Lopsan in the courtyard of the Aldan-Maadyr Museum. Kyzyl, 2000.

plaque with raised gold lettering: "Entrance to Doctor of Historical Sciences, Living Treasure of Shamanism, Mr. Mongush Borakhovich Kenin-Lopsan. Entrance fee: 10 rubles." According to another sign that adorned the lobby of Kenin-Lopsan's shamanic clinic in downtown Kyzyl, the Dünggür Society (*dünggür* is the Tuvan name for the shaman's drum), the designation "Living Treasure of Shamanism" is the highest award of the Foundation for Shamanic Studies in Mill Valley, California—an award, as the sign notes, that has been given to only three other people on earth.[7]

When it was my turn to see Kenin-Lopsan, an assistant ushered me into the office, where the Living Treasure of Shamanism brooded over a desk in the far corner, peering up through thick glasses as I entered the room.

"When did you arrive in Kyzyl?" Kenin-Lopsan asked slowly and loudly, motioning for me to sit in a chair in front of his desk but not rising or offering his hand.

"Late last night. Today is my first day here."

"What presents did you bring me?"

"I didn't bring you any presents," I stammered. "I just stopped in to see you while walking around town. I didn't even know if you'd be in today."

"Two years ago, you had some photographs taken of us. Where are those photographs?" Kenin-Lopsan asked menacingly.

"They're at home," I replied, looking at my feet. Indeed, I had forgotten about the photos—an inexcusable oversight for an ethnographer.

"That's very bad, Professor Levin," said Kenin-Lopsan, his eyes narrowing. "You get a D."

"I'll send them to you as soon as I return home," I said in an upbeat voice.

Kenin-Lopsan frowned again. "I'm old. I have a bad heart. I'm not going to live long." He swiveled around in his chair and took a small box of index cards from a shelf behind him. Shuffling through the cards, he pulled one out and placed it on his desk. On it, in my handwriting, was my name and academic affiliation, transliterated into Cyrillic. To the side, Kenin-Lopsan had written in Russian: "b. 1951, 9 August in America. Rabbit." Next to that was the date of my last visit.

"I work according to the stars," said Kenin-Lopsan dramatically, explaining about the rabbit—the astrological animal corresponding to my year of birth.

Kenin-Lopsan's bellicose theatrics belied his hardnosed approach to the topic that had occupied him for more than fifty years: Tuvan shamanism. Born in a small settlement in central Tuva to a mother whose own mother had been a well-known shaman, and educated in Saint Petersburg, Kenin-Lopsan was at once an insider and outsider in the world of shamanism, and the chief architect of its revival and transformation into a contemporary clinical practice in Tuva.[8] His network of clinics, where certified shamans treated ailments ranging from alcoholism to mastitis and performed a range of other shamanic services, did a brisk business not only in Kyzyl but also in towns throughout Tuva. "I have ten shamans in Kyzyl-Majalyk, around ten in Samagaltai, and six shamans in Ak-Dovurak," Kenin-Lopsan boasted to a journalist who phoned from England in the middle of our conversation. All had received their certification after passing a practical examination in healing. Shamans in the Dünggür Society reported different versions of the exam, most of them involving treatment of Kenin-Lopsan himself. One shaman was asked to lower the high blood pressure that caused Kenin-Lopsan problems with his eyes. Another had been asked to relieve headaches, and a third, to heal a burn.

Beyond his entrepreneurial activities, Kenin-Lopsan had made major contributions to serious scholarship on shamanism, most notably his collections of *algysh* texts, or what he called "shamanic hymns."[9] At the same time, his claims to shamanic powers were viewed with skepticism by some Tuvans. Kenin-Lopsan seemed to relish the aura of enigma that surrounded his public life. He was at once shaman and wry trickster, and in his presence, one was never sure which role he was playing.

Kenin-Lopsan had strong opinions about the primacy of the shamanic tradition in Tuvan culture. "We Tuvans are pagans," he said with exaggerated slowness, as if to underscore the authority of his statement. "We've lived through Buddhism and Orthodox Christianity. But for us, the primordial religion, the native religion, the archaic religion, is shamanism. Tuvans respect and believe in shamans, and that's why shamanism has been preserved here in its original form. What's preserved here represents the childhood of humanity.

"Buddhism, of course, was very powerful. The first Buddhist temple was built here in 1772. That was the beginning of the rise of Buddhism in Tuva. Up until 1932, we had thirty-four Buddhist temples. All of them were destroyed and burned. Wonderful examples of wooden architecture were lost, and now, unfortunately, we can't show a single temple to our children. After 1914, Russian churches appeared. But in the history of the Tuvans, both Buddhism and Christianity are young religions. Buddhism was quickly forgotten because its language is FOREIGN." Kenin-Lopsan practically shouted the word "foreign."

"Tibetan! Books were written in Tibetan. Books were written in Chinese. Books were written in Mongolian. Not everyone had a command of these languages—there were never more than 6,000 monks here. But everyone spoke Tuvan. Yes, there was political repression, the communist terror. They oppressed well-known shamans. Some were killed outright. Some died behind barbed wire. And most tragic for Tuvan society, the children of shamans didn't have a chance to learn from them. But despite the repression, Tuvans preserved their ancient religion because shamans conduct their rituals in their native language. Tuvan was the language of folksongs, stories, the great shamanic hymns. For shamans, words are like drugs. They can kill, or they can save. That's the great power of the shamanic hymns."

Gently I interrupted Kenin-Lopsan's peroration and steered him back to the topic I had come to ask about. "What is the role of animals and animal sounds in the shaman's craft?" I asked.

"Shamans are great masters of imitating voices," Kenin-Lopsan replied without a pause. "For example, I can imitate a raven." Kenin-Lopsan did a convincing *caw-caw-caw*. "I can imitate an eagle owl. '*Ha-hoo, Ha-hoo, Ha-*

hoo.' I can imitate a cuckoo bird. And I can imitate various animals. Here's a dog barking." Sitting before me, Kenin-Lopsan instantaneously transformed himself into an aggressive canine. He didn't just make completely realistic sounds, but, like the protagonist of Bulgakov's magical-realist play, *The Dog's Heart*, he assumed the character of a dog. A shiver rippled through me. If spirits exist, then Kenin-Lopsan's mimetic voices would surely reach them. In that instant, the respect and fear that has traditionally surrounded shamans became clearer.

Reappearing in human form, Kenin-Lopsan continued his discourse. "Shamans have *sygyt*," he said, whistling eerily to illustrate what he meant by *sygyt*, the term that Tuvans typically use to describe the high, whistle-like style of throat-singing. "Before a séance, shamans always whistle to call their helpers, their spirits. Their whistling rings across the landscape and spirits hear it and come running to the shaman. And that's why ordinary people don't whistle. Only shamans whistle. If an ordinary person whistles, he'll fall sick. With time, the sound of whistling evolved into something else—throat-singing—and people also called this sound *sygyt*. Shamans, you could say, are founders of *xöömei*, of *sygyt*." Not all Tuvan music specialists would agree with Kenin-Lopsan, and in any event, his claim can be neither proved nor disproved. It is possible, however, that the whistling of shamans, along with the whistling of wind, birds, and mountains, was one of the sounds that inspired the earliest throat-singers.

In the voluminous bibliography on Inner Asian shamanism, there has been scant attention to the shaman as sound-maker. This lacuna is odd, given the fundamental importance of sound technology in shamanic tradecraft. One exception is the work of Leonid Pavlovich Potapov, an eminent Russian ethnographer who made a detailed study of the shaman's drum, called *düng-gür, tünggür,* and other cognate names.[10] Potapov, who conducted fieldwork in the Altai beginning in the 1920s and extending for more than fifty years, showed that shamans name their drums after the animals whose skins are stretched across their frames.[11] Sounding the drum animates or "enlivens" it, giving voice to the spirit of the animal whose skin is struck with the beater. In the same way, the use of horsehide, horsehair, and horse figurines on bowed fiddles—*morin huur, igil, byzaanchy*—is believed to animate the spirit of a horse.

These days, the link between bowed fiddles and animal spirits has been folklorized in some performance traditions, for example, in Mongolia, where *morin huur* players add horse "sound effects" to music that represents horses. But in Central Asia, even with its still-potent legacy of Soviet-imposed folklorization, two-stringed fiddles have maintained their bona fide connection to the spirit world. In Kazakhstan and Kyrgyzstan, where nomads were coercively sedentarized during the Soviet era, folklorization largely passed over the marginalized *qyl-qobyz* (Kazakh) and *qyl qiyak* (Kyrgyz) in favor of more fetching targets, for example, plucked lutes like the *dombra* and *komuz,* with their virtuosic performance techniques and dramatic arm gestures. These days, both *qyl-qobyz* and *qyl qiyak* have been the object of active, if limited, revival movements.[12]

Through Abdulhamit Raimbergenov, the *dombra* virtuoso in Almaty described in the previous chapter, I had seen a video of a young *qyl-qobyz* player with great talent. Her name was Raushan Orazbaeva, and one evening, Abdulhamit invited her to join us in his office at Kökil Music College. Raushan was thirty years old, petite, with straight brown hair tied in a ponytail that swung over her shoulder and reached below her waist when she sat with her instrument. She had studied *qyl-qobyz* in a music school, and later at the Conservatory in Almaty, but Abdulhamit explained that the *qyl-qobyz* wasn't the sort of instrument that just anyone can pick up and learn to play. "It used to be an instrument that people were afraid to take in their hands because it was considered sacred. Only shamans, or people who were close to the spirits, could play it.[13] And the fact that Raushan plays *qyl-qobyz* is not accidental, because her grandmother was a famous shaman. Her clan is from around Qyzyl-Orda, where Qorqut, the first Kazakh shaman, is buried."

I asked Abdulhamit how shamans give voice to spirits on the *qyl-qobyz.* "Instrumental pieces about animals are connected with totemic representations in legends," he said. "There are *kui*s [instrumental pieces] that are named after animals. For example, there's 'Kaskyr,' (The Wolf) and 'Kuu' (The Swan). Until recently, a lot of shamans, when they conducted a séance, would dress in the skins of a swan, and they'd make themselves out to be a swan.[14] A lot of people think that the instrument itself, the *qobyz ,* transforms itself into a swan, that the soul flies away together with a swan. Even now, hunters don't kill swans. They're sacred animals. The *qobyz* is an instrument that has preserved music in a form that hasn't changed for thousands of years. If something were to change in this music, then people would consider that it had lost its power, its sacred meaning."

Abdulhamit's explanation about shamans transforming themselves into swans touched on one of the core elements of shamanic craft. Zoomorphic transformation is common in accounts of traditional Siberian shamanism—not only the swan, but the goose, eagle, and falcon are frequently mentioned, as well as game animals such as elk and bear.[15] This theme has been addressed in great depth by the French scholar Roberte Hamayon in her study of Buryat shamanism, *La chasse à l'âme* [The hunt for the soul]. Hamayon's interpretation of shamans' transformations into birds and animals, shaped by the ideas of French structuralist anthropology, is that at root these transformations represent a process of exchange that emerged in archaic hunting societies. That is, shamans symbolically marry the spirits of birds and animals in order to win them over and assure success in the hunt. In this view, sound-making can be understood as one of the ways in which shamans imitate, and thus become like, their "in-laws."[16] Shamans must balance the process of exchange by which spirits give game to humans, and in return, are nourished with human flesh and blood, a source of illness in hunting communities.

"Have you heard anything about shamans healing with the *qyl-qobyz*?" I asked Raushan.

"I believe that they did, because I always feel this quality in the instrument—that it's a healing instrument."

"How does that quality manifest itself?" I asked.

"When I go into trance—I don't know how else to explain it—when I reach a kind of summit; when I'm really alone in myself and no one else is interfering; when I detach myself—then I really give myself with my soul and heart to this instrument.[17] I know that I serve the instrument. You have to play it with a clean, true heart. If you play it just as work, just to earn money, then the instrument will never open itself up to you. The more you play, the more you have the desire to search; you feel there's something inside, and you're trying to get at it and get it to open up. You have to work at it, you have to think. It's a philosophy. You can't just give in to contemporary life if you want to stay on this path. So of course the *qobyz* can heal. I believe that because I feel it myself."

The body of the *qyl-qobyz* is shaped like a heart. The lower part of the face, where the two sides come together, is covered by animal skin, but the upper part is open. Inside, embedded in the wooden shell of Raushan's instrument, were two small diamond-shaped mirrors.[18] Oblong metal jangles that looked like long, narrow earrings dangled over the open shell. I asked Raushan about the mirrors, which I assumed to be linked to the mirrors used by shamans to see spirits.

"Yes, it's true that shamans call spirits with mirrors. At the same time, I'm a performer and when you perform, people get very curious, and some of them can cast the evil eye, so the mirrors protect you from the evil eye. It turns the evil eye back so it can't get to you. In the past, there weren't any Muslims among the Kazakhs. Qorqut believed in spirits, in the sun, in the moon. Nature is all here in this instrument. There are only two strings, but you can show everything that humanity lives on and is connected with—you can show all of this inside the instrument."

Raushan performed two *kuis*, each of which represented the spirit of an animal. In "The Wolf," a pack of wolves stalks and then attacks and fights with its prey. Raushan simulated the howling of the wolves by sliding her fingers in ever-so-slowly descending intervals along the *qyl-qobyz*'s horsehair strings, and at the dénouement, created a fearsome fight scene by bearing down on the strings in a dissonant, screeching tremolo. "The White Swan" used a variety of textures and techniques—bouncing the fingers off the strings to simulate the sound of wings flapping, lyrical melody, repeated rhythmic figures, harmonics—to represent the sounds and movements of the bird. During her performance, Raushan seemed indeed to interiorize herself in the instrument and its mimetic sound.

Raushan Orazbaeva performs "The White Swan" on the *qyl-qobyz* (Video File, track 11).

Raushan's playing beautifully illustrates the animation or "enlivening" of a swan spirit through the *qyl-qobyz*. While shamans honed such spirit enliv-ening into a reliable technology that became a part of their ritual practice, the line between sound technology and sound art disappears in the hands of a master performer like Raushan. Her ability to transmit the feeling of an animal and the voice of its spirit depends not on formal shamanic initiation but on artistic talent and an empathy for the natural world.

The *qyl-qobyz* and shaman's drum are not the only instruments believed to enliven sound with a living spiritual presence. In *Sound and Symbol,* the philosopher Victor Zuckerkandl, grounded in European classical music, de-scribed what he called "dynamic symbols" in music as a parallel to religious symbols. "The symbol is the representation of a supermaterial—that is, physically indemonstrable—force in a material form," Zuckerkandl wrote. "The religious symbol is not a sign that merely indicates the divine being to the believer. Rather, the deity is directly present *in* the symbol, is one with it, and is also directly beheld in the symbol by the believer."[19] While Zuckerkandl was surely not thinking of shaman drums and horsehead fiddles when he wrote about sound symbolism, his characterization is useful in explaining why performers and listeners hearing these instruments can have such a strong sense that their sounds are the voices of spirits—not that they "rep-resent" these voices, but that they *are* the voices. And as Zuckerkandl adds, "What does disbelief prove against belief? . . . To him who opens himself without reservations to symbols, their meaning will gradually become clear of itself. . . . Because music exists, the tangible and visible cannot be the whole of the given world. The intangible and invisible is itself a part of this world, something we encounter, something to which we respond."[20]

SIGNALING AND SINGING TO ANIMALS

Summoning and enlivening animal spirits with the voice or musical instruments draws on the same mimetic principles as other kinds of sound and music described in this work. Whether performed in the guise of sound technology as part of a shamanic healing séance, or as musical art by someone "close to the spirits," as Abdulhamit had characterized *qyl-qobyz* players, these performances all use sound mimesis as a means of forging links between humans and animals. The animals most commonly represented are those whose spirits are most powerful or effective in a given situation.

An entirely different realm of human-animal communication exists in pastoralists' relationship specifically to domesticated animals: sheep, goats, cows, horses, camels, yaks, and reindeer, depending on the climatic zone. Here the aim is not to appeal to the spirit of an animal, whether to cure an illness, sanctify a hunt, or conduct other shamanic business, but to support the day-to-day work of herders. Such work includes controlling the movement of herds or individual animals through signals, facilitating the nursing of newborn animals by their sometimes-reluctant mothers, and, on the perceiving end, staying tuned to changes in the sounds made by animals (including wild animals) that might aid in weather forecasting. In the days before meteorology and radios, this was a constant concern of herders whose livelihood depended on maximizing the economic efficiency of their herds in an unforgiving environment.

The history and prehistory of animal domestication is of great interest to archaeologists, anthropologists, biologists, and geographers, who have produced a large bibliography on the subject.[21] Archaeological excavations of Neolithic sites suggests that animals were first domesticated in the eighth and seventh millennia BCE in western Asia, when hunter-gatherers began to keep goats and sheep to assure a steady supply of meat.[22] The domestication of equids came somewhat later, in the sixth millennium[23] (see plate 22). Pastoralists subsequently spread westward to Europe and eastward to other parts of Asia. The ability to domesticate animals depended on keen observation of animal behavior. For example, herd animals are distinguished by whether they have a dominance hierarchy and follow a single dominant leader, like sheep and goats, or whether they defend a specific territory, like deer. Animals in the first category are far easier to domesticate than those in the second. In *A Natural History of Domesticated Mammals,* Juliet Clutton-Brock suggests that the domestication of goats and sheep took place in two ways: "One was by the herding and controlling of wild flocks that were perhaps kept in a favoured situation such as near a supply of water simply by habituation of a herdsman with a group of wild animals. The second method was by the taming and rearing of young animals that were imprinted on humans as their leaders."[24] However it took place, domestication required humans to learn to command and control herd animals, constituting what Siberian musical ethnographer Yuri Sheikin has called a "paleosonoric system."[25]

Human-animal communication occupies a semiotic domain that is at once paralinguistic and paramusical, yet intimately linked to both. Intoned speech, rhythmic incantations, whistling, throat-singing, and signals that include calls, cries, shouts, onomatopoetic words, and sui generis nonlinguistic vocalizations exist alongside melodic song and instrumental music. One consequence of this double liminality is that human-animal communication as a topic of scholarly research has been largely shunned by both linguists and music specialists (by contrast, intraspecies animal communication has of late become a subject of intense interest to biologists, evolutionary psychologists, and, increasingly, linguists).[26] An exception is the French Turcologist Rémy Dor, who devoted a carefully researched series of articles to human-animal communication among Turkic herders.[27] As a general term to describe the sounds that comprise this communicative domain, Dor came up with *huchement* (from French *hucher,* "to call with cries or whistling"), an onomatopoetic neologism that does not have a good English translation, but that Dor defines as "a vocal sound whose aim is to influence the behavior of an animal."[28] Dor's exhaustive phonetic and morphological analysis of *huchements* used by herders who spoke twenty different Turkic languages and dialects, ranging geographically from Anatolia to the Sakha Republic in north central Siberia, led him to postulate a classification for this vast inventory that suggests common origins and underlying linguistic consanguinities. These consanguinities fuel Dor's hypothesis that *huchements* are the vestige of an archaic system of communication between man and domestic animals "whose fundamental processes are probably universal."[29]

Among Dor's *huchements* are sounds whose origin seems clearly mimetic, for example, onomatopoetic words based on sounds made by animals themselves, or nonarticulated utterances based on what Dor calls the "phonic sensation" of animal sounds—utterances, he notes, "which change little from one culture to another."[30] *Huchements* also include what he calls "descriptives," that is, the name of a particular species or an individual animal, or references to the physical traits or comportment of these animals. Such descriptives are the least represented among the various groups in his classificatory scheme, notes Dor, and are linguistically the most strongly marked.

In another category, Dor places imperatives (in particular, "come!"), adverbs of place ("here!" "there!"), and what he calls "prepositional syntagmas" (e.g., "in," "over").[31] Articulatory speech can be transcribed using the International Phonetic Alphabet developed by linguists, but Dor's *huchements* include a large number of nonlinguisticized sounds not easily represented by either the phonetic symbols of language or conventional notation systems of music. To grasp these sounds, it is better to hear them, and a number of them appear in the audio files online.

The source of the first group of recordings is Dari Bandi, a Dörvöd Mongol from Uvs Aimag, in the Mongolian west, who earns his living as a telegraph operator but also keeps herd animals and serves as a praise-singer (*eroolch*) at weddings, ceremonies to dedicate a new yurt, celebrations of the birth of a child, and so on. Born in 1966, the year of the horse, as Bandi pointed out, he had become an important tradition-bearer in his native Türgen District, and he generously shared his knowledge with members of our Trans-Altai research group (see plate 23).

Bandi wanted to show us how animals have served as the inspiration for music, and to make his point, he performed a short song (*magtaar*) called "Black-Spotted Yak" (Hartai sarlag), which combines text and melody with a refrain of yak-calling (*höörvöl-höörvöl*). The text is transcribed and translated below.[32] Bandi told us that from the time yaks are very young, they learn that the sound of this song means they should come together. The tremulous cry at the end does not imitate any animal source sounds, but is purely a human-inspired signal (Audio File, track 32).

Black-spotted yak	*Hartai sarlag n'-i*
Höörvöl-höörvöl	*Höörvöl-höörvöl*
My dear one	*Hairtai ter min'-i*
Come here, come here	*Naariich, naariich*
Yak with many spots	*Bügentei sarlag n'-i*
Höörvöl-höörvöl	*Höörvöl-höörvöl*
Before it gets dark	*Bürenhii bolvol*
Come here, come here.	*Naariich, naariich.*

Bandi then ran through a sequence of whistles and vocalizations that he uses to signal animals. "From ancient times, nomads have known that these sounds influence animals," Bandi told us. "Animals know the calls of different herders from the same region because their calls are similar. But the calls differ from one region to another. They're related to different peoples and their linguistic dialects." Following is the sequence of calls that Bandi demonstrated as it appears in the audio files online (track 33).

Time Code:	Description
0:00–0:23	Whistle for sending horses to pasture.
0:27–0:50	Variant form containing words as well as whistling for sending horses to pasture.
	Horses recognize the interpolated words and move more quickly. Bandi's command "chü!" corresponds precisely to the *huchements* provided by Dor for "stimulating" horses among various groups of Inner Asian Turkic-speakers (Dor notes that "chü" is also used by Halh Mongols, and is transformed into "shu" among Tuvans. A contemporary throat-singing group, Shudee [meaning "giddyup!"] took its name from this expression). Dor adds that in the form "chuh," the expression was attested by Mahmud Kashgari, the ninth-century scholar who created the first known lexicon of ancient Turkic.[33]
0:52–1:18	Whistle to signal horses to drink water.
	Compared to the whistle in example 1, this whistle is more relaxed. Bandi's understanding of the signal's effect is that the whistle imitates the sound of wind, calming the horses and giving them pleasure, and horses learn to connect the wind imitation with water.
1:21–1:46	Sheep and goats are sent to pasture.
1:50–2:11	Cows are sent to pasture.
2:12–2:33	Order to horses to slow down on the way to pasture.
2:36–3:00	Calling sheep and then goats from pasture.
3:04–3:12	Calling cows from pasture.
3:13–3:19	Goats: come to me. (Different for goats and sheep; other sounds are the same for both.)
3:19–3:24	Goats: turn around.
3:28–3:34	Goats: go to pasture.
3:35–4:00	Calling cows from pasture.

Systems of *huchements* analogous to Dari Bandi's exist throughout the Altai region.[34] Valentina Süzükei noted that among Tuvan herders, signals to move farther away or come closer have a number of gradations and variations. For example, the verb *daigyrar* means "to shout to animals in a way that makes them gradually turn around and return toward the yurt." "My grandmother used to make that sound," said Valentina. "It sounded something like 'Ho-wow-wow-wow-trrrrr.' It depends on the echo of the land, but the herd hears it and they'll begin to come back—not right away, but gradually.

"The jew's harp can also act on animals," Valentina added. "It was once used by shamans to heal animals, but herders use it too. I remember that in the evening, my mother would call to our herd, and sometimes only the sheep would come down, and the goats stayed up there. But when I started to play the jew's harp, the goats came down as well. There are stories that hunters played the *igil* and jew's harp to lure animals." Carole Pegg reported that camel and yak herders in western Mongolia use throat-singing to call animals.[35]

Pastoralists also use sound to encourage herd animals to suckle newborn offspring. These sounds are not signals or cries, but more like chants or incantations. Typically performed by women, they accompany physical measures to attract a female animal to nurse a newborn that may or may not be her own. Often, young animals born in the cold weather of early spring are initially kept inside a warm yurt and brought to their mothers only for feeding. Sensing that they smell different as a result of proximity to humans, mothers will sometimes refuse to nurse these newborns. To neutralize unfamiliar smells, salt water or milk from the mother is rubbed on the young animal's tail and hindquarter, and as it tries to nurse, specific syllables and verses are intoned. Tuvans call these interventions by the general term *mal alzyry*—"animal domestication." The name of a specific animal may be substituted for *mal*, thus *xoi alzyry* (sheep domestication), *öshkü alzyry* (goat domestication), and so on.[36]

Formulaic chants and melodies vary for domesticating different kinds of animals, and even for the same animal, may vary from one group of pastoralists to the next. For example, sheep domestication songs that I recorded in 1988 in Erzin, in southern Tuva, just across the border from Mongolia, are markedly different from those recorded in Davst Sum, on the Mongolian side of the Tuvan-Mongolian border, about a hundred miles west of Erzin in summer 2000. The two recordings appear in the audio files online (track 34, from Mongolia; track 35, from Tuva).

The Mongolian version is much more song-like, with a verse-refrain structure and a regular metrical pattern in the texted portion. By contrast, the Tuvan variant resembles not so much a song as an incantatory recitative: it is limited to the range of a tritone and built exclusively around vocalizations, with no actual text. Aksenov wrote in his description of domestication songs in *Tuvan Folk Music* that they sound remarkably similar to lullabies. "Tuvans say that from afar, it's impossible to tell whether they're lulling a baby to sleep or domesticating a sheep, goat, or calf."[37]

Mongolian ethnomusicologist Erdenechimig transcribes a song text from Gombo-surengiin Begzjav (b. 1931). Davst Sum, Uvs Aimag, Mongolia, 2000.

Two respected ethnographers who wrote about cattle incantations among Altai herders concluded that the incantations were intended to have a "magical" influence on the animals.[38] While the choice of sounds used for different kinds of animal domestication rituals may ultimately be arbitrary, the use of these sounds seems much more grounded in empiricism than magic. If you ask herders why they use a specific type of sound to elicit a response from a particular kind of animal, they will confirm that their animals give milk only to that sound and not to any other. Just as lullabies calm babies, repetitive melodies seem to relax animals and make them more likely to nurse.

A closely related use of sound technology consists of songs sung to animals as they are being milked, also with the aim of relaxing the animal and making the milk flow more freely. An example is a yak-milking song sung by Tuvans living in Buyant District of western Mongolia, recorded in summer 2000 (Audio File, track 36).

In the recording, a man (Tserenedimit, age 31) sings while his wife (Nyaama, age 34) does the milking (the voice of their daughter, Aldyn-Shagaa, also appears in the background). The discovery of such "sound therapy" for animals is most surely ancient, extending back to the dawn of pastoralism, and illustrates another form of sound technology that is an intimate part of the daily lives of herders.

LISTENING TO ANIMALS

Herders not only use sound and music to influence the behavior of animals but also listen attentively to sounds made by animals, both domestic and wild, as one element of the crucial task of weather forecasting. Herders in the Altai region have traditionally practiced transhumant pastoralism—a seasonal rotation of pasture areas that exploits differences in elevation to maximize grazing efficiency. Since temperatures and weather patterns can vary dramatically from year to year, no fixed calendar regulates seasonal movements. Rather, herders must pay close attention to the condition of grasses in a pasturage area and, to the best of their ability, take into account environmental clues about weather patterns. Will snow come early, necessitating a move to the relative shelter of river valleys, or to forested mountain slopes that offer protection from harsh weather as well as proximity to wind-blown snow-free areas where grass is accessible? When will spring appear, making it safe to leave the winter herding station and migrate to pasturages where grasses have grown sufficiently to sustain hungry animals? These are the sorts of questions to which wrong answers can have serious consequences for a herding family.

Valentina Süzükei has used the term "sound calendar" to describe a repeating yearly cycle of seasonally specific environmental sounds whose observation yields information meaningful to herders. She has noted that in contrast to the lunar calendar, which objectively marks a universal temporal unit, sound calendars are intrinsically local and pragmatic, linking herders through collective sensory knowledge to the natural environment of specific places. The yearly nomadic cycle has been the subject of extensive research and a fine publication by ethnographer Sevyan Vainshtein, translated into English as *Nomads of South Siberia: The Pastoral Economies of Tuva*.[39] Vainshtein details various forms of Tuvan pastoralism, but neither he nor other ethnographers have much to say about the abundant information that herders extract from the sounding world.

During recording work in Tuva in spring 1998, Valentina Süzükei and I met an exceptionally knowledgeable young herder and hunter from Kungurtug, an isolated settlement in the extreme southeast of Tuva, who was spending a few weeks in Kyzyl. In a series of conversations, Ochur Arakchaa (b. 1971) explained the cycle of the nomadic year as he had experienced it with his own family in the Tuvan southeast, and in particular, the role of animal sounds and behavior in providing clues about the proper time to shift from one seasonal camp to another. The following synopsis of the annual nomadic cycle is based on these conversations, as well as on information from other sources provided by Valentina Süzükei.[40] The cycle is divided into the four seasons, each of which corresponds to a distinct pasturage. In some regions, different seasonal pasturages are practically adjacent, while in others, moving herds from one pasturage to another requires a journey of several days or a week. In any event, none of these seasonal movements involve epic migrations over long distances of the sort that have become a popular, if unrepresentative, sine qua non of "nomadism."

WINTER

At the winter herding station (*kyshtag*), where both people and animals are most vulnerable to the danger of sudden weather changes, herders pay particular attention to the sound of crows and woodpeckers as signals of bad weather. The cry of crows can indicate a storm or approaching cold front. Kenin-Lopsan recounted in a collection of autobiographical sketches how his grandmother distinguished different song patterns of the woodpecker. "If the voice of the woodpecker is high and shrill, it means that it will get cold, and if it is low, like *kargyraa*, then it will stay warm." Kenin-Lopsan continued, "In those unforgettable years of childhood, when I heard the high voice of the woodpecker, I didn't go far and mainly played around the yurt. If I heard the *kargyraa* of the woodpecker, then I ran to the river and played there, and brought back ice for boiling tea."[41] Other sonic signs of spring include sparrows singing at dawn, choirs of chirping gophers emerging from hibernation, and the sounds of migratory birds returning from the south.

Rabbits provide another sound clue that winter is receding. In the evening, and just before dawn, from inside a yurt, herders could hear rabbits slapping their front paws together in a sound that resembles the beating of a shaman's drum. This "*dot-dot-dot*" sound became the basis for a chanted text, or incantation, that represents rabbits as shamans. In the text, which exists in variant forms, the rabbit speaks to the snow and, summoning shamanic powers, excoriates and banishes it. Following is a version recorded from Kaigal-ool Xovalyg's great uncle, Ochur-ool Mongush, born in 1928 in Xündergei, Chöön-Xemchik Region. At the end of the performance, Ochur-ool wipes his face in imitation of the rabbit, who personifies the shaman as he banishes the snow.

Ochur-ool Mongush performs "The Rabbit-Shaman" (Video File, track 12).

Oh, dot dot dot	*Oh, dot dot dot*
My tree tops and	*Arga bajym saagaindyr*
My dead larch tree tops,	*Syra bajym syyngaindir,*
Start to sway.	*Aga berem dot dot dot.*

You [snow] will lie here only a short time	*Kezek kada chydar-dyr sen*
Dot dot dot	*Dot dot dot*
And what will happen in the end, I don't know.	*Kedi bajyng bilbein-dir men.*
Dot dot dot	*Dot dot dot*
While you are lying here	*Amdyzynda chydar-dyr sen*
Dot dot dot	*Dot dot dot*
I don't know what will happen in the end.	*Alys bajyng bilbein-dir men.*
Dot dot dot	*Dot dot dot*
Though you have a beautiful snow-white color	*Akkir chaagai öngnüg-daa bol*
Dot dot dot	*Dot dot dot*
Inside you are a black scoundrel.	*Alys özün kara kulugur sen.*
Dot dot dot	*Dot dot dot*
You tormented	*Albatyny xoor chonnu*
A lot of people.	*Xinchekteen sen.*
Dot dot dot	*Dot dot dot*
You made the milk-filled livestock	*Aar süttüg arbyn maldy*
Grow thin and ragged.	*Argyskan sen, chudatkan sen.*
Dot dot dot	*Dot dot dot*
Go far away and disappear.	*Yrap-la kör, arlyp-la kör.*
Dot dot dot	*Dot dot dot*

SPRING

The migration to the spring camp (*chazag*) takes place when the food supply in the winter camp is close to being exhausted, but before new growth has appeared there—typically as the snows melt in late April or early May. Herders tried to move as early as possible in order to keep herds from eating new growth that will be needed the following winter. One of the sure signs that warmer weather has come to stay is the return of migratory birds—first the scoters, followed by geese, ducks, wagtails, jackdaws, and others. The singing of the bird that Tuvans call *baa-saryg*, literally, "yellow-breasted," indicates that it is safe to plant grain. Sowing and planting have to take place before the sound of the cuckoo bird signals the end of the moist winds (*chig salgyn*). With the end of that work, it becomes necessary to migrate quickly to the summer pasturage in order to fatten the livestock, particularly young animals, on fresh grasses.

SUMMER

At the summer camp (*chailag*), the final arrival of warm weather is confirmed by the sound of the black kite, the last of the migratory birds to return, and by the warble of larks. Animals tend to be sonically most active during their mating season, and in summer, the loudest mating-related sound is the

Summer herding camp (*chailag*) near Kyzyl-Xaya, southwestern Tuva.
Note winter camp (*kyshtag*) in the background, set on a protected bluff
at a slightly higher elevation than the summer camp. 2003.

roar of bulls—in particular, bull yaks. The awe-inspiring bull roar has been
represented in Tuvan music in the form of an instrumental piece performed
on the *igil*, "Bùga Bustugary." The approach of bad weather is signaled by the
whistling of the chipmunk, a sure sign of rain. The singing of the quail indicates that grains are ripening and that it is time for the harvest. The crackle
of crickets marks the start of autumn, and the rutting calls of male red deer
in the taiga forest signals the beginning of the autumn hunting season, and
preparation for the move to the autumn herding camp.

AUTUMN

The short stay at the autumn camp (*küzeg*) serves as a period of intensive
preparation for winter when warm clothes are readied, yurts are renovated,
new felt is prepared, animal pens are fixed, and winter food supplies are laid
in. The move to the winter camp is timed according to the sounds and behavior of migratory birds and wild animals. For example, the harvest should
be completed and final preparations made for moving to the winter camp
before the cranes fly south. When ponds and lakes freeze over, the ducks and
geese finally leave—the last of the migratory birds. "Domestic herds feel very
acutely when it's time to move," Ochur Arakchaa told us. "If you want to stay

put, the herd itself will tell you that it's time to go—in particular, the cows; sheep are less edgy. The horses also want to push on to the winter location.

"Just as herders pay attention to the sounds of their animals, domesticated animals have to get accustomed to the sound of being around humans," Ochur added. "For example, when a horse is loaded and moving along, it pulls a board along the ground that makes a sound. The board serves as a ramp to load a yurt or other goods onto the horse's back. So that the animals won't be afraid of this sound, they're acclimated to it by pulling cans over rocks. Afterward, they're very calm about such sounds. During the migrations from one pasturage to the next, if a horse isn't loaded, people put empty dishes on him so that he'll constantly have this clanking sound.

"There are a lot of sounds of birds and wild animals that have particular meanings," Ochur concluded. Here, as one thought led to another, he mixed together what seemed like genuine knowledge with what were surely false beliefs. For example, he said, "If an owl hoots at the same time that a dog barks, it's a bad sign." But then came an insightful observation: "Owls make different kinds of sounds. Basically, an owl remembers the sounds and voices that it hears during the day, and at night, it imitates these sounds to scare little animals. In the taiga it's interesting when you come to the place where you think the owl is crying from, and in fact that owl can be three or four kilometers away."

The son of a veterinarian, and an accomplished landscape painter as well as a herder, Ochur Arakchaa was finely tuned to the seasonal cycle of nomadic life. "In recent years, the spirits of various places have been disturbed due to abuse of the nomadic cycle," he said lugubriously. "For example, there used to be a lot of mountain goats, but now they're rare. They're being eaten by vultures. Big mountain birds never used to come near human encampments, but in the last few years, there have been incidents when they've flown down and taken away domestic animals. Snow leopards are coming closer to human civilization. It used to be that even a hunter would rarely see them, but now they're attacking livestock. Livestock behave differently now as a result of cross-breeding with animals from other parts of Russia. They don't behave like Tuvan sheep, goats, and bulls. They don't make the proper sounds at the proper time of year."

ANIMALS IN MUSIC

Like other aspects of the natural and human environment represented in the nomadic sound world, the representation of animals extends along a continuum that ranges from spontaneous mimetic caricatures and imitations at one end to fully musical narrative at the other. Mimetic instrumental pieces like "The White Swan" and "The Wolf," performed on the *qyl-qobyz* by Kazakh musician Raushan Orazbaeva, are plentiful throughout the Inner Asian nomadic world. In Tuva, they are often linked to a specific narrative plot that is recited by a musician before performing it. One such instrumental piece recounts a humorous episode in the life of a horse named Chyraa-Bora. Following is a transcription of the story as performed by *igil* player Aldar Tamdyn.

Aldar Tamdyn performs "Chyraa-Bora" on the *igil* (Video File, track 13).

An exhausted horseback rider,	*Pazyryktyg izig xovaa,*
His head drooping and jerking up with a start,	*A'ttyg kiji udumzurap*
Moves slowly across	*Bajy ol bo xalangainyp*
The hot kurgan-strewn steppe.	*Al-la shag chok chortup choraan.*
Suddenly he hears a sound "shyg"	*"Shyg" deen soonda artynda bir*
That comes from something heavy landing behind him.	*Aar chuve ushkajypkan.*
Chyraa-Bora whinnied and bolted.	*Chyraa-Bora kishtei kaapkash yngai bolgan.*
The horseback rider got frightened,	*Erning ku'du chashtai bergesh,*
Pushed his feet against the stirrups, grabbed the horn of the saddle, and turned around.	*Ezengige xere tepkesh xaya köörge.*
Behind him a huge eagle had landed.	*Artynda bo kara ezir olurup tur.*
As he smacked it with his hand,	*Xolu bile chaya shaapkan,*
The huge eagle, without falling to the ground,	*Ulug ezir cherge chetpein.*
Took off and, climbing higher,	*Ujup ünüp bedii bergesh,*
Screamed with indignation.	*Xomudaanzyg kyshkyrgylaan.*
The horseback rider noticed	*Kaigal erning xoinun orta*
That a small bird had landed and was hiding itself	*Bichii kushkash xorui bergen*
Inside his robe.	*Olurup tur.*
The eagle had tried to catch the bird,	*Ezir onu sürüp kelgesh,*
And dived behind the horseback rider.	*Ezer soonga orup tup tur.*

The same mimetic impulse that drives performers of bowed fiddles to represent horses also inspires performers on other instruments. Yedil Huseinov, a Kazakh musician and composer who is a virtuoso performer on the jew's harp (Kazakh, *shang-qobyz*), has exploited both the instrument's articulatory power and its rich timbral palette to create an expressive portrait of a winged horse called "The Gallop of Tulpar." Huseinov, who plays jew's harp in a Ka-

145

Aldar Tamdyn playing the *igil*. Near Kyzyl, 2003.

zakh rock band called Roksonaki, which uses traditional music and musical instruments as a resource for contemporary songwriting, explained to me that when he plays his composition, it is as if he becomes Tulpar. "It's not like I'm looking at a horse from the side. I *am* the horse," he said. "I get tired, I have feelings. At the end of the piece, the horse flies up to the sky, and you hear the sound of wind. It's interesting what a horse thinks about us. The ancient Turks worshipped horses. Horses were gods. So the roots of my thinking are in that belief. It's not my idea. It's in the psychology of the nomad."

Yedil Huseinov performs "The Gallop of Tulpar" on the jew's harp (Video File, track 14).

Huseinov also uses his jew's harp to provide musical accompaniment for animal marionettes that are made to dance by jerking on a string. The animal figure—in this case a mountain goat—is constructed from pieces of wood loosely attached to one another, like the dancing limberjack of Appalachian folklore in the southeastern United States. Husein-ov controls the string at the same time that he plays the jew's harp.

Yedil Huseinov is what some American folklor-ists and ethnomusicologists would call a "reviv-alist" (see plate 24). That is, he did not learn his traditional art through a family lineage or in a community in which it was a living practice. Rather, his parents were professional musicians and music educators trained both in Western music and Soviet-style Europeanized Kazakh music. "It was Soviet times," Yedil explained, "and it was fashionable to study piano, not *dombra*. I was a pianist, then studied theory and com-position at the conservatory, and graduated as a composer. But on a genetic level, Kazakh traditions were always alive in me. We had relatives who lived in the *auls* [herding camps], and they'd frequently come to visit us. I'd drunk *qïmïz* [fermented mare's milk], seen how horses galloped, and felt the cold of winter from inside a yurt. I always loved to travel to backwoods places. I preferred going to western Mongolia than to Paris. But it wasn't until I met Bulat Sarybaev, a great folklorist who taught at the conservatory and had a collection of ancient instruments, that I became interested in old music.

Yedil Huseinov performs "Danc-ing Mountain Goat" on the jew's harp (Video File, track 15).

"In 1991, I went to Yakutsk, to the International Congress of the Jew's Harp, sponsored by the Sakha Ministry of Culture, and that's where I really began to understand the potential of the jew's harp.[42] After that, I started to work seriously. The problem is that for ancient instruments, there's no rep-ertoire. You have to think it up. I make my own repertoire—I'm a composer, so it's easier. I have compositions in which I use old instruments, but since we live in the contemporary world, I want to make these instruments acces-sible to everyone, not just to specialists. The key to contemporary music, of course, is pop. My mission, like it or not, is to propagandize old instruments, and so I put rock instruments together with traditional instruments and create a synthesis."

For herders accustomed to the subtle and gentle sounds of older jew's harp styles, like the Tuvan "sketches of nature" discussed in chapter 3, Yedil Huseinov's assertively rhythmic portrait of Tulpar may leave too little to the imagination (like the neighing *morin huur* riffs popular in Mongolia). But Yedil knows his audience, and it is largely young Kazakhs like himself—"as-phalt Kazakhs," as they are known—who grew up in the cities, not the steppe. Yedil's music self-consciously preserves the equine sound imagery and sym-bolism of the ancient Turks in a more contemporary form.

The same reflex characterizes many songs in the concert repertoire of Huun-Huur-Tu, whose music has become known among some American fans as "Country and Eastern." Huun-Huur-Tu uses not only the jew's harp and *igil,* but the plucked, banjo-like, long-necked lute called *doshpuluur* or *toshpuluur,* to simulate the sound of various horse gaits. One of their favorite pieces in this genre is "Chyraa-Xor" (The Yellow Pacer) (Audio File, track 37).

In the middle of the yellow steppe, Chyraa-Xor	*Saryg xovu ortuzunda, Chyraa-Xor*
A lone pine tree stands and sways, Chyraa-Xor	*Saglalchyngnap janggys xady, Chyraa-Xor*
Permeated by a light wind, Chyraa-Xor	*Salgyn syryn aidyzangan, Chyraa-Xor*
I travel with a peaceful spirit, Chyraa-Xor.	*Sagysh amyr chorumal bodum, Chyraa-Xor.*
In the grass-covered river valley, Chyraa-Xor	*Köktüg-shyktyg shynaalarga, Chyraa-Xor*
Resting in the cool shade, Chyraa-Xor	*Xölbeng bazyp choraanyngny, Chyraa-Xor*
Freshened by a light, juniper-infused wind, Chyraa-Xor	*Xölegege seriidengen, Chyraa-Xor*
I am a happy traveler, Chyraa-Xor,	*Xöglüg omak chorumal bodum, Chyraa-Xor.*

"Chyraa-Xor" is like a cowboy song whose clomping rhythms sonically stereotype a horse in slow motion. But it is throat-singing that provides a more authentic representation of a horse's gait. Before throat-singing became largely a performance art, it was often done in the saddle when the rider, inspired by the beauty of a landscape, would spontaneously break into song. It is rare to hear mounted singers now, but once I did during a trip with Huun-Huur-Tu to Chadaana, in central Tuva.

"Listen to how the rhythm changes when a singer is riding," Kaigal-ool had observed. And that had planted the idea of trying to record throat-singing performed on horseback. Recording engineer Joel Gordon furnished Tolya Kuular with a microphone attached to a length of plastic pipe that he held in front of him while he rode. A microphone cable ran to a DAT tape recorder in a knapsack on Tolya's back. Kaigal-ool rode another horse alongside Tolya. The results of that experiment, in which the rhythm of the throat-singing synchronizes to the rhythm of the various horse gaits as the horses speed up, is presented in the audio files online (track 38).

The sound of boots clacking rhythmically in stirrups has also been stylized in Tuvan throat-singing under the name *ezenggileer,* "stirrup." In a 1988 recording of master throat-singer Marjymal Ondar, Marjymal accentuated the clacking rhythm by snapping his finger against a tea bowl as he sang. The recording is reproduced in the audio files online (track 39).

Throat-singing is also frequently connected with the representation of birdsong, in particular, in the Tuvan style known as *sygyt*. Having spent much of their lives outdoors on the grasslands and in the taiga, many herders are excellent amateur ornithologists. They identify a range of birds with ease, know their habits, and can mimic their calls with great accuracy. These various calls, however, are not distinguished one from another in throat-singing.[43] Even with all of the timbral and rhythmic modulations accessible to an experienced singer, throat-singing is a medium that lends itself better to stylization than to precise imitation. As Valentina Süzükei said, "listeners hear what they want to hear."

"ANIMAL-STYLE" ART AND MUSIC

The imaginative stylization that so gracefully balances the naturalistic and narrative element in musical representations of animals has an equally rich analogue in material culture. Clothing, horse trappings, textiles, jewelry, and decorative objects abound in images of animals. In Tuva, for example, skilled sculptors carve animal figurines in blocks of soft white stone. Animal motifs turn up frequently in wood carving, felt appliqué, leather art, and ceramics. And of course, many of the objects that pastoralists use in their daily lives are—or were—made from animal parts or products: wool, hair, bone, gut, hide.

Traditional nomadic artisanry and craftsmanship are still strong in parts of Inner Asia, assisted these days by a growing number of cooperatives and nongovernmental organizations that market indigenous art and craftwork to foreign buyers. But the most artistically spectacular animal-centered objects to come from the steppe lands were produced by nomads of antiquity—Scytho-Siberians, Sarmatians, Xiongnu, and other groups, whose cultural contacts spanned much of Eurasia in the middle and end of the first millennium BCE. Archaeologists excavating burial sites that range geographically from the Black Sea to Inner Mongolia have turned up troves of decorative objects made from wood and precious metals with zoomorphic motifs that collectively have become known as "animal-style" (or "animal-style") art.[44] Before the fluorescence of animal-style art, a still-earlier tradition of zoomorphic imagery found expression in petroglyphs—graphic images carved in rocks, cliffs, and caves, many of which feature scenes of hunting and animal combat. Rock art continued to be produced by successive nomadic inhabitants of the Altai Region right up to the beginning of the twentieth century.[45]

What might one learn from a comparison of animal-style art with animal-

A contemporary Kyrgyz felt textile (*shyrdaq*) uses felt appliqué to create an image of stylized rams' horns.

style music? Each in its own artistic realm embodies the natural and super-natural vitality of animals that has been an enduring force in the lives of Inner Asian pastoralist-hunters. In an introductory essay to the Metropolitan Mu-seum of Art exhibition catalogue *Nomadic Art of the Eastern Eurasian Steppes*, art historian Emma Bunker notes wisely: "The art of the steppe peoples was created to transmit information to those who saw and wore it, both the living and the dead, but if we try to attribute specific meanings to the various motifs and symbols, we run the risk of being profoundly wrong. Their meanings were not meant for us and can probably never be retrieved."[46]

Bunker is right, yet animal-style art and animal-style music complement one another in a way that can expand our knowledge of both. Expressive culture—music, epic, legend, and the diverse forms of sound mimesis—can animate the latent spiritual vitality that lies mute in physical objects. For example, the story of Ösküs-ool and his magical winged horse provides one possible narrative program for the quasi-fantastical winged ungulates excavated by archaeologists.[47] At the same time, physical objects that have survived from the distant past provide a window into the artistic style and sensibility of a historical era whose sounds were evanescent.

A bronze belt plaque from North China, dated first–second century A.D. shows confronted rams. The Metropolitan Museum of Art, Gift of Mr. and Mrs. Eugene V. Thaw, 2002 (2002.201.134). Photograph © 2001 The Metropolitan Museum of Art.

Searching for ideas, *Weltanschauung*s, and expressive languages that shape both the art and music of a society or historical period is nothing new. In graduate school, our group of music historians read art historian Erwin Panofsky's *Gothic Architecture and Scholasticism* as a way into the aesthetics of medieval liturgical music, and we read Carl Schorske's *Fin-de-Siècle Vienna* for its elucidation of links between expressionism in the work of painters such as Gustav Klimt and the atonal music of Arnold Schoenberg. Music historian Richard Taruskin has analyzed the relationship between Stravinsky's music and the works of early-twentieth-century Russian painters.[48] In Indic musicology and art history, Harold Powers wrote about the iconic relationship between *rāgas* and *rāgamālā* painting.[49] All of these art-music connections, however, take as their starting point artistic vocabularies that developed not only in the same cultural milieu but also in the same era. Can one learn anything of value from comparing animal-style art produced

151

more than two millennia ago within a vast geographical terrain by myriad groups whose relationship one to another is largely a matter of speculation, and animal-style music, whose documentation began little more than a century ago? My answer is a tentative "yes."

The key unifying principles and points of contact between the two artistic spheres are a penchant for narrativity, strong emphasis on the representational rendered through a mixture of naturalism and stylization, and the joining of the realistic and the fantastic. In ancient textiles and tapestries, for example, exuberant color schemes often bear no relation to the natural color of the objects being represented.[50] In Scytho-Siberian animal-style sculpture, deer, felines, and mythical hybrids like griffins are represented by twisted, coiled, and contorted torsos or with distorted proportions such as the exaggerated, spiraled antlers that top the heads of stags. "Ancient artists attempted to make the animal figures as realistic as possible, but they modified and distorted proportions to fit the animal to its decorative purpose," wrote art historian Liudmila Barkova in the Metropolitan Museum exhibition catalogue, *The Golden Deer of Eurasia*.[51] Analogously, musical depictions of animals juxtapose a seemingly real being in a realistic setting, for example, the steed of Öskü-ool, the poor Tuvan herder, with the fantastical imagery of the winged horse. The same fusion of naturalism and stylization animates the musical representation of other natural sound motifs. For example, Anatoli Kuular's mimesis of flowing water in rhythmicized throat-singing mixes timbral and rhythmic verisimilitude with the whimsical use of reinforced harmonics to provide a stylized, abstract interpretation of the source sounds.

One of the most widespread motifs in animal-style art is animal combat: wild animals attacking domestic animals, wild animals attacking one another, hybrid mythical animals attacking wild and domestic animals. The animal combat motif also turns up in music, as in Raushan Orazbaeva's performance of "The Wolf" on the *qyl-qobyz*, in which a pack of wolves attacks and fights with its prey. Art historian Esther Jacobson, a specialist in Scytho-Siberian art, has pointed out that depictions of animals attacking and being attacked, and of human hunters pursuing animals, have an even more archaic source than the portable objects attributed to the Scythians and their contemporaries. Petroglyphs in the Altai region dating from the end of the second millennium and beginning of the first millennium BCE are full of such scenarios or "mythographies."[52] Jacobson argues that these scenarios pictorially represent "an ancient oral tradition involving a great hunter, an animal with magical powers, and a powerful deity."[53] Thus it is possible that graphic and musical narratives may have been different ways of telling the same stories—a principle that ought to make sense to anyone who has ever listened to movie soundtracks.

Belt plaque with fighting stallions. Southern Siberia, second century B.C.E. In *Nomadic Art of the Eastern Eurasian Steppes,* Emma C. Bunker notes that the short, upright manes identify the animals as Przewalski horses. She also notes that "numerous examples of this plaque have been found throughout Buryatia and southern Siberia in graves associated with Xiongnu" (132). The Metropolitan Museum of Art, Gift of Mr. and Mrs. Eugene V. Thaw, 2002 (2002.201.121). Photograph © 2001 The Metropolitan Museum of Art.

The representational, narrative style of nomadic art, both visual and musical, offers a stark contrast to the nonrepresentational, highly abstract language typical of both art and music that arose under the cultural influence of Islamic civilization among sedentary dwellers who lived south of the steppe, in the riverine and oasis towns and cities of Central Asia. An aesthetic abyss separates the nomadic world from the Central Asian Islamic sensibility. Islamic decorative arts, textiles, and ceramics all draw on a common artistic vocabulary rooted in the infinite variation of floral and arabesque patterns, elaborate ornamentation and embellishment, and disembodied, geometricized bird and animal motifs. Sculpture, the representational medium par excellence, is all but nonexistent in Islamic art. Conversely, architecture, which unites the greatest achievements of Islamic science and civilization, never evolved among nomads beyond the creation of portable housing—a significant achievement, to be sure, but in the vast realm of architecture, a highly specific one.[54]

The same principles of abstraction, dense ornamentation, and infinite variation of motif and pattern at the core of Islamic visual arts also shape many forms of music and sacred chant in the Islamic world. These principles are particularly evident in the recitation of the Qur'an and in the classical vocal and instrumental traditions known collectively as *maqâm* that have

153

flourished in Islamic cities from Casablanca to Kashgar.[55] *Maqâm* has as little in common with the *kui* and *küü* of Kazakh and Kyrgyz music and the throat-singing, jew's harp melodies, and bowed fiddle narratives of the Altai Turks and Mongolians as do Bukharan carpets with Scythian deer figurines.

Differences between the music of pastoralists and sedentary dwellers do not imply an absence of historical contact between the two groups. On the contrary, such contact has been well documented in the realms of both commerce and culture, and musical exchange was unquestionably a part of it.[56] For example, it is likely that fiddles, with their strong horse symbolism and various horse-derived components, passed from nomads to sedentary dwellers. Yet a Mongolian *tatlaga* performed on the *morin huur* could not be more different from an Azeri *mughâm* performed on the *kemenche* (spike fiddle). Conversely, lutes, for which archaeological evidence of great antiquity exists in the Middle East, were most likely an invention of sedentary peoples that was later passed to nomads. But the contemplative art music performed on an Iranian *setâr* is a world apart from the kinetic dynamism of a Kazakh *dombra*. When musical instruments cross from one cultural domain into another, they are adapted to the performance of different musical styles and repertories, and to different sensibilities.

It is only recent history—the legacy of czarist Russia and the Soviet Union—that has placed much of the Inner Asian nomadic world so firmly within the political and cultural orbit of "Islamic" Central Asia, which contemporary geopolitics has cast once again in its traditional role as a buffer zone between empires. Ancient cultural and commercial relationships that existed long before the rise of Islam may reveal a far more influential and enduring musical link between pastoralists and sedentary culture—namely, the sedentary culture of China. A clue to that link is provided by Emma Bunker in her catalogue for *Nomadic Art of the Eastern Eurasian Steppes*, the exhibition staged at the Metropolitan Museum of Art in 2002.

Exhibition item 178 in the catalogue is identified as "Tuning key for a *qin*," referring to the Chinese zither that was the musical instrument par excellence of the learned Chinese in a tradition leading back to Confucius himself. Item 179 is a "*Se* string anchor" (the *se* is a kind of zither), and item 180 is a "Zither string anchor."[57] Each of these musical instrument accessories is adorned with zoomorphic motifs that Bunker relates to northern traditions beyond the boundaries of China, which is to say, to pastoralists. The *qin* tuning key consists of a bear perched atop the shaft of the tuning key, with the key placed over a tuning peg similar to the piano-tuning hammers of today. The *se* string anchor is described as a "spectacular gilded-bronze mountain with jagged peaks inhabited by wild beasts."[58] The zither string anchor presents a "mythological ungulate with inverted hindquarters."[59]

Bronze tuning key for a *qin*, with a bear perched atop the shaft of the tuning key. North China, third–second century B.C.E. The Metropolitan Museum of Art, Gift of Mr. and Mrs. Eugene V. Thaw, 2002. (2002.201.150). Photograph © 2001 The Metropolitan Museum of Art.

In her catalogue description for the *se* string anchor, Bunker writes, "The recent suggestion that stringed instruments in ancient China may possibly have had a northern origin hints at an interesting new interpretation of the Han image of the mountain inhabited by wild animals. This theory is supported by the innumerable mountain-shaped censers and jars that display such imagery which appeared at a time when the Han Chinese were in close association with the nearby pastoral world. . . . The strong parallels between early Han landscapes in the round and pastoral imagery may have been a major catalyst to the integrated development of pictorial Chinese landscape representation rather than the art of the ancient Near East, which is frequently cited but exhibits no parallels."[60]

Bunker's linking of nomadic animal-style art and pictorial Chinese land-scape representation through evidence provided by a musical instrument accessory is telling, for this link has a clear analogue in music itself. The mimetic principle and narrative style at the root of nomadic music is also at the core of much Chinese music, in particular classical instrumental music like that commonly performed on the *qin* and the *pipa*, a short-necked lute. The *pipa* is itself an instrument with a strong connection to the nomadic world (nomads may in turn have adopted short-necked lutes from the Persian *barbat,* the ancestor of the Middle Eastern *'ud* and European lute). The very name *"pi-pa,"* which describes the upward and downward strokes of the plectrum, suggests foreign origin, and Chinese documents record it as having been brought to China by "northern barbarians," that is, nomads.[61]

An important part of the classical repertory for the *pipa* consists of musical illustrations of landscape or landscape paintings. Composers of these pieces aimed to render a landscape, whether actual or painted, through musical sound and gesture.[62] The mimetic principle here is analogous to Tuvan musician Grigori Mongush's transformations of landscape into whistling, described in the last chapter. In broad strokes, the representational strategies of nomadic music and Chinese classical music offer persuasive parallels, particularly when compared with the strong contrast between nomadic music and the nonrepresentational art music traditions of sedentary Islamic culture to the south and southwest.

Archaeology and art history have provided evidence and interpretations of ancient animal-centered art. For music of the same period, evidence of course excludes sound itself and is limited to objects, the most important of which are musical instruments found in archaeological excavations. One such instrument, the so-called Pazyryk harp, was recovered from a fourth-century BCE burial site at Pazyryk, in the present-day Altai Republic. Single-headed, hourglass-shaped drums were also retrieved from the site.[63] Musical instruments, however, can at most provide a starting point for reconstructing music itself, as I learned during an evening séance with local musical enthusiasts in Barnaul, capital of Russia's Altai Krai, who had reconstructed the Pazyryk harp and composed music for it and other instruments, such as flutes and drums, which may have existed in the Altai in the fourth century BCE. The music had a spare, earthy quality and a catchy rhythmic groove—to this listener it sounded not unlike early rural blues from the southern United States. It was lovely to the ear, but there is no reason to think that it resembles Pazyryk music of 2,500 years ago, nor did the players make such a claim.

An account of the connection between contemporary nomadic sound

Alexander Gnezdilov holding
his reconstructed Pazyryk
harp. Photo courtesy of
Alexander Gnezdilov, 2000.

art and its ancient roots is only as plausible as the larger story in which the
connection is embedded. Since we have neither recordings nor other direct
empirical evidence of ancient music, one must ask whether it is more likely
than not that there is such a connection in light of the inferential and other
evidence we do have—what philosophers call "inference to the best explanation." In this view, there is every reason to believe that the sophisticated fusion
of naturalism and abstraction in animal-style art must have had a parallel
in animal-style music created by musicians who represented the world in
sound with a degree of imagination equal to that with which their sculptor
and rock-carving contemporaries rendered it in objects.

An animist view of the world in which the power of nature—landscape,
animals, and the spirits of natural places and beings—serves as a vital life
force has continually replicated a particular kind of artistic inspiration
among the Inner Asian pastoralists. It would be far-fetched to suggest that
a coherent artistic tradition was passed down from the Scytho-Siberian no-

157

mads of antiquity to the Turkic and Mongolian nomads of yesterday and today across vast gulfs of time and the cyclical rise and fall of steppe empires. Yet, despite differences in form, style, and medium, nomadic art and music reveal an underlying continuity that must arise from the shared experience of steppe pastoralism—an experience shaped by perceptions of space, time, sound, and color, and by spending the days and nights of a lifetime surrounded by animals. Valentina Süzükei had said that you cannot destroy the timbre-centered system at the center of nomadic music because the sounds are lodged in the cultural memory of nomads; that it will survive as long as herders live in nature and listen to the sounds of the taiga and the steppe, birds and animals, water and wind. That centuries and millennia of nomadic civilization seem to have come up with such similar means of artistic expression suggests that she is right.

6

AN ANIMIST VIEW
OF THE WORLD

HUUN-HUUR-TU AT HOME

KYZYL: AUGUST 2003

If you stroll slowly along the central part of Kochetova Street, Kyzyl's congestion-free main thoroughfare, sooner or later you'll run into everyone you know—or so it seemed during my visit in the sunny days of Siberian midsummer. I had spotted Kaigal-ool Xovalyg three times in as many mornings. Now here he was again, leaning pensively against the front door of his car, ever-present cigarette dangling from the corner of his mouth, as he waited for his wife Anya to emerge from an office building. The car was not the beat-up Zhiguli he had driven in 1998 but a shiny white Toyota station wagon imported from Japan. Kaigal-ool and Anya were preparing for a trip to Krasnoyarsk, 400 miles to the north, where their eighteen-year-old daughter would soon begin studies at a management institute. Meanwhile, Kaigal-ool was also finalizing arrangements to purchase an apartment in Kyzyl for his son, who planned to return to Tuva after graduating from law school in Moscow.

These two summer weeks between concert tours were filled with chores and family obligations that had accumulated while Kaigal-ool had been on the road with Huun-Huur-Tu and also with his new band, Malerija. Malerija (rhymes with "galleria") performs a techno version of Huun-Huur-Tu's repertory that combines Kaigal-ool's voice and *igil* with electric guitar, synthesizer, and drums played by Sayan Bapa and two Russian musicians. Most recently, they had performed at a world music festival on the island of Borneo, where according to Kaigal-ool, the young, mostly Indonesian audience danced enthusiastically to the band's galloping rhythms and heavy metal covers of Tuvan songs.

Kaigal-ool was tired. The trip to Borneo came in the middle of a tour itinerary that had started in May at a festival on the Reunion Islands, off the coast of Madagascar, and continued on to France, Norway, Germany, Malaysia, and Singapore. Then had come a recording session in Saint Petersburg, interrupted midway by a single concert appearance in London. Another round of concerts in Norway and France followed the recording session, and after a final concert in Denmark, Huun-Huur-Tu returned to Moscow, whence they'd flown with me to Abakan, Xakasia, arriving in the middle of the night and immediately transferring to a taxi for a five-hour ride over the Sayan Mountains to Kyzyl. Earlier in the year, they had also performed in the United States, Canada, Ireland, Italy, Switzerland, and the Czech Republic.

I had last met with Huun-Huur-Tu a year ago at the previous summer's Philadelphia Folk Festival. Onstage during that festival, Huun-Huur-Tu looked exhausted, and later, when we met at the suburban Holiday Inn where they were staying, my impression was confirmed. "You need to get off the road for a while and recharge your batteries," was my unsolicited advice. We agreed to meet in Tuva the following August and do some leisurely fieldwork together. But now that we were there, the month-long window of opportunity I had envisaged for our travels had been politely, yet firmly, condensed into less than a fortnight by Huun-Huur-Tu's Moscow-based manager, Sasha Cheparukhin. Sasha sent me e-mails describing a series of important performance opportunities in Greece and Germany that Huun-Huur-Tu could ill-afford to turn down. Moreover, since the previous summer, Huun-Huur-Tu had undergone a transformation. In spring 2003, Tolya Kuular had left the group.

"We didn't have any arguments or disagreements," Tolya told me one afternoon when we met in Valentina Süzükei's office at the Tuvan Institute for Humanities Research on the east end of Kochetova Street. "I had told them the previous spring that I'd play with them for one more year, and that I wanted to leave after that. We traveled together for ten years. That's not a small amount of time. It was rare that we had a chance just to stay here in Tuva and hang out with musicians. There are a lot of old people—they're not going to live forever—and I wanted time to talk with them and learn from them. I want to work with hunters, for example, recording the *amyrga* as they actually use it during a hunt. And there's a great singer who wants me to play *igil* and *byzaanchy* to accompany shamanic songs. For us young people, our work is here in Tuva."

Explaining Tolya's departure from Huun-Huur-Tu's perspective, Kaigal-ool drew a laconic analogy to horses. "Old Tuvans say that if you leave one stallion in the same herd for too long, you won't have good results. It was the same with Tolya. We needed fresh blood—someone who wanted to develop himself artistically. I didn't feel that Tolya was trying to break new ground."

Anatoli Kuular (bottom row, second from left) with Sayan Bapa and Kaigal-ool
Xovalyg, lending a hand to Tolya's relatives during haying season in Xorum-Dag,
Chüün-Xemchik Region, late summer 1996.

For Huun-Huur-Tu, "breaking new ground" had come to mean not simply
rediscovering traditional Tuvan songs, reviving lost instruments, or redefin-
ing the stylistic boundaries of throat-singing but rather experimenting with
plugged-in arrangements of their repertory, sophisticated mixing techniques,
and cross-cultural fusion projects. Much of their touring schedule was filled
with hybrid musical events organized by a coterie of impresarios, freelance
producers, promoters, record companies, and Western-based musicians
who viewed Tuvan music—and invariably throat-singing in particular—as
an elixir that could rejuvenate their own musical endeavors. Huun-Huur-
Tu had recorded and concertized with the Bulgarian female vocal ensemble
Angelite, the jazz-inspired Moscow Art Trio, and the monarchs of classical-
world music crossover, the Kronos Quartet. Just before returning to Tuva in
August 2003, Huun-Huur-Tu played a concert in Copenhagen with the hy-
bridized East-West percussionist Trilok Gurtu and his ensemble. Kaigal-ool
belonged to Veshki da Koreshki, a fusion group that included a Senegalese
kora player and a Russian accordionist; he also worked with Sayan in Malerija,
the plugged-in doppelganger of Huun-Huur-Tu.

The challenge of joining musical inspiration from traditional sources
to the often-quirky projects proposed by outsiders had become a leitmotif

161

in the creative lives of the members of Huun-Huur-Tu. How could music linked to the beauty of natural landscapes and the reassuring presence of herd animals, the importance of humility before the spirit-masters and respect for the values of family life, be expressed in the hybrid musical idioms and crossover styles that epitomized contemporary world music? Huun-Huur-Tu, of course, was not alone in trying to reconcile the competing forces of the cultural marketplace. Nourishing global connections while maintaining the integrity of art rooted in an authentic tradition is a challenge for musicians everywhere, and young musicians all over the Altai region are only too well aware of the benefits of getting connected. In these conditions, what is the future of the animist view of the world that first inspired music-making among the south Siberian pastoralists?

Examples of bad outcomes are not hard to find. Some musicians lose their spiritual equilibrium and descend into a spiral of alcoholism and depression. Others lose their aesthetic equilibrium and transform tradition into kitsch, embracing hybrid styles where subtleties of timbre, rhythm, and melody that evolved over centuries or millennia are summarily trammeled by thumping bass guitars, synthesized drones, and robotic drum machines. But what about tradition-bearers who successfully manage the relationship between global connections and local roots—producing music and other forms of expressive culture that can be exported, yet also maintain their authority among a local audience?

Huun-Huur-Tu provided an enviable model of achievement. They had deftly negotiated the Janus-faced demands of world music musicianship, and their success beyond the borders of Tuva had brought them rock star status at home, even though—or perhaps because—they rarely performed there. Huun-Huur-Tu's cachet as hometown heroes was ratcheted even higher when, following Tolya Kuular's departure, they inducted into the group a local heartthrob, twenty-six-year-old Andrei Mongush. Mongush's arrangement of a recently composed song "Men Tyva Men" (I am a Tuvan) had become a chartbuster after he turned it up during a visit to the Tuvans of Tsengel Sum in 1999 and arranged it in the style of *estrada,* or pop music. In Kyzyl there was talk about designating "Men Tyva Men" as Tuva's "national" anthem.[1]

The enthusiastic worldwide reception of Tuvan music created a fertile climate for musical revivalism in Tuva itself, where new ensembles sprang up like wildflowers. By one count, Kyzyl alone boasted twenty traditional music ensembles, the vast majority of them featuring young performers. The energy of Tuva's musical renascence reverberated throughout the Altai region and encouraged nascent revivalists beyond Tuva's borders. In Xakasia and

Plate 17. Narantsogt and members of his family. Meeren, Duut Sum, Hovd Aimag, Mongolia, 2000.

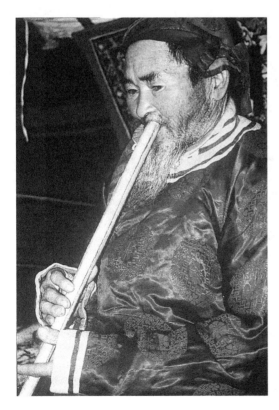

Plate 18. Narantsogt playing the *tsuur* inside his *ger* (yurt). Meeren, Duut Sum, Hovd Aimag, Mongolia, 2000.

Plate 19. Pasturage on the outskirts of Hovd City, Mongolia, 2000.

Plate 20. Xakas musician Evgeni (Zhenya) Ulugbashev plays the *chatxan*. The movable bridges under each string are made from sheep knee bones. Abakan, Xakasia, 2000.

Plate 21. The red "shaman" after placing a curse on us. Tsengel Sum, Bayan-Ölgii Aimag, Mongolia, 2000.

Plate 22. Horses are driven toward microphones held by sound engineer Joel Gordon during the recording of the Smithsonian Folkways compact disc, *Tuva, Among the Spirits*. Central Tuva, 1998.

Plate 23. Praise-singer Dari Bandi performing "The Black-Spotted Yak" for a video shoot. Türgen Sum, Uvs Aimag, Mongolia, 2000.

Plate 24. Kazakh musician Yedil Huseinov. Photo by Chloé Drieu, 2001.

Plate 25. Sabjilar: from left, Sergei Charkhov, Anna Burnakova, Slava Kuchenov. Xakasia, 2003.

Plate 26. One of eighteen giant stones at the Great Salbyk Kurgan in Xakasia, 2003.

Plate 27. Lazo Mongush divining with stones in his treatment room at the Dünggür Society. Kyzyl, 2003.

Plate 28. Shaman Kara-ool Dopchuur-ool demonstrating how different drum sounds are used in a purification ritual. Kyzyl, 2003.

Plate 29. Shamans of the Dünggür Society pose for a photo outside their building. Ai-Chürek Oyun is seated in the middle. Kyzyl, 1998.

Plate 30. Rysbek Jumabaev, Yo-Yo Ma, and Nurlanbek Nyshanov during a Silk Road Project residency at the Peabody Essex Museum, Salem, Massachusetts, January 2004.

Plate 31. Tyva Kyzy during a recording session near Kyzyl. From left: Ailang Ondar, Shoraana Kuular, Ailangmaa Damyrang, Choduraa Tumat, 2003.

Plate 32. Kongar-ool Ondar (right), with Kaigal-ool Xovalyg and Anatoli Kuular, Boston, Massachusetts. Photo by Clark Quin, 1993.

the Altai Republic, singer-songwriters and epic reciters, seers and shamans, prophets and poets all emerged to claim their place in the bustling market-place of post-Soviet neotraditionalism—a marketplace that catered both to indigenous peoples and to outsiders from European Russia, the West, and Japan. Meanwhile, in Kyrgyzstan, customarily linked to the cultural sphere of "Islamic" Central Asia, Kyrgyz cultural revivalists, at least in the northern half of the country, looked not southwest toward the core Islamic world, but northeast, toward their ancient animistic roots in the Altai. With the aim of learning more about the animist view of the world that seemed so alive in the expressive culture of the larger Altai region, and also among the Kyrygz, whose *Volkswanderung* had led them out of the Altai and into the Tien Shan, I set out on a series of travels in the summers of 2000 and 2003. In both years, one of my principal destinations was Abakan, capital of the Republic of Xakasia, and home to a remarkable musical ensemble called Sabjilar.

EPIC DREAMS

"Go to our website and click on 'tour schedule,'" Slava Kuchenov, founder and leader of Sabjilar e-mailed in response to my query about coming for a visit. "You'll see when we're going to be on the road, and then you can make your own plans." Good advice, as it turned out. Sabjilar indeed had a busy concert season ahead: several weeks in Europe as part of an East-West fusion music project called Tien Shan Express, conceived and funded by a Swiss impresario, followed by a break, and then several more weeks of touring in Central Asia. I was fortunate to be able to snag Sabjilar for a few days in mid-August, between concert tours.

In addition to Slava Kuchenov, Sabjilar consists of Slava's wife Anya Bur-nakova, who plays jew's harp, traditional percussion instruments, and sings, and Sergei Charkhov, a vocalist and multi-instrumentalist who also builds finely crafted shaman drums and *chatxans*—the Xakas plucked zither. Slava serves as lead singer and backup *chatxan* player (see plate 25). I met Sabjilar in summer 2000, when Liesbet Nyssen, a young Belgian ethnomusicologist doing fieldwork on Xakas music, offered to introduce me to her circle of musical friends in Abakan, a city of around 170,000 that lies 250 miles north of Kyzyl. I was seduced by Sabjilar's gutsy arrangements of traditional material and newly composed music for voices, *chatxan, yyx* (two-stringed fiddle), jew's harp, and percussion and invited them to come to Washington, D.C. in summer 2002 to participate in the Smithsonian Folklife Festival, whose theme that year was the Silk Road.

The Xakas are a small minority in their own republic, which is a land of farmers and stockbreeders, almost all of them sedentarized, that extends westward from the Yenisei River as it flows out of the Tuvan grasslands and transects the Sayan Mountains en route to the distant Arctic Sea. Of a total population of 600,000, only 11 percent, or around 70,000, identify themselves as Xakas. The rest of the population is mostly Slavic. Xakas, like Tuvans, have a complex ethnogenesis originating in a confederation of tribal groups that assumed the form of a national identity only in relatively recent times. Unlike the Tuvans, however, who came under the sphere of Russian influence in the early twentieth century following the breakup of the Qing Dynasty, the four feudal princes who reigned over the Xakas signed a treaty and united with Russia in 1726.[2] These days, many Xakas do not speak their own language, and in an authoritative critical edition of Xakas heroic epic published by the Siberian branch of the Russian Academy of Sciences in 1997, the author of an introductory essay wrote, "At present, only one master is known who commands the art of improvising *xai*"—the raspy, guttural vocal style used by epic reciters.[3]

Sabjilar performs their arrangment of a Xakas folksong, "Pis Kildibis" (Video File, track 17).

The loss of language and expressive culture is a source of angst among Xakas cultural revivalists. The members of Sabjilar decided that an ensemble trying to reclaim Xakas traditional music should not have performers with Russian names like Slava, Anya, and Sergei, so for stage purposes they took Xakas names. Anya is Altyn Tan Xargha, Sergei is Shibetei Xyrghys, and Slava is Ai Charyx Saiyn. "In fact, my father wanted to call me Ai Charyx," Slava told me, "but when he went to register me at the office of birth registration, they said, 'What kind of a crazy name is that? Pick a Russian name.' So he wrote down the first name that came into his head, and that was Vyacheslav" ("Slava" for short). Friends and family still call the members of Sabjilar Slava, Anya, and Sergei.

As much as I enjoyed Sabjilar as an ensemble, the focus of my visit to Abakan was Slava Kuchenov himself. Slava had mentioned casually during a conversation the year before that he had composed an epic poem—or more precisely, that he had "received" an epic poem, as he put it, in a visionary dream. During the Smithsonian Folklife Festival, I had proposed to Slava that he perform his epic on stage, and he had quickly demurred. "It's not for performance," he said cryptically. "I'll explain later." Amid the bustle of the festival, we never managed to continue that conversation, and that was why in August 2003 I was sitting on the floor of the bare living room in Slava's telephoneless apartment (at the time he was number 14,230 on Abakan's waiting list for a phone) taking notes on my laptop as Slava recounted the story of his life as a musician and a *xaijy,* or Xakas epic reciter.

"I was born in 1969 in a village called Uty, in Beisk Region," Slava began. "When I was five, my mother died and my father went to a different place, so I was raised by my grandmother. She was blind, and at night she told stories, and she'd force me to listen to them. I'd be falling asleep, and she'd hit me to wake me up. She was a pensioner on a collective farm, and she tried to transmit what she knew to me, but out of everything she told me, I remember little.

"From sixth or seventh grade, I began to show talent in art. I went to a children's art school in Abakan, and when I was fifteen, I went to Leningrad to study sculpture. I graduated from the Repin Academy in 1994 and returned to Xakasia. I beat the pavement, trying to find work as a sculptor, but no one needed my sculpture here. I was an orphan and at that time, orphans were supposed to receive apartments. But there weren't any apartments available. I asked the Union of Artists for work, and they didn't have any. Finally, a teacher's college invited me to teach anatomical drawing. I needed to bring my diploma to register for this job, but the diploma was in my village. There wasn't any bus that went all the way to the village, so I took a bus to Esin, and from there I went on foot to my village. There was a strong rain and I got really soaked. I came home late, ate supper, and in the morning, I was supposed to go back to Esin and return to Abakan to bring the diploma. I needed to have dry shoes to leave in the morning, and I left my boots by the stove, and went to sleep.

"That night I had a dream. In my dream I saw a shadow. The shadow looked like my uncle—my mother's brother—and it was if he were speaking to me. 'Get up. I have to talk to you,' he said. I knew that he had already died, and I couldn't say no to him. I got up, took my shoes, and we went to a certain kurgan. Then we went to a place called Shazoi, where members of our clan have always offered prayers. After that, we went to Arghyzhyg, which is a place where two rivers merge. There, the shadow started to tell me that I should be a bard—that I should sing, play the *chatxan* or jew's harp, and recite *xai*. I objected. I had never played a *chatxan* or jew's harp, and I'd never sung *xai*. The shadow said that if I didn't do this I'd have a strong illness, and could even die. And then after that, he showed me how *xai* should sound, how the *chatxan* should be played. He said, 'You'll learn all of this.' It was a long dream that went all night, and then I went back to the house and went to sleep.

"In the morning, I woke up and wondered, 'What was that strange dream?' I got up and went to take my shoes to go out to the toilet. The shoes were all dirty and wet. I asked my aunt—my father's younger sister—'Did I get up and go anywhere in the night?' Normally, if anyone gets up, she wakes up too. I had heard that people who have these kinds of dreams sometimes become shamans, and that if they refuse to follow the commands of the dream, they can die. So I decided to try singing *xai,* and found that I could do it. And when I went back to Abakan on the bus, suddenly an epic tale was churning around in my head. I'd never known any of these tales, but suddenly there it was. The text was called 'Ai Charyx Khan on a Grey Horse.' I've looked at a lot of epic texts, but never found this one, even though it has an ancient form. It might well have existed earlier and just not have been written down. A lot of words and expressions I didn't understand myself. It was about an hour's worth of recitation, and I received it all at once. At first, I would close my eyes, so that no one would bother me, and the text would come on its own. Later, I started to add my own improvisations on the text, but realized that it was like patching pants, and I stopped doing that. I ordered instruments—a jew's harp and a *chatxan.* People were surprised. I'd never sung before, and suddenly, I began to sing.[4]

"When I came from the village to Abakan, I was half-atheist, or maybe wholly an atheist. I didn't give much meaning to stories, and didn't think much about stories. But in Abakan, I had a dream in which I saw three horse-back riders running after me and whipping me with a horsewhip. I had lines across my forehead and chest from the whippings. And it was after that dream that I ordered the instruments and began to sing. It still happens after a long time when I haven't recited *xai,* that the three horseback riders come with their horsewhips and beat me. So that was the beginning of my musical work. Before that I'd tried to learn to play the guitar when I was in Leningrad, and nothing came of it. I tried for half a year to learn the guitar, and I just couldn't figure it out. Musicians told me that I didn't have a good ear.

"When my first dream appeared, the shadow said that I should turn my palms toward people, not toward myself. What he meant, probably, was that I should turn my soul outward toward other people—that I should serve as a kind of guide. To avoid the awkwardness of always performing with my palms outward, I put a stamp of my palm on the back of all the instruments I play." Slava picked up a *topchy xomys* (long-necked lute) and showed me the palm-print on the back of the body of the instrument that had been outlined from his own hand.

"Later I received another text, 'Siber Chyltys on a Sixty-Foot-Long Brown Horse.'[5] It's not complete. There's maybe one-fifth of it—an hour-and-fif-teen-minutes or so. Of course I could complete what I have, but I don't want to do it artificially. I think that if I wait, I'll receive the rest of the text, and so I'm waiting. I tried to compose the rest, but it was silly. There's no sense in hurrying. You just have to wait until it comes to you. The text comes at a moment when you're not expecting it—in a dream, or when you're thinking about something completely different. This second text came in parts. After

Slava Kuchenov playing the *chatxan*. Note wolf and horse images on the side of the instrument. Xakasia, 2003.

I started trying to compose it myself, I got really sick, and had to have an operation. That was a message, I think. It happened twice that I started to compose text, and both times I got sick and had to have an operation. During these nine years, I've received two texts, and that's all. I don't perform these texts with Sabjilar."

"Why not?" I asked, returning to the question that had come up at the Folklife Festival in Washington, D.C. the previous year.

Slava responded, "Once I went to Japan and performed my text with some improvisations, and on the way home on the train, again, I got really sick. After that I decided that it was too risky to perform these texts in concerts. I'm sure that the reason I got sick was that I'd performed the text in the wrong surroundings. But if you recite the text in a village, it all goes very easily. And another thing—if I start to sing the text, I have to finish the performance. I can't perform just a section of it and leave it at that. There's an impresario in the Netherlands who was always asking me to perform a little section of it, and it was awkward, because later in the evening, I'd have to sit up alone and perform the rest. The full moon and new moon are good times for performances, and when they occur, I try to perform both texts. I don't have any explanation for why they're good times, but one of the traditional roles of the *xaijy* was to protect people from bad spirits. Some people say that at the full moon, bad spirits are most active, and *xai* threatens them. It's true that at the full moon, my *xai* has a harder edge to it, while at the new moon, it becomes softer, more cultured. The changes are completely unconscious."

"So a *xaijy* is like a type of shaman?" I asked.

"Yes, except that shamans have more functions," Slava said. "A *xaijy* offers prophylaxis, but a shaman is like a surgeon."

It was time to pose the question that had motivated my visit to Abakan. I looked Slava in the eye and asked, "How would you feel about my videotaping a performance of a brief excerpt from 'Siber Chyltys'?"

Slava was silent for what seemed a long time. Did he feel ambushed by my request? In our e-mail correspondence about my visit, I had mentioned my interest in his epic, but never stated outright that I hoped to videotape it.

"If you'd rather that I not tape it, that's okay," I said deferentially, anticipating that I was about to be turned down. "But I'd love at least a chance to hear it." Finally Slava spoke.

"Okay," he said. "But not here. We have to go to a special place."

That special place was a site of spiritual power known as the Great Salbyk Kurgan, a Stonehenge-like circle of eighteen enormous, crudely sculpted rocks set on a broad plain between mountain ranges, located fifty-odd miles northwest of Abakan. Archaeologists first excavated the site in the 1950s and attributed it to the Tagar people, who inhabited the territory of present-day Xakasia in the third century BCE (see plate 26).

An unmarked dirt track led away from the paved road toward the kurgan, and Slava steered his car carefully to avoid sinking into the muddy ruts. Slava had invited fellow Sabjilar members Anya and Sergei to join us so that I could videotape a song or two by the ensemble after Slava had performed an excerpt from his epic. Fortunately, we were alone at the kurgan on this opalescent August afternoon, but previous visitors had left their mark: the remains of offerings to spirits scattered around a fire pit, a ring of colored fabric strips tied around one of the rocks, and on another rock, fading graffiti. When I read the graffiti aloud, Slava scowled. "It was probably done by kids, but the worst graffiti is over there." He pointed to an iron plaque screwed into one of the rocks that acknowledged the achievement of Russian-led archaeologists who had dug up the kurgan. "How could they deface these sacred rocks?" Slava asked, anger flashing across his face.

Slava lit a small fire in the fire pit and made an offering to the spirit-master of the kurgan. Then, while I set up a tape

Slava Kuchenov performs an excerpt from "Siber Chyltys," using the vocal technique known as *xai* and accompanying himself on the *chatxan* (Video File, track 16).

recorder and video camera for the performance, he tuned his *chatxan*. The opening section of "Siber Chyltys" that Slava chanted and recited appears below.[6]

Siber Chyltys on a Sixty-Foot-Long Brown Horse	Toghys Xulas Küreng Attygh Siber Chyltys
1. When the universe first appeared	*Ax chaian chir ailanyp syxanynda*
2. And the black earth mixed together,	*Xara palghas pylghal paryptyr*
3. On the black earth	*Xara palghas üstünde*
4. Under the great sky	*Xan tigyrnyng altynda*
5. Arose snowy white peaks.	*Ax synnar pütklep parybystyr.*
6. Cold streams trickled down	*Ax synnarnyng pastarynang*
7. From the summits of the snowy white peaks	*Kök mustarnyng sughlarynang*
8. And from the blue icy water.	*Xara sughlar axlap syghymtyr.*
9. Streams converged	*Xara sughlar pirigip*
10. Cold waters flowed together,	*Soox sughlar xozylyp*
11. Turning into rushing rivers.	*Aghyn sughlar polyp paryptyr.*

(Recitative [lines 12–22] repeats previous 11 lines)

(*Xai* continues)

23. In the rushing rivers	*Aghyn sughlarda*
24. Different kinds of fish	*Aimax pasxa palyxtar*
25. Began to live.	*Churtaghlap syghyptyr*
26. Catching these fish	*Ol palyxtarny tudup-y*
27. Killing these water worms*	*Sugh xurtaryn soghyp*
28. The Tadar** people began to live.	*Tadar chony churtapchadadyr.*
29. The herds of the Tadar people	*Tadar chonyng mallary*
30. The sheep of the people with the wide stride***	*Xalyx chonyng xoilary*
31. Grazed on the green steppe.	*Kök chazylarja ottapchadadyr.*

(Recitative [lines 32–52] elaborates on preceding 9 lines)

32. The rushing rivers diverged sixty times	*Aghyn sughlar alton ailanyp*
33. Seventy times they mixed together	*Chiton pylghalyp axlapchadyr*
34. Spreading out along the green steppe	*Kök chazylarcha chaiypchadyr*
35. Resounding over the white steppe.	*Ax chazylarcha orlapchadadyr.*
36. In deep hollows	*Oiym chirlerde*
37. Quiet lakes were formed.	*Amyr köller pol parchadadyr*
38. In rocky places	*Tastygh chirlerde*
39. Rushing rivers flowed.	*Xazyr sughlar axlapchadyr*
40. In the quiet lakes	*Amyr köllerde*
41. Lived slow-moving fish.	*Maiyng paryxtar churtapchadyr.*
42. In fast-flowing places	*Xazyr chirlerde*

43. Were quick-moving fish
44. That gleamed in the sun's rays.
45. Catching these fish
46. Killing the water worms [i.e., fishing]
47. Along the banks of the wide rivers
48. The great Tadar people made their livelihood.
49. The herds of the great people
50. The sheep of the people with the wide stride
51. Spread out along the green steppe
52. And grazed on the white steppe.

43. *Chapchang palyxtar*
44. *Kün sustaryna chyltyrapchadyr.*
45. *Ol palyxtarny tudup*
46. *Sugh xurtaryn soghyp*
47. *Aghyn sughlarnyng xastada*
48. *Ilbek Tadar chony churtapchadyr.*
49. *Ilbek Tadar chonyng mallary*
50. *Xalyx chonyng xoilary*
51. *Kök chazylarja chaiylchadadyr*
52. *Ax chazylarja otap chörchededir.*

(*Xai* continues)

53. Siber Chyltys became
54. The owner of these herds and
55. The leader of the people with the wide stride.
56. Ai-Arygh became
57. The wife of Siber Chyltys,
58. The beloved of Siber Chyltys.
59. The two first people lived
60. Without any sorrows.
61. These two strong worlds lived
62. Without any want.

53. *Ol malardyng eezi*
54. *Xalyx chonyng pigi*
55. *Siber Chyltys pol paryptyr.*
56. *Siber Chyltystyng alghany*
57. *Siber Chyltystyng xynghany*
58. *Ai-Arygh polyptyi.*
59. *Iki alyp pir dee nime*
60. *Chobalanmin churtapchaty.*
61. *Iki külük pir dee nime*
62. *Xyzylbin churt salyptyi.*

(Recitative [lines 63–73] repeats and elaborates on previous 10 lines)

63. Astride a sixty-foot-long brown horse
64. Siber Chyltys became
65. The owner of these herds and
66. The leader of the people with the wide stride.
67. Ai-Arygh became
68. The chosen wife of Siber Chyltys
69. The beloved of Siber Chyltys.
70. The first two people didn't grieve for anything
71. They lived with no want of anything
72. The three-year-old children grew older****
73. And raised an only son.

63. *Ol mallerdyng eezi*
64. *Xalyx chonyng pigi*
65. *Toghys xulas küreng attyg*
66. *Siber Chyltys polyptyr.*
67. *Siber Chyltystyng alghany*
68. *Siber Chyltystynhg xynghany*
69. *Ai-Arygh poltyr.*
70. *Iki alyp pirdee nime chobalanmin*
71. *Pir dee nime xyzylbin chutapchatyrlar*
72. *Üs chastygh palalaryn öskirchetirler*
73. *Chalghys oollaryn azyrapchatyrlar.*

* "water worm" is a synonym for "fish"
** "Tadar" is a self-identifying ethnonym used by the Xakas
*** "People with the wide stride" expresses the idea that they are a free people
**** "three-year-old-son" means an eighteen-year-old, since one year in epic time was equal to six actual years

"What I've performed," said Slava, putting down his *chatxan*, "is the beginning of a heroic epic. Siber Chyltys defends his people. His enemies try to trick him and lie to him; later there are descriptions of fights and battles, but Siber Chyltys maintains his power to the end. He's a real hero. This text is from 1996. Once when I performed it, it went on for nine hours and fifteen minutes. I sat in the evening and started to write the words, and then it was morning. I haven't been able to repeat that. If you try to think something up, if it's not 'given,' it's obvious right away. It's like the difference between a natural food and a synthetic one. Writers told me that I'm an amateur poet, that my text was crude, and that I needed to fix it up. I tried that—I tried making it more poetic in a modern sense. But it always ended badly for me. My soul completely rejects that kind of approach."

Initiatory dreams and visions are common—in fact, they are essential—among bards and minstrels in the Turkic-language epic and storytelling traditions of Eurasia, just as they are among shamans and healers. Folklorist Natalie Moyle, who studied the Turkish minstrel-tale tradition in the 1970s, explains the significance of the initiatory dream as a means of augmenting the authority of the performer. "Drawing attention away from the mundane drudgery of slowly learning the techniques of the profession and making minstrelsy seem a product of inspiration alone certainly enhances its stature. What is more, this increases the relative importance of the initiatory dream and emphasizes the element of divine sanction."[7] Or as stated by the literary critic Northrop Frye, writing about William Blake, "Inspiration is the artist's empirical proof of the divinity of his imagination."[8]

Moyle's larger point is that, while dreams may inspire bards and minstrels to choose their profession, "all real minstrels train and practice before they can perform in front of an audience. Remnants of a formal apprenticeship system still exist despite evidence of the profession's decline."[9] In a recent book on heroic poetry, Karl Reichl, a medievalist and leading scholar of Central Asian oral epic, corroborates Moyle's conclusion: "A professional singer has typically learned his profession from another singer, and may remain with his master for years before becoming an independent performer."[10] Moyle and Reichl's generalizations stem from the study of oral literature in historically Islamic cultural milieus, where the master-disciple (or master-apprentice) model of oral transmission, known in Persian and Central Asian Turkic languages as *ustaz-shagird*, is indeed ubiquitous. But farther north, among the Altai pastoralists, the convention of *ustaz-shagird* seems to have been all but nonexistent.

"Who is your teacher?" I continually asked the throat-singers and *igil* players I met during my early trips to Tuva. When they shrugged their shoulders, or looked uninterested in my question, I thought that perhaps I had not pronounced the words correctly, and asked again. Then, apparently not wanting to disappoint me, the musicians would come up with a perfunctory answer: "My uncle used to throat-sing, and I learned from him." Or, "My grandfather was a well-known musician, and he'd sing in our yurt."

Only later did I see the pattern: in the Altai region, not only throat-singers but also musicians in general typically do not learn from a teacher or master in the sense that Indian, Iranian, Uzbek, or, for that matter, American and European professional musicians do. There is no formal acceptance into an apprenticeship nor is there any rite of passage at the end to mark its conclusion. Most important, there is not the sense that a musician's authority depends on the pedigree of a lineage. "So-and-so studied with X and Y" is the standard formula of professional musical resumés, whether in New York or New Delhi. Autodidacts, by contrast, are viewed with a certain suspicion.

In the Altai, the formula is reversed. Music connoisseurs regard a musician whose performances are the result of formal instruction, music notation, or written texts as inauthentic, while spirit-inspired autodidacticism is the norm. Slava Kuchenov's insistence that he rely exclusively on oneiric inspiration to "receive" his epic, and that what he produces through his own conscious agency is inescapably deficient, seems unremarkable in the context of present-day musical revivalism. Moreover, his reliance on inspiration rather than on acquiring tradecraft and technique is not simply a ploy to promote his own originality. Quite the contrary; even a cursory examination of his text shows that it relies heavily on formulaic imagery that would be obvious to any culturally informed listener. The opening section of Slava's "Siber Chyltys," for example, bears an uncanny resemblance to the beginning of "Ai-Xuuchyn," a well-known Xakas heroic epic recently published in a book-length critical edition by the Russian Academy of Sciences.[11] Like "Siber Chyltys," "Ai-Xuuchyn" opens with the beginning of the world, describing rushing rivers, pastoral grazing lands, multitudes of livestock, and a rider on a sixty-foot-long horse. Are the texts that Slava "received" merely a paraphrase of older material shaken loose from his memory—for example, the tales he heard as a child, when he was beaten to stay awake at night and listen to his blind grandmother? Or do they stem from a less direct source in what the eminent Jungian psychologist Erich Neumann called the "archetypal canon of the prevailing culture"?[12]

Scholars who have analyzed epic and folktale traditions would be quick to point out the telltale mechanisms of oral composition: formulas and patterns, versions and variants, models and motifs. Yet what is most interesting about

Slava's text is not its actual sources—evidently stories like "Siber Chyltys," as well as perhaps a broader cultural narrative about heroes, horses, and epic reciters, must have infiltrated his consciousness and served as a model for his "revelation." Rather, the interest is in how this process of unpremeditated inspiration exemplifies a reawakening of the animist view of the world at the heart of Siberian cultural revivalism. Why does a successful sculptor like Slava Kuchenov suddenly experience a prophetic revelation in which he is told to become a *xaiïy*, compose an epic poem, and begin a new life as a musician? A pragmatic, or perhaps cynical, explanation might point to the lure of the marketplace—the success of music from Tuva, Xakasia, Mongolia, and Sakha in attracting worldwide interest among a clientele of seekers interested in shamans and spirits. But the emergence of so many talented musicians in one place at one time cannot be the result of the marketplace alone. The appearance of musicians like Slava—a sculptor who becomes an epic reciter, inspired by a dream—must be linked to a deeper social need.

I would be far from the first ethnographer to note that spiritual callings, whether that of prophet, poet, mystic, or musician, blossom in times of trouble. Roberte Hamayon, the French scholar of Inner Asian shamanism, wrote about the "latent availability of shamanic practices in all types of society." This availability," she suggested, "becomes manifest especially in crisis periods, when such practices easily revive or emerge."[13] By any account, the decade that followed the breakup of the Soviet Union was such a period, and Hamayon's observation was indeed borne out. People calling themselves shamans were not the only ones to rise from the crisis and offer succor. Anyone who could persuasively claim contact with the spirit world was thrust into a position of authority—an authority amplified by the disintegration of the material world that, even in the "period of stagnation" of the U.S.S.R.'s final years, had provided social stability.

Not only shamanism, but music, with its intrinsic closeness to the spirit world and ability to empower charismatic personalities, became a medium of social salvation. One society's response to crisis, though, is another's cultural chic. Shamans and musicians in the Altai region who answered the call to help restore spiritual equilibrium in a society torn asunder quickly found themselves fetishized from afar. "These people have a kind of knowledge for which there's a real need now in the West," was how one young seeker I met summed up his reason for following the meridian lines of global shamanism that extended from California to Kyzyl. That seeker had plenty of company, particularly in the days following the Second International Symposium of Shamans and Shamanologists that convened in Tuva in August 2003. And that was how it came to be that on a sunny August morning I sat in the treatment room of Tuvan shaman Lazo Mongush, sharing a bowl of mutton parts with an acupuncturist from Hawaii and a former military doctor from Novosibirsk who ran a center of Eastern medicine there, while in the anteroom, an art student from Finland waited her turn for a consultation.

SHAMANS AND CHAMPAGNE

When Valentina Süzükei and I pulled up in front of the complex of small wooden buildings that serves as headquarters for the Dünggür Society, the chain of shamanic clinics founded by Mongush Kenin-Lopsan, Lazo greeted me like an old friend. Before he became a shaman, Lazo had been a throat-singer, and in 1988, he and I had sung together on Tuvan television. I had forgotten about that television debut, which occurred in the days before throat-singing enthusiasts far more serious and skilled than I began visiting Tuva, and the threshold for local excitement about throat-singing foreigners had been significantly raised. I had not seen Lazo in fifteen years, and the gaunt figure of my memory had grown more rotund, the face puffier. We made small talk, and after a respectable interval, the acupuncturist and military doctor excused themselves, leaving Valentina and me alone with Lazo and the mutton parts. I asked him to talk about his career change.

"It's not so much that I changed my career," Lazo replied. "I'd always shamanized in secret, when it was forbidden. I can't even remember the first time I healed someone, but I was born near a well known *ovaa*, and my great-grandfather was a shaman, so for me, shamanizing is hereditary."

"Did you know your great-grandfather?" I asked.

"I remember him, but he died when I was six [Lazo was born in 1950]. I was raised by an aunt—my father's sister. My father was a victim of Stalin's terror. He served ten years in a labor camp in the far north of Siberia for selling seed that should have been given to the government. People were starving, and he was trying to take care of his family. After he was released, it took him three years to get home. On the way back to Tuva, he married a Russian woman, but then discovered that she had another husband who was in prison. So he left and made his way to Abakan. From Abakan he joined a caravan. One of the caravan drivers died, and my father was given his horse. My aunt brought me here to Kyzyl, and we found my father working in a cafeteria. Meanwhile, my mother moved away and remarried. I kept in touch with her. She told me that after I was forty, my life was going to be hard, and she was right. I developed a thyroid problem and had to have an operation on my throat. The doctor told me to forget about throat-singing. So I became a journalist, and in 1993, a policeman beat me almost to death.

The headquarters of the Dünggür Society in Kyzyl the week after an international conference, summer 2003.

I had written an article about a colonel in the police who was poaching, and I'd snapped pictures of him through a telephoto lens. Several months passed after the article came out, and nothing happened. I thought people had forgotten about it, and then came the beating. Ever since then, I've been registered as a second-class invalid. But I surmounted all these difficulties. Becoming a shaman isn't simple. There has to be some kind of difficult journey, and if you survive it, you'll be okay.

"My mother had foretold that I'd become a healer, but that I'd only hold a shaman drum after I was forty-eight years old. At age forty-nine, I began to use the drum, and I've been using it now for four years. The drum you see there is one I made myself." Lazo pointed to a large frame drum hanging from the wall. "I've made four drums. On the second one, a figure drew itself in the patterns of the drum skin, which was made from the hide of a yak. I think it's my great-grandfather. When the drum was in good condition, the image was very clear. Now it's ripped and the image is beginning to disappear. A drum is a living organism. You have to feed it and take care of it."

Lazo rose from the bearskin cushion on which he had been seated, picked up the larger of two silver bowls from the corner of his desk, and filled it with milk from a refrigerator in the corner. He sprinkled powdered juniper on the milk, stirred it in with a twig, and added water. "This is the best *arzhaan* [mineral or spring water] for a shaman." Lazo picked up a wooden beater and struck the bowl on its four sides. As it began to resonate, he traced the circumference of the top of the bowl with the beater, producing a chain reaction of shimmering overtones that piled up on top of one another until the bowl was ringing loudly. The excitation of the bowl made the milk "boil" and sizzle.

"When you drink this, it purifies the human organism from the inside," Lazo said, motioning for me to take a sip.

"It's like a Tibetan singing bowl!" I exclaimed.

"The Tibetans don't use it correctly," Lazo replied sharply. "Shamans used these bowls before Buddhist monks, although I was the one who thought up the idea of filling it with milk. I haven't seen others do this. Silver is one of the nine valuable things that a shaman should have, and this bowl is one of my attributes—an *eeren*." *Eeren*s are physical objects that represent spirit-helpers called upon to assist a shaman with particular tasks or rituals. Lazo's *eeren*s hung from the sawed-off stubs of a thin tree branch anchored in a weighted stand on his desk: bells, teeth, feathers, a bag of juniper powder, various colored threads and beads (see plate 27). Other *eeren*s—most prominently a wolf skull—were affixed to the back of the shaman's coat that hung from a hook on the wall. A brown kangaroo hide pinned up behind his desk—a gift from a Novosibirsk-based "extra-sense," as New Age healers and parapsychologists are generically called in Russian—rounded out the *eeren*s. "Different kinds of animal skins help a shaman overcome any barrier or difficulty," Lazo said, when I asked him about the healing effects of kangaroos.

Valentina and I had come to Lazo to ask about the role of sound-making in his shamanic work. In the practices of traditional healers around the world, sound and music are a ubiquitous presence.[14] Their role seems to be to help induce the nonordinary states of consciousness often grouped together as "trance," in which the relationship of mind and body can become momentarily freed from habit and realigned to startling physical and psychological effect. Scholars who have studied music associated with trance practices have pointed to the cognitive complexity of the relationship between music and trance, to the diversity of forms in which trance music is expressed, and to the resistance of trance phenomena to reductionist explanatory models.[15] As a result of these challenges, recent scholarship by ethnomusicologists has tended to focus on observable aspects of social behavior, for example, on music's role in the social construction of trance experiences, rather than on the internal physical and physiological mechanisms through which sound and music act on listeners to facilitate entry into nonordinary states. Yet where science and scholarship demur, shamans tread intrepidly. The clinicians at the Düng-gür Society had no shortage of ideas about the healing power of sound and music. Indeed, anyone who has ever experienced shamanic sound-making up close cannot help but be affected, whether therapeutically or not. I am no exception.

"Hold the talisman between your hands and think positive thoughts," the female shaman ordered me as I sat in one of the Dünggür Society's treatment rooms. The sound of the drum seemed to come from everywhere as the sha-man held it close to the back of my head, then far away, then gliding around in front of me. I opened my eyes and noticed that her face was close to the surface of the drum and that she was singing directly at the drumhead. The sound was comforting as it swirled around the room, the thud of the drum blending with the deep growl of her voice. "I'm no singer," said the shaman after the ritual was over, "but the spirits help me."

In that moment I had what was perhaps an epiphany of the obvious: that the drum and the rich array of sound-making accoutrements attached to the shaman's cloak act to mask our perception of the sounds that ordinarily surround us, thus intensifying the internal aural and visual imagery iden-tified with shamanic "trance." Was this fleeting thought a hypothesis that could be empirically confirmed or disproved? Could it be framed as a ques-tion that could be meaningfully put to Lazo or his colleagues? Could Lazo comment on the effects of the drum, and of the different timbres and rhyth-mic patterns that characterize its use? What about other types of shamanic sound-making, such as bells, jingles, clackers, throat-singing, imitations of animal sounds, and of course, *algyshtar*—the shamanic hymns, as Kenin-Lopsan had called them.

Lazo seemed impatient with our questions, and his responses were frus-tratingly cryptic. "The drum purifies, but the shaman adds his own energy," he said with an air of finality. "If you just beat on the drum without that energy, nothing will happen."

"How can you tell whether a shaman really has that energy?" I asked.

"Empiricism," Lazo replied. "If someone's sick, and a person is able to get rid of the problem, then of course this person is a real shaman. And no matter how many drums you show up with, if you can't cure the illness, then you're not a shaman."

"But surely even a real shaman can't heal everyone?" I said.

"Yes, that's the point. Not everyone can be healed. The spirits decide who will live." Lazo stood and began to tidy up his desk. "Look, I'm not going to be able to explain this by talking to you. If you want to understand how a shaman works, come and watch me do a purification ritual."

Valentina's face broke into a smile. This invitation was what we had hoped for. "When do we leave?" she asked.

"I'll meet you here tomorrow morning at nine o'clock. We'll drive across the river to an *arzhaan* [spring]. You'll need to bring offerings—a kilogram of meat, clarified butter, *kurut* [dried cottage cheese], *dalgan* [roasted ground wheat or barley], an apple, cookies, and a half-kilo of toffee candy. I'll take care of the rest."

Lazo's description of an "*arzhaan* across the river"—by which he meant the Yenisei River—was vague enough, but once we turned off the main road just after crossing the Yenisei and began to follow a dirt track that ran along the high bluffs on the river's north bank, I knew exactly where we were headed. Valentina and I had been to that *arzhaan* three years earlier with another shaman. It was the closest site to Kyzyl that offered ready access to the spirit world, and it was heavily used not only by shamans but also by people who simply wanted to make offerings at a spring and relax around a fire. Colored strips of cloth (*chalama*) left as offerings were tied in dense clusters to trees on either side of the spring, and they were also packed together along a rope strung between them. A pile of garbage moldered behind a bush near the fire pit. Candy wrappers and empty plastic bottles and cups lay among the stones, fouling the water that trickled down from the spring toward the Yenisei far below. A short distance from the fire pit, a large wooden cross had been dug into the ground. Lazo grimaced. "It's Russians who did that," he said. "They know this is a place used by shamans."

Lazo gave me a strip of cloth with a piece of *artysh* tied to it and took another one himself. We hung the strips on a branch of the tree aside the spring, then washed our hands. Next, Lazo burned *artysh* and spread the smoke around the fire pit to purify it. Then he built a log cabin–style fire with split pieces of log that he stripped off with a sharp knife, packing leaves and grass among the logs to create smoke. The raw meat was imbedded in a lower layer of the log cabin, and on the top he placed the other foodstuffs. Finally, he poured milk in a silver bowl, stirred it with a piece of *artysh,* and threw the liquid to the four compass points. The purification ritual was about to begin.

Lazo took a large piece of *artysh* and lit it. As crackling flames consumed the dry juniper bough, he waved it gracefully along the underside of his arms, grasping the *artysh* first with one hand, then the other. The flames appeared to surround his arms, but there was no sign that he was being burned. After laying the piece of *artysh* atop the ensemble of logs and food offerings, he retreated to a bush near the fire pit where his shamanic accoutrements were laid out on the ground and hung from the branches of an adjacent tree.

Lazo had prepared the fire wearing his shaman's feathered headdress and

Offerings surround the spring where Lazo Mongush performed a
purification ritual near Kyzyl, 2003.

street clothes—a green T-shirt and dungarees—but as the smoke from the
fire began to thicken, he slipped a bracelet onto each forearm and pulled his
heavy shaman coat up over his shoulders, adjusting the fit as he slid his arms
into the sleeves. He replaced his sneakers with black boots, and to the front
of the costume he tied a belt with a string of jingles that clattered loudly as
he shook the coat from side to side to test the sound. Affixed to the end of
the belt was a massive bear claw—an important *eeren* that would facilitate
contact with the bear spirit. Twirling a *kuduk* (a mop-like wand of braided
string) from different positions around the fire pit to stir up the smoke, he
whistled a series of rapid, descending cadences. Then he took his drum from
its perch on a tree branch and used the beater (*orba*) to sprinkle milk from
the silver bowl over its skin. He rubbed the milk into the skin with his hand
and held it over the fire to dry, beating the head intermittently and tapping
with his fingers to test the tightness. The beater was also purified by shaking
it over the flame. As Lazo moved the wooden beater with quick, short strokes
while simultaneously jiggling the drum and twisting his headdress-bedecked
head, tiny bells attached to the back of the beater joined the clamorous sound
emanating from the bells and jingles on his coat, headdress, and drum. Lazo
had turned himself into a human idiophone.

An abridged version of Lazo Mongush's performance of a shamanic purification ritual is included in the video files online, track 18. The full text is transcribed below.

Now he stood by the fire and began beating the center of the drum. Not satisfied with the timbre, he held the drum over the fire to heat the skin so it would be still more taut. Then, to the accompaniment of rapid strokes of the beater to various parts of the drumhead, Lazo began to chant and sing an *algysh*.

Shaking the beater, I get ready to shamanize	*Orba chaiyp xamnaarym ol*
Sit, be seated	*Olurungar, saadangar, ooi*
Be respectful and free up the road	*Oran-Tangdym eeleringe*
For the spirit-masters of my Oran Tangdy.	*Oruk chailap bolgaanyngar, ooi.*
Beating the drum, I get ready to shamanize	*Dünggür soktap xamnaarym ol*
Be seated, and be patient	*Tüveksinmein saadangar, ooi*
Be respectful and free up the road	*Dündük deerning eeleringe*
For the spirit-masters of the sky.	*Oruk chailap bolgaanyngar, ooi.*
My nine wooded mountains, my Ursa Major	*Tos-la tangdym Dolaan Burgan*
My moon, my sun, my golden land	*Aiym, xünüm, aldyn cherim*
My land is my mother, my sky is my father	*Ie cherim, deer adam*
The Pleiades and the polestar are my eyes.	*Ülger sholban karaktarym.*
Spirit-masters of the underworld	*Aldyy cherning azalary*
Sit on your horse, and put on your robe	*A'ttanyngar, tonanyngar*
We'll travel around the *aals* and the yurts	*Aaldar, ögler keziilinger*
We'll free and purify those	*Ajyg, shüjüg tutturganga*
Who are seized by grief and sadness.	*Avyraldap aktaalyngar.*
We'll establish peace and tranquility	*Amyr taibyng turguzaaly*
So that work can proceed	*Ajyl-ishti chogudaaly*
Spirit-masters of my Oran-Tangdy	*Oran-Tangdym eeleri*
Spirit-masters of my fire and hearth	*Odum-közüm eeleri*
Master-spirits of the earth and water	*Cherning-sugnung eeleri*
Now I bow down to you to the ground.	*Cherge chedir mögeidim-ne.*
Now I burn my *artysh* and Siberian juniper	*Artysh shaanaam kyvystym-na*
I toss my spring water and milk in the air	*Arzhaan südüm örü chashtym*
Give freedom and forgiveness	*Avyraldap örsheenger-le*
Take pity on children.	*Azhy-töldü keergenger.*
Spirit-masters of my Oran-Tangdy	*Oran-Tangdym eeleri*
Spirit-masters of my birthplace	*Oran churtum eeleri*
Spirit-masters of my land and water	*Cherning sugnum eeleri*
Now I bow down to you to the ground	*Cherge chedir mögeidim-ne*
Take pity on us and forgive us.	*Cher-le keergep örsheenger-le.*

Help yourself to the food that we put in the fire	*Otka salgan a'shty-chemni*
And let us depart	*Orta chooglap örsheenger-le*
Open my road and let me accomplish what I want to do	*Oruk choruum ajydyngar*
Don't let me have any accidents along the way.	*Ozal-ondak boldurbangar.*

Spirit-masters of my sky and my taiga	*Kudai tangdym eeleri*
Spirit-masters of *kurbustu* [the upper sky]	*Kurbustunung eeleri*
I sing, swinging the *kuduk**	*Kuduk chaiyp yrlap tur menxi*
Don't allow any sadness.	*Kudaraldy boldurbangar.*
* A wand of braided string.	

Help yourself to the food that we put in the fire	*Otka salgan a'shty-chemni*
And let us depart	*Orta chooglap örsheenger-le*
Open my road and let me accomplish what I want to do	*Oruk choruum ajydyngar*
Don't let me have any accidents along the way.	*Ozal-ondak boldurbangar.*

Spirit-masters of fire and hearth	*Odum-közüm eeleri*
Spirit-masters of my Oran-Tangdy*	*Oran-Tangdym eeleri*
Spirit-masters of spring water	*Arjaan sugnung eeleri*
Spirit-masters of golden water	*Aldyn sugnung eeleri*
I bless and praise you	*Algap iöreep maktap tur men*
Protect and forgive us.	*Avyraldap örsheenger-le.*
* A place with high mountains	

I purify the flowing spring water	*Agyp chydar kara sugnu*
With my *artysh* and *aitys* [powdered juniper]	*Artyjadym aityzadym*
I purify my mineral water and spring water	*Arjaan suumnu kara suumnu*
With my *artysh* and *aitys*.	*Aityzadym artyjadym.*

Ribbons that represent my *eerens*	*Charnym bajyn chara baskan*
Hanging from my shoulder blades	*Chavagalar eerennerim*
Don't allow any laziness	*Chalgaa choruk boldurbangar*
And don't allow any conflicts.	*Chargy chaaly ündürbenger.*

(First two lines are undecipherable)	(undecipherable)
People who have come from far and near	*Yrak chooktan kelgen chonu*
Let them sing and not be wanting.	*Yrlap turzun, todug turzun.*

For him who carries misfortune on his back	*Bachyt xalap chüktep algan*
Let bad habits stay far away	*Bagai changchyl yngai turzun*
For him who carries black misfortune on his back	*Kara xalap chüktep algan*
Let the dark forces stay far away.	*Kara küshter yngai turzun.*

Let my people live well	*Arat chonum eki chorzun*
Let their work go well	*Ajyl-iji chogup chorzun*
Let children live well	*Ajy-tölüm eki chorzun*
Let life be without obstacles.	*Amydyral ajyk bolzun.*

Let suffering not surround	*Kachygdaldy körüp choruur*
The black-haired child of humanity	*Kara bashtyg kiji tölü*
Let dark forces not envelop	*Kara küshke bürgetpezin*
He who is entrapped by suffering.	*Kachygdalga tutturbazyn.*
Let poverty not surround	*Türegdeldi körüp choruur*
The human child with hair on his head	*Düktüg bashtyg kiji tölü*
Let the dark night not crush him	*Dümbei düne bastyrbazyn*
Let the cyclone wind not carry him away.	*Düvü xatka alyspazyn.*
Let evil forces not close his road	*Bachyttyglar oruk dozup*
And spread their bad influence [to him]	*Bala chyvaan xaldatpazyn*
Let misfortune not weigh on his head	*Bagai choruk bashka xaldap*
And spread its bad influence.	*Bala chyvaan xaldatpazyn.*
Help yourself to my offerings	*Ajym chemim deejizin*
And bless us again	*Am-daa chooglap örsheenger-le*
With respect I give you my offerings of	*Artysh shaanaam arzhaan südüm*
Artysh, my juniper, my spring water,	*Avyraldap chajyp tür men.*
and my milk.	
Spirits of my upper world and taiga,	*Kudai tangdym eeleri*
Don't allow sadness	*Kudaraldy boldurbangar*
Spirit-masters of earth and water,	*Cherning sugnung eeleri*
Don't allow unfortunate events.	*Cherle xalap boldurbangar.*
Let the middle *aza** which blocks my fire	*Odum közüm bajyn doskan*
Stand far away	*Ortun aza yngai turzun*
Aza spirits that awaited my help	*Chaglak manaan aza chetker*
Can I fufill your wish?	*Sagyjyngar ajyttym be?*
* malevolent or demonic spirit	
(First two lines are undecipherable)	(undecipherable)
Spirit-masters of my taiga	*Oran tangdym eeleri*
Actually noticed me.	*Okta körüp amyrady.*
Spirit-masters of my land and my birthplace	*Cherim churtum eeleri*
Don't forget about me	*Cherle ojaap örsheenger-le*
Don't allow death and loss	*Ölüm chidim boldurbangar*
And don't allow enmity.	*Öjen kylyk ööskütpenger.*
Spirits of the spring	*Kara-sugnung eeleri*
Take me into account from time to time	*Xaigaarangar tegeeringer*
Don't allow dark forces	*Xai-la bachyt kara küshtü*
Suffering, and sadness.	*Kachygdaldy boldurbangar.*
Spirit of my upper world and taiga	*Kudai tangdym eeleri*
Don't allow misfortune and sadness	*Kudaraldy boldurbangar*
Don't allow the *aza* spirit to become active	*Aza chetker doyuldurup*
So that they can cause illness.	*Aaryg arjyk boldurbangar.*

Spirit-masters of my golden taiga	*Aldyn tangdym eeleri*
Take me under your protection and forgive me	*Avyraldap örsheenger-le*
Please give happiness	*Arat chonum aas-kejiin*
To my people.	*Ala chaigaar xaiyrlangar.*

Spirit-masters of the upper sky	*Kurbustunung eeleri*
I bow to my waist	*Kurlak chedir mögeidim-ne*
Push away sadness	*Kudaraldy chailadyngar*
And let there be laughter and joy.	*Katky xögnü boldurungar.*

Spirit-masters of earth and water	*Cherning sugnung eeleri*
I bow to the ground	*Cherge chedir mögeidim-ne*
Ensure that the blue-eyed wild *aza*	*Cherlik aza karaa köktü*
Does not have success.	*Chedimche chok boldurungar.*

After around ten minutes of texted singing, Lazo beat the drum for a long time and then, to the accompaniment of the drum, began throat-singing in a guttural *kargyraa* style, continuing for several minutes without words. At the first sound of the *kargyraa*, Valentina and I both looked up from our video cameras at the same moment. Throat-singing by shamans was a controversial topic. Some shamans believe that real shamans don't throat-sing. "They use it like a 'show,'" complained Kara-ool Dopchuur-ool, a member of the Adyg-Eeren (Bear Eeren) Society that had broken off from the Dünggür group to which Lazo belonged. "It's art," Kara-ool scoffed. "Every shaman *can* use it, of course, but my grandmother, who was a great shaman, said that it's forbidden." Lazo evidently disagreed. When I asked him about it later, he had a straightforward explanation. "*Kargyraa* takes away stress."

The ceremony ended abruptly. After finishing a quatrain of text, Lazo beat the *dünggür* quietly for another half-minute, stopped, twirled the instrument around so that the bells jingled, and set it down on the ground. Picking up the silver bowl filled with milk, he used a sprig of *artysh* to sprinkle liquid on the fire, then flicked it in different directions, and finally daubed milk on Valentina's hands and then on my hands. We rubbed the liquid into our skin, leaving a sticky coating. I eyed the fresh spring water, but the point of the ritual was of course not to wash off the milk. Lazo poured the remaining contents of the silver bowl on the burning embers and the hot rocks that lined the fire pit. Then he rang a bell over each of our heads, brushed our clothes and hair with the belted bear claw that he had detached from his costume, and jingled the bells on the bear claw belt around our bodies.

As Lazo took off his headdress and boots and folded his shaman coat, Valentina and I put away our video cameras. Neither of us spoke. Maybe it was just the absence of the pounding drum, but I felt a deep silence in my body—and yes, a sort of purification. The loud drumming and chanting, the clanging of bells and crackle of burning wood, the pungent smell of smoke and burning *artysh* had indeed driven tension away and left me utterly calm. I had not the slightest desire to move from our idyllic perch overlooking the Yenisei, but Lazo had picked up his things and was heading back up the steep embankment to his car. Valentina and I grabbed what was left of our gear and followed behind him. Lazo stowed his shaman costume in the trunk, climbed into the driver's seat, and navigated slowly along the dirt road back to the main highway to Kyzyl. As we approached the bridge across the Yenisei, he turned on the radio. A Tuvan pop song was playing, and Lazo hummed along.

Back at the Dünggür Society, Lazo, Valentina, and I made our way to Lazo's treatment room through a knot of anxious-looking clients gathered around the receptionist's desk. Lazo shut the door. While Valentina and I made ourselves comfortable, he checked messages on the cellphone lying on his desk, then retrieved a bottle of champagne from a table in the back corner. Popping the cork, he filled a white mug on his desk labeled "Scorpio" in Russian and pushed it toward me.

"Do you drink champagne?" he asked.

"Yes, if it's good."

"Don't worry, I only drink good champagne." Lazo searched for a knife and stirred the warm liquid around in his mug until it fizzled. "Here, try this." I drank a mouthful and passed the cup back to Lazo, who sipped it like coffee as we continued to talk. Veuve Clicquot it was not.

"When I see our shamans drunk, I get really angry," said Lazo, whose shamanic antennae had perhaps picked up the question I was silently asking. "Sometimes Mongush Borakhovich [Kenin-Lopsan] sends people over—they beg to work with us. They say, 'Let's work together.' They're persistent, and he sends them over, and I ask them, 'How many days a month do you drink? How many days are you sober?' And I check everything. And if it doesn't check out, I send them away. Or a shaman is invited to a memorial feast, and he sees a beautiful girl and says, 'Oh, a bad spirit has gone to that girl. She has to come to me.' The girl gets scared and goes to the shaman, but he has something else in mind. There are a lot of charlatans."

These days, the issue of charlatanism versus authenticity among shamans and others with claims of access to the spirit world is hotly debated. Kenin-Lopsan's Dünggür Society, with its red membership cards (modeled after the cards once issued to Communist Party members), year-long probationary period for shaman-clinicians, and strict rules of conduct ("We don't take alcoholics," Kenin-Lopsan had assured me when I asked about the selection process) was intended to establish a rigorous standard of certification for all practitioners within his sprawling clinic system. But fractures had grown among the shamans, and splinter groups had broken off. Some shamans accused others of devoting too much attention to foreigners at the expense of the local population, or of shamanizing for personal profit—an animistic version of simony. Lazo had brought up this theme in one of our conversations. "A lot of people in Tuva are suffering," he said. "They're poor, they're hungry. For a shaman to earn from these people. . . ." He shook his head. "I try to take less. People ask you to come and get rid of some horror, and to add to this horror by taking a lot of money—that's terrible."

Kara-ool Dopchuur-ool, the shaman from the competing Adyg-Eeren Society, had been generally skeptical about the foreigners who streamed into Kyzyl to learn the secrets of Tuvan shamans (see plate 28). "To become a shaman you have to live here for several years and give your all," he said sternly to Valentina and me. "You have to know the voices of nature and the language of spirits. You have to listen to the rippling of a brook, the sound of a river at night, the echo in a mountain ravine—you have to hear those things. And nature spirits are called through text, not just imitation of their sounds. So you have to know our language. Every people has its own language, and to heal someone, you have to know the words of that language —that's simple psychology. The foreigners who come here—they've gathered a lot of information from informants and written it down, and they know how to beat a drum. But when they play the drum, there's no energy. There's no truth. They're just making noise."

Ai-Chürek Oyun, a vivacious young shaman who has become one of the principal links between Tuvan shamans and their American acolytes, had a more positive outlook (see plate 29). When I asked her, shortly before she set out on a trip to Mill Valley, California (see her web page at www.pure-naturemusic.com/ai-churek.htm), whether Americans could be shamans, her eyes lit up. "Yes, why not?" she replied. "America has a great energy." Ai-Chürek (her name means "moon heart") was looking forward to her trip and to spending a little time away from Tuva. "It's hard to be a shaman here," she told me. "There are a lot of bad spirits. The land is pure, but people pollute it." Sounding momentarily weary, she pointed to the door beyond which a throng of clients waited for treatment. "It's not interesting, day after day, trying to purify these people."

The different views articulated by Ai-Chürek and Kara-ool each represent a legitimate take on Tuvan contemporaneity. Kara-ool, for his part, is no xenophobe. He had boasted about having clients from Russia and even abroad. But he was disturbed by the fawning deference to foreigners that he perceived among some of his fellow shamans; by the commodification and franchising of practices that were a response to Tuva's own social chaos and misfortune. Ai-Chürek, by contrast, feared the trivialization of the spirit world that had become endemic among Tuvans themselves. Many clients came to her to ask for purification not of their road toward health, spiritual harmony, or safe travels to a foreign land but rather toward earning more money, winning the lottery, or avoiding mishaps in an expensive new car.[16]

Tuvan shamanism has always had a practical side. Outsiders have been attracted to the High Church shamanic healing rituals that feature plenty of smoke and incense and, of course, drumming. The workaday world of the shaman, however, is much more prosaic: purifying apartments and new cars (for the best residual effect, some shamans advise hanging a compact disc from the rearview mirror to deflect the evil eye), finding lost items, determining whether something has been lost or stolen, or summoning the spirit of financial profit to reign over business enterprises and lottery entries.

Tuvans are very matter-of-fact about using the service of shamans, and they invite them to make house calls in the same way that Americans phone the plumber or electrician. Valentina Süzükei told about calling a shaman to help her husband find his lost keys. She believes fully in the power of certain people to perceive auras and finer energies that most people cannot see. Svetlana Bapa, Sayan's wife, recounted how she had dealt with the problem of purifying their new apartment. She is trained as a nurse and has a modern, rational view of the world. "I don't know whether or not I believe," she confided in me. "But Sayan was concerned that bad spirits may be lingering in our apartment. The family that lived here before us included a man who had been ill for two years, and finally died right in the apartment. Sayan asked me before he left for the United States to take care of the problem.

"I thought about calling a shaman to perform a purification ritual, but I was worried about disturbing the neighbors with all the noise. Not long ago someone in our building bought a new car and invited a shaman to purify it so that it wouldn't have any breakdowns or accidents. He must have beat on that drum—what do you call it, a *dünggür*—for two hours. I was worried that if I invited a shaman, he'd go on and on, and I wouldn't be able to tell him to stop when I—and the neighbors—had had enough. So I decided to go to church instead [Svetlana's mother is Russian]. I hadn't been in years, but I went and talked to the priest. I had to stand for hours while he was busy leading a service. Then I waited for him behind a young Russian with a thick gold chain around his neck, who took the priest outside to where a shiny new car was parked, and the priest blessed the car. Finally he came to me and asked whether I was a Christian, and whether I'd been baptized. 'Do you have your cross with you?' he asked. I showed it to him, and he told me that he'd come to the apartment the following week—he'd say some prayers, and hopefully, that would take care of the problem."

For Svetlana, the priest was a surrogate shaman. The choice of one or the other was not a matter of principle, but of expediency—not disturbing the neighbors. "There's a Tuvan saying," Svetlana said during our discussion. "'The poorer the people, the more shamans appear.' People are out of work. They have nothing to do, and nothing to hope for. Tuberculosis is epidemic here. People are dying from drinking industrial alcohol because it's a third the price of vodka. Families are in terrible shape from alcoholism. I saw a television program which said that these days in Tuva, if you reach the age of sixty, you're considered to be long-lived—like those people in the Caucasus who live to be a hundred by eating a lot of yogurt. So what do people who live in these conditions do? They go to the shaman."

In "Magic and Dependence," the second part of an acerbic essay about the intellectual and moral failings of contemporary India, V. S. Naipaul wrote, "Magic is an Indian need. It simplifies the world and makes it safe."[17] Naipaul's point was that such simplification is the enemy of progress, and that India will only advance to the extent that its inhabitants reject myth and ritual and embrace a Western-style modernity grounded in receptivity to thought. Indians, of course, are not alone in grappling with the tensions between ritual and rationality, and magicians are hardly the only contemporary actors who appeal to a yearning for simplicity and safety in a dangerous world. In the West, that function falls more commonly to politicians and preachers and, increasingly these days, to chimerical hybrids of the two. Americans at the beginning of the twenty-first century live in a country whose president has declared his belief in the Biblical account of creation and where, according to surveys, "many more people believe in the Virgin Birth than in Darwin's theory of evolution."[18] Naipaul's stark partition between the way of magic and the way of thought seems incompatible with both history and human nature. The intermingling of rational and irrational beliefs in the human psyche is surely universal, and the blend of magic and empiricism that infuses Tuvan neoshamanism is replicated in contemporary beliefs about healing and spirituality that range widely through class, culture, and educational background in the West no less than the East.

Tuva's neoshamans are worldly and intelligent. Lazo Mongush was a successful journalist before changing careers. Kara-ool Dopchuur-ool had been the director of a hunting cooperative. The doyen of them all, Mongush Kenin-Lopsan, is a celebrated novelist, a doctor of science graduate of Leningrad University, and, as he can never let any visitor forget, one of Tuva's "People of the Century." Like Western self-help gurus, neoshamans offer their own lives as testimony to the possibility of salvation. But salvation invariably comes at a price, both psychic and pecuniary, and if the transformation of spiritual power into commerce leaves some observers of Tuva's neoshamanism with a feeling of queasiness, there are other spirit-inspired domains of neotraditionalism in which commerce has played a lesser role. Most active among these in the realm of expressive culture is the performance of oral epic.

Slava Kuchenov, the Xakas sculptor-turned-*xaiji*, exemplifies the reemergent vitality of epic reciters as contemporary performance artists.[19] Slava, however, is a solitary revivalist as well as a neophyte in the world of Xakas epic, and his dream-induced tale of the horse-mounted hero Siber Chyltys is an epigonic facsimile of the great epic texts. By contrast, the Kyrgyz epic reciter Rysbek Jumabaev belongs to the venerable guild of the *manaschi*—a reciter of the *Manas,* whose thousandth anniversary, however dubious the dating, was celebrated in the Republic of Kyrgyzstan with great fanfare in 1995.

THE SPIRIT OF MANAS

I met Rysbek in Bishkek, Kyrgyzstan's capital, in the winter of 2003. Nurlanbek Nyshanov, whose jew's harp playing is discussed in chapter 4, had invited Rysbek to perform in a small concert at the American University. When Rysbek appeared alone on stage, his gaunt face set off by a blue kerchief knotted around short-cropped hair, and began to perform an excerpt from the *Manas* with a Dionysian ardor both thrilling and terrifying, I knew that I was in the presence of a great talent. The *Manas,* which recounts the exploits of its eponymous hero as he battles a range of foes and unites the Kyrgyz clans, was systematically transcribed by Soviet scholars from the recitation of leading *manaschis* beginning in the 1930s.[20] The longest of these transcriptions, from the recitation of Sayakbay Karalaev (1894–1972), includes some 500,000 lines of verse (by comparison, the *Mahabharata* contains around 200,000 lines and the *Iliad* around 16,000). Published transcriptions have served as a source for a new generation of younger *manaschis* to learn the epic, but Rysbek derisively dismisses such performers as "Philharmonia *manaschis*"—academicized performers tainted by the inauthenticity of learning oral poetry from written sources. Rysbek prides himself on having "received" the *Manas* rather than having read it.

"It all began when I was eleven and had a dream in which the famous *manaschi* Sayakbay recited the *Manas,*" Rysbek told me during the first of many meetings that began in Bishkek, later moved to Rysbek's austere home

Rysbek Jumabaev standing in
the courtyard of his house.
Darxan, Kyrgyzstan, 2003.

in the village of Darxan, on the south shore of Kyrgyzstan's Lake Issyq-Qul,
and following that, to the United States, where Rysbek came to perform
with Yo-Yo Ma's Silk Road Ensemble. "My father knew some episodes from
the *Manas,* and when I was four years old, Sayakbay came to my house and
blessed me so that I would become a *manaschi.* He had a strong effect on me.
I was scared of him, but I really wanted to be like him. I consider Sayakbay
my teacher, even though I didn't study with him directly."

"Why did Sayakbay choose you in particular?" I asked.

"It was a gift of God. If a person has God-given talent, he comes to the
Manas himself. People aren't taught in a formal sense. I started performing
at small gatherings when I was sixteen, and at first I performed as an amateur. Then, in 1983, I started having stomach aches. I couldn't eat, I couldn't
sleep. I went to various doctors and they gave me drugs, but nothing helped.
I had stopped reciting the *Manas* because there weren't any invitations. No
concerts, no festivals. Finally, I went to a clairvoyant who lives in Karakol—

his name is Mirbek—and asked why I had fallen into this state. Mirbek said that I had become ill because I had stopped reciting. He told me that I had to go to a *mazar* near Darxan, slaughter a sheep as an offering, spend the night there, and rededicate myself to the *Manas*."

Mazar is a word of Arabic origin that means "place of visitation." In Central Asia, *mazar*s are typically shrines to Islamic saints. There is no institutional mechanism in Islam for canonizing saints, as there is, for example, in Catholicism. A Muslim saint is not beatified by ecclesiastical authority, but elevated to sainthood by popular zeal. For Muslims, saints are people venerated and revered for their wisdom, beneficence, or miraculous acts, and *mazar*s are typically physical structures erected at or near the burial site—or alleged burial site—of a saint that serve as a locus of pilgrimage. Some *mazar*s are modest, purely local affairs, while others are grandiose and attract pilgrims from afar (for example, Mazar-i Sharif, the major city of northern Afghanistan, is built around a shrine to Ali, the son-in-law of the Prophet).

For the Kyrgyz, however, *mazar* has assumed a double meaning. In one sense, it corresponds to the conventional understanding of a physical structure marking the burial site of a saint. In another sense—what some Kyrgyz scholars have called a "natural" *mazar*—it refers to a site of spiritual power marked by a distinctive natural phenomenon: a spring or cave, a distinctive geological formation or botanical oddity, such as a grove of trees amid a landscape of barren steppe. In this second sense, *mazar* overlaps with the Tuvan term *xaiyrakan* (described in chapter 2). But whereas the concept of *xaiyrakan* is purely animistic, with its primary meaning denoting the spirit-essence of bears, the notion of "natural" *mazar* accounts for animistic beliefs within an Islamic frame of reference. For Kyrgyz, the two kinds of *mazar*s—built *mazar*s and natural *mazar*s—often coincide in one and the same physical site. Veneration of saints is thus physically linked with offerings to spirits, and this linkage is a defining feature of the syncretic Islamic-animistic practices and beliefs of many Kyrgyz.[21]

On August 17, 1983, after two months during which Rysbek said he was neither able to eat or sleep, he obeyed the oracular advice of Mirbek, and went to the *mazar* near his home in Darxan to prepare a sacrifice with the hope of recovering his health and restoring his connection with the spirit of *Manas*. The Darxan *mazar* boasts no link to a saint, but centers around an ancient poplar tree that rises from a plain of scrubby grass and bushes on the southern bank of Lake Issyq-Qul. Close by, four lesser poplars, evidently seedlings of the original tree, spread their roots, but beyond this small grove, no other trees are visible for miles in any direction. The *mazar* was protected by spirit-masters, Rysbek told me, who assumed the form of an old man named Egizbek, an old woman named Segizbek, and a young child with a camel.

"I took seven people with me on that evening in 1983," Rysbek recounted. "We slaughtered a lamb and boiled it, and for the first time in months, I ate meat and fell soundly asleep. During the night, while I slept, my companions were awakened by a tremendous whooshing noise coming from the mountains. They woke me up, and I heard it, too. I couldn't believe my ears. My companions said that it was the sound of a spirit. I don't know, it was some kind of sign from God that a road was being opened."

"After what happened at the *mazar,* did it become easier for you to recite the *Manas?*" I asked.

"Yes. Before going to the *mazar,* I had become very weak. I was living alone—my parents had both died—and after the night at the *mazar,* everything changed. It was as if I'd bumped up against something that led to an opening. Soon after that, a film crew came and filmed me. And I had more dreams in which I saw Sayakbay reciting the *Manas* in a beautiful form—one of the largest parts of the *Manas*—and in the dream, Manas's forty knights came to me. I married and had children. I had three girls, and after I started to recite, I had a son. I answered the call of God and was rewarded. I named my son Syrghak, one of the main characters in the epic.

"Until 1995, I performed at small events—my interest in the *Manas* was more an inner one—but in 1995, Kyrgyzstan celebrated a thousand years of the *Manas,* and that was the first time that I performed for a large audience.[22] I won second place in a *Manas* competition for young performers in Bishkek. It was also in 1995 that I had another strong dream, in which Sayakbay and Saghimbay (1867–1930) led me to two great *manaschis*, Shaabai Azizov (b. 1927) and Choyuke Omur-uulu (1863–1925). They grabbed me and put me on the street, as if to open the road for me. I had been working as a construction worker, a tractor driver, a herder—all the rural professions. I left these professions and became a *manaschi.* This is the profession that best suits me.

"Everything went well for a while, but then again the spirit of Manas began to grow more distant and it became difficult to recite. The stomach aches came back. I suffered for a long time, and finally, I went again to Mirbek, and in January 2001, he took me to the *mazar* of a holy man named Manjaly-*ata.* No one knows exactly when Manjaly-*ata* lived, or where he was buried, but in 1999, they celebrated 5,000 years of Manjaly-*ata.* He was an *oluya*—a person loved by God. His *mazar* is in a willow grove surrounded by clay hills on the south shore of Issyq-Qul. Willows don't grow anywhere else around that place. All you have there is scrubby plants growing out of the clay.

"Mirbek took me there, and he asked me, 'Do you feel anything special here? Do you see something, or maybe hear some kind of echo?' I didn't see anything out of the ordinary, but twice, I heard an echo coming from afar—from the mountains. It was the echo of herders on the move. There were camels, horses, old men and women. A young child was crying hard. Mirbek was testing me, to see whether I had the spirit of Manas. After I heard the echo, he said to me, 'You have something. Those herders you heard are the herders of Manas.' He told me how I should live—what I had to do. He said that I'd experience a lot of wonders—that I'd go to Europe and to America. It seemed ridiculous at the time. But look what's happened. Everything he predicted is coming true.

"It was around this time that I learned I had chronic ulcers, and the doctors told me I had to have an operation. I consulted again with Mirbek, and he said his ancestors had told him that you can be treated for ulcers by urinary therapy. You have to drink your own urine for two-and-a-half months. Mirbek told me to take the therapy and to keep reciting the *Manas,* and not to stop. I did this—I drank urine at five o'clock in the morning every day from the beginning of February to the middle of April, and the ulcers went completely away. I was completely cured. Since then, the road has been open to me. Sometimes I can't sleep all night. I hear the words of the *Manas,* the voices. And in the morning, I begin to recite. I receive information from the heavens. It's not my information. It's like a spirit that comes to me inside. A motive comes to me in a twilight state between wakefulness and sleep. Or sometimes I'll be sweeping the courtyard at home and I begin to recite. I cry out, and people gather. Now I've started to take a piece of paper and write down the information when it comes to me. I have several notebooks like that. But the information comes at such a fast tempo that I'm not able to write it all down."

I asked Rysbek, "Now that you have a family to support, how do you balance family responsibilities with being a *manaschi?*"

"I have this talent, but I don't have any material things. I just don't seem to be very good at earning money," Rysbek lamented. "It's hard for my children—there was a time when they wanted milk and I didn't have enough money to get it for them. I'd like to buy a cow—a dairy cow costs around three hundred dollars. I hope we'll be able to afford it during the next year. But I have to keep myself clean. I can't steal or lie, because I'll be punished. I have to be grateful for this richness that's completely separate from the material world. The *Manas* is given only to certain people. People who are connected to *Manas* have a patron-protector [*koldolchuu*]. It can be a dead ancestor, or one of the companions of *Manas,* or some spirit. But the patron-protector only takes care of people who are clean."[23]

Rysbek had shared these thoughts as we sipped tea in the simple guest-room of his house in Darxan, a village of 1,500 families who keep animals and coax small crops of potatoes from the arid plain south of Lake Issyq-Qul. I had come to Darxan not only to speak with Rysbek but also to make a video recording of his *Manas* recitation at the nearby *mazar*, where, in 1983, he had renewed his devotion to the spirit of Manas. Rysbek had invited me to visit Darxan in May 2003 during a meeting in Bishkek, and we had set a date for early September, when I was scheduled to be back in Kyrgyzstan. But in mid-summer, a cruel event had taken place at the Darxan *mazar*. When I showed up in Darxan in September, Rysbek explained what had happened.

"Around a year ago, a new mosque was built in Darxan with help from Saudi Arabia," said Rysbek. "The Saudis want the Kyrgyz to become more reli-gious. They train religious teachers and build mosques, but in Darxan almost no one goes to that mosque. It's a strange thing about the Kyrgyz—you can't really say that we're Muslims. But then again, you can't really say that we're not Muslims. Anyway, one night, some young people from the mosque came to the *mazar* and cut down most of the old poplar tree. And they cut down the four smaller poplar trees next to it. In the mosque, they had learned that God is one, and that it was blasphemous to pray to spirits. They got the idea to destroy this tree, where people came to make offerings and tie strips of cloth [*chüpürök*]. They came at night and sawed most of it down, and hauled away the pieces. When I heard about it, I cried."

"Are you absolutely sure that it was people from the mosque?" I asked Rysbek.

"Absolutely. It was a group of young people. It's known who they were."

Nurlanbek Nyshanov, who had accompanied me to Darxan, chimed in, "People think of nomads as barbarians, but it's my generation of village and city people who are the barbarians. What they have done to nature and the natural world is indescribable. The old people who lived in yurts whom I knew as a kid—they were very soft, and fine. They had a wonderful relation-ship with children. When it was forty degrees below zero, they'd go to their horses to take care of them at night. Respect for nature was a crucial part of their worldview. For example, I wasn't allowed to cut living trees. We only used wood from fallen trees, even if it meant bringing it from far away."

Rysbek had a pained look as we approached the *mazar* with my video camera. "It was once such a beautiful tree, and now look at it." The poplar's branchless trunk rose bleakly about fifteen feet out of the ground and ended abruptly in a small clump of leaves. Rysbek spread a blanket on the ground beneath the tree and I set up my video camera and tape recorder.

"What section of the *Manas* are you going to recite?" I asked Rysbek.

"I don't know yet. I have to prepare myself to perform. If people tell me,

'You have to perform this place or that place,' nothing will happen. I need freedom to choose the place. Depending on the listeners, I have a sense of which way to go with the performance."

In the past, Rysbek told me, the majority of *manaschis* recited without music. But there were some who accompanied themselves on the *qyl qiyak,* the two-string upright fiddle that is similar to the Kazakh *qyl-qobyz.*[24] Rysbek does not play an instrument in order to leave his hands free for gestural miming. For him, gesture is a central part of performing the *Manas.* There are conventional gestures, for example, knocking hands together to symbolize the bow and arrow, but Rysbek has added many gestures of his own.

As I readied my equipment, Rysbek assumed a theatrical pose, his arms outstretched to the side, his face peering skyward, as if poised to download the *Manas* text from a heavenly source. After a quarter-minute of silent gesticulating, he began to recite. The section of the *Manas* he had chosen is the story of Almambet, the son of a Chinese ruler who meets Kökchö, a companion of Manas. After hearing about the feats of the Kyrgyz hero, Almambet converts to Islam and himself becomes a companion of Manas. Transcribed below is the excerpt of the *Manas* that Rysbek recited at the *mazar.*

Rysbek Jumabaev performs an excerpt from the Kyrgyz epic, *Manas* (Video File, track 19).

The Story of Almambet	**Almambettin oquyiasy**
From Qoqand, where a big battle was in full swing,	*Baatyr kayinap jatqan Qoqondon*
Only two of us managed to escape,	*Oshondon ekööbüz gana arang qachyp qutulup,*
Oh, fickle fate!	*Atangdyn görü dünüyiö.*
(lit., "world like your father's grave")	
Crossing rounded mountains,	*Tompoyigon gana toonu ashyp*
Crossing icy ridges,	*Tongup jatqan qoonu ashyp*
Crossing countless places,	*Ächen böksö jer ashyp*
Fording a cool desert,	*Muzdagyraaq chöl kechip*
Fording countless rivers and waters,	*Ächen dayira suu kechip*
Oh fickle fate!	*Atangdyn görü dünüyiö.*
I skirted the land of Ak Talaa.*	*Men Ak talaa boyiloyi ashypmyn.*
When I had gone further,	*Aryragyraaq ashkanda*
Oh, fickle fate!	*Atangdyn görü dünüyiö.*
Accompanied by Er Majit,**	*Ärchitkenim Är Majit*
Becoming lost, I went as far as Altai,	*Men Altayiga kettim adashyp*
And while I was wandering around,	*Men adashyp jürgöndö*

* Ak Talaa: a valley in Naryn Region, near China.
** "Er" means "courageous," thus "courageous Majit."

I turned [my horse] Sarala's head,	Saralang oozun burganda
Oh, fickle fate!	Atangdyn görü dünüyiö.
[And found myself among the people] of that Sary-Arka*	Bayiagy Sary-Arqany jerdegen
Who were fought against but never beaten,	Salyshyp ushu adam jengbegen
Whose wives are praised like young girls,	Ayialyn qyzdai maktagan
Whose barley is husked white like stone,	Taruusun tashtayi aktagan
Whose grain is sown in autumn,	Ashtygyn küzdö ayidagan
Whose forefathers are from the Alash [clan],	Tüp atasy Alashtan
Whose yurt frames are made from wood.	Keregesi jygachtan.
Aidarhan's Kökchö,	Ayidarqandyn kökchösü
Shin of blue boots,	Kök ötüktün ökchösü
The friend of the very Alooqe,	Oshol Alooqengdin ökchösü
At that moment I came across him	Oshondo kelip tush boldum
In the riverbed running through Sary-Arka.	Sary-Arqanyn sayiynda.
In the broad steppe	Bayagy tüzdük talaada
It was lying stretched out,	Oshondo jatkan äken jayikalyp
As you have seen yourself, old man,	Özüng körgön jaryqtyq
The very place Sary Arka!	Oshol kezde Sary-Arka.
Oh, fickle fate!	Atangdyn görü dünüyiö,
And then you'll see, you'll glimpse	Myna oshondo qarasang
What a commotion he raised,	Milte tartyp, duu kylyp
Shooting his rifle, making noise,	Ayiabagan chuu qylyp
Sixty tigers, a hundred bears	Altymysh jolbors, jüz ayiuu
He managed to shoot.	Atyp alyp aldyryp.
The very Er Kökchö whom you saw	Özüng görgön Är kökchö
Took six strong men and forty knights	Alty balban, qyrk choro
Along with him as company.	Janyna joldosh alyptyr
The very Er Kökchö whom you saw	Özüng körgön är Kökchö
Came hunting,	Oshondong uuga kelip qalyptyr
Making such a commotion	Ayiabagan duu kylyp
That echoed along the open steppe.	Ayi-talaany jangyrtyp
Er Kökchö, khan of the Kazakhs	Qazaqtyng qanyng Är kökchö
Was on the hunt then,	Oshondo uuda jürgön kezi äken
And it was then that I myself,	Osho kezde men özüm
Oh, fickle fate!	Atangdyn görü dünüyiö.
Saw the khan of the Kazakhs,	Qazaqtyn qany Kökchönü
Saw Er Kökchö.	Är Kökchönü körgöndö.
And Er Majit was with me,	Ärchitkenim Är Majit
I turned [my horse] Sarala's head.	Saralang oozun burgamyn
On my broad back was a rifle.	Ayi dalyda syr barang
I grabbed my rifle,	Syr barang alyp turgamyn
And then I myself	Myna oshondong men özüm
scratched and put an ember [in my rifle],	Kyryp iyiip, chok koyiup

* Sary-Arka: the steppes of present-day Kazakhstan.

Filling its barrel with a bullet.	*Miltesine ok koyiup.*
Oh, fickle fate!	*Atangdyn görü dünüyiö.*
At the deer from the nearest mountains	*Budurudagy bugunu*
I shot again and again	*Atkylap osho kezde men özüm*
And killed a countless number of deer	*Oshondo bugunu atyp jayinattym*
And tigers on the hills.	*Adyrdagy sherlerdi.*
It was then that I myself	*Oshol kezde men özüm*
Was shooting and going on a rampage,	*Atkylap shorun qayinattym*
Oh, fickle fate!	*Atangdyn görü dünüyiö.*
All the bears that I shot	*Atkan ayiuu barysyn*
I packed and bound up for Er Kökchö.	*Är kökchögö bayilattym*
Seeing such feats of mine,	*Bul ärdigim görgöndö*
Ayidarqan's Kökchö,	*Ayidarqandyn kökchösü*
Shin of blue boots,	*Kök ötüktün ökchösü*
Began his words from afar,	*Qyngayigan sözdön bashtady*
And then the words he wanted to say	*Oshondo ayita turgan sözdörün*
He threw in front of us,	*Ortogo qoyiup, tashtady*
Oh, fickle fate!	*Atangdyn görü dünüyiö.*
Leave your Kalmyks	*Sen qalmagyngan kayit dedi*
And accept the Muslim faith.	*Bul musulman dinge kir dedi*
And at that time this very Kökchö	*Osho kezde al Kökchö*
If you ask about him,	*Kökchönün jayiyn surasang*
Oh, fickle fate!	*Atangdyn körü dünüyiö!*
The one who finishes the race alone,	*Bu jeke chygat jaryshtan*
Who has very good eyesight,	*Közü göröt alystan*
If you ask about Kökchö's situation,	*Bu kökchönün jaiyn surasang*
Shin of blue boots,	*Kök ötüktün ökchösü*
Aydarqan's Kökchö,	*Ayidarqandyn Kökchösü*
Quoting a lot from the *Sharī ʾa*,	*Shariattan göp süyilöp*
He spoke like a Mullah.	*Moldolugu bar äken*
He could speak like a charm,	*Jangylbagan jez tangdayi*
He was like an orator,	*Munun chechendigi bar äken*
That uncle of yours,	*Al akengdin jayiy osho*
When I came to Kökchö	*Men Kökchögö kelgende*
And served him six years,	*Alty jyl qyzmat kylganda*
Oh, fickle fate!	*Atangdyn görü dünüyiö.*
So when I came to Kökchö	*Osho men Kökchögö kelgende*
I covered his *tuurduq** with fat	*Tuurdugun mayi qyldym*
To let everyone know that Kökchö	*Tyshta uqanga Kökchönü*
Became khan of many places.	*Tush-tush jerge Qan qyldym.*

* *tuurduq*: the outer felt covering of a yurt. To cover the *tuurduq* with fat means to enrich the owner of the yurt.

A day after performing the *Manas* for me beneath the sawed-off poplar tree near Darxan, Rysbek performed again at the *mazar* of Manjaly-*ata*, where he had his second reinspiration in 1999. As a *mazar* linked both to the veneration of a saintly person and to nature spirits manifested in the botanical oddity of the lone willow grove, Manjaly was not in danger of the kind of desecration that had befallen the poplar trees at Darxan. On the contrary, the site was all set up for pilgrims: to the side of the willow grove a lean-to sheltered fire pits where sacrificed animals were prepared, and directly under the willows was an elevated wooden platform where visitors spread out their festive meals. One such meal of boiled mutton was being laid out as Rysbek and I, along with our traveling companions Nurlanbek and Raziya, and our driver, Volodya, approached the willow grove. The five of us were warmly welcomed to join the feast by complete strangers—an extended family that had come to give thanks for the birth of a new child after the parents, long unable to conceive, had visited the *mazar* and prayed to have children.

Rysbek had been solicitous of my interest in his *Manas* performance, and he was generous in recounting his life story and performing innumerable retakes of the recitation necessitated by my novice videography skills. "I can feel people's auras," Rysbek told me as we sat in the lobby of the Hyatt Regency Hotel in Bishkek near the end of one of my visits. American servicemen from the nearby airbase lolled at the bar while we sat at a small table talking about spirits, visions, and a thousand-year-old epic. "Sometimes I can feel the future, and I can feel right away whether a person who's standing next to me is a good person or a bad person. You're a good person," Rysbek assured me.

Rysbek's sunny assessment was flattering, but was it ingenuous, ironic, or mildly calculating? I could not tell, and that made me uncomfortable. I wanted Rysbek's respect, not his obeisance. And yet, as much as I would have done anything to change it, our relationship was an asymmetrical one. I lived in a wealthy country, Rysbek in a poor one. I came to Kyrgyzstan representing not only myself, but organizations that offered potentially life-changing opportunities to performers like Rysbek. Rysbek, by contrast, was a loner; or, if one wanted to extend him the benefit of the doubt, his accomplices were a gaggle of mercurial spirits as notable for their absence as for their appearance. I had asked Rysbek to make the long trip from Darxan to Bishkek not only to seek his help with my book manuscript but also to extend an invitation from cellist Yo-Yo Ma to come to the United States, together with Nurlanbek Nyshanov, to participate in an innovative musical residency organized by the Silk Road Project, the transnational arts initiative that Ma founded and directs.

Rysbek and Nurlanbek had performed briefly during a reception following a Silk Road Project concert in Bishkek the previous spring, and Yo-Yo Ma and his fellow musicians had been powerfully moved by the performance. The invitation to join the musical residency program—a two-week-long series of gallery performances and cross-cultural, improvisatory music-making inspired by exhibition objects at the Peabody Essex Museum in Salem, Massachusetts—had grown out of that brief contact. If the Peabody Essex residency went well, other performance opportunities around the world were sure to follow (see plate 30).

Listening to my description of the residency program, Rysbek could contain neither his excitement nor his conviction that the journey to the United States had been foreordained, both by Mirbek, the clairvoyant who had advised him to visit the *mazars*, and by his dreams. "I dreamed that I would come to the United States and recite the *Manas*," Rysbek said triumphantly, "and everything that I dreamed has come true!" But how would performing in the West affect Rysbek? And how would it affect the tradition of the *Manas* itself? Would Rysbek turn into a neo-*manaschi* version of the neoshamans in Tuva whose fawning to foreigners had drawn the ire of Kara-ool Dopchuur-ool? Or worse, a Kyrgyz variant of the Tuvan throat-singers whose immersion in the world music marketplace had fractured their spiritual equilibrium and sent them rocketing toward alcoholism and, in too many cases, an early death? (Indeed, several months after the Silk Road Project residency program, Rysbek's friend, Nurlanbek, complained to me that Rysbek was suffering from "star disease." As this book goes to press, Rysbek had recently completed performances of *Manas at* Carnegie Hall and at the London Coliseum, among other venues in the West. He had agreed to the Carnegie Hall event reluctantly, however, because it took place the same weekend as a *manaschi* contest in Kyrgyzstan that he had long planned to enter.)

The Silk Road Project was dedicated to reinvigorating cultural exchange, and to the belief that artistic innovation and imagination are nourished by the cross-cultural circulation of ideas, technologies, and fashions. There was no question that putting Rysbek and his exceptional artistic gift into wider circulation would enrich the imagination of artists and audiences in other locales. But beyond assuring Rysbek the purchase of his much-wanted dairy cow, what would the swirl of cross-cultural music-making contribute to his own tradition? Would Manas, the ancient hero who vanquished countless enemies, fall victim to the marketplace's voracious appetite for new talent, turning it into entertainment "product" and "content"? Or might fresh impressions spur Rysbek, as well as other tradition-bearers, to search for the roots of artistic evolution within their own expressive culture, and in so doing, challenge convention and break taboos?

WOMEN ARE NOT SUPPOSED TO DO THIS

One enduring convention in the expressive culture of the Altai region concerns the gendering of performance. For example, while women commonly perform a variety of vocal genres, play jew's harps and plucked zithers like the *chatxan* and *yatga,* excel at strummed lutes like *komuz* and *dombra,* and, more rarely, play fiddles such as the *igil* and *qyl qiyak,* epic performance and throat-singing in all their diverse forms are overwhelmingly dominated by men. During my first visit to Tuva in 1987, I had naively asked a male throat-singer why women did not throat-sing, and I can still visualize the smirk on his face as he pronounced the answer: "Because throat-singing makes women barren!" He said those words with an air of incredulity at my ignorance.

The notion that throat-singing causes infertility in women was not the only male-inspired canard about *xöömei* and gender. Another common male riff was that the manipulation of facial muscles involved in throat-singing contorts a woman's face and spoils her beauty. Underlying these explanations, however, was a more basic objection that rested on grounds of unnaturalness. "Making those kinds of low guttural sounds—women are not supposed to do this," one old singer told me solemnly. "It's embarrassing, and if women don't have enough sense not to do it, then their husbands ought to forbid them. If their husbands won't forbid them, then there ought to be a law against women throat-singing in public."

None of the invective against female throat-singers deterred Choduraa Tumat, an energetic Tuvan woman with long braided hair and delicate features, who leads the all-female ensemble Tyva Kyzy—"Daughters of Tuva" (see plate 31). Choduraa and her fellow band members, Ailangmaa Damyrang, Ailang Ondar, and Shoraana Kuular, were all born in the mid-1970s and attended the High School of Arts in Kyzyl, where they met and started to make music together. During a conversation in summer 2003, Choduraa recalled the group's early years. "It was around 1997 and we were all working in different places in Kyzyl. I was working in a teacher's college, Ailangmaa and Ailang were working in a music school, and we started to think about participating in the Xöömei Symposium that was to take place in 1998. We thought it would be a good idea to create a women's ensemble. There were women who had been soloists such as Valentina Chuldum and Shanchalai Oorzhak, but never an entire group consisting of women.

"In March 1998 we met for the first time. We met a second time in June, three weeks before the symposium. We were seven then, and wanted to find a name. Konushtar-ool [Oorzhak—a famous throat-singer who died in 1993] had dreamed about starting an ensemble called Tyva Kyzy, and we chose that name. Konushtar-ool taught *xöömei* in the High School of Arts for a brief period. He started in September 1992, and in January he got sick and died. He was the only one among men who supported the idea of a women's ensemble. He was very wise. With regard to performing *xöömei*, he looked at women and men as equals. Still, Ailangmaa and Shanchalai were the only girls at the school who sang *xöömei*."

"My first lesson with Konushtar-ool was in a park," Ailangmaa added. "He wanted to teach singing in a place where there was nature, which was perfect for me, because I was shy and didn't want to sing in front of other people. I had learned a little *kargyraa* from listening to my grandfather. I didn't even know it was throat-singing. I just sang that way because I liked it. I didn't know that I could produce those sounds. The first time I sang for Konushtar-ool, I sang with my back to him because I was too shy to face him."

Choduraa continued her account of the group's history. "In 1999, we made our first trip out of Russia, to the Gdansk Festival in Poland, and in 2000, we went to Osaka and Tokyo. The next year we went to Finland, and then to Berlin and Switzerland. In all these places, we were received with admiration and surprise. On our first trip to Poland, we didn't know that there would also be a male ensemble from Tuva at the Gdansk Festival—we'd arrived a little late, and one of the artists from that ensemble had already told the audience that in Tuva, women weren't allowed to sing *xöömei*.

"It wasn't until 2002 that we gave our first solo concert in Kyzyl. It was in a theater with 640 seats, and more than half of them were filled. One of the newspaper reviewers interviewed an old man who said, 'Why did I come to this concert? Girls are not supposed to do this.' But most of the reviews were positive. Some people came to the concert because they didn't believe that women could sing *xöömei* and wanted to see for themselves. Last year we were hired by five or six candidates running for seats in the Parliament to go on the road with them and play music after they gave speeches. There are always some men in the audience who object to what we do, and sometimes we're uncomfortable about performing. But the main thing is, we don't have any fear before the spirits."

"Which spirits?" I asked Choduraa.

"Not long ago I went to my homeland—the place where my grandparents used to herd—and sang there so that the spirits of my homeland would always defend me. I went to the River Xemchik and stood on the bank of the river and sang *xöömei,* and played the *igil*. It's normal when you sing by a river and make an offering. The place where my family herded is called Xür Taiga. It's higher even than Kyzyl Taiga, and I went up there and sang without any fear of spirits. When my brother died, I thought that it might have been because of my throat-singing. We invited a shaman on the seventh day and on the forty-ninth day after his death, but the shaman didn't say anything about my singing. There have been no bad results from it. The spirit of the apartment where we rehearse should be happy that we're singing, and should listen to this music."

The members of Tyva Kyzy were eager to have me video a performance. They were searching for a new manager, having fired their previous one because they weren't getting enough invitations to perform abroad. In return for filming rights, I agreed to make the video available to whomever they asked me to send it to, and Choduraa and I exchanged e-mail addresses. The video filming was done inside a yurt set up in a tourist camp a little north of Kyzyl. In addition to a *kojamyk*—a light-hearted song that included different techniques of throat-singing—Tyva Kyzy sang a magnificent lullaby that featured dark, luxuriant vocal harmonies in a conventional singing voice, but no throat-singing.

Trying to shed all preconceptions about the propriety of women performing throat-singing, I still found that the lullaby suited Tyva Kyzy far better than the *kojamyk* saturated with throat-singing. Such a judgment, however, is purely a matter of taste. Is there anything ultimately more "natural" about men singing reinforced harmonics than women? The answer has to be no. Moreover, in at least one other example of a traditional musical style centered around the use of reinforced harmonics—the *umngqokolo* technique of the Xhosa people of eastern South Africa—the singers are exclusively women and girls.[25]

The ensemble Tyva Kyzy performs a *kojamyk* and a lullaby whose texts are transcribed below (Video Files, tracks 20 and 21).

Kojamyk: "Setkilimden Sergek Yr-Dyr"

My *sygyt* carries a light wind	*Sygydymga ooi syrynnaly eei*
From my soul comes a cheerful song	*Setkilimden ooi sergek yr-dyr eei*
As soon as I begin to sing *borbangnadyr*	*Borbangymga oi bodu kelir ei*
My melody becomes a beautiful song.	*Ayan yrlyg oi ayalgam-dyr ei.*
Like a lullaby for my beloved	*Xöömeiimge oi xongnun chazaan ei*
My *xöömei* raises his spirits	*Xööküiümnüng oi öpeii-dir, ei*
From the cradle, my talent was	*Kargyraamga chazalgham-dyr, ei*
To raise my spirits with *kargyraa*.	*Kavailyymdan, oi chayaalgam-dyr, ei.*

"Lullaby: Öpei Yry"

I'm rocking you, my sweet little jumper	*Uvailaiang ovai opang saryym ovai opeilengim ovai*
My son, the jumper, my sweetie that I'm rocking	*Uvai oglum xopang saryym opeilengim ovai*
The mother's youngest son	*Iezining xeimer oglu*
Without shoes, what will he wear?	*Idii-le chok chünü keder?*
In two beautiful trunks	*Iyi kyzyl aptarada*
Is there leather with which to sew shoes?	*Idik kylyr bylgaar bar be?*
Öpei, öpei, öpei, my little one	*Öpei, öpei, öpei sarrym*
Please fall asleep	*Uduy berem ökpejigim*
So that I can finish what I'm doing	*Kylyr ijim doozup alyin*
Please fall asleep, my youngest son	*Udui berem xeimer oglum*
Öpei, öpei ooi öpei, my little one	*Öpei öpei ooi öpei saryym eei*
Look at how the moon is shining	*Örü körem aining chyryyn*
The sun will shine even more brightly	*Oon artyk xününg chyryy*
My son, it will come to you tomorrow	*Oglum sengee erten kelir*
The beautiful house that your father built	*Achang tutkan charash tuduun*
You will widen and develop	*Algydar sen xögjüder sen*
Let your mother and her lullaby	*Avangnyng meeng öpei yrym*
Be a gift for your peace and rest.	*Amyr dyshtyng belee bolzun.*

During travels around the Altai region in the summer of 2000, I met another musician, Raisa Modorova (b. 1967), who, like the members of Tyva Kyzy, had challenged the gender taboos embedded in traditional expressive culture. Raisa lived in Gorno-Altaisk, the capital of the Altai Republic, which borders Tuva on the west, but is accessible from Tuva only by means of jeep tracks that twist through high mountain passes along the remote boundary between the two republics (the route taken by our Trans-Altai Research Group in summer 2000). Access to the Altai Republic—not to be confused with the Altai Krai, a separate territory of the Russian Federation —is much easier from the north, where a good road links Gorno-Altaisk with the Russian cities of Biysk, Barnaul, and Novosibirsk. The proximity of Altai to Novosibirsk, one of southern Siberia's main transportation hubs, has produced a thriving tourism industry.

Altai has much the same image among urban Russians as does New Mexico among Americans: a land of spectacular natural beauty infused with the mysteries of native religion and archaic culture. The Russian-American painter, adventurer, and spiritualist Nicholas Roerich published a rapturous account of a visit to Altai in 1926 that has become scripture for a new generation of Russian artists, trekkers, and seekers who travel there to camp in the fresh alpine air, commune with nature, and patronize Altai's rich assortment

Raisa Modorova plays the *topshuur* near the bank of the Katyn River outside Gorno-Altaisk. Altai Republic, 2000.

of native healers and religious prophets.[26] Russian Orthodox schismatics, devotees of shamans, Mongolian Buddhists, and members of hybrid religious movements such as Tengrianism and White Faith (*Ak Jang*) or Burkhanism, as it has been called by Russian scholars, all thrive among the Republic of Altai's population of around 200,000.[27]

Like many present-day neotraditionalists, Raisa Modorova returned to her cultural roots only after formal study of a European art form—in her case, opera, which she studied in Moscow and Saint Petersburg. Later she began writing pop songs and performed with an *estrada* ensemble in Gorno-Altaisk. In 1995, she had a dream in which she saw herself playing the *topshuur* and singing *kai*—the guttural vocal style used to perform oral poetry. "That dream was a signal to me to order a *topshuur*. I'd wanted to sing *kai* for a long time, and finally I decided to go ahead and do it. I learned to play the *topshuur,* and went to a festival in Almaty, Kazakhstan, where I sang three songs with *kai*. People responded well. After that, I started to sing publicly, but not with courage. People are just starting to react to what I do. They can't decide whether it's good or bad. Old people say that Altai is too sacred a place for women to sing *kai*—they say that it will be the end of Altai. It's hard being the only woman who does it here."

Raisa agreed to perform her music for my tape recorder and Dutch colleague Mark van Tongeren's video camera, and after long discussion about an appropriate location for the recording session, Raisa finally suggested a spot on the bank of the Katun River a little south of Gorno-Altaisk. It was apparent, though, that she had reservations about her choice.

"What's the matter?" I asked. "Are you concerned about noise from the road, or from sunbathers?"

"No, I'm afraid that there may be bad consequences if I sing so close to the river. The spirit-master of the Katun is very powerful, and may be displeased by a woman singing *kai*."

"We can go somewhere else if you'd like," I told Raisa.

She thought for a moment, then shook her head. "No, let's stay here. I believe in what I'm doing. I think the spirits will support me." Raisa tuned up her *topshuur* and, in a transformation that seemed truly shamanic, launched into a performance of a praise-song, "I Ask Permission of My Altai" (*Altaiymnang surap*), using the *kai* technique. The text is transliterated and translated below.

Raisa Modorova performs an Altai praise-song, accompanying herself on the *topshuur* (Video File, track 22).

I praise the river which flows in my Altai,	*Altaiymnyi ichindede burlap iatkan suularyna*
And ask a blessing from the mountains that stretch out around me,	*Alkysh byxtan aidyp iadym tuularynaa köstöp iadym*
Forgive me for the sins I have committed.	*Iamanymdy tashtazyn dep, bui, bui, bui, bui*
I praise the trees so that their tops will reach toward the sky,	*Örö özüp chykkan taldaryna agash tajynn mürgüp iadym*
I want to reveal something to them that comes from my heart.	*Aidagan sözimdi aidyp alym aidy-kuunai kuudim iadym, bui, bui, bui, bui, bui, bui*
I bow down to my blue sky,	*Kök bütken bu tengerimge*
I beg it to excuse the mistakes that people make in this life.	*Aldyma men mürgüp iadym kilinchek albatyn bu buruzym*
The tastiest offerings of the Altai lie before me,	*Kök changkyrga aidyn iadym alama shikir aldymaiadyp iady*
To them I bow down.	*Bash bolzyn, oi, oi*
To the rivers that flow through the valleys,	*Agyp iatkan suularyna*
To the voice of the cuckoo bird in the mountains,	*Küüktii üni bu aldyna*
I offer a prayer and begin to sing my *kai*.	*Mürgüp iadym bash bolzynda, kojoi kaiym torgul iadym.*

Raisa seemed to reassure herself through her performance. "Some people say that women aren't supposed to do this," she said, repeating the mantra of male authority that she felt compelled to challenge. "But I have to do what works for *me*. It doesn't matter whether you're a man or a woman. What's important is to believe in the spirits of these rivers and springs and mountains, to go to the springs and drink pure water, and to fill your *kai* with that purity so the spirits accept your offering."

Raisa's offering appears to have been accepted. Not only did no harm come to her from our recording session, but not long afterward, she remarried and bore a child.

THE ONDAR PHENOMENON

Unlike Raisa Modorova, who seemed more concerned about how her *kai* would be received among the spirits than about its reception among her fellow Altaians, Tuvan throat-singer Kongar-ool Ondar reveled in the attention of human listeners—and the more, the better. At least that was how I remembered Ondar, as he had become known in the West, in the tradition of one-name pop stars like Prince, Madonna, and Bjork. I had seen little of him since 1993, when Ondar—the last-minute replacement for Gennadi Tumat—traveled to the United States with Kaigal-ool Xovalyg and Tolya Kuular to throat-sing on horseback in the Rose Bowl Parade.

When I ran into Ondar on Kochetova Street just after arriving in Kyzyl in summer 2003, he looked less fierce than the pugnacious cowboy of my memory, his erstwhile *kejege*—the shaved crown *cum* braided ponytail that is the traditional coiffure of Tuvan men—replaced by a combed-over receding hairline (see plate 32). Ondar had adopted the gracious, jaunty persona of a celebrity, which indeed he was after a decade of highly publicized antics. Ondar carried the Olympic torch in a segment of the cross-country marathon preceding the 1996 Atlanta summer games, advertised Oldsmobiles, made the rounds of television talk shows, and flew from Tuva to New York for a long weekend to promote digital recording studio mixing consoles for AT&T ("Singing two notes at once may not be revolutionary for the people of South Siberia, but a system that can be analog and digital at the same time could revolutionize New York, Nashville, London, and L.A.," read the promo brochure). Later, Ondar became known as costar of the highly successful documentary film *Genghis Blues* and also as a recording artist whose Warner Brothers Records compact disc, *Back Tuva Future,* with Willie Nelson and Randy Scruggs, was included by the *New York Post* in its 1999 list of the year's ten best CDs. Ondar's fame in the West reverberated strongly in Tuva, where he was elected a deputy in the Parliament and founded a respected program in traditional music at the High School of Arts. There, a classroom houses Ondar memorabilia, a collection of musical instruments he commissioned, and a floor-to-ceiling hourglass fashioned from boughs of willow wood that symbolizes the link between past and future—a metaphor for tradition in Ondar's understanding.

More than any other Tuvan, Kongar-ool Ondar has emplanted throat-singing in the sphere of American popular culture, and his efforts have drawn both plaudits and groans from fellow throat-singers. Some regard his work as the purest of kitsch. Others accept it as a necessary evil—the price a small Siberian culture has to pay for a stake in the global musical marketplace. And still others view Ondar as an imaginative neotraditionalist who has harnessed the power of popular culture to preserve an endangered tradition. During Ondar's years of throat-singing celebrity, our paths had rarely crossed. Now I wanted to hear how Ondar himself assessed what he had contributed to Tuvan music by bringing it so colorfully—or, depending on one's point of view, kitschfully—to the West.

"It's no secret that when you came to Tuva the first time [in 1987], the reason that we didn't meet was that I was in a camp," Ondar said forthrightly as we sat in his memorabilia-filled classroom-museum in Kyzyl's High School of Arts. "I had been in a fight and my father's friend was the prosecutor of Bai-Taiga Region. He promised to get me off if I admitted my guilt, but he didn't keep his promise, and I was convicted. I spent four years and seven days in jail. After that, I was paroled, but had to work in a brick factory where they employed only ex-convicts.

"I never knew my father, and was raised by my grandparents. During the summers, I'd go to stay with my grandfather where he was herding. In the evenings, they'd drink a little and start singing, and they'd go all night. If you asked my grandfather to sing when he was sober, he'd never do it. He always drank, and then in the morning, he'd go to work. I grew up with those sounds in my ears, and when I was in ninth grade, I began singing myself.

"I really wanted to be a musician, and after I was freed from prison, I went to see Gennadi Tumat [the founder of the Tuva Ensemble]. Tumat talked about how the Sayan Ensemble received invitations to go abroad mainly because of throat-singing, but the throat-singers in the group got the lowest pay and performed the fewest numbers. Tumat said that people called them 'street singers' because they didn't have diplomas. During the show, it was the ballet dancers with diplomas who performed the most. Tumat described how the Sayan Ensemble had gone to Japan and been invited out to dinner, and he had started to eat a napkin, and been laughed at. After that Tumat had thought, 'Let's start our own ensemble. We don't need a tour bus, we don't need anything.' He said to me, 'If you join us, we'll create an ensemble that sings like our ancestors. It will be as if we're sitting around a campfire and singing with one another.' So we started dreaming of having our own independent ensemble. It was just the beginning of the times when we could do that. Zoya Kyrgys put me on a halftime salary at the High School of Arts, and we started to put a repertory together. Zoya suggested that we chant a Buddhist prayer, and she found a Tibetan sacred text. I remembered a few couplets of the song 'Beijing,' about the caravan drivers who traveled from Tuva to China, and we tried to find someone who knew more of the couplets. We made different kinds of jew's harps. There was a shaman who came out on stage while we changed our costumes. That was the beginning of the Tuva Ensemble.

"When we toured in Tuva, old people would cry when they heard our songs, which reminded them of their youth. And they'd say, 'You forgot this couplet or that couplet.' They gave us words, and they said, 'You have to dress in national clothes,' and they gave us their boots and their robes, and their trunks to keep them in. When we had toured for the second or third time, there were already little kids who were imitating us. Then we went to Holland, Belgium, Germany, and I thought, if we're going to have professional throat-singers, they should really be professionals. So in 1992 I left the ensemble and started a program at this school. I've worked here for eleven years. It's been hard, because there's no textbook. The school requires solfeggio—European solfeggio—and the students read notation. They can do arranging; there's a national orchestra and they all play in that orchestra. The school also teaches piano, but we don't have any results with piano students. They study for eleven years and at the end, there's nothing. It's not that the teachers are bad, but the piano is a European instrument. With *xöömei*, it's different. We have real results."

"If you believe so strongly that Tuvan kids should focus on their own traditions, why have you devoted so much of your time to crossover and fusion projects with Western artists?" I asked.

"There are people who like to hear folklore and there are people who like to hear pop. You can't leave those pop listeners out of the picture. If I don't do music that interests them, someone else will. We need time to get to the stage of blues, rock, jazz, but we're not going to lag behind the civilized world."

Ondar's reasoning was not unsound. It was the same reasoning I had used in agreeing to allow Smithsonian Folkways to license throat-singing for the Swedish cheese snack commercial. I had argued that the appropria-

Ayan-ool Sam, a student
of Kongar-ool Ondar, sports
a traditional Tuvan haircut
(*kejege*) popular among
younger musicians. Kyzyl,
2003.

tion of Tuvan music by Western musicians and media companies is ethically
neutral and in any event, unstoppable; that the most one could do was to
ensure that musical sacrilege was avoided, and that Tuvan musicians were
fairly compensated. Ondar, however, had been more than an accomplice
in a licensing deal. He had actively sought opportunities to commercialize
Tuvan music in forms that radically decontextualized and repackaged it as
an attention-grabbing special effect. Was there really a musical or cultural
point to Ondar's collaboration with Willie Nelson in "Where Has My Country Gone? (Kongurei)" on *Back Tuva Future*? Did it open up new vistas for
Tuvan music? Did dressing up throat-singing in the safe and familiar style
of a musical brand name like country and western offer a way to attract new
listeners who would subsequently become curious about Tuvan music on its
own terms? This, after all, was one of the bedrock beliefs of the world music
industry—an end-justifies-the-means argument that has led many artists to

submit to the caprice of producers who promise fame and fortune with the addition of synthesizers, drum machines, bass guitars, and plenty of digital reverb. Musicians, for their part, have typically been only too eager to lard up their recordings with extra effects in search of larger audiences and more touring opportunities.

I had discussed these issues with the members of Huun-Huur-Tu and had been blunt about my reservations concerning some of their recent fusion and crossover projects. These discussions had been lively and constructive, and for my part, I had come to understand that in the case of Huun-Huur-Tu, fusion and crossover were not temporary aberrations in the life of a "traditional" music group but represented a fundamental shift in their own sense of artistic mission. I wanted to observe this increasingly central part of their musical lives up close, not simply through the filter of recordings. E-mailing Huun-Huur-Tu's manager, Sasha Cheparukhin, I asked whether he could recommend an upcoming tour with collaborative concerts on which I might tag along. Sasha's response was immediate: "Best place to see new Huun-Huur-Tu style is Greece. They have concerts with Ross Daly 'Labyrinth' group on Crete and in outdoor amphitheater in Elefsina [the ancient Eleusis], near Athens in early September. You can travel together from Tuva after your fieldwork."

CRETE

SEPTEMBER 2003

The village of Houdetsi's albescent stone and plaster houses hug the contours of a rocky escarpment along the narrow road that weaves southward through dry hill country from Heraklion, the largest city on the island of Crete. The most imposing of these dwellings is a spacious two-story villa set behind a walled-in terrace and tree-shaded lawn just opposite the tiny village square. The villa has been transformed into the headquarters of Ross Daly, a charismatic Irish musician and world music impresario who has lived in Greece for the last twenty-eight years and become an accomplished performer of its traditional music. Daly, fifty-one, is tall and thin with biblical locks of flowing, sun-bleached hair, now greying, which hang down to his shoulders and frame his deep-set eyes. At first sight, he could be mistaken for a superannuated apparition of Yanni, the New Age Greek pop idol, except that Daly's casual dress and tousled mane seem unselfconscious rather than the issue of a fashion stylist. Daly lived in Athens until four years ago, when, through an old friendship with the mayor of Houdetsi, he came to the vil-

Ross Daly and fellow musicians rehearse their concert program with Huun-Huur-Tu. Houdetsi, Crete, 2003.

lage, took a lease on the villa, and began converting it into a museum for his substantial personal collection of musical instruments, as well as a center for workshops, lawn concerts, and cross-cultural musical encounters such as the one to which Huun-Huur-Tu had been invited in the infernally hot days of late summer.

Huun-Huur-Tu had come to Daly's Cretan world music emporium not simply as a traditional music group from Siberia. In Greece, they are rock stars. If in most countries where they have toured, Huun-Huur-Tu's audience has grown from a grassroots base of throat-singing aficionados, worldbeat buffs, and New Agers, in Greece their fame started with soccer. Specifically, it started with a television advertisement for Pro Po, the country's most popular soccer lottery, in which a barber shaves a man's head to resemble a soccer ball, with its black and white patches, to the accompaniment of a soundtrack featuring Huun-Huur-Tu's up-tempo, popular encore piece, "Eki Attar" (Good Horses).

The Pro Po ad featuring Huun-Huur-Tu performing "Eki Attar" is included in the video files online, track 25.

The ad was created in 2001 by Pro Po's advertising agency, Kino TV and Movie Productions SA, whose music department was managed by a world music fan named Manos Andriotis. Andriotis had heard Huun-Huur-Tu's music on recordings, and he selected "Eki Attar" for its "positive energy and tempo, and the wonderful, weird sound of the voices," Andriotis later wrote me.[28] Andriotis was sure that the ad would be a hit and open the way for "Eki Attar" to have a life of its own as a dance remix. His insight led to the release of a compact disc single by Protasis Records and Eros Music that featured four DJ mixes of "Eki Attar." Soon another record company with a competing claim to the publishing rights of "Eki Attar" released its own compact disc with five more dance remixes of "Eki Attar." "Television, radio, and the biggest newspapers in Greece were confused about where Huun-Huur-Tu was from," Andriotis recalled in an e-mail, "and were calling them 'the group from Mongolia' or 'Huun-Huur-Tu from Lapony' [Lapland]. I was yelling to journalists that the group came from Tuva, and they were asking me, 'Are they from Cuba?'"

Huun-Huur-Tu's manager, Sasha Cheparukhin, described what happened next. "With so much attention focused on 'Eki Attar,' one of the remixes fell into first place on the Greek pop charts. Huun-Huur-Tu came into the charts in March 2002, and for a month, 'Eki Attar' was outselling Madonna, the Beatles, and Britney Spears. There were other remixes that were in third place, in fifth place. No one dared to remix another song, because it was not Huun-Huur-Tu that was popular, but 'Eki Attar.' The Greek national lottery organization ordered 50,000 CD singles of 'Eki Attar' as promos for their clients. Then the idea arose to do a tour of Greece. Ross Daly and a concert agency he worked with, Protasis, were the first to organize a tour. When we arrived at Athens airport and I told the immigration officials who I was with, they said, 'Wow, Huun-Huur-Tu!' and immediately abandoned stamping passports and rushed out to ask for autographs. There was pandemonium. Immigration officers, customs officers, passengers—they were all crowding around Huun-Huur-Tu asking for autographs, and for ten minutes, no one could get a passport stamped. The first concert in Athens had three or four thousand people. The next day there was a concert in Salonika, where there were also 3,000 people. When Huun-Huur-Tu played 'Eki Attar,' everyone in the theater stood up and waved their arms and screamed. It was then that we understood what pop fame was."

Huun-Huur-Tu's trip to Greece in September 2003 was not to plug "Eki Attar" and play solo concerts but to participate in a Tuvan-Cretan-Iranian musical collaboration organized by Ross Daly that included, in addition to Huun-Huur-Tu, Daly's group, Labyrinth, and a family percussion trio headed by Iranian *zarb* player Jamshid Chemirani. Daly and members of Labyrinth had jammed with Huun-Huur-Tu during the Tuvans' previous visits to Greece. There had been good chemistry between the groups, and Daly had invited the Tuvans back for a more structured exploration of musical common ground. Three days of rehearsal would precede an outdoor concert on Daly's large lawn in Houdetsi, and, two evenings later, a second concert in Elefsina, on the outskirts of Athens.

While Huun-Huur-Tu caught up on sleep—the journey from Tuva had taken fifty-four hours spread over three days and nights—other musicians arrived and began rehearsing. Rehearsals took place in a square, whitewashed room on the second floor of Daly's villa that was filled with cushions, chairs, and stringed instruments stashed in the corners. At the beginning of the first formal rehearsal session, Daly outlined his plan for the concert program in a mixture of Greek and English. He proposed that Huun-Huur-Tu perform a few solo numbers and suggested some songs he liked from their repertory. He didn't know the names of the songs, but he located them on a mini compact disc player and then played the beginning of each one on a boom box. Sayan nodded his head as the pieces came on one by one.

Daly then introduced his idea for how the musicians from Greece, Iran, and Tuva would play together. "For the third piece, it would be nice to go into the 'Orphan's Lament' [one of Huun-Huur-Tu's signature songs], with some of us accompanying on clarinet, *lyra,* and other instruments. We have a Greek song that's also about orphans, so I thought it would be nice to go into that." Another of Daly's suggestions was to blend together Huun-Huur-Tu's "Kaldak Xamar," an agitprop song from the 1930s about building a road through a mountain pass in the south of Tuva, with two energetic, Indian-flavored unison melodies that he had composed just the day before and that, like "Kaldak Xamar," were based on pentatonic modes. Daly studied sitar for four years before becoming interested in Greek music, and in the arrangement, Huun-Huur-Tu was joined by *lyra, lauta, santuri,* drum, *kopuz,* and *tarhu*—a hybrid spike fiddle that was the invention of an Australian instrument-maker, and whose name combines the Arabic and Chinese words for "string" (*tar* plus *hu*). Daly's musical direction was low-key. He proposed his arrangement to the Tuvans but added emphatically that if they didn't like it, they should feel free to suggest something else.

When the rehearsal came to an end just before the start of a late dinner in a local cafe, I asked Kaigal-ool what he had thought of the "Kaldak Xamar" medley. "I don't know," he replied. "What did you think?"

My reaction was positive. "The sounds of the instruments work well together and the melodies cohere, even though they come from very different traditions. Ross has good taste." Kaigal-ool nodded his head, as I sat poised over my notebook.

"You can write that I share your opinion," he said. Then he added, "It's nice that Ross can invite the musicians he likes, and it's no accident that he invited us a couple of times. He hears something in our music. But it will be even nicer when *we* are the ones doing the inviting—inviting the musicians that *we* find interesting to play with."

I had translated Kaigal-ool's answer for Jamchid Chemirani, the Iranian *zarb* player, who was sitting across from Kaigal-ool, and Chemirani continued Kaigal-ool's line of thought. "You can't really escape participating in these events. This is what people are doing now, and in any case, I like these kinds of projects because they're a way of keeping in contact beyond one's own tradition. Ross's approach is good because it's about trying to approach one another—a meeting rather than a fusion. Nothing is forced. There aren't artificial attempts to impose one music on another. Instead, he brings different music into proximity in order to allow listeners to make up their own minds about how they're similar and different."

As the sky darkened on the evening of the concert, Ross Daly's sun-bleached yard was transformed into an alluring concert venue. The terrace became a carpet-covered stage set against the backdrop of the stone villa awash in pale red light. Thirteen hundred folding chairs had been set up on the lawn, but these were not enough to accommodate the crowd of around 2,000 that overflowed the yard, perched on the surrounding stone wall, and mingled in the square beyond, filling the tavernas beyond capacity. The audience was diverse—craggy villagers from Houdetsi mixed with soigné couples from Heraklion. Teenagers and young children sat among old people. The summer concerts in Houdetsi normally attract around 500 listeners, and when I asked Ross Daly to speculate on the reason for the large attendance he replied right away, "Huun-Huur-Tu, of course."

The concert started at 10:15 PM, forty-five minutes late, and the second set didn't begin until after midnight. Few people left early. During the first half, when Daly's ensemble, Labyrinth, played virtuosic arrangements of Cretan folk music that sounded like a sewing machine with its pedal pushed to the floor, an undercurrent of low conversation rose from the lawn. But when Huun-Huur-Tu opened the second half with the powerful roar of "Mörgül," their musical arrangement of a Buddhist prayer, the lawn became instantly silent. Later, the horse-clopping rhythms of "Eki Attar," the song from the soccer lottery advertisement, evoked loud cheers of recognition that shot into the air like fireworks. The performance of the collaborative Cretan-Tuvan-Iranian pieces was tight, and drew good audience response, but the applause seemed more from politeness than passion.

On the day following the concert, Huun-Huur-Tu arose late. The sky was overcast, and the temperature had dropped precipitously from the previous day's scorching heat. In early afternoon, all the musicians were rounded up and taken to a village a few kilometers away, where at a scenic picnic spot, two sheep were lying on the grass waiting to be turned into lunch. A crowd of village men eagerly brandished knives, and when Ross pointed out that Tuvans also spend a lot of time around sheep, a workshop in cross-cultural sheep-slaughtering was quickly organized. Kaigal-ool, Alexei, and Andrei are all as much at home holding a butcher's knife as a *byzaanchy* or *igil,* and Kaigal-ool, the elder of the group, chose himself to wield the knife. The Cretans looked on with horror as one of the sheep was pinned on its back and Kaigal-ool cut a short slit in its belly, thrust his arm into the incision, and quickly pinched the aorta, instantly killing the sheep. When he pulled his blood-covered arm out of the incision, the Cretans gasped. "*Varvaroi!* [barbarians]" one of them was heard to whisper loudly. In ancient Greece, *varvaros* referred to people who didn't speak Greek or act like Greeks, among whom were nomads, but in modern Greek, the word has the same extended meaning as in English.

Next it was the Cretans' turn to demonstrate their own method of slaughter. Crete was long under Ottoman rule, and the Muslim (and Jewish) tradition of animal slaughter, in which the animal's throat is slit and the blood drained away and discarded, remains the norm. By contrast, nomads in the Altai region, who were never Islamized, use sheep blood to make blood sausage, an important source of nutrients in their diet. After the second sheep's throat was cut, the animal lay heaving on the ground, its limbs jerking intermittently as the blood slowly drained out of the gash in its throat. "Let the blood run like a river!" shouted one of the butchers. Andrei Mongush sidled up next to me, a look of horror on his face. "It's barbaric, what they did," said Andrei, an experienced sheep slaughterer. "I've never seen anything like it. They have no respect for the spirit of the animal."

While the meal was being prepared, I pulled Ross aside and asked him to assess the results of the cross-cultural musical exchange that had transpired during the rehearsals and performance. Had his expectations for the event been met? Did the different kinds of music enhance one another? And how does one even begin to evaluate cross-cultural music that lies beyond the aesthetic canons of specific traditions?

"I wasn't looking for fusion, but for what you could call common ground," Ross replied assuredly. "In my view, nomads are very practical people. They're not interested in ideology, and so the common ground I sought had to be straightforward and obvious. The most obvious common ground between Tuvan and Cretan music lies in their use of pentatonic scales, and of rhythms that suggest horses. I'm not sure that's what the rhythms initially represented in Cretan music, but there's unquestionably a similarity, and the Iranian *zarb* works very well with Tuvan music, the way it marks the rhythm. Also, the mixture of fiddles sounds very nice, and the Tuvan overtones sounded good in one of the Greek songs. It's not that complicated. In the end, the question is, are the musicians enjoying themselves? Are they having a good time playing together? For all the participants, the answer seems to have been an unqualified 'yes.'"

Ross's hallowed "common ground" was indeed carved out of the vast pan-Eurasian territory of modal music—pentatonic and otherwise—whose central axis extends from the Balkans through Turkey, Iran, and Central Asia all the way to India. Notwithstanding the enormous musical diversity of this region, commonalities do exist, among them a tendency for instrumental improvisation to take the form of running up and down minor scales with great rhythmic vigor. Yet for all its alacrity, this approach did not allow the Tuvan music a sustained opportunity to speak in its own voice, to take listeners into the interior of its own world. At best, the audience was offered a brief glimpse of this world, for example, in Kaigal-ool's masterpiece, "The Orphan's Lament." What the musicians created together, at least to my ears, added up to less than the sum of the parts.

Each ensemble and, indeed, each musician had a distinctive flavor to contribute to the Greek salad, but the effect of combining them was to diminish their individual pungency. That was my own view, but I wanted to know Huun-Huur-Tu's. I had barely had a chance to speak with them, aside from brief exchanges with the always laconic Kaigal-ool, who maintained a remarkable inner focus through the hectic regimen of travel, rehearsals, and performances—three days into our stay on Crete, he had looked up from the newspaper he'd been reading ever since leaving Moscow and asked, "What's the name of this island we're on?" As we prepared to take the night ferry from Heraklion to Epirus for the next evening's concert in Elefsina, I sat with Huun-Huur-Tu and turned on a tape recorder. Mostly it was Sayan who spoke.

"So what's really being exchanged when you play with Ross and his musicians?" I asked, trying to get the conversation rolling. "I sat and listened to you performing together. In the beginning, they played, and then you played, and they accompanied you with a drone. Then they played again and you accompanied them with a drone. And it goes like that. Is there really some kind of exchange or syncretism or synthesis? Or is it like when you're sitting around a campfire and you have a song swap?"

"That's the perpetual question around our collaborations," Sayan answered. "People are always saying to us, 'Oh, you're hanging around with all these famous musicians,' but from the very beginning, we got involved with these people not because of an interest in collaboration per se. The issue for us is about choosing our influences. The main influence that you find between musicians is freedom. You play with someone else, and you improvise. He makes you free, and you make him free. It's not about digging for details in the other person's music. Here, for example, I don't see that Ross and his group literally know our material, and maybe they don't want to. And maybe I don't know their material and don't want to—or maybe I want to but don't have time. The point is that for me, it's not necessary right now. You listen to it, and that's enough. I don't intend to learn their pieces and they don't intend to learn mine. But if there's a common search—a search for the emotion that's in real music—then people can play together even if they come from very different backgrounds. I'm interested in emotion. If it touches me, I like it. And if musicians like something, they'll play it freely, with feeling."

"So your role in this improvisation is to give freedom to others?" I asked.

"Absolutely. Because they feel that freedom in our music—in our instruments, our voices, our songs, our words. They feel the emotion. Some people cry, some get contemplative, some laugh, some get silent and sad. They don't understand a single word, right? But something's going on in the music, and they feel it in their heart, not in their head."

"And that's true for all Tuvan music?"

"I think so. We've talked about how it's a culture where people spend a lot of time alone, and where they make music for themselves. When you do that, you don't lie to yourself, and from those conditions come real emotions. If you're a musician who wants to be well known, you'll sit and think like a composer, 'Now what should I do so that people will like this? What words should I write?' But from the beginning, our music has expressed emotions that people receive from nature. If someone has an emotion, he immediately puts all of it into lines of poetry, into a song, into sounds. Tuvan music is full of emotions, but not just anyone can express them. You have to be immersed in the instruments, in the way of producing sounds."

"So what about people who aren't Tuvans—people who are searching for something in Tuvan music that can be useful for them. You're the chief object of that process. People think that if they only invite Huun-Huur-Tu, your magic will work on them."

"You can't judge people for that. Influences are a necessity for any musician. I realized that even when I was working in the Ayan Ensemble and hanging around with older musicians. I understood that if I spent time with them and listened to their music, I'd fall under their magical influence and start using their material. It's natural. But you're right—we meet people every single month who come up after a concert and ask, 'Can we do such-and-such a project with you?' A lot of people think that once they've grabbed onto us, everything will take care of itself. That's really dumb. They don't come to us through our own material, through our own old people. They want to jump right into working with us. You shouldn't judge them, but smart people, like Ross, swim around in the material for a long time. They ask themselves, 'What's going on in this music? What kind of mode is this?' A good musician always tries to go deep from the very start. That's his interest, his curiosity—he's been touched, and he wants to understand why."

"Okay," I said. "I'll grant you that there are better and worse ways of collaborating. But whenever I've heard Tuvan music blended or fused with some other kind of music, I can't escape the feeling that it's more interesting when you hear it on its own." Extending my point beyond cross-cultural collaborations, I took a swipe at the efforts of Huun-Huur-Tu and its clone, Malerija, to attract young listeners by plugging in and tarting up their newest recordings with gratuitous studio effects. "The way to attract new listeners is to perform music at an extremely high level and let the music speak for itself. Outstanding performers will always attract debutante listeners," I said. "Look at the example of Ravi Shankar."

"Yes, look at the example of Ravi Shankar!" countered Sayan. Who would have heard of Ravi Shankar had it not been for George Harrison? It would have taken 300 years for Shankar's music to get out to the kind of audience that assembled almost instantly as the result of George Harrison's intervention. Some of the people who found their way to Indian classical music through the Beatles later became devotees of Indian classical music in its pure form. It's the same with Tuvan music. Even with outstanding performers, not everyone can come and spend years in Tuva studying our music, and it's difficult to get across the essence of the older musical forms on recordings. We have to meet our audience at least halfway."

Or do they? I am not so sure, but let listeners judge for themselves. Malerija's plugged-in performance of "Ancestors," a Tuvan folk song first arranged and performed by Huun-Huur-Tu, is included in the audio files online (track 40). In my view, it represents the best work that Malerija has done. A translation of the text appears below:

> The Yenisei, Sayan and Tandim are our ancient places
> Soft and soulful *sygyt* and *xöömei* are the ancient songs of our people
> The ancestors of our *kargyraa* long ago became like gravestones on the steppe
> But our hearts are proud that among us are still *xöömei* singers.

POSTLUDE
Appropriation and Its Discontents

In concerts and on recordings, Huun-Huur-Tu could exert a measure of artistic control over collaborative performances. Ross Daly, after all, had been generous in soliciting Huun-Huur-Tu's input during the rehearsals on Crete. As for collaborative recordings, Huun-Huur-Tu did its best to retain approval rights over final mixes. But when other musicians sampled or licensed Huun-Huur-Tu's recordings, working through record companies, agents, or attorneys to acquire rights without necessarily notifying Huun-Huur-Tu, artistic control over the group's work passed into other people's hands.

Smithsonian Folkways, which licensed an excerpt of throat-singing for use in a Swedish cheese snack commercial (Video File, track 24), is exceptional in its practice of consulting with artists or producers about licensing requests even after the term of a recording contract has expired. Once artists are no longer under contract and artist relations are no longer a consideration, record companies overwhelmingly approach licensing purely as a business opportunity. In the realm of world music, the most lucrative licensing contracts invariably result from the use of traditional music in television advertisements and films. Knowing of my interest in appropriations of Tuvan music, friends, colleagues, and students kept me well informed about new sightings in the world of mass media and popular culture. By the late 1990s, the frequency of such sightings was so great that I had become blasé. But when a new film with Huun-Huur-Tu's music on the soundtrack opened in one of New York City's premier cinemas, I took note. The film was *The Fast Runner* (*Atanarjuat*), and in 2001 it appeared out of nowhere to win the Caméra d'Or Award for best first feature film at the Cannes International Film Festival.

Coproduced by Igloolik Isuma Productions and the National Film Board of Canada, *The Fast Runner* was filmed in the Canadian Arctic, and might be described as an ethnographic thriller. Amid sweeping panoramas of snow-fields and ice floes, an Inuit clan, their native Inuktitut language tersely subtitled in English, is hexed by a shamanic curse and disemboweled by jealousy and murderous revenge, yet they emerge from these challenges to their survival by exorcising evil spirits and turning to the wisdom of tradition. A dramatic escape by Atanarjuat, the male lead, who is chased naked across snow and icy pools of water by three rivals who have just murdered his brother, gives the film its name. In keeping with the film's austere setting, the soundtrack is spare. Consisting mostly of original music and digital sound effects composed by Chris Crilly, it also includes excerpts from performances by Huun-Huur-Tu and their artistic collaborators, the Bulgarian women's choir Angelite. Credits at the end identified the Huun-Huur-Tu excerpt as having been licensed from Shanachie Entertainment, the independent record label in New Jersey that released Huun-Huur-Tu's first four recordings.

After viewing *The Fast Runner,* I contacted Huun-Huur-Tu's manager, Sasha Cheparukhin, to ask whether he and Huun-Huur-Tu were aware that the group's music appeared in the film. Sasha responded that they were not. The licensing deal had been arranged between Shanachie and the Canadian production company, and neither party had contacted Huun-Huur-Tu or its manager. The credits list two tracks with Huun-Huur-Tu's music: "Fly, Fly, My Sadness," performed by Huun-Huur-Tu and the Bulgarian Voices [sic], and "Prayer," performed by Huun-Huur-Tu alone. It is the use of "Prayer" that raised the Tuvans' hackles.

"Prayer" is a translation of the Tuvan word *Mörgül,* which refers not to any prayer, but to a Buddhist prayer. The text and musical arrangement that Huun-Huur-Tu recorded for Shanachie was first performed by the Tuva Ensemble, the group organized at the beginning of the 1990s by Gennadi Tumat with help from Zoya Kyrgys. Kyrgys had found the text of *Mörgül* in a collection of Buddhist sutras, and she helped Tumat arrange the text in a style that evoked the basso profundo, unison overtone chanting of Tibetan monks. Huun-Huur-Tu modified this arrangement by splitting the unison chanting into angular harmonies that reinforced the parallel fifth sound of drone against reinforced overtone. Excerpts of "Prayer" are heard at several points in the film. The first of these excerpts occurs one hour and twenty minutes into the film, when "Prayer" provides musical accompaniment to an image of Atanarjuat and his brother, Amaqjuat, urinating in the snow shortly before Amaqjuat is murdered.

Huun-Huur-Tu viewed *The Fast Runner* after it was released on DVD in late 2002, and during our long conversation on Crete, I asked the musicians about their reaction.

"What the film did was a cultural insult because of the context in which our music was used," Sayan said. "That context mutilates the music. And it's not the first time that a film director has used 'Prayer.' There was a Bulgarian director who also used it. It was awful what he did: he put our prayer in the mouth of the devil, because to a simple listener, it sounds powerful and menacing. The director was an educated person, and he should have known better. But he used the music absolutely out of context as a kind of special effect to reap a dividend for himself. If you use someone's music, first of all, you ask the people who made it—you explain where you'd like to use it, and you ask whether it's okay to use it there. You ask what the music is about and why it was created. That's what happens in a normal, sensible society."

Though Sayan was annoyed about the use of Huun-Huur-Tu's music in *The Fast Runner,* he wasn't above acknowledging the two-edged sword of appropriation. "On the other hand," he continued, "emotionally speaking, you could say that our music touched that film director. He felt something, and he thought to himself, 'Why not put that music just here.' And he chose a place where there's a kind of harmonization with nature—even when there's a guy urinating, that's also part of nature. I don't know—I watched the film, and it's unpleasant to look on while Mörgül, a Buddhist prayer, provides the soundtrack for someone urinating. You could say that it's unaesthetic. I wouldn't go into a Protestant church and urinate in the corner during a service. There's some kind of limit, and if the film director didn't figure it out for himself from an emotional standpoint, what can you do? It means that he's deformed—morally, physically. He doesn't feel those limits. The other song he used—'Orphan's Lament' [renamed "Fly, Fly My Sadness" on the collaborative recording with the Bulgarian choir]—there was some kind of context for it. There was a murder in the family, and someone is left alone. Here again we're speaking about emotions. The person who chose that music didn't know the words, but understood that it was a deep and serious song, and that it would be appropriate for this situation. And it worked."

Sayan concluded, "Nothing is going to happen to 'Mörgül' as a result of the film." As he spoke his jaw tightened in defiance. "And nothing's going to happen to the other pieces of ours that people use. People do what they need to do for their own purposes. They draw the material toward themselves. I know that you can't hold back the world. I know that someone could turn an arrangement of 'Mörgül' out of any computer tomorrow—they could do whatever they want with it. My life wouldn't be long enough for all the lawsuits you'd have to bring against people who misuse your music. But that's not my business. In the end, you can't insult our music. It's stood for a thousand years, and, despite all the people who misuse it and rename it and make up for it some new philosophy and new categories, it will stand for a thousand years more."

NORWICH, VERMONT: JANUARY 2004

Kaigal-ool, Sayan, Alexei Saryglar, and Andrei Mongush huddled around the woodstove in the 200-year-old converted barn I call home. They had bunked down for a few days at the start of yet another long tour of North America that would take them from the Maritime Provinces of Canada to Hawaii. From their perch by the woodstove, they could see my neighbor's horses in a corral across the dirt lane from the barn, and in the distance, a sheep pasture bordered by tall pine trees aglow in the late afternoon sunlight. The thermometer outside the kitchen window registered 20 degrees below zero.

"It feels like the outskirts of Kyzyl here," said Sayan. We joked about the idea of nomads migrating all the way from Tuva to northern New England only to find the same hills and fields, the same animals, the same dirt roads, and the same frigid temperatures they have at home.

"Why should we do all that hard traveling just to end up back where we began?" Kaigal-ool hammed.

The irony of Kaigal-ool's quip came not only from the obvious fact that, similarity of landscape aside, Vermont is not Tuva, but also from our shared understanding that Huun-Huur-Tu's global nomadizing had nothing to do with pastoral landscapes and animals. Rather, the ensemble's members are examples of what the French writer Jacques Attali calls "hypernomads" in his work *L'homme nomade,* a panoramic world history of nomadism and its place in humanity's future. Hypernomads are voluntary nomads, as distinguished from involuntary nomads or "infranomads," whom Attali divides into "nomads by heritage" and "nomads by constraint" (e.g., refugees, immigrant workers, and homeless people).[1] In Attali's scheme, hypernomads comprise a peripatetic creative class who are "masters of globalization" and whose discoveries and innovations, in a replay of earlier eras of globalization, strongly influence sedentary societies.

Huun-Huur-Tu seems emblematic of this new nomadism—or to be more precise, its members represent a bridge between the mobile pastoralists of Inner Asian tradition and the hypernomads of today and tomorrow. The group's migratory routes are deterritorialized, determined not by the turning of seasons and ripening of grasses but by the exigencies of commerce—the release dates of recordings, the contracts of festival programmers, or the collaborative proposals of artists higher up in the pecking order of the music business. Yet it is not as if their beliefs in old things or the power of spirits has vanished. As Sayan put it, "We have a feeling of taste, of limits, of love for our music. We're not about to throw it just anywhere. No, we'll try to make it contemporary, but only in a way that is useful, only within a golden mean."

The golden mean is elusive, however, in music so radically decontextualized. What measures provide the basis for limits and taste? Or for meaning and meaningfulness? These questions concern not only Huun-Huur-Tu in its work as neotraditionalists, but all the appropriators, recontextualizers, and recyclers of the world who have used Tuvan music as a raw material in their own cultural production. About all of these, Huun-Huur-Tu had plenty of reservations, despite their display of public forbearance. These reservations arose not from a nationalistic reflex of control, like that still evident among politicians and cultural bureaucrats who support licensing throat-singers to perform beyond Tuva's borders. Rather, Huun-Huur-Tu's reservations arose from years on the front lines of transnational cultural exchange.

"Why are Americans attracted to overtone singing?" asked Sayan rhetorically, repeating my question in one of our discussions about the issue. "I don't know. I think they feel some kind of emotionality in overtones, but in their overtone singing, I don't hear any emotions. It sounds like someone thumping a cup. It rings, and that's it. Overtones should have emotions, just like any other kind of music. A lot of our followers exclaim, 'Listen! I can do it!' as soon as they're able to produce an audible overtone. They're all wrapped up in the production of the sounds. For Tuvans, producing a sound is just the beginning. Overtones are connected to words, to texts. There's always a 'why' in singing with overtones that one is trying to answer. It's like playing any instrument—you have to put emotion into it, for example, as if those sounds were a flute. I don't feel that in a lot of the Westerners who are doing overtone singing. I don't feel any emotion."

Sayan's reservations became even more pronounced when he discussed the appropriation of throat-singing by people trafficking in the alleged healing power of harmonics—a recurring theme in our conversations. "A lot of people do throat-singing for the wrong reason and in the wrong place," said Sayan. "They use it to draw attention to themselves. They want people to notice them, so they start singing unexpectedly—in a crowd of people, or while traveling—and of course it can have the wrong effect. Shamans are right when they say that if you sing this way, you'll frighten the spirits. Throat-singing didn't come into being for that—to draw attention to yourself—and if you use it with the wrong feeling, or with the wrong intention, it will have the wrong effect. It's like black magic and white magic. Of course sounds can heal, but they can also cripple and mutilate. People don't understand that. They think that they can make any kind of god-awful harmonic sounds and a sick person will stand up and be healed. They're liable to harm themselves psychologically because they don't understand what they're dealing with. A lot of people in the West sing aggressively—you can see it in the way they hold their bodies, and feel it in their sound. Of course this kind of music won't heal anyone."

"Where do you think those wrong-headed ideas come from?" I asked Sayan.

"They speak to the fact that something's not right in your country, and in other countries in the West. There's a curiosity and a hunger for innovation that starts to devour everything. Innovation is like a narcotic. You hear some kind of music and you say, 'Oh, I got a buzz from that . . .' and you immediately want to try it yourself. We were just in Spain, and there were people hanging around us talking about healing with harmonics. It's very serious there—sound therapy is everywhere, and I said to those people, 'Go ahead and heal, but it's not really our thing. We don't know where and how harmonics act. We act on our feelings, we play our music, and if it has a positive result for anyone else, so much the better.'"

For Sayan, the aggressive sounds made by healers reflect an aggressiveness that characterizes Western music more generally—or at least Western music of European origin—and sets it apart from Tuvan music. "Wood, skin, and hair—these are the materials at the root of music," said Sayan. "I played string bass for years in an orchestra, and I got to the point where I couldn't stand the sound of a violin. The whole point of the violin is fighting against iron. You try to overcome the metallic, unnatural sound of playing on metal strings. Our music is a lot more natural, and real Tuvan music—the kind that Kaigal-ool makes—isn't aggressive. It's not performing for someone else, but first and foremost, for oneself. It's self-contained and intimate. And what's strange is that these sounds that are made for oneself end up being much stronger and carrying much farther than when you try to shout. Kaigal-ool, even when he recorded against the cliff, sang in a very measured way. He didn't shout, but the sound nonetheless had an enormous power."

Sayan is at once both insider and outsider in Tuvan music, reflecting his mixed Tuvan-Russian parentage. He grew up in western Tuva, where his parents were teachers, but he graduated from a music high school in Mineralnye Vody, in the Caucasus, where he developed a strong interest in jazz and jazz rock. Asked to list important influences on his musical development, he names Joe Zawinul and Wayne Shorter of the group Weather Report, John

McLaughlin, and Frank Zappa. After returning to Tuva in 1990 to focus on traditional music, Sayan made no attempt to conceal these influences. At the same time, he was not afraid to point out the limitations of Western-trained musicians' ability to understand the nuances of Tuvan music. More than most of his compatriots, he was ideally poised to serve as a musical bridge between Tuva and the West. Still, the constant crossing back and forth was hard on him and also on his family. Weeks and months away from home, and the physical burden of traveling on the cheap in an effort to cut road expenses to a minimum, had taken their toll. Meanwhile, back in Kyzyl, his family faced other concerns. One summer night in 2000, Svetlana Bapa described some of these issues as we shared a dinner of fried fish and chicken soup while Sayan was away on tour.

"Our lifestyle is very average," said Svetlana. "Especially if you compare us, say, to the people around the President [of Tuva]—the kind who build three-story cottages at the drop of a hat. But Kyzyl is a small place, and everyone knows about my husband's work. Not long ago, I got a call from a woman friend I hadn't seen in two years. She said that she was planning to go to a spa in Yalta, that it would cost five thousand rubles, and that she was a bit short of what she needed to make the trip. She wondered if I might be able to help. Thinking she might be just thirty or forty rubles short, I asked her how much money she still needed. 'Five thousand rubles,' she said. I couldn't believe it. What nerve! We have problems enough just trying to support all the relatives who come to us—cousins, nephews and nieces, great aunts and uncles—people we barely know. Sometimes people show up here and ask to be fed for days at a time because they don't have money for food. Or they ask help for medical treatment or paying for their kid's school. How can you say no when people ask you that? There's a saying in Russian: 'You have only to come into money to discover poor relatives.' As soon as Sayan returns from the West, people start phoning and dropping by. The whole situation creates a lot of tension, and he starts to drink. I don't blame him. It's the only way he can relax."

In Tuva, as elsewhere in Russia, the manly drink of choice is vodka, and in Kyzyl, vodka is a staple of commerce. From the shelves of food markets, convenience stores, and kiosks, dozens of competing brands assault the buyer's eye: Prince Alexander, Pushkin, Old Russia (the label shows an Orthodox church), Russian Size (big), Masculine Dignity, Just Vodka, and a brand whose labels consist of men's names: Boris, Igor, Dmitri, Nikolai, Aleksei. Alcoholism is pandemic in Tuva. It transcends boundaries of ethnicity, nationality, age, gender, and profession. Musicians seem particularly vulnerable, and among them, the most vulnerable are those on the road. The members of Huun-Huur-Tu are no exception.

"Kaigal-ool had a vision while he was stopped in a car in a mountain pass," Sayan recounted. "In the vision, Gennadi Tumat and Oleg Kuular came up to him from behind and told him to follow them. Tumat and Kuular are dead. They were both brilliant throat-singers who died in their early thirties from the stresses of becoming music stars. Kuular hanged himself, and Tumat drank himself to death. That's what happens here. People with talent are raised up on a pedestal, but no one is really thinking of their well-being."

Concerned about Huun-Huur-Tu's future, and about some personal issues of his own, Sayan had gone to see Rosa, a well-known shaman in Kyzyl. As Sayan recounted the conversation, Rosa told him that the danger for musicians who spend much of their time touring is that they put all of their energy into music and, as a result, become exhausted and spiritually depleted. Then, in order to recharge themselves, they turn to alcohol and other destructive things. Sayan acknowledged that he understood from his own experience what Rosa was talking about—the feeling of giving one's all to the music, becoming spiritually drained, and not having the inner resources to recharge. "Rosa said that you have to fill that emptiness with something," Sayan added. "And of course it's with nature that we should fill it."

"Rosa's right," I said. "Traditionally, nomadic musicians recharged themselves by drawing inspiration from the land. Shamans make frequent trips to spiritual sites for the same purpose. But what can you do when you spend most of your time performing in cities?"

"Of course you can't escape the times we live in," Sayan replied. "But our music is so rich that you can't exhaust it. There's enough in it for three Moscows, four New Yorks, ten Los Angeleses, and thirty Londons. Let the concerts be in concert halls, churches, or wherever you want. The problem is not with cities, but with people's souls. It's not about where you are, but about what you carry inside you. You don't need cities, and you don't need yurts. Wherever you are, your plot of land is right here." Sayan pointed to his chest. "You're the master of your own heart, and to feel this music, that's all you need."

"There's a lot of rigidity these days," Sayan opined. "But I like the Buddhist-animist approach—you let things happen and evolve, and you don't destroy. The nomadic way of life is set up for that. You put up your yurt and you haven't harmed anything—not the grass, not the sunlight. It's the same when you play music: you've taken from nature, and you give back to it. Everything passes through you, and in the end, you're back to zero—a big and beautiful zero."

GLOSSARY

aal (*ail*) (*aul*)*	A small group of households herding and migrating together. (Tuvan, Mongol, Kazakh)
adyg	Zoological term for "bear." (Tuvan)
aimag	In Mongolia, an administrative subdivision that designates a region or province.
aitys (*aitysh*)	A Kazakh (Kyrgyz) term for a poetry competition.
aitysh	Powdered juniper burned in ritual ceremonies and offerings for its pleasing aroma.
albys	A type of spirit, either male or female, characterized by seductive beauty. (Tuvan)
algysh (*alkysh*)	A Tuvan (Altai) term for a shamanic hymn.
Ak Jang	"White Faith," also known as Burkhanism. A native religious movement in the Altai Republic.
amyrga	A hunting horn used to attract male red deer in rutting season. (Tuvan)
ang-meng mal-magan öttüneri	"Imitation of wild and domestic animals." (Tuvan)
artysh	Twigs of juniper burned in ritual ceremonies and offerings for their pleasing aroma. (Tuvan)
arzhaan	Tuvan word for a spring with healing or curative waters. (Tuvan)

* Words in parentheses signify cognate terms in other languages.

ayalga	"Melody," "motif," "dialect," "accent," or "pronunciation." (Tuvan)
aza	A malicious spirit. (Tuvan)
bayan	A small accordion. (Russian)
bie (alternate form, *biyelgee*)	A form of mimetic dance in which stylized movements of the hands, arms, and upper torso represent scenes of work and play or narrate the events of myths and legends. (Mongolian)
boidus churumaly	Sonic sketches of nature. (Tuvan)
borbangnadyr	Technique of throat-singing in Tuva, from the verb *borbangnaar*, a causative verb form that means "to cause to roll," "revolve," or "spin."
burxan	A sky deity; god, divinity. (Tuvan and Mongolian)
byzaanchy	Tuvan bowl-bodied fiddle with four horsehair strings.
chadagan	Tuvan name for a plucked zither with movable bridges.
chalama	Strips of cloth affixed to trees, bushes, or lengths of rope as an offering to spirits. (Tuvan)
chanzy	Tuvan three-stringed unfretted long-necked lute.
chatxan	Xakas name for a plucked zither with movable bridges.
choor	Kyrgyz name for an end-blown flute made from reed or wood with four or five holes.
chylandyk	A style of throat-singing in Tuva that imitates the sound of a bird by the same name.
deel	Traditional robe or gown worn by men and women. (Mongolian)
dombra	Kazakh two-stringed fretted long-necked lute. May refer to other types of Central Asian long-necked lutes, both with and without frets.
doshpuluur	Tuvan two-stringed long-necked unfretted lute.
dünggür	Frame drum played by shamans. (Tuvan)
dutâr	Designates different kinds of two-stringed long-necked fretted lutes among Uzbeks, Tajiks, Turkmens, Qaraqalpaks, Uyghurs, and other groups.

ediski	Small reed made from a folded piece of birch bark used to mimic wild goats or female musk deer. (Tuvan)
ee (*ezen*)	Local spirit-host or spirit-master. (Tuvan/Mongolian)
eeren	Physical object that represents a spirit-helper called upon to assist shamans with particular tasks or rituals. (Tuvan)
eroolch	Praise-singer who performs praise-songs at weddings and other festivities. (Mongolian)
ezenggileer	Style of throat-singing in Tuva that represents the sound of boots clacking in stirrups.
ger	Yurt. (Mongolian)
hargaa	Style of throat-singing in Mongolia—a "light" form of *harhiraa* used in Buddhist temple rituals.
harhiraa	Mongolian term (used by Sengedorj) to describe non-melodic style of throat-singing used by reciters of oral epic and also to accompany the *tsuur*.
höömii	General term for throat-singing. (Mongolian)
höömiich	Throat-singer. (Mongolian)
igil (*ikil*)	Two-stringed upright fiddle with horsehair strings. (Tuvan, West Mongolian)
jetigen	Kazakh name for a plucked zither with movable bridges.
kai	Guttural Altai vocal style used for performance of oral poetry.
kanzyp	Individual style of throat-singing in Tuva with an elegiac character.
kargyraa	Technique of throat-singing characterized by an extremely low-pitched fundamental drone. (Tuvan)
kejege	Traditional coiffure of Tuvan men featuring a shaved crown and braided ponytail.
kemanche	Spike fiddle used in Iranian and Azeri classical music.
kojamyk	Light-hearted song expressing a personal point of view, often performed antiphonally. (Tuvan)

kol oinotuu	"Dance of the hand." The Kyrgyz term that describes hand and arm gestures integral to the performance of instrumental music.
komuz	Three-stringed fretless long-necked lute that is the main folk instrument of the Kyrgyz.
kongguraa	Rattle, especially a rattle used by shamans.
kui	Kazakh term for a narrative instrumental piece traditionally performed by a solo player.
küü	Kyrgyz term for a narrative instrumental piece traditionally performed by a solo player.
limbi	Tuvan term for a wooden side-blown flute.
magtaal	In Mongolia, a praise-song.
magtaar	In western Mongolia, a short-song.
Manas	The Kyrgyz national epic that recounts the life story of its eponymous hero.
manaschi	A reciter of the *Manas*.
maqām	The modal principle in Turco-Arabic and Persian art music; in Central Asia, a classical suite form.
mazar	A physical structure marking the burial site of a saint; also, among the Kyrgyz, a site of spiritual power marked by a distinctive natural phenomenon.
morin huur	Mongolian two-stringed horsehead fiddle.
noyon	A member of the land-owning nobility in presocialist Tuva.
oboo	A rock cairn that marks a site of spiritual power, often in a mountain pass. (Mongolian)
oluya	A saintly person. (Kyrgyz)
orba	Fur-covered drumstick used to beat a shaman's drum.
ovaa	A rock cairn that marks a site of spiritual power, often in a mountain pass. (Tuvan)
pipa	Chinese short-necked fretted lute.
qin	Chinese plucked zither.

qyl qiyak	Kyrgyz variant of a bowl-bodied fiddle with two horse-hair strings.
qyl-qobyz	Kazakh variant of a bowl-bodied fiddle with two horse-hair strings.
samodeyatel'nost	Amateur arts programs in the Soviet Union and its successor states.
se	A Chinese zither.
shang-qobyz	Jew's harp. (Kazakh)
shingen höömi	"Liquid throat-singing," a term coined by Mongolian throat-singer Sengedorj.
shoor	Tuvan name for an end-blown flute made from reed or wood with three holes.
shuluraash	Onomatopoetic word that describes sound of flowing water.
sum	In Mongolia, an administrative subdivision of an *aimag*.
sybyzghy	Kazakh name for an end-blown flute made from reed or wood with three holes.
sygyt	One of the principal styles of throat-singing in Tuva, characterized by a fundamental pitch in the baritone register and high, piercing harmonics.
tartys (tartysh)	Kazakh (Kyrgyz) name for a competition among performers of instrumental music.
tatlaga	Bowing technique for Mongolian horsehead fiddle marked by strong rhythmic accentuation that represents rhythms of horse gaits or other animals.
temir komuz	Metal jew's harp. (Kyrgyz)
tespeng xöömei	Individual style ofthroat-singing in Tuva.
topshuur	Long-necked fretted lute played by Altai musicians.
toshpuluur	Variant spelling of *doshpuluur*. (Tuvan long-necked lute)
tsuur	Mongolian name for end-blown flute with three holes.
urtyn duu	Long-song. (Mongolian)

ustaz-shagird	"Master-apprentice." Term used to describe system of traditional oral musical transmission by Muslim musicians in Central, West, and South Asia.
uzun xoyug	Tuvan instrumental music genre analogous to Kyrgyz *küü* and Kazakh *kui*.
uzun yr	Long-song. (Tuvan)
xai	Guttural Xakas vocal style used for performance of oral poetry.
xaiji	A performer of *xai*. (Xakas)
xaiyrakan	A pseudonym for "bear." A sacred topography inhabited by a bear spirit, often shaped like a bear. (Tuvan)
xam	Shaman. (Tuvan)
xapchyk	Rattle consisting of sheep knee bones inside a bull scrotum. (Tuvan)
xem	River. (Tuvan)
xirlee	Children's toy consisting of a wooden propeller or button spun around on a piece of string to imitate the sound of wind. (Tuvan).
xoluraash	Onomatopoetic term describing the sound of flowing water. (Tuvan)
xomus	Jew's harp. (Tuvan)
xöömei	General term for throat-singing. (Tuvan)
xörekteer	A Tuvan neologism for "throat-singing." From *xörek*, "chest."
xovu kargyraazy	Steppe *kargyraa*: a style of throat-singing that represents the acoustical ambience of the steppe. (Tuvan)
xün xürtü	Sun-propeller; the vertical separation of light rays just after sunrise or before sunset. (Tuvan)
yatga	Mongolian name for a plucked zither with movable bridges.
yyx	Xakas bowl-bodied fiddle with horsehair strings, similar to *igil*.

NOTES

PREFACE

1. As a result of new archaeological discoveries, interest in nomads has extended to a group that really did vanish: the Scyths, who in recent years have been the subject of a *National Geographic* article ("Unearthing Siberian Gold," June 2003) and three highly publicized museum exhibitions: "Nomadic Art of the Eastern Eurasian Steppes" (Metropolitan Museum of Art, 2002); "The Golden Deer of Eurasia" (Metropolitan Museum of Art, 2000); and "Scythian Gold" (San Antonio Museum of Art, Los Angeles County Museum of Art, Brooklyn Museum of Art, et al., 1999–2001).

2. *Tuvan Folk Music* is a translation of the Russian title of Aleksei Nikolaevich Aksenov, *Tuvinskaia narodnaia muzyka* (Moscow: Muzyka, 1964). *Kyrgyz Folk Musical Art* is a translation of the Russian title of the work by Kamchybek Diushaliev and Ekaterina Luzanova, *Kyrgyzkoe narodnoe muzykal'noe tvorchestvo* (Bishkek: Soros Fund-Kyrgyzstan, 1999).

3. On music in Uzbekistan and Tajikistan, see my monograph, *The Hundred Thousand Fools of God: Musical Travels in Central Asia (and Queens, New York)* (Bloomington: Indiana University Press, 1996).

4. See, for example, Caroline Humphrey and David Sneath, *The End of Nomadism?* (Durham, N.C.: Duke University Press and Cambridge: White Horse Press, 1999), 1.

5. "Tuva" is a Russification of what in Tuvan is pronounced "Tyva" (written in Cyrillic as Тыва). The widespread use of "Tuva," however, offers a persuasive reason to adopt it in this work.

6. Until the 1990s, the primary English-language source for information on Tuvan music was a brief excerpt from A. N. Aksenov's *Tuvinskaia narodnaia muzyka* [Tuvan folk music], translated by ethnomusicologist Mark Slobin in *Asian Music* 4:2 (1973): 7–18.

7. From 1980 to 1985, I was a member of the Harmonic Choir, a New York–based overtone-singing group founded and directed by David Hykes. Hykes's work with overtones was sui generis—as a singer, he was self-taught, and Hykes often pointed out that the music he created with the Harmonic Choir was not beholden in form, style, or technique to the Tuvan, or any other Inner Asian overtone-singing tradition. As Hykes put it, harmonics were like gravity—the consequence of universal physical laws that made them available to anyone in any culture who wanted to use them as a source for musical creativity.

8. The 1990 recording is *Tuva: Voices from the Center of Asia,* released by Smithsonian Folkways (SF CD 40017).

9. As this book goes to press, Valentina Süzükei has completed her own book-length manuscript, *Muzykal'naia kul'tura Tuvy v dvatsatom stoletii* [The musical culture of Tuva in the twentieth century] (forthcoming).

10. Zoia Anaiban, "The Republic of Tuva: A Model of Ethnological Monitoring," *Anthropology and Archeology of Eurasia* 37:3 (1998–99): 61–62.

1. FINDING THE FIELD

1. Otto Mänchen-Helfen, *Journey to Tuva,* trans. Alan Leighton (Los Angeles: Ethnographics Press, 1992): 39–40. Originally published as *Reise ins asiatische Tuwa* (Berlin: Der Bücherkreis, 1931).

2. For Tuvan demographic data through 1996, see Anaiban, "The Republic of Tuva: A Model of Ethnological Monitoring." Data from the 2002 Russian census is available at http://www.gks.ru/PEREPIS/t1.htm.

3. The name "Tanna-Tuva People's Republic" (in Tuvan, *Tangdy-Tyva Ulus Respublika*) was later shortened to "Tuva People's Republic" (*Tyva Arat Respublika*).

4. Mänchen-Helfen, *Journey to Tuva,* 6.

5. Sakha is the ethnonym that has superseded the Russian-inspired "Yakut" as a means of self-identification among members of the titular ethnos of the Republic of Sakha, a part of the Russian Federation.

6. A good description of the role of the shaman's assistant appears in Sergei Shirokogoroff [Shirokogorov], "The Shaman's Assistant," in Jeremy Narby and Francis Huxley, eds., *Shamans Through Time: 500 Years on the Path to Knowledge* (New York: Jeremy Tarcher/Putnam, 2001), 90–93. Shirokogoroff's brief piece is excerpted from his classic work, *Psychomental Complex of the Tungus* (London: Kegan Paul, 1935; reprint, AMS Press, New York, 1982), a pioneering study of shamanism in Siberia.

7. For more on Idamchap, see the section in chapter 3, "Timbre-Centered Music."

8. Shamanism in Siberia has spawned a large literature—much of it in Russian—that ranges from rigorous ethnographic accounts and source-critical studies to highly personal and experiential narratives. A good entry point into the English-language scholarly literature is Marjorie Mandelstam Balzer, ed., *Shamanic Worlds: Rituals and Lore of Siberia and Central Asia* (Armonk, N.Y.: M. E. Sharpe, 1997). See also Balzer's contribution, "The Poetry of Shamanism," in Tae-gon Kim and Mihály Hoppál, eds., *Shamanism in Performing Arts* (Budapest: Akadémiai Kiadó, 1995), 171–187. On Tuvan shamanism, see Mongush B. Kenin-Lopsan, "Tuvan Shamanic Folklore," in Balzer, *Shamanic Worlds,* 110–152. For a more extensive bibliography of work on Tuvan, Altai, and Xakas shamanism, see chapter 5, n. 2. A useful compendium of Russian-language ethnographic work translated into English is Andrei A. Znamenski, *Shamanism in Siberia: Russian Records of Indigenous Spirituality* (Dordrecht, The Netherlands: Kluwer Academic Publishers, 2003). Notwithstanding recent critical reassessment, Mircea Eliade's *Shamanism: Archaic Techniques of Ecstasy* (Princeton, N.J.: Princeton University Press, 1964) remains an important source more than a half-century after it first appeared in French (for an interesting contemporary gloss on Eliade's work, see Mark Sedgwick, *Against the Modern World: Traditionalism and the Secret Intellectual History of the Twentieth Century* (New York: Oxford University Press, 2004). For a recent overview of shamanism and neoshamanism in East and West,

see Merete Demant Jakobsen, *Shamanism: Traditional and Contemporary Approaches to the Mastery of Spirits and Healing* (New York and Oxford: Berghahn Books, 1999). A recent book by Judith Becker, *Deep Listeners: Music, Emotion, and Trancing* (Bloomington: Indiana University Press, 2004), does not address Siberian shamanism directly, but it outlines "universals of trance experience" (29 ff.) that may be useful in thinking about how Siberian shamanism is both like and unlike other practices glossed as "trance."

9. Zoya Kyrgys translated this text from Tuvan to Russian, and I translated it from Russian to English. The original Tuvan has unfortunately been lost.

10. See Levin, *The Hundred Thousand Fools of God,* especially chap. 1.

11. The expression "brother Russians" refers ironically to the Soviet slogan, "brotherhood among Soviet peoples," in which Russians were depicted as "big brothers," and non-Russians, in particular, the native peoples of Siberia, were depicted as "little brothers." The anti-Russian sentiment expressed by the Tuvan speaker must be understood in the political climate of the late 1980s and early 1990s, when nativist sentiment in Tuvan welled up into a nascent secessionist movement. For a brief overview of this period in Tuvan history, see Marjorie Mandelstam Balzer, introduction to "The Republic of Tyva (Tuva): From Romanticism to Realism," *Anthropology and Archeology of Eurasia* 37:3 (1998–99): 5–12. For a broader view of interethnic relations in Siberia, see also Balzer, "Hot and Cold: Interethnic Relations in Siberia," in Bartholomew Dean and Jerome M. Levi, eds., *At the Risk of Being Heard: Identity, Indigenous Rights, and Postcolonial States* (Ann Arbor: University of Michigan Press, 2003), 112–141.

12. For a more detailed discussion of the Tuva Ensemble, see Mark C. van Tongeren, *Overtone Singing: Physics and Metaphysics of Harmonics in East and West,* rev. 2d ed. (Amsterdam: Fusica, 2004), 100–103.

13. Kuular, Ondar, and Xovalyg were not the first Tuvan musicians to perform in the United States. That honor goes to Gennadi Chash (1961–1998), who appeared at the Smithsonian Folklife Festival of 1988.

14. Andrew Higgins, "Tunes of War as Throat-Singers Go for the Jugular," *The Independent,* London, April 27, 1995. The motive for Sherig-ool's comment seems to have been a general concern for maintaining the dignity and integrity of Tuva's cultural patrimony and spiritual culture as a bulwark against exploitation by outsiders, whether colonizers or globalizers. Comments by other officials, however, suggest that the Tuvan government viewed itself as the lawful beneficiary of profits accruing from the public performance of its cultural patrimony beyond the borders of Tuva. For an erudite theorization of the role of spiritual culture in forming national identity, see Partha Chatterjee, *The Nation and Its Fragments: Colonial and Postcolonial Histories,* in *The Partha Chatterjee Omnibus* (New Delhi: Oxford University Press, 1999), 6–9.

15. For a historical study of Buddhism among the Tuvans, see Marina Vasil'evna Mongush, *Istoriia Buddizma v Tuve* [The history of Buddhism in Tuva] (Novosibirsk: Nauka, 2001). See also N. L. Zhukovskaia, "Lamaism in Tuva," *Anthropology and Archeology of Eurasia* 39:4 (2001): 48–49.

16. A. N. Aksenov was one of a pleiad of mid-twentieth-century Russian musical ethnographers—others included Viktor A. Uspensky (1879–1949), Viktor Beliaev (1888–1968), and A. V. Zataevich (1869–1936)—who used concepts of scale, mode, genre, and style derived from Russian musicology and folkloristics to study indigenous music in Siberia and Central Asia. Though aspects of their methodologies may seem dated, the ethnographic value of their published work has not diminished. See, for example, the recent new edition of Uspensky and Beliaev's two-volume *Turkmenskaia muzyka* [Turkmen

music], ed. Shakhym Gullyev (Almaty: Soros Fund—Kazakhstan, 2003; first published in 1928 [vol. 1] and 1936 [vol. 2]). Aksenov's *Tuvinskaia narodnaia muzyka* [Tuvan folk music] remains a model of musicological rigor, whose breadth in surveying diverse genres of Tuvan music has not been surpassed in the forty years since its publication.

17. Statistics concerning percentages of Tuvan and non-Tuvan populations in different years and in different regions of Tuva are available in Anaibin, "The Republic of Tuva: A Model of Ethnological Monitoring," 18–30.

2. THE WORLD IS ALIVE WITH THE MUSIC OF SOUND

1. According to linguist David Harrison (personal communication), the second of the onomatopoetic water sounds that Tolya Kuular illustrates, *shuluraash,* has many phonetic variants. Harrison provided a list of onomatopoetic words he has collected in Tuva, which includes the following: *shylyreesh, shölyreesh, shaluraash,* and *sholuraash,* each with a slightly different sound reference. Harrison points out that shifting vowels within one and the same consonant structure is a typical Tuvan strategy for forming onomatopoeias. The same process exists in English to a more limited extent, e.g., "babbling," "burbling," "bubbling."

The subtitled text that Tolya Kuular speaks is the following:

> "This kind of stream usually appears after a strong rain in the mountains, and the sound of the stream is different in different places. Since the stream isn't permanent, the rocks are not firmly set, and quite often they get dislodged. The sound of rocks falling and hitting other rocks combined with the sound of flowing water is called *xoluraash.*"

(second episode):
"Here the sound is lower, and in contrast to *xoluraash,* the water speaks. This is called *shuluraash.* If you listen carefully, it's as if the water is carrying on a conversation. Compared with the human voice, it's like a middle voice. You can also use *shuluraash* to describe a very talkative person."

2. The Tuvan word *"ee"* has cognates with similar or identical meanings in other Inner Asian Turkic languages, as well as in Mongolian (*ezen*).

3. For another evocation of the power of the river spirit, see Zoya Kyrgys's description of how swimmers pour milk into a river and sing a song as an offering to the local spirit-master before entering the water. *Tuvinskoe gorlovoe penie* [Tuvan throat-singing] (hereinafter, work will be referred to as "Tuvan Throat-Singing") (Novosibirsk: Nauka, 2002), 70.

4. It is hard to say what percentage of contemporary Tuvans embrace what I am calling a traditional worldview and believe in spirits. Anecdotal evidence suggests that among young people, many still adhere to these beliefs, while others are aggressively apostate. "Shamanism is total nonsense," a young Tuvan woman in Kyzyl once told me. "Most shamans are just in it for money."

5. For a comparison to Buryat *oboo* rituals, see Caroline Humphrey, *Marx Went Away—But Karl Stayed Behind* (Ann Arbor: University of Michigan Press, 1998), 378.

6. Reverence for trees is discussed more broadly in Tsui Yenhu, "A Comparative Study of the Attitudes of the Peoples of Pastoral Areas of Inner Asia Towards Their Environ-

ments," in Caroline Humphrey and David Sneath, eds., *Culture and Environment in Inner Asia*, vol. 2 (Cambridge: White Horse Press, 1996), 1–24.

7. For a comparative description of how body parts are metaphorically mapped onto land among herders in several different regions of Mongolia, see Caroline Humphrey, "Chiefly and Shamanist Landscapes in Mongolia," in Eric Hirsch and Michael O'Hanlon, eds., *The Anthropology of Landscape: Perspectives on Place and Space* (Oxford: Clarendon Press, 1995), 144.

8. Valentina Süzükei, *Tuvinskie traditsionnye muzykal'nye instrumenty* [Tuvan traditional musical instruments] (hereinafter, work will be referred to as "Tuvan Traditional Musical Instruments") (Kyzyl: Tuvinskii nauchno-issledovatel'skii institut iazyka, literatury, i istorii, 1989), 29–31. See also Kenin-Lopsang, "The Drum in the Cave," recorded in 1992 from Amin Ondar, in *Shamanic Songs and Myths of Tuva* (Budapest: Akadémiai Kiadó, and Los Angeles: International Society for Trans-Oceanic Research, 1997), 82. In Mongolia there are also many legends about the origin of the *igil* (Mongolian, *ikil*).

9. These musical-environmental recordings became the compact disc *"Tuva, Among the Spirits,"* released by Smithsonian Folkways.

10. Tuvan scholar Mongush B. Kenin-Lopsan elaborates on the definition of the word *"xaiyrakan"* in the glossary to his work, *Shamanic Songs and Myths of Tuva:* "This word is sacred for Bear and Dragon deities. It is not so much a word for god, as it is to differentiate between that which is human and of this world and that which is sacred, holy and above normal human beings. Refers to a deity which dwells in the Upper Skies. Perhaps not the highest deity, but the most well known" (114). Sacred words, concepts, and ceremonies concerning the bear are the subject of A. Irving Hallowell's authoritative monograph, "Bear Ceremonialism in the Western Hemisphere," *American Anthropologist* 28:1 (1926): 1–175.

11. The syncretic religious practices common among Tuvans are discussed in V. P. D'iakonova, "Lamaism and Its Influence on the Worldview and Religious Cults of the Tuvans," *Anthropology and Archeology of Eurasia* 39:4 (2001), 53–75.

12. Gombosurengiin Begzjav, b. 1931, Davst Sum, June 20, 2000.

13. Sayan's comment is interesting in its emphasis on respect for sacred landscape as a criterion for being a "real" Tuvan; however, it was not clear from the context whether he was contrasting "real" Tuvans with non-Tuvans, i.e., Russians, or whether he was lamenting the decline of traditional mores.

14. Russian folk music also has "long-songs" (*protiazhnie pesni*), but these belong musically to an entirely different genre and style.

15. For more on the relationship of long-song contour to topography based on discussions with Mongolians representing a variety of different social groups and geographical locations, see Carole Pegg, *Mongolian Music, Dance, and Oral Narrative* (Seattle: University of Washington Press, 2001), 106.

16. Valentina Süzükei recounts a similar story in *Tuvan Traditional Musical Instruments* (45). In the story, wind excites the strings of a zither (*chadagan*) placed atop a yurt so that the strings could dry, whereupon an old man takes it up and plays it, and by making beautiful music, he is able to convince an unwilling mother to breastfeed the future heir to the khan.

17. The summer 2000 expedition was supported by the National Geographic Society's Committee for Research and Exploration and included Mongolian musicologist Erdenechimig, videographer Bill Gaspirini, sound engineer Joel Gordon, linguist David

Harrison, ethnomusicologist Peter Marsh, and interpreter Sansargereltekh (the latter is a talented pianist, composer, and artist).

18. Carole Pegg quotes Sengedorj as saying that the wind may be held for four to five hours, while Tserendavaa, a musician and herder who lives in Chandman, said that it can be held for twenty-four hours and "sometimes for as long as three days" (*Mongolian Music*, 103).

19. Tserendavaa's career and musical ideas are extensively described in Pegg, ibid., 62 ff.

20. Pegg's account of Bazarsad is similar (ibid., 61). Galdan Khan is discussed in David Morgan, *The Mongols* (Oxford: Blackwell, 1990), 205.

INTERLUDE

1. Since 1995, many more recordings of Tuvan music have been released. While cassettes of contemporary Tuvan singer-songwriters are widely available in Kyzyl, the only internationally distributed compact disc for sale is an unlicensed version of twenty tracks from the Smithsonian Folkways release *Tuva: Voices from the Center of Asia*, supplemented by fourteen additional tracks taken from local archives. The disc is titled *Xörekteer: Virtuozy tuvinskogo gorlovogo peniia* [Xörekteer: Tuvan throat-singing virtuosos] and credits Zoya Kyrgys as the producer.

3. LISTENING THE TUVAN WAY

1. The use of analogy and metaphor to explain timbre is not unusual. In "The Paradox of Timbre" (*Ethnomusicology* 46:1 [2002]: 56–95), a study that draws extensively on African music, Cornelia Fales points out, "With no domain-specific adjectives, timbre must be described in metaphor or by analogy to other senses, and this is true in many, many languages of the world" (57).

2. Idamchap is described in chapter 1 as the performer of a shamanic purification ritual. His photo, reproduced in this work as plate 5, appears on the cover of the Smithsonian Folkways compact disc *Tuva: Voices from the Center of Asia*.

3. Valentina Süzükei used the term "undertone" not to characterize an acoustic phenomenon, but rather, a perceptual one. Musicians sometimes use "undertone" to describe resonances that seem to be lower than the fundamental pitch of a sound. Such perceptions, however, invariably result from a misidentification of the fundamental frequency, which can only produce overtones, not undertones.

4. Anthropologist Marjorie Balzer, an expert on Siberian shamanism, notes that the free and flexible sense of time and space described by Valentina Süzükei in relation to timbre-centered music and to oral epic is also a shamanic concept (personal communication).

5. In this statement, Valentina Süzükei is of course not making a metaphysical claim about access to the Unfiltered, but rather, she is suggesting that it is possible to listen in a way that is relatively more attentive.

6. Fales, "The Paradox of Timbre," *Ethnomusicology* 46:1 (2002): 68.

7. Ibid., 73, 78, 87.

8. Sendenžavyn Dulam, "Conte, chant et instruments de musique: quelques légendes d'origine mongoles," *Etudes mongoles* 18 (1987): 33–47, cited in Alain Desjacques, "La

Dimension orphique de la musique mongole," *Cahiers de Musiques Traditionnelles* 3 (1990): 104.

9. "Thing-in-itself" is a free translation of the Tuvan "noun + *bodu*" construction. It has no connection with the English translation of Kant's *Ding an sich*, also rendered as "thing-in-itself."

10. I do not mean to suggest that any interest in the prehistory of music is purely romantic. For example, Eduard Alekseyev, in *Ranne fol'klornoe intonirovanie* [The pitch aspect of primitive singing] (Moscow: Sovetskii Kompozitor, 1986), offered a rigorous theory about the genesis and evolution of tonal systems based on decades of research on music in Inner Asia as well as analysis of transcriptions and recordings of sources from other parts of the world. In his work, Alekseyev hypothesized that fixed pitch systems such as pentatonicism and diatonicism evolved from archaic forms of tonality, in which pitches tended toward fluidity rather than fixity, and timbre served as the preeminent parameter of sound organization. There appears to be a wide gulf, however, between the methodologies of scholars such as Alekseyev, who work backward toward prehistory from studies of extant musical systems, and those whose speculations about the origins of music come from evidence outside of music itself. For example, contributors to a recent edited volume, *The Origins of Music,* Nils L. Wallin, Björn Merker, and Steven Brown, eds. (Cambridge, Mass.: MIT Press, 2000), draw on evidence from anthropology, bioacoustics, evolutionary psychology, ethology, neurobiology, and zoology, while ethnomusicologists are scarcely represented among the authors, and little of the diverse and interesting material in the book addresses music per se.

11. Throat-singers and ethnographers of throat-singing are far from the only ones interested in the musical representation of water. Western music has a long history of "water music" that continues to the present. Recent works of interest in this vein are Tan Dun's "Water Passion after St. Matthew" (commissioned in 2000 by the International Bach Academy of Stuttgart, Germany to commemorate the 250th anniversary of Bach's death) and Tristan Murail's "Partage des Eaux" (1996).

12. A good example of a nineteenth-century European song cycle in which flowing water is represented instrumentally is Schubert's *Die schöne Müllerin* [The fair maid of the mill]. In the opening song, "Das Wandern" [Wandering], the flow of a brook is represented by a steady stream of sixteenth-notes on the piano, while in the penultimate song, "Der Müller und der Bach" [The miller and the brook], the brook is represented by flowing, bubbling gestures in a major key, in contrast to the slow, minor-key music that represents the miller. For these insights, I am grateful to my Dartmouth College colleague, pianist Sally Pinkas, and to program notes for her performance of *Die schöne Müllerin* on November 23, 2003 (program notes by Kathryn L. Shanks Libin of Vassar College).

13. For the results of this work, see the recording *Tuva, Among the Spirits.*

14. Zoya Kyrgys, in *Tuvan Throat-Singing,* confirms Kaigal-ool's account with the following quotation from an informant, Andrei Mongush: "The closer you come to a stream, the stronger its humming becomes, and there's the urge to sing so that your voice can become louder." Kyrgys notes, "It's interesting that frequently throat-singers sitting on opposite banks of a river would engage in a competition. Each tried to outdo his rivals in achieving a more exact imitation of the hum of the river" (73).

15. For a more detailed explanation of this process, see Theodore Levin and Michael Edgerton, "The Throat Singers of Tuva," *Scientific American* 281:3 (September 1999): 70–77.

16. See van Tongeren, *Overtone Singing,* chap. 1, "Singing Harmonics," for an explanation and description of various styles of reinforced overtone vocal production. See also Trân Quang Hai, "A la découverte du chant diphonique," in Guy Cornut, ed., *Moyens d'investigation et pédagogie de la voix chantée: actes du colloque tenu les 8, 9 et 10 février 2001 au Conservatoire national de région de Lyon* (Lyon: Symétrie, 2002), 117–132; Hugo Zemp and Trân Quang Hai, "Recherches expérimentales sur le chant diphonique," *Cahiers de Musiques Traditionnelles* 4 (1991): 27–68; and Gerrit Bloothooft, Eldrid Bringmann, Marieke van Capellen, Jolanda B. van Luipen, and Koen P. Thomassen, "Acoustics and Perception of Overtone Singing," part 1, *Journal of the Acoustical Society of America* 92:4 (Oct. 1992): 1827–1836.

17. van Tongeren, *Overtone Singing,* 27–28.

18. For a detailed elaboration of *kai,* see Y(uri) I. Sheikin and V. S. Nikiforova, "Altaiskoe epicheskoe intonirovanie" [Altai epic intonation], in *Altaiskie geroicheskie skazaniia Ochi-Bala [i] Kan-Altyn* [The Altai heroic tales Ochi-Bala and Kan-Altyn], vol. 15 of *Pamiatniki fol'klora narodov sibiri i dal'nego vostoka* [Monuments of the folklore of Siberian and far eastern peoples], Russian Academy of Sciences, Siberian Branch, Institute of Philology (Novosibirsk: Nauka, 1997), 47–70.

19. The Altai term *"alkysh"* is cognate with Tuvan *algysh,* Sakha *algys,* and Evenki *alga,* all of which have similar or identical meanings.

20. See Huston Smith, Kenneth N. Stevens, and Raymond S. Tomlinson, "On an Unusual Mode of Chanting by Certain Tibetan Lamas," *Journal of the Acoustical Society of America* 41:5 (May 1967): 1262–1264; and Huston Smith and Kenneth Stevens, "Unique Vocal Abilities of Certain Tibetan Lamas," *American Anthropologist* 69:2 (April 1967): 209–212.

21. Kyrgys, *Tuvan Throat-Singing,* 45.

22. van Tongeren, *Overtone Singing,* 29. See also ibid., chapter 4, "Overtone Singing in Other Traditional Music," "Tibet: Sound and Symbol," 145–154.

23. Kyrgys, *Tuvan Throat-Singing,* 7.

24. Ibid., 81–82.

25. Kombu (1892–1944) was a well-known throat-singer from Xorum-Dag and Bayan-Dugai, Chöön-Xemchik *kojuun.* He was Kaigal-ool Xovalyg's great-uncle (the brother of his paternal grandfather). Vladimir Oidupaa (b. 1951) is a controversial figure in Tuva. Imprisoned several times for violent crimes, he is currently serving a long sentence, and he produces his music from prison (see http:www.tarbagan.com/oidupaa.htm [accessed May 30, 2005]). His signature style of throat-singing includes accompaniment on the *bayan,* a small accordion, and though he is denounced by Tuvan cultural officials, his music remains immensely popular and widely imitated. See van Tongeren, *Overtone Singing,* 96–99.

26. Kyrgyz, *Tuvan Throat-Singing,* 77.

27. Pegg, *Mongolian Music,* 62.

28. Tserendavaa apparently adopted the term *hosmoljin* after it was used by researchers in Ulaanbaatar. Pegg, ibid., notes that this style also includes speaking, singing, humming, and long-song melodies (62). The style categories that Tserendavaa wrote in my field notebook in 2000 distinguished between glottal (*bagalzuuryn*) and throat (*hooloin*) *höömii,* while in Pegg's book, they are grouped together under one and the same style.

29. Sengedorj's system is not among those described by Pegg.

30. Performances of "Gooj Nanaa" by Sengedorj, and of "Buyant Gol" by Yanjiv Tsogt-

baatar, both recorded in 1994, appear on the compact disc *Jargalant Altai: Xöömii and Other Vocal and Instrumental Music from Mongolia* (Pan Records 2050, 1996), produced by Chris Johnston.

31. Conversation with Tserendavaa, Chandman Sum, June 2000.

32. Zoya Kyrgys provides an exhaustive account of the early ethnographies and recordings in the first chapter of *Tuvan Throat-Singing.*

33. Kyrgys, *Tuvan Throat-Singing,* 118.

34. Caroline Humphrey, introduction to Sevyan Vainshtein, in *Nomads of South Siberia* (Cambridge: Cambridge University Press, 1980), 25.

35. Tozhu-Tuvans speak a dialect of Tuvan that is mostly comprehensible by other Tuvan speakers. For a recent ethnographic study of Tozhu reindeer herders, see Brian Donohoe, "'Hey, You! Get Offa My Taiga!' Comparing the Sense of Property Rights Among the Tofa and Tozhu-Tyva," Max Planck Institute for Social Anthropology Working Paper Series, no. 38, Halle/Saale, Germany, 2002. An older ethnography is Sevyan Vainshtein's *Tuvintsy-Todzhintsy* [The Tuvan-Todzhins] (Moscow: Vostochnoi Literatury, 1961).

36. See the website of David Harrison's Altai-Sayan Language and Ethnography Project at http://www.swarthmore.edu/SocSci/Linguistics/aslep/quickfacts.php (accessed on May 30, 2005) (funded by Volkswagen Stiftung).

37. Zoya Kyrgys proposes that throat-singing in Todzhu existed prior to settlement of the region by Russians in the nineteenth century, saying that it gradually disappeared as a result of the "collapse of a style of life and tradition" (*Tuvan Throat-Singing,* 118). This explanation seems unlikely, however, since Russian settlement in Todzhu was extremely limited compared to the vastness of the territory, and Todzhu-Tuvans preserved many other aspects of traditional life, including the structure and function of the clan system. See Sevyan Vainshtein, *Nomads of South Siberia* (Cambridge: Cambridge University Press, 1980), 238.

38. Linguist David Harrison, who participated in the summer 2000 visit to Tsengel *sum,* returned to Tsengel in 2002. On that visit, he was introduced to Batsukh Dorzhu-oglu (b. 1990), a Tuvan boy regarded by the local population as a rising throat-singing talent (oral communication, David Harrison).

39. Pegg, *Mongolian Music,* 65, 253–297.

40. Ibid., 60.

41. S[evyan] I. Vainshtein, "A Musical Phenomenon Born in the Steppes," *Soviet Anthropology and Archeology* 18:3 (1979–80): 68–81. Originally published as "Fenomen muzykal'nogo iskusstva, rozhdennyi v stepiakh," *Sovetskaia etnografiia,* no 1 (1980): 149–159.

4. SOUND MIMESIS

1. In *Mimesis and Alterity* (New York: Routledge, 1993), a political and social history of mimesis, anthropologist Michael Taussig singles out Darwin's description of his encounter with the Fuegians for extended critique. Taussig reads the episode as a political statement about the relation between colonizers and colonized, in which "civilization takes measure of its difference through its reflection in primitives." Taussig then provides the following exegesis: "So deeply invested is this scene in Western cultural patrimony, and hence selfhood, that it cannot be shrugged aside or calmly studied from a distance because it enters in all manner of subtle ways into that very Self, into the apparatus that might attempt the

shrugging and, most pertinent of all, into its very philosophy of the senses and of copying the real—all the more baffling on account of the way by which mimesis entertains bewildering reciprocities, mixes them with sentience, with pleasures, with pain, and with the 'ludicrous' and 'odd mixture of surprise and imitation'" (79).

2. Charles Darwin, *The Descent of Man, and Selection in Relation to Sex* (New York: New York University Press, 1989), 875–881.

3. See Geoffrey Miller, "Evolution of Human Music through Sexual Selection," in *The Origins of Music,* ed. Nils L. Wallin, Björn Merker, and Steven Brown (Cambridge, Mass.: MIT Press, 2000), 329–360.

4. For this insight, I am indebted to Merlin Donald's *Origins of the Modern Mind* (Cambridge, Mass.: Harvard University Press, 1991), 167. For a recent hypothesis about the role of imitation in the evolutionary path leading to language, see Michael A. Arbib, "The Mirror System, Imitation, and the Evolution of Language," in *Imitation in Animals and Artifacts,* ed. Kerstin Dautenhahn and Chrystopher L. Nehaniv (Cambridge, Mass.: MIT Press, 2002), 229–280.

5. Donald, *Origins of the Modern Mind.* See also Donald's more recent *A Mind So Rare: The Evolution of Human Consciousness* (New York: Norton, 2001), and "Imitation and Mimesis," in *Perspectives on Imitation: From Neuroscience to Social Science,* vol. 2, ed. Susan Hurley and Nick Chater (Cambridge, Mass.: MIT Press, 2005), 283–300.

6. Donald defines culture as "a collective system of knowledge and behavior." *Origins of the Modern Mind,* 148.

7. Ibid., 269, 370. The quotations from Donald's *Origins of the Modern Mind* in the next paragraph are all drawn from 168–169.

8. Curiously, the relation of mimesis and music is little discussed in Wallin, Merker, and Brown, *The Origins of Music,* which brings together contributions from biologists, linguists, psychologists, anthropologists, and others. Beyond studies of mimicry per se, the only extensive discussion of mimesis is in Jean Molino's "Toward an Evolutionary Theory of Music and Language" (165–176).

9. My thinking about sound metaphors and the cultural construction of meaning has been influenced by James W. Fernandez's edited volume, *Beyond Metaphor: The Theory of Tropes in Anthropology* (Stanford: Stanford University Press, 1991) and, in particular, by Terrence Turner's contribution to this volume, "'We Are Parrots,' 'Twins Are Birds': Play of Tropes as Operational Structure" (121–158). In thinking more generally about symbol and metaphor in music, I have been influenced by the work of Russian music theorist Boris Asaf'ev, whose seminal publication, *Muzykal'naia forma kak protsess* [Musical form as process] (Moscow: Izdatel'stvo Akademii Nauk SSSR, 1957), and in particular the second of its three parts, *Intonatsia,* proposes an important but still too little known theory of musical meaning. In discussing the representational strategies of sound mimesis, I have not included any discussion of how sound and music may embody myth. This is not because mythic thought does not lend itself to musical or other sonic representation—on the contrary, the relation between myth and music is territory that has been well trodden, both by scholars and by musicians and composers themselves (for scholarship, good examples are Claude Levi-Strauss, *The Raw and the Cooked* [New York: Harper and Row, 1969] and Steven Feld, *Song and Sentiment* [Philadelphia: University of Pennsylvania Press, 1982]). Rather, I have not discussed myth because, in my own field research, I did not find musical representations of myths. While musical representations of legends and stories are common in Inner Asia, these legends and stories do not constitute myths in the archetypal sense in which that term is commonly understood.

10. For an enlightening discussion of Cage's work, see Lewis Hyde, *Trickster Makes this World: Mischief, Myth, and Art* (New York: Farrar, Straus and Giroux, 1998), 141–150. Hyde makes the important observation that, for Cage, chance operations represented a spiritual practice or discipline. Hyde finds support for this interpretation in Cage's frequent quotation of Meister Eckhart, "We are made perfect by what happens to us rather than by what we do" (142).

11. For insight into the three works by John Adams, I am grateful to Daniel Colvard, whose 2004 honors thesis at Dartmouth College, "Three Works by John Adams," provided fresh and original insight as well as access to unpublished or unrecorded compositions.

12. Igor Stravinsky, *An Autobiography* (New York: W. W. Norton, 1962), 53.

13. Scholars engaged in the study of musical semiotics have devoted a great deal of attention to the mechanisms by which autonomous musical works operate as a system of acoustical signs. Jean-Jacques Nattiez, arguably musicology's foremost exponent of musical semiotics, argues that formal and asemantic theories such as those of Stravinsky do not preclude the possibility of identifying semiotic processes within aesthetically autonomous musical works, in particular processes concerned with "identity, equivalence, and contrast between the internal sonic phenomena of a work" (Nattiez, "The Contribution of Musical Semiotics to the Semiotic Discussion in General," in Thomas A. Sebeok, ed., *A Perfusion of Signs* [Bloomington: Indiana University Press, 1977], 127).

14. Plato, *The Republic of Plato,* trans. Francis MacDonald Cornford (New York: Oxford University Press, 1945), 83.

15. For a summary of the speculative tradition of music in Western esotericism, see Joscelyn Godwin, *Harmonies of Heaven and Earth: The Spiritual Dimension of Music from Antiquity to the Avant-Garde* (Rochester, Vt.: Inner Traditions International and New York: Harper and Row, 1987).

16. I use the term "imaginal" in the sense employed by the French philosopher of religion Henri Corbin to denote the inhabitants of a *mundus imaginalis*—an imaginal world that has its own reality and that coexists with the everyday world of ordinary consciousness.

17. Based on musical fieldwork in Mongolia, Alain Desjacques ("La Dimension orphique de la musique mongole," *Cahiers de musiques traditionnelles* 3:90 [1990]: 105) has proposed a taxonomy of imitation whose categories include imitation of sounds—natural, animal, or human; imitation based on observation of animal or human movements; imitation based on observation of a form, relief, or place; and imitation based on observation of an animal or human psychological trait. Desjacques's taxonomy, presented in schematic form and without illustrative examples of all of his categories, nonetheless provides independent support for a metatheory of sound mimesis similar to that proposed here.

18. Anatoly M. Khazanov, *Nomads and the Outside World,* trans. Julia Crookenden (Cambridge: Cambridge University Press, 1984), 94. For a complementary hypothesis about the origin of nomadic pastoralism that draws on genetic geography, see L. Luca Cavalli-Sforza, "The Spread of Agriculture and Nomadic Pastoralism: Insights from Genetics, Linguistics, and Archaeology," in David R. Harris, ed., *The Origins and Spread of Agriculture and Pastoralism in Eurasia* (Washington, D.C.: Smithsonian Institution Press, 1996), in particular, 54–57. On the role of hunting among nomads, see Sevyan Vainshtein, *Nomads of South Siberia,* chap. 5, 166–188.

19. Yuri I. Sheikin notes that deer horns made from both birch bark and wood are found throughout Siberia, and comprise one of the oldest and most representative examples of what Sheikin calls "luring sound-imitation" [*mankovoe zvukopodrazhanie*] used by hunt-

ers. Sheikin provides a detailed taxonomy of such instruments in *Istoriia muzykal'noi kul'tury narodov sibiri* [History of the musical culture of Siberian peoples] (Moscow: Vostochnaia literatura, 2002), 169–189.

20. Valentina Süzükei, *Tuvinskie traditsionnye muzykal'nye instrumenty* [Tuvan Traditional Musical Instruments], 80. See also Kyrgys, *Tuvan Throat-Singing*, 56.

21. In *Mongolian Music, Dance, and Oral Narrative*, Carole Pegg discusses analogous sound-luring techniques among the Mongols as well as a form of dance and gestural mimesis used for hunting marmots (245–246).

22. The Kazakh *sybyzghy* and Bashkir *kurai* are identical to the *shoor/tsuur*. The recently revived Kyrgyz *choor* is also the same instrument as *shoor and tsuur*, but in the performance of revivalists, it is not accompanied by a vocal drone produced by the player.

23. Süzükei, *Tuvan Traditional Musical Instruments*, 72 ff.

24. Pegg, *Mongolian Music, Dance, and Oral Narrative*, 242, recorded a version of the same legend in western Mongolia that recounts the origin of the strummed lute *tovshuur*. She notes that she heard a version of the same myth from Narantsogt, the *tsuur* player from Hovd Aimag.

25. Pegg includes a recording of Narantsogt playing the *tsuur* on the compact disc published with *Mongolian Music, Dance, and Oral Narrative* (track 25).

26. Alain Desjacques, "La Dimension orphique de la musique mongole," *Cahiers de musiques traditionnelles* 3 (1990): 97–107.

27. On the central role of the ludic among the Inner Asian pastoralists, see Iwona Kabzínska-Stawarz, *Games of Mongolian Shepherds* (Warsaw: Institute of the History of Material Culture, Polish Academy of Sciences, 1991). See also A. M. Sagalaev and I. V. Oktiabr'skaia, *Traditsionnoe mirovozzrenie tiurkov Iuzhnoi Sibiri: Znak i ritual* [The traditional worldview of the Turks of South Siberia: Sign and ritual] (Novosibirsk: Nauka, 1990), 120–136.

28. In many cultures, epilepsy is connected with shamanic powers or shamanic lineage. See Mircea Eliade, *Shamanism, Archaic Techniques of Ecstasy*, 15, 20, 24 ff.

29. Wolf-skull *eerens* are depicted in the video files online, track 18, where they hang from the back of Tuvan shaman Lazo Mongush's coat as he performs a purification ritual. Among Turkic peoples, the wolf is a key symbol of transnational solidarity. On wolf imitations, see also chapter 5, "Animal Spirits."

30. For a useful cultural comparison to landscape-oriented music in the Altai, see ethnomusicologist Hugo Zemp's twenty-three-minute film, "Head Voice, Chest Voice," on Alpine singing in Switzerland (coproduced by Ateliers d'ethnomusicologie [Geneva] and CNRS Audiovisuel).

31. In the waning years of the Soviet Union and especially after its breakup, a nativist ecology movement in Siberia has addressed the local legacy of Soviet economic policies that took a heavy toll on the natural environment and on the health of indigenous populations. As in the West, musicians and other artists have turned their performance skills to the support of ecological awareness and activism. In Tuva, the most notable of these was the late Gennadi Chash (1961–1998), an outstanding throat-singer as well as an ardent defender of Tuva's natural resources.

32. Pegg, *Mongolian Music*, 105–106, discusses the same phenomenon in performances of Mongolian long-song and short-song, as well as in dance (*bie*).

33. A fuller portrait of a different Xakas *xaijy*, Vyachaslav Kuchenov, appears in chapter 6, "Epic Dreams."

34. While the Aboriginal concept of "songlines" is best known to the general public from Bruce Chatwin's fictional book of the same name (*The Songlines* [New York: Viking, 1987]), Australian scholars have produced much ethnographic research on Aboriginal music and on the role of sound and music in Aboriginal religion. For an entry point into this bibliography, see T.G.H. Strehlow, *Songs of Central Australia* (Sydney: Angus and Robertson, 1971), W.E.H. Stanner, *On Aboriginal Religion* (Sydney: University of Sydney, 1989), and the bibliography for Allan Marett et al., "Traditional Australian Music," in *The Garland Encyclopedia of World Music,* vol. 9, *Australia and the Pacific Islands,* ed. Adrienne L. Kaeppler and J. W. Love (New York: Garland Publishing, 1998), 447–449.

35. For a discussion of recovering the past through music in an Apache community, see David W. Samuels, *Putting a Song on Top of It: Expression and Identity on the San Carlos Apache Reservation* (Tucson: University of Arizona Press, 2004), esp. 123–148. Samuels notes an "antinostalgia" in such recoverability, which is "mediated through the affective response to expressive forms" (138).

36. "Waterfalls of Song: An Acoustemology of Place Resounding in Bosavi, Papua New Guinea," in Steven Feld and Keith Basso, eds., *Senses of Place* (Santa Fe, N.M.: School of American Research Press, 1996), 100.

37. Ibid., 114.

38. For another example of rainforest acoustemology, see Marina Roseman, *Healing Sounds from the Malaysian Rainforest: Temiar Music and Medicine* (Los Angeles: University of California Press, 1991), in particular, chap. 3, section 3, "Singers of the Landscape," 63–71. See also Roseman's recording, *Dream Songs and Healing Sounds in the Rainforests of Malaysia,* Smithsonian Folkways SF 40417 (1995).

39. Witness, for example, the brouhaha raised by Susan McClary's interpretation of the recapitulation in the first movement of Beethoven's Ninth Symphony as signifying "one of the most horrifyingly violent episodes in the history of music" (*Feminine Endings: Music, Gender, and Sexuality* [Minneapolis: University of Minnesota Press, 1991], 128) or the controversy that still swirls around Solomon Volkov's *Testimony: The Memoirs of Dmitri Shostakovich,* trans. Antonina W. Bouis (New York: Harper and Row, 1979). In *Testimony,* Volkov claims that much of Shostakovich's work comprises a form of veiled protest against Stalinism and the Soviet regime.

40. The programmatic quality of instrumental music is discussed en passant in Alma Kunanbaeva, "Kazakh Music," in *The Garland Encyclopedia of World Music,* vol. 6, *The Middle East,* 956–958. Kyrgyz musicologist Kamchybek Dyushaliev also touches on this topic in chapter 6 of *Kyrgyzskoe narodnoe muzykal'noe tvorchestvo* [Kyrgyz folk musical art] (Bishkek: Soros Fund—Kyrgyzstan, 1999), as does Kyrgyz organologist Sagynaly Subanaliev in *Traditsionnaia instrumental'naia muzyka i instrumentarii kyrgyzov* [Traditional instrumental music and instruments of the Kyrgyz] (Bishkek: Uchkun, 2003). By contrast, text-based narrative genres in Inner Asia, in particular, oral epic, have long been the object of scholarly attention. Russian and German scholars took an early lead in these studies. In the last third of the nineteenth century and first third of the twentieth century, Radlov, Budukov, Vladimirtsov, Poppe, and Zhirmunsky collected, transcribed, and published important collections of oral poetry. Later came Karl Reichl, Yuri Sheikin, and native scholars such as V. E. Mainogasheva (Xakasia), S. S. Surazakov, S. M. Kamashev (Altai), and S. M. Orus-ool (Tuva). In recent years, the Siberian branch of the Russian Academy of Sciences with its base in Novosibirsk has published critical editions of oral poetry from Xakasia, Altai, Tuva, and Buryatia.

41. A version of this piece, "Qâradali," is performed on the *dutar* by Shuqqrat Razakov on the compact disc *Uzbekistan: Music of Khorezm,* track 9 (UNESCO/Auvidis, 1996, recordings and commentary by Otanazar Matyakubov and Theodore Levin). The tradition of conveying ideas and suggestions to kings through music was not restricted to nomads. Persian music specialist Margaret Caton notes that the same phenomenon existed in Sasanian Iran, and that Iranians attribute its origin to Bârbad, the court musician who some consider the founder of Iranian classical music ("Performance Practice in Iran: *Radīf* and Improvisation," in *The Garland Encyclopedia of World Music,* vol. 6, *The Middle East,* 131).

42. During the Soviet era, Kazakhstan was regarded as a buffer zone connected to Central Asia but not formerly part of it. The region was known in Soviet geopolitics as "Central Asia and Kazakhstan." The nation now called Kyrgyzstan was known in Soviet times as Kyrgyzia.

43. For a discussion of the "autochthonic theory," see Tyntchtykbek Tchoroev, "Historiography of Post-Soviet Kyrgyzstan," *International Journal of Middle Eastern Studies* 34 (2002): 355.

44. On the role of "play" in the spiritual and expressive culture of Inner Asian pastoralists, see Roberte Hamayon, "Des usages de 'jeu' dans le vocabulaire rituel du monde altaïque," *Études mongoles et sibériennes* 30–31 (*Jeux rituels*) (1999–2000): 11–45.

45. *Aitys* and *tartys* are the Kazakh forms of the words. In Kyrgyz, they are pronounced *aitysh* and *tartysh.*

46. Kunanbaeva, "Kazakh Music," 953.

47. Ibid., 955.

48. B. Amanov, *Tartys kak spetsificheskaia forma muzitsirovaniia v muzykal'noi kul'ture kazakhov* [Tartys as a specific form of music-making in Kazakh musical culture], in A. Muxambetova, ed., *Instrumental'naia muzyka kazaxskogo naroda* [Instrumental music of the kazakh people] (Alma-Ata: Oner, 1985), 31.

49. Nurlanbek Nyshanov noted that only "happy music" is performed with gestures, and that "sad music" is never so performed.

50. On Qurmanghazy, see Asiya Muxambetova, ed., *Kurmangazy i traditsionnaia muzyka na rubezhe tysiacheletii* [Qurmanghazy and traditional music at the turn of the millennium: proceedings of an international conference dedicated to the 175th anniversary of Qurmanghazy's birth, Almaty, November 9–11, 1998] (Almaty: Daik-Press, 1998).

51. The most prolific transcriber of Kyrgyz folk music was Aleksandr Viktorovich Zataevich (1869–1936), who began his work among the Kyrgyz in 1920. His publications include *1000 pesen kirgizskogo naroda* [1000 songs of the Kyrgyz people] (Orenburg: n.p., 1925), which consists of both Kyrgyz and Kazakh music; *500 kazakhskikh pesen i kuiev* [500 Kazakh songs and *kuis*] (Alma-Ata: n.p., 1931); and *250 kirgizskikh instrumental'nykh p'es i napevov* [250 Kyrgyz instrumental songs and tunes] (Moscow: n.p., 1934). After Zataevich's death, a collection of his transcriptions was compiled and edited by V. Vinogradov (A. Zataevich, *Kirgizskie instrumental'nye p'esy i napevy* [Kyrgyz instrumental songs and tunes] [Moscow: n.p., 1971]).

52. This biographical information comes from Kamchybek Diushaliev and Ekaterina Luzanova's *Kyrgyzskoe narodnoe muzykal'noe tvorchestvo* [Kyrgyz folk musical art], a history of Kyrgyz music written for college and conservatory students (197).

53. The text spoken by Namazbek Uraliev before he performs the piece is as follows (this text appears in subtitles in the video files online):

Atai said, "Ak-Tamak is the wife, Kök-Tamak is the husband. They lived at the wide bend of a river, in Talas, on the very plane tree on which our sister Ai-Chürek sometimes landed." (Ai-Chürek was the wife of Semetei, who was the son of Manas. She transformed herself into a swan while still alive, flew around the world and saw everything, and then changed herself back into a beautiful woman). "And there they built a nest and lived happily. One day, Ak-Tamak began an argument and said to her husband, 'Here in Talas, there aren't any fruit and berries growing. Let's resettle in the direction of Aksy, where there are fruits and vegetables.' And Kök-Tamak said to her, 'Eh, old woman, no let's not leave Talas. You know very well that in his time, our father, Manas, loved Talas. Let's not leave here. Around the Ala-Too mountain ridge, whose summits are eternally covered in white snow, even in the middle of summer, it's not terribly hot.' Not being able to agree, they decided to compete in song, and whoever sang better, would choose whether to stay put or fly away. Ak-Tamak said, 'You sing first,' and here Kök-Tamak begins to sing."

"Ak-Tamak asks, 'Have you finished your song?'"

"'Yes, now it's your turn.' And here's what Ak-Tamak sang."

"In a transparent spring, washing her wings, she sang as follows."

"And here, flying to the top of the plane tree, she looked around and decided they'd go toward Kara-Buura and Chatkal. And thus she beat her husband, and from the expanses of Talas, they took off. And it's said that in that way, they flew away."

54. My English translation corresponds to the version printed in Valentina Süzükei's book, *Tuvan Traditional Musical Instruments* (28–29). In the book, however, the story is attributed to throat-singer Kombu Oorzhak, Süzükei Ondar's uncle, who also knew it. This attribution was suggested by a former director of the Institute of Language, Literature, and History, who was concerned that Dr. Süzükei not give the appearance that her fieldwork was conducted exclusively within her own family. It was customary, however, for Tuvan ethnographers to interview members of their own family, who often served as rich sources of information. In retrospect, Valentina Süzükei regrets not having credited her mother, who was indeed the source of the particular version paraphrased in her book.

55. For a study of the *morin huur* and its central role in the enforced modernization of musical practice that took place in Mongolia throughout the twentieth century, see Peter Marsh, *The Horse-head Fiddle and the Cosmopolitan Reimagination of Tradition in Mongolia* (New York: Routledge, 2005).

56. Valentina's comment that "people hear what they want to hear" illuminates an important semiotic principle of sound mimesis, namely, that the particular set of features selected as a basis for iconic representation through sound and music is at least partially arbitrary, thus reinforcing the essentially symbolic nature of sound mimesis. The symbolic properties of mimesis are mitigated, however, when performers prime listeners with specific interpretations of musical narratives. After such priming, listeners are more likely to hear what they have been told they will hear, and thus music will appear more mimetic than it would otherwise. Priming also accounts for the contextual specificity of mimetic representation. Sound mimesis makes most sense to listeners who share—or are directed to—an experience of the landscapes and soundscapes that it references.

57. *Bie* is used by Oirats, *biyelgee* by Halhas. Carole Pegg lists a number of different kinds of *bie* (*biy,* in her transcription) in *Mongolian Music,* 90–93.

58. A pertinent analogy to the rhythmic asymmetries that pervade nomadic sound mimesis is the aesthetics of irregularity so central to Japanese arts, both visual and aural, for which natural landscapes and soundscapes provide much of the imagery (or in the case of gardens, the content itself). In *The Unknown Craftsman: A Japanese Insight into Beauty* (Tokyo/New York/London: Kodansha International, 1989 [1972]), Sōetsu Yanagi, founder of the Japanese craft movement, writes about the beauty of irregularity in the making of tea bowls. "The beauty of irregularity—which in its true form is actually liberated from both regularity and irregularity—the asymmetric principle contains the seed of the highest form of beauty known to man" (126).

59. Roberte Hamayon sees dance among the Inner Asian pastoralists as a form of ritualized play whose inspiration is at root shamanic. Furthermore, Hamayon views music as having developed to fill a gap created by the retreat of this shamanic "play" ("Des usages de 'jeu' dans le vocabulaire rituel du monde altaïque," *Jeux Rituels,* 39). Linking dance among Turkic and Mongol pastoralists first and foremost to ritualized play, as opposed to autonomous music, make sense on the evidence of practices that continue today, for example, the dialogue songs (*oyïn*) of the Northern Xakas, and the *ohuokai* (also transcribed as *osuoxai*) circle dance-songs of the Sakha. On *osuoxai,* see A. S. Larionova, "Yakuty," in *Muzykal'naia kul'tura sibiri* [The musical culture of Siberia], vol. 1 (Novosibirsk: Novosibirsk State Conservatory, 1997), 185–208. See also Eduard E. Alekseev, "*Est' li u yakutov mnogogolosie?*" [Do the Yakuts have polyphony?], *Sovetskaia muzyka,* no. 5 (1967): 97–105.

60. Jean During, *Musiques d'Asie Centrale: l'esprit d'une tradition* (Paris: Cité de la Musique/Actes Sud, 1998), 21.

61. In *Mille plateaux,* Deleuze and Guattari credit composer and music theorist Pierre Boulez with being the first to develop the implications of the "smooth" and the "striated" in music. "In the simplest terms," Deleuze and Guattari wrote, "Boulez says that in a smooth space-time one occupies without counting, whereas in a striated space-time one counts in order to occupy. He makes palpable or perceptible the difference between nonmetric and metric multiplicities, directional and dimensional spaces. He renders them sonorous or musical. Undoubtedly, his personal work is composed of these relations, created or recreated musically" (477). For Boulez's characterization of smooth and striated space, see "Musical Space" in Pierre Boulez, *Boulez on Music Today,* trans. Susan Bradshaw and Richard Rodney Bennett (Cambridge, Mass.: Harvard University Press, 1971), 83–98. For information about Deleuze's interest in nomadic music, I am indebted to André Bernold, who sent Deleuze the Tuvan ensemble Huun-Huur-Tu's recording, *The Orphan's Lament,* and later told me that Deleuze had written him to say that he had found the recording "very impressive" (personal communication).

62. Deleuze and Guattari note that in smooth space, perception "is based on symptoms and evaluations rather than measures and properties. That is why smooth space is occupied by intensities, wind and noise, forces, and sonorous and tactile qualities, as in the desert, steppe, or ice. Striated space, on the contrary, is canopied by the sky as measure and by the measurable visual qualities deriving from it" (*A Thousand Plateaus,* 479). The distinction between the centrality of measurement in striated space as opposed to the continuous evaluation of sensory input in smooth space correlates well with the distinction developed in this work between pitch-centered listening and timbral listening, and helps explain why the latter plays such an important role in sound mimesis.

63. As During points out in a detailed study of rhythm in "trance" music of the Baluch and in the Uzbek-Tajik "limping" metro-rhythmic genre called Talqin, Talqincha, or Chapandâz (also known as *aksak* among Turkish musicians), asymmetrical rhythms may be metrically framed, and it is precisely the tension between systematic asymmetry and the attempt to represent this asymmetry metrically that may help to induce trance states ("Rhythmes ovoïdes et quadrature du cycle," *Cahiers de Musiques Traditionnelles* 10 [1997]: 17–36).

64. One may observe exactly such a process of "sedentarization" in the music of Kyrgyz musician Nurlanbek Nyshanov, discussed earlier in this chapter. Nyshanov grew up in a rural, mountainous region of Kyrgyzstan, and his early musical life was centered around solo performance on jew's harp and *komuz*. Later he moved to Kyrgyzstan's capital city, Bishkek, and in the conditions of urbanity he felt drawn to ensemble performance. Nyshanov himself remarked that the "ensemblization" of Kyrgyz music seemed a natural and inevitable response to the migration of musicians from countryside to city (personal communication, October 2004). For an example of Nyshanov's oeuvre for ensemble, see the recording *Tengir-Too: Mountain Music from Kyrgyzstan* (Smithsonian Folkways).

65. Valentina Süzükei, *Tuvan Traditional Musical Instruments*, 84.

66. See J. W. Love et al., "Musical Instruments," in *The Garland Encyclopedia of World Music*, vol. 9, *Australia and the Pacific Islands*, 395.

67. Jamtsyn Badraa, "*Xöömei i 'Urtyn-duu': spetsificheskie iavleniia mongol'skoi traditsionnoi klassicheskoi muzyki*,"[Xöömei and Urtyn-duu: a specific phenomenon of Mongolian traditional classical music] in *Professional'naia muzyka ustnoi traditsii narodov blizhnego, srednego vostoka i sovremenost'* [Professional oral tradition music of the peoples of the Near East and Central Asia and modernity], 117–118.

68. René Grousset, *The Empire of the Steppes*, 538.

69. An important body of research on the folklore of the Tsengel Tuvans has been produced by German scholar Erika Taube, whose many publications, particularly on fairy tales, provide an invaluable resource for students of Tuvan language and literature. For an introduction to her work, see Erika Taube, *Sovremennoe sostoyanie traditsionnykh form byta i kul'tury tsengel'skikh tuvintsev* [The contemporary state of traditional forms of life and culture among the Tsengel Tuvans] (Warsaw: Etnografia Polska, 1981), and *Skazki i predaniye altaiskikh tuvintsev* (Tales and legends of the Altai Tuvans (Moscow: Vostochnoi Literatury, 1994). See also Marina Mongush, *Tuvintsy mongolii i kitaia* [The Tuvans of Mongolia and China] (Novosibirsk: Nauka, 2002), and Marina Mongush, "The Tuvinians in China: Aspects of Their History, Language, and Culture," in Humphrey and Sneath, eds., *Culture and Environment in Inner Asia*, vol. 2, 116–133.

70. The most recent groups of Tuvans to arrive in Tsengel from Xinjiang came in the 1940s as a result of unfavorable political conditions in China (Boris Tatarintsev, *Tuvinskoe gorlovoe penie: problemy proiskhozhdeniia* [Problems of the origins of Tuvan throat-singing] (Kyzyl: Mezhdunarodnyi Nauchnyi Tsentr "Xöömei," 1998), 11.

71. Pegg, *Mongolian Music*, 18.

72. Pegg reports hearing a performance of the piece from Narantsogt (*Mongolian Music*, 19). She includes a performance of the melody on the *igil* by a different performer, Horloo, on the compact disc that accompanies her book (track 3).

73. Yerlan Arynov, "On Bayan-Ölgii and its Kazakhs," trans. Paul D. Buell (Aziya 48 [November 1993]): 4.

74. The photo was used on the cover of the Smithsonian Folkways compact disc *The Silk Road: A Musical Caravan*.

5. MUSIC, SOUND, AND ANIMALS

1. See S[evyan] I. Vajnsteijn [Vainshtein], "The Êrens in Tuvan Shamanism," in V. Diószegi and M. Hoppál, eds., *Shamanism in Siberia* (Budapest: Akadémiai Kiadó, 1978), 457–476.

2. Ethnographic accounts of Tuvan, Altai, and Xakas shamanism and its attendant spirit world are overwhelmingly in Russian. The works of Kenin-Lopsan and Leonid Pavlovich Potapov—in particular, his book *Altaiskii Shamanizm* [Altai Shamanism] (Leningrad: Nauka, 1991)—hold a key place in this corpus. Kenin-Lopsan's most important Russian-language books on shamanism include: *Algyshi tuvinskikh shamanov* [*Algysh* of Tuvan shamans] (Kyzyl: Novosti Tuvy, 1995); *Mify tuvinskikh shamanov* [Myths of Tuvan shamans] (Kyzyl: Novosti Tuvy, 2002); *Obryadovaia praktika i fol'klor tuvinskogo shamanizma* [Ritual practice and folklore of Tuvan shamanism] (Novosibirsk: Nauka, 1987); *Magiya tuvinskikh shamanov* [The Magic of Tuvan shamans] (Kyzyl: Novosti Tuvy, 1993); and *Tuvinskie shamany* [Tuvan shamans] (Moscow: Transpersonal Institute, 1999). For works of Kenin-Lopsan in English, see his *Shamanic Songs and Myths of Tuva;* and see also "Tuvan Shamanic Folklore," in Marjorie Balzer, ed., *Shamanic Worlds.* For works of Potapov in English, see "The Shaman Drum as a Source of Ethnographical History," in V. Diószegi and M. Hoppál, eds., *Shamanism in Siberia.*

3. According to Shirokogoroff, *burxan* is a Mongol term that is a modification of "Buddha" (*The Psychomental Complex of the Tungus,* 277). Shirokogoroff provides evidence of the many different ways in which the term is used (as *burkan*) among the Tungus (see "Index of Spirits," 452). *Burxan* also gave its name to the nativist religious movement among the Altai people known (in Russian) as Burkhanism. On Burkhanism, see Sergei Filatov, "Altai Burkhanism: Faith or a Dream of Faith?" *Anthropology and Archeology of Eurasia* 39:4 (2001): 76–91. See also Lawrence Krader, "A Nativistic Movement in Western Siberia," *American Anthropologist* 58 (1956): 282–292.

4. This is a schematic presentation of a complex pantheon; specialists will recognize that many nuances are missing. Spirits are called differently among different Turkic peoples, and not all beliefs are identical. But ethnographers who have delved into the subject have concluded that in its broad outlines, Inner Asian Turkic beliefs about the spirit pantheon are extremely similar, lending more evidence to support the view that their expressive culture emerged from common origins.

5. Kenin-Lopsan, "Tuvan Shamanic Folklore," in Balzer, *Shamanic Worlds,* 132.

6. For a brief biography of Kenin-Lopsan, see Mihály Hoppál, "Life and Works of Mongush B. Kenin-Lopsan" in Kenin-Lopsan, *Shamanic Songs and Myths of Tuva,* xix–xxiii. For a portrait of figures who occupy roles somewhat parallel to that of Kenin-Lopsan in the Sakha Republic, see Marjorie Balzer's study of Vladimir Kondakov, founder of the Association of Folk Medicine, and Andrei Borisov, the Sakha Minister of Culture, "Two Urban Shamans: Unmasking Leadership in Fin-de-Soviet Siberia," in George E. Marcus, ed., *Perilous States* (Chicago: University of Chicago Press, 1993), 131–164.

7. The Foundation for Shamanic Studies (http://www.shamanism.org [accessed on May 30, 2005]), founded by anthropologist Michael Harner, offers workshops in "Core Shamanism" and "Advanced Shamanism" and maintains an online shop that sells "Shamanic Supplies." The foundation has also produced two videos on shamanism in Tuva: *Healing Rituals of the Tuvan Shamans,* filmed in California during a workshop sponsored by the foundation, and *Tuva: Shamans and Spirits,* filmed in Tuva in 1993.

8. For a recent overview of shamanic revivalism in the Altai region, see Kira Van Deusen, *Singing, Story, Healing Drum: Shamans and Storytellers of Turkic Siberia* (Montreal: McGill-Queen's University Press/Seattle: University of Washington Press, 2004), in particular chapter 7, "Contemporary Shamans in Tuva and Khakassia," 163–178.

9. For works by Kenin-Lopsan, see n. 2.

10. See Potapov's *Altaiskii Shamanizm* [Altai shamanism]. An abridged form in English that addresses the same theme appears in "The Shaman Drum as a Source of Ethnographical History," in Diószegi and Hopál, eds., *Shamanism in Siberia*. For a comparative taxonomy of Siberian shaman drums, see Sheikin, *History of the Musical Culture of Siberian Peoples,* 69–86.

11. Potapov demonstrated that some of these names represent archaic terms for draught animals, such as camels, that were unknown to the shamans who used them. These shamans represented hunting cultures, and Potapov concluded that the names must be vestiges of a time past when those hunters were herders (hunters in northern Inner Asia do not use camels). In other words, Potapov suggested that pastoralists might have become hunters, not only the reverse, which is typically taken as an orthodoxy in studies of Inner Asian pastoralism.

12. *Qiyak* is a transliteration of Kyrgyz кыяк and thus should properly be written "*qyyak*." I have replaced the initial "y" with "i" to simplify pronunciation for English readers. Kyrgyz organologist Sagynaly Subanaliev proposes that the term *qiyak* is cognate with *ghijak*, the spike fiddle played among sedentary dwellers in Transoxania, and that the similarity of names explains similarities in the morphology of the instruments. This similarity, he suggests, is an indication that the *qiyak* entered the Kyrgyz instrumentarium in the twelfth and thirteenth centuries, after the Kyrgyz migrated out of the Altai region to the territory of present-day Kyrgyzstan. Subanaliev draws support for his hypothesis by pointing to clear morphological differences between the *qyl qiyak* (*qyl* means "hair") and two-stringed fiddles from south Siberia (*Traditsionnaia instrumental'naia muzyka i instrumentarii kyrgyzov* [Traditional instrumental music and instruments of the Kyrgyz] [Bishkek: Uchkun, 2003]), 128. *Qyl-qobyz* and *qyl qiyak*, like other Central Asian fiddles and lutes, did experience folklorization beginning in the 1930s, when they were cloned into instrumental consorts modeled on those of European music. However, prima, alto, bass, and contrabass *qobyz* and *qiyak* were never widely embraced, and they remained within the purview of the official folk orchestra movement. On these consortized instruments, see K. Vertov, G. Blagodatov, and E. Iazovitskaia, *Atlas muzykal'nykh instrumentov narodov sssr* (Moscow: State Musical Press, 1963), 131–133.

13. For a discussion of the *qobyź,* its zoomorphic qualities, and its relationship to the supernatural, see Xavier Hallez and Saïra and Abdulkhamit Raïmbergenov, *Le chant des steppes: musique et chants du Kazakhstan* (Paris: Editions du Layeur, 2002), 14–16.

14. For a study of the role of animals in origin legends among Turkic and Mongol peoples—in particular, the wolf and the swan—see Jean-Paul Roux, *La religion des turcs et des mongols* (Paris: Payot, 1984), 177–199. For Roux's views on animal imitations in shamanic dance, see also his "La Danse Chamanique de l'Asie Centrale," in *Les Danses Sacrées* (Paris: Éditions du Seuil, 1963).

15. For an overview of zoomorphic transformation in Sakha shamanism, see Marjorie Balzer, "Flights of the Sacred: Symbolism and Theory in Siberian Shamanism," *American Anthropologist* 98:2 (1996): 305–318. On shamans' transformations into birds, see also Caroline Humphrey with Urgunge Onon, *Shamans and Elders: Experience, Knowledge, and Power among the Daur Mongols* (Oxford and New York: Clarendon Press, 1996).

16. Roberte Hamayon, *La chasse à l'âme: Esquisse d'une théorie du chamanisme sibérien* (Nanterre: Société d'ethnologie, 1990). A synopsis of Hamayon's theories appears in English in "Shamanism in Siberia: From Partnership in Supernature to Counter-Power in Society," in Nicholas Thomas and Caroline Humphrey, eds., *Shamanism, History, and the State* (Ann Arbor: University of Michigan Press, 1996). Hamayon's focus on the origins of shamanism in the role of transformation and exchange in archaic hunting societies is rooted in an evolutionist perspective that has been abandoned by some other scholars. See, for example, Thomas and Humphrey, "Introduction," in *Shamanism, History, and the State*, 1–12.

17. Speaking in Russian, Raushan Orazbaeva used the Russian cognate for "trance" [*trans*]. Her effort to define what she meant by "trance" in the rest of the sentence suggests that she felt some unease using a term with such a great range of cross-cultural meanings to describe her own experience. For a discussion of "trance" in cross-cultural perspective, see Judith Becker, *Deep Listeners: Music, Emotion, and Trancing*, chap. 1, "Rethinking 'Trance,'" 25–44.

18. For Kazakh terms that refer to the various parts of the *kobyz*, see Patrick Garrone, *Chamanisme et islam en asie centrale* (Paris: Librairie d'Amérique et d'Orient/Jean Maisonneuve Successeur, 2000), 188–193. See also Vladimir N. Basilov, "Bowed Musical Instruments," in Vladimir N. Basilov, ed., *Nomads of Eurasia*, trans. Mary Fleming Zirin (Seattle: University of Washington Press/Natural History Museum of Los Angeles County, 1989), 153–158. In Basilov's view, the *kobyz* is a descendant of the two-stringed "Scythian harp" excavated in Pazyryk (described later in this chapter).

19. Victor Zuckerkandl, *Sound and Symbol*, trans. Willard R. Trask (New York: Pantheon Books, 1956), 69.

20. Ibid., 69.

21. For an introduction to this bibliography, see in particular Juliet Clutton-Brock, *Horse Power: A History of the Horse and the Donkey in Human Societies* (Cambridge, Mass.: Harvard University Press, 1992), and also her *A Natural History of Domesticated Animals* (Cambridge: Cambridge University Press, 1999). For a broader archaeological perspective, see André Leroi-Gourhan, *Gesture and Speech*, trans. Anna Bostock Berger from *Le Geste et la parole* (Cambridge, Mass.: MIT Press, 1993).

22. Clutton-Brock, *A Natural History of Domesticated Animals*, 74.

23. Clutton-Brock, *Horse Power*, 11.

24. Clutton-Brock, *A Natural History of Domesticated Animals*, 74.

25. Sheikin, *History of the Musical Culture of Siberian Peoples*, 167.

26. See, for example, Nicholas Wade, "Early Voices: the Leap to Language," *New York Times*, July 15, 2003, Science Section.

27. Remy Dor, "Les huchements du berger turc 1: interpellatifs adressés aux animaux de la cour et de la demeure," *Journal Asiatique* 273:3–4 (1985): 371–424; "Les huchements du berger turc 2: du huchement-aux-morts à l'appel des chevaux," in G. Veinstein, ed., *Les Ottomans et la mort* (Leiden: Brill, 1996); "Les huchements du berger turc 3: interpellatifs adressés au gros bétail," *Turcica* 27 (1995): 199–222; "A la recherche d'un proto-langage: analyse de quelques huchements turcs relatifs au petit bétail," *Bulletin de la Société de linguistique de Paris* 98 (2003): fasc. 1, 385–408.

28. Dor, "Les huchements du berger turc [2]: Du huchement-aux-morts à l'appel des chevaux," 46.

29. Dor, "Les huchements du berger turc [3]: Interpellatifs adressés au gros bétail," 202.

30. Dor, "Les huchements du berger turc [2]: Du huchement-aux-morts à l'appel des chevaux," 48.

31. Dor, ibid., 2: 48.

32. Pegg (*Mongolian Music,* 236) includes a Hoton version of the same song (*Hartai Sarlag*), although with somewhat different words. A musical comparison of the two versions is not possible because Pegg provides neither a recording nor a transcription of the melody.

33. Dor, "Les huchements," 3: 206. Evidently the use of these *huchements* also spread beyond Turkic speakers. Dor notes that the Even, a Tungusic reindeer-herding people, use *"chö"* to stimulate their deer.

34. For a study of human-animal communication among the Xakas, see V. N. Shevtsov, *"Okhotnich'e-skotovodcheskie zvukopodrazhaniia i vozglasy u khakasov"* [Hunting and cattle-raising sound imitations and cries among the Khakas], in Iu. I. Sheikin, ed., *Muzykal'naia etnografiia severnoi azii* [Musical ethnography of northern Asia], vol. 10 (Novosibirsk: Novosibirsk State Conservatory named after Glinka, 1988), 108–129.

35. Pegg, *Mongolian Music,* 236.

36. *Alzyry* is a noun produced from the verb *alyr,* "to take," thus the expression *mal alzyry* literally means something like "the taking of a domestic animal." Zoya Kyrgys notes in *Pesennaia kul'tura tuvinskogo naroda* (Kyzyl: Tuvinskoe Knizhnoe Izdatel'stvo, 1992), 23, that A. N. Aksenov mistranslated the term into Russian in *Tuvinskaia narodnaia muzyka* as *priruchenie* (domestication) rather than *priuchenie* (training, schooling). In the present case, however, the meaning of "training" or "schooling" is precisely "domestication," and thus I follow Aksenov's practice in referring to *mal alzyry* as domestication songs.

37. A. N. Aksenov, *Tuvinskaia narodnaia muzyka,* 20.

38. Natalia M. Kondratieva and Vladimir V. Mazepus, "Cattle Incantations in the Culture of the Altaians," *Altaica* 3 (1993): 40–49.

39. Vainstein, *Nomads of South Siberia: The Pastoral Economies of Tuva,* ed. and with an introduction by Caroline Humphrey, trans. Michael Colenso (Cambridge: Cambridge University Press, 1980).

40. Valentina Süzükei has presented her own "sound calendar" in an unpublished article, *"Xudozhestvennaia transformatsiia zvukov prirody v muzykalnom fol'klore tuvintsev (o zvukovom kalendare kochevnika)"* [The Artistic transformation of natural sounds in Tuvan musical folklore (on the nomadic sound calendar)]. The sound calendar in the present work relies heavily on the information in Süzükei's article.

41. Kenin-Lopsan, *Chogaaldar chyyndyzy* [Collected works] (Kyzyl: Novosti Tuvy, 1992), 350–351.

42. Yakutsk has become the epicenter of a pan-Siberian jew's harp revival. The production of high quality instruments, a sizeable cadre of excellent musicians, and the activities of the International Museum of the Xomus, founded by jew's harp scholar and performer Ivan Alekseev and sponsored by the Sakha Ministry of Culture, all provide impetus to the revival movement. Moreover, in this supportive atmosphere of revivalism, jew's harps have become reconnected to what was surely one of their traditional functions: shamanic curing and healing. For a description of a contemporary music therapy session in Sakha, see Balzer, "Flights of the Sacred: Symbolism and Theory in Siberian Shamanism," 312.

43. One exception is the sound of the nightjar or goatsucker (*Caprimulgus europees*), which is represented by an eponymous style of throat-singing, *chylandyk.* But in the opinion of some throat-singers, as explained earlier, *chylandyk* is a "mimesis of mimesis": not

the representation of a bird, but the sound of a beginning throat-singer imitating an adult, and in so doing, producing a sound like the *chylandyk.*

44. For recent exhibition catalogues of animal-style art, see Emma C. Bunker, *Nomadic Art of the Eastern Eurasian Steppes: The Eugene V. Thaw and Other New York Collections* (New York: Metropolitan Museum of Art, 2002); Joan Aruz et al., eds., *The Golden Deer of Eurasia: Scythian and Sarmatian Treasures from the Russian Steppes* (New York: Metropolitan Museum of Art/New Haven, Conn.: Yale University Press, 2000); and Ellen D. Reeder, ed., *Scythian Gold: Treasures from Ancient Ukraine* (New York: Harry N. Abrams, 1999). A somewhat older catalogue is Basilov, ed., *Nomads of Eurasia.*

45. Marianne Devlet, *Petroglify na dne sayanskogo morya* [Petroglyphs on the bottom of the Sayan Sea] (Moscow: Russian Academy of Sciences, Institute of Archaeology, 1998), 194. A full English translation of Devlet's book appears in *Anthropology and Archeology of Eurasia* 40:1–2 (2001).

46. Bunker, *Nomadic Art,* 33.

47. The same idea has been proposed by Ann Farkas, "Filippovka and the Art of the Steppes," in Aruz et al., eds., *The Golden Deer of Eurasia: Scythian and Sarmatian Treasures from the Russian Steppes,* 17. Farkas writes: "A folk song from Tuva, in the Sayan Mountains, tells of a poor Tuvan shepherd whose horse was killed by a cruel Mongolian prince. The horse came to the shepherd in a dream and told him to make a musical instrument from the hair of its mane and tail. When the shepherd made the instrument and played it, a thousand horses fell from the sky. If one substitutes a deer for the horse and a bow for the musical instrument and twenty-six deer for the thousand horses, the Filippovka discoveries could illustrate the words of a similar song, but it is unlikely that one would think of deer falling from heaven without knowing that there was such a song."

48. Richard Taruskin, *Stravinsky and the Russian Traditions* (Berkeley: University of California Press, 1996).

49. Harold Powers, "Illustrated Inventories of Indian Rāgamālā Painting," *Journal of the American Oriental Society* 100:4 (1980): 473–493. See also John Andrew Grieg, "Rāgamālā Painting," in *The Garland Encyclopedia of World Music,* vol. 5, *South Asia,* ed. Alison Arnold (New York: Garland Publishing, 2000), 312–318.

50. James C. Y. Watt, "The Legacy of Nomadic Art in China and Eastern Central Asia," in Bunker, *Nomadic Art,* 208.

51. Liudmila Barkova, "The Nomadic Culture of the Altai and the Animal Style," in Aruz et al., eds., *The Golden Deer of Eurasia,* 246. A recent analysis of animal-style art as an "art of expressive deformations" has also been presented by Russian art historian V. A. Koreniako in "Nomadic Animalistic Art: Its Origins and Historical Destinies," *Anthropology and Archeology of Eurasia* 38:1 (1999): 73–94.

52. The term "mythography" comes from the French archaeologist and art historian André Leroi-Gourhan, *Gesture and Speech,* 196.

53. Esther Jacobson, "Early Nomadic Sources for Scythian Art," in E. Reeder, ed., *Scythian Gold,* 67.

54. The notion that nomadic civilization never developed architecture is presently an area of sensitivity in parts of Inner Asia. In Kazakhstan, recent archaeological excavations have uncovered the remains of Saraishyq, a city built in the thirteenth through sixteenth centuries that provides Kazakhs with evidence of their forbears' mastery of sophisticated urban living, including adobe architecture. See Imangali Tasmagambetov and Zainolla Samashev, *Saraishyq/Saraichik* (Almaty: Berel, 2001). In Mongolia, the remains of Qaraqo-

rum, the city built in the mid-thirteenth century under orders of Ögedei, the third son of Chingis Khan, are offered as evidence of the same idea: that nomads were not devoid of urban sophistication.

55. For a précis of how Islamic aesthetic principles are manifested in sound, see "*Handasah Al Sawt* or The Art of Sound" (chap. 23) in Isma'il R. al-Faruqi and Lois Lamya' al-Faruqi, *The Cultural Atlas of Islam* (New York: Macmillan, 1986), 441–477. On the relationship of Islamic metaphysics and music, see also Jean During, "The Symbolic Universe of Music in Islamic Societies," in *The Garland Encyclopedia of World Music,* vol. 6, *The Middle East* (New York: Routledge, 2002), 177–188.

56. See Edward H. Schafer, *The Golden Peaches of Samarkand: A Study of T'ang Exotics* (Berkeley and Los Angeles: University of California Press, 1963), esp. 50–57. See also Annette L. Juliano and Judith A. Lerner, eds., *Monks and Merchants along the Silk Road* (New York: Harry N. Abrams with the Asia Society, 2001), and Luce Boulnois, *Silk Road: Monks, Warriors and Merchants on the Silk Road,* trans. Helen Loveday with additional material by Bradley Mayhew and Angela Sheng (Hong Kong: Odyssey Books and Guides, 2004, distributed by W. W. Norton), 72, 115, 207, 263.

57. Bunker, *Nomadic Art,* 187–189.

58. Ibid., 188.

59. Ibid., 189.

60. Ibid., 189.

61. See Laurence E. R. Picken, "The Origin of the Short Lute," *Galpin Society Journal* 8 (1966): 32–42.

62. See John Myers, "Instruments: *Pipa,*" in *The Garland Encyclopedia of World Music,* vol. 7, *East Asia: China, Japan, and Korea,* ed. Robert C. Provine, Yosihiko Tokumaru, and J. Lawrence Witzleben (New York: Routledge, 2002), 167–170.

63. On the Pazyryk harp, see Bo Lawergren, "The Ancient Harp from Pazyryk," *Beitrage zur allgemeinen und vergleichenden Archäologie* 9–10 (1990): 111–118. See also Sergei I. Rudenko, *Frozen Tombs of Siberia,* trans. M. W. Thompson (Berkeley and Los Angeles: University of California Press, 1970), 277–278.

6. AN ANIMIST VIEW OF THE WORLD

1. "Men Tyva Men" and its message of pride in a neotraditional cultural identity has analogues elsewhere in Inner Asia, for example, in the song "Xakasia," by Xakas musician German Tanbaev, and in the book *Min Sakhabyn* [I am a Sakha], the autobiography of Sakha writer Ivan Nikolaev, who writes under the pen name Ukhaan. For a broader look at political and cultural neotraditionalism in Siberia, see Aleksandr Pika, ed., *Neotraditionalism in the Russian North* (Edmonton: Canadian Circumpolar Institute Press and Seattle: University of Washington Press, 1999).

2. For an authoritative history of Xakasia written by a collective of local scholars, see the Xakas Institute of Language, Literature and History's *Istoriia xakasii s drevneishikh vremen do 1917 goda* [The history of Xakasia from the earliest times until 1917] (Moscow: Nauka/Vostochnaia Literatura, 1993). On Xakas self-identity, see *Anthropology and Archeology of Eurasia* 33:1 (1994), devoted to "Ethnonyms and Origins."

3. V. E. Mainogasheva, "O Xakasskom geroicheskom epose i alyptyx nymaxe 'Aï-Xuuchin'" [On Xakas heroic epic and the heroic tale Ai-Xuuchyn], in *Xakasskii geroicheskii*

epos Ai-Xuuchyn [The Xakas heroic epic Ai-Xuuchyn], vol. 16 of *Pamyatniki fol'klora narodov sibiri i dal'nego vostoka* [Monuments of the folklore of Siberian and Far Eastern peoples] (Novosibirsk: Nauka, 1997), 14.

4. A condensed account of Slava Kuchenov's dream was published by Kira van Deusen in *Singing Story, Healing Drum: Shamans and Storytellers of Turkic Siberia,* 75–77, as well as in "The Shamanic Gift and the Performing Arts in Siberia," in *Shamanskii dar* [The shamanic gift] (Moscow: Institute of Ethnology and Anthropology of the Russian Academy of Sciences, 2000), 223–239.

5. In the Xakas original, a "nine-*xulas*-long horse," *xulas* being a measure equivalent to the Russian *sazhen'*, or 2.17 meters—approximately the length of a man's arm span.

6. Slava Kuchenov performed his text in the Sagai dialect of Xakas.

7. Natalie Kononenko Moyle, *The Turkish Minstrel Tale Tradition* (New York: Garland Publishing, 1990), 84.

8. Northrop Frye, *Fearful Symmetry: A Study of William Blake* (Princeton, N.J.: Princeton University Press, 1947, 91).

9. Moyle, *The Turkish Minstrel Tale Tradition,* 84.

10. Karl Reichl, *Singing the Past: Turkic and Medieval Heroic Poetry* (Ithaca, N.Y.: Cornell University Press, 2000), 37.

11. *Xakasskii geroicheskii epos Ai-Xuuchyn.* [The Xakas heroic epic Ai-Xuuchyn].

12. Erich Neumann, *Art and the Creative Unconscious* (Princeton, N.J.: Princeton University Press, 1959), 178.

13. Hamayon, "Shamanism in Siberia: From Partnership in Supernature to Counter-Power in Society," in Thomas and Humphrey, eds., *Shamanism, History, and the State,* 76.

14. See Judith Becker, *Deep Listeners,* 1–4.

15. Ibid., 3, 25–27.

16. For reports on neotraditional shamanism in other cultures, see Marjorie Mandelstam Balzer, "The Poetry of Sakha (Siberian Yakut) Shamanism," in John Leavitt, ed., *Poetry and Prophecy: The Anthropology of Inspiration* (Ann Arbor, Mich.: University of Michigan Press, 1997), 93–127; and Balzer, "Healing Failed Faith? Contemporary Siberian Shamanism," *Anthropology and Humanism* 26:2 (2001): 134–149; Laura Kendall, "Korean Shamans and the Spirits of Capitalism," *American Anthropologist* 98:3 (1996): 512–527; Galina Lindquist, *Shamanic Performances on the Urban Scene: Neoshamanism in Contemporary Sweden* (Stockholm: Stockholm University, Stockholm Studies in Social Anthropology, no. 39, 1997); and Merete Demant Jakobsen, *Shamanism: Traditional and Contemporary Approaches to the Mastery of Spirits and Healing.*

17. V. S. Naipaul, "A Second Visit," in *The Writer and the World* (New York: Knopf, 2002), 24.

18. Gary Wills, "The Day the Enlightenment Went Out," *New York Times,* November 4, 2004, op-ed page.

19. The revival of epic storytelling is much stronger in some parts of Inner Asia than others. In the Sakha Republic, for example, *olonkho* (epic) singing competitions are now held not only at the yearly *yhyakh* festival, which has been made a republic-wide holiday, but also in the new Center for Spiritual Development (*Archy d'ete*) in Yakutsk. (Marjorie Balzer, personal communication, 2004). By contrast, in Tuva, while throat-singing flourishes, "epic storytelling is now a seriously endangered genre," according to Tuvan language and literature specialist David Harrison. In "A Tuvan Hero Tale with Commentary, Morphemic Analysis and Translation" (*Journal of the American Oriental Society,* forthcoming), Harrison writes, "Tuvan youth with talent are increasingly drawn exclu-

sively to throat-singing and its promise of a lucrative stage career, leading to a neglect of epic genres. One genre is now thriving while the other withers away" (David Harrison, personal communication, December 21, 2004).

20. Before the Soviet era, partial transcriptions of the *Manas* had been made in 1856 by Chokan Valichanov and also beginning in 1862 by the great turcologist Wilhelm Radloff (1837–1918). See Arthur T. Hatto, ed. and trans., *The Manas of Wilhelm Radloff* (Wiesbaden: Otto Harrassowitz, 1990), 9–16.

21. On syncretic Islamic-shamanic *mazar*s, see Vladimir N. Basilov, *Shamanstvo u narodov Srednei Azii i Kazakhstana* [Shamanism among the peoples of Central Asia and Kazakhstan] (Moscow: Nauka, 1992). See also Basilov's "Chosen by the Spirits," in Balzer, *Shamanic Worlds,* 38–46, on the fusion between shamanism and Islam, Buddhism, and Christianity. For an ethnography of analogous syncretic practices at the opposite end of the core Islamic world, see Edward Westermarck's classic *Ritual and Belief in Morocco* (London: Macmillan, 1926).

22. Later I learned that from 1985–1987 Rysbek studied acting at a theater school in Moscow (*Teatralnoe uchilishche im. Shchukina*) because he believed that *manaschis* are actors and that his own performance would improve with professional study. He left the school without completing his degree.

23. Every person has such a patron protector, explained Raziya Syrdybaeva, a Kyrgyz folklorist and musicologist who works as local coordinator for the Aga Khan Music Initiative in Central Asia. Syrdybaeva traveled with me to visit Rysbek Jumabaev. "Some people listen to this patron and some don't," Syrdybaeva told me. "Sometimes the patron-protector can be an animal. My grandfather has a patron-protector that was a white rabbit. The patron-protector of sheep is *cholpan-ata,* of cows, *zangi baba,* of girls, *kyngyr ata,* of horses, *jylkynyn piri kambar ata.* Old people say that before death, there's a shadow formed around a person. If you see that shadow, it means that the person doesn't have long to live."

24. Kenje Kara, who lived at the end of the nineteenth century, was one well-known *manaschi* who accompanied himself on the *qyl qiyak.*

25. The following references to work on Xhosa music come from van Tongeren, *Overtone Singing,* 158: David Dargie, *Xhosa Music* (Cape Town and Johannesburg: David Philip, 1988); Dargie, "Umngqoolo: Xhosa Overtone Singing and the Song Nondel'ekhaya," *African Music* 7:1 (1991): 33–47.

26. Nicholas Roerich, *Altai-Himalaya: A Travel Diary* (New York: Frederick A. Stokes, 1929; reprint, Brookfield, Conn.: Arun Press, 1983).

27. For a study of the encounter of different belief systems in Altai, see A. Znamenski, *Shamanism and Christianity: Native Encounters with Russian Orthodox Missions in Siberia and Alaska, 1820–1917* (Westport, Conn.: Greenwood Press, 1999). For a detailed study of "White Faith," see Andrei Vinogradov, "Ak Jang in the Context of Altai Religious Tradition" (master's degree thesis, University of Saskatchewan, 2003). For a contemporary study of the interaction of Buddhism, shamanism, and Burkhanism in Altai, see Abnieszka Halemba, "Contemporary Religious Life in the Republic of Altai: The Interaction of Buddhism and Shamanism," *Sibirica* 3:2 (2003): 165–182.

28. Manos Andriotis, personal communication, December 23, 2003.

POSTLUDE

1. Jacque Attali, *L'homme nomade* (Paris: Fayard, 2003), 356.

BIBLIOGRAPHY

Aksenov, Aleksei Nikolaevich. "Tuvan folk music." Trans. Mark Slobin. *Asian Music* 4, no. 2 (1973): 7–18.

———. *Tuvinskaia narodnaia muzyka* [Tuvan folk music]. Moscow: Muzyka, 1964.

Alekseyev, Eduard. "Est' li u yakutov mnogogolosie?" [Do the Yakuts have polyphony?]. *Sovetskaia muzyka* no. 5 (1967): 97–105.

———. "Ranne fol'klornoe intonirovanie" [The pitch aspect of primitive singing]. Moscow: Sovetskii Kompozitor, 1986.

Al-Faruqi, Isma'il R., and Lois Lamya' al-Faruqi. *The Cultural Atlas of Islam*. New York: Macmillan, 1986.

Amanov, B. "Tartys kak spetsificheskaia forma muzitsirovaniia v muzykal'noi kul'ture kazakhov" [Tartys as a specific form of music-making in Kazakh musical culture]. In *Instrumental'naia muzyka kazaxskogo naroda* [Instrumental music of the Kazakh people], ed. Asiya Muxambetova, 25–38. Alma-Ata: Öner, 1985.

Anaiban, Zoia. "The Republic of Tuva: A Model of Ethnological Monitoring." *Anthropology and Archeology of Eurasia* 37, no. 3 (1998–99): 13–96.

Arbib, Michael A. "The Mirror System, Imitation, and the Evolution of Language." In *Imitation in Animals and Artifacts*, ed. Kerstin Dautenhahn and Chrystopher L. Nehaniv, 229–280. Cambridge, Mass.: MIT Press, 2002.

Aruz, Joan, et al., eds. *The Golden Deer of Eurasia: Scythian and Sarmatian Treasures from the Russian Steppes*. New York: Metropolitan Museum of Art and New Haven, Conn.: Yale University Press, 2000.

Arynov, Yerlan. "On Bayan-Ölgii and Its Kazakhs." Trans. Paul D. Buell. *Aziya* 48 (November 1993): 4.

Asaf'ev, Boris. *Muzykal'naia forma kak protsess* [Musical form as process]. In *Izbrannye trudy* [Collected works], vol. 5. Moscow: Izdatel'stvo Akademii Nauk SSSR, 1957.

Attali, Jacques. *L'homme nomade*. Paris: Fayard, 2003.

Badraa, Jamtsyn. "Xöömei i 'Urtyn-duu': spetsificheskie iavleniia mongol'skoi traditsionnoi klassicheskoi muzyki" [Xöömei and Urtyn-duu: specific phenomena of Mongolian traditional classical music]. In *Professional'naia muzyka ustnoi traditsii narodov blizhnego, srednego vostoka i sovremenost'* [Professional oral tradition music of the peoples of the Near and Middle East and modernity], 116–119. Tashkent: Izdatel'stvo literatury i iskusstva im. Gafura Guliama, 1981.

Balzer, Marjorie Mandelstam. "Flights of the Sacred: Symbolism and Theory in Siberian Shamanism." *American Anthropologist* 98, no. 2 (1996): 305–318.

———. "Healing Failed Faith? Contemporary Siberian Shamanism." *Anthropology and Humanism* 26, no. 2 (2001): 134–149.

———. "Hot and Cold: Interethnic Relations in Siberia." In *At the Risk of Being Heard: Identity, Indigenous Rights, and Postcolonial States,* ed. Bartholomew Dean and Jerome M. Levi, 112–141. Ann Arbor: University of Michigan Press, 2003.

———. Introduction to "The Republic of Tyva (Tuva): From Romanticism to Realism." *Anthropology and Archeology of Eurasia* 37, no. 3 (1998–99): 5–12.

———. The Poetry of Sakha (Siberian Yakut) Shamanism." In *Poetry and Prophecy: The Anthropology of Inspiration,* ed. John Leavitt, 93–127. Ann Arbor: University of Michigan Press, 1997.

———. "The Poetry of Shamanism." In *Shamanism in Performing Arts,* ed. Tae-gon Kim and Mihály Hoppál, 171–187. Budapest: Akadémiai Kiadó, 1995.

———. *Shamanic Worlds: Rituals and Lore of Siberia and Central Asia.* Armonk, N.Y.: M. E. Sharpe, 1997.

———. "Two Urban Shamans: Unmasking Leadership in Fin-de-Soviet Siberia. In *Perilous States,* ed. George E. Marcus, 131–164. Chicago: University of Chicago Press, 1993.

Barkova, Liudmila. "The Nomadic Culture of the Altai and the Animal Style." In Aruz et al., eds., *The Golden Deer of Eurasia: Scythian and Sarmatian Treasures from the Russian Steppes,* 241–247.

Basilov, Vladimir N. "Bowed Musical Instruments." In *Nomads of Eurasia,* ed. Vladimir N. Basilov, trans. Mary Fleming Zirin. Seattle: University of Washington Press and Los Angeles: Natural History Museum of Los Angeles County, 1989.

———. "Chosen by the Spirits." In Balzer, *Shamanic Worlds,* 38–46.

———. *Shamanstvo u narodov Srednei Azii i Kazakhstana* [Shamanism among the peoples of Central Asia and Kazakhstan]. Moscow: Nauka. 1992.

Becker, Judith. *Deep Listeners: Music, Emotion, and Trancing.* Bloomington: Indiana University Press, 2004.

Bloothooft, Gerrit, Eldrid Bringmann, Marieke van Capellen, Jolanda B. van Luipen, and Koen P. Thomassen. "Acoustics and Perception of Overtone Singing." *Journal of the Acoustical Society of America* 92, vol. 4, part 1 (1992): 1827–1836.

Boulez, Pierre. *Boulez on Music Today.* Trans. Susan Bradshaw and Richard Rodney Bennett. Cambridge, Mass.: Harvard University Press, 1971.

Boulnois, Luce. *Silk Road: Monks, Warriors and Merchants on the Silk Road.* Trans. Helen Loveday with additional material by Bradley Mayhew and Angela Sheng. Hong Kong: Odyssey Books and Guides, distributed by W. W. Norton, 2004.

Bunker, Emma, ed. *Nomadic Art of the Eastern Eurasian Steppes: The Eugene V. Thaw and Other New York Collections.* New York: Metropolitan Museum of Art, 2002.

Caton, Margaret. "Performance Practice in Iran: *Radīf* and Improvisation." In Danielson et al., eds., *The Garland Encyclopedia of World Music.* Vol. 6, *The Middle East,* 129–143. New York: Routledge, 2002.

Cavalli-Sforza, L. Luca. "The Spread of Agriculture and Nomadic Pastoralism: Insights from Genetics, Linguistics and Archaeology." In *The Origins and Spread of Agriculture and Pastoralism in Eurasia,* ed. David R. Harris, 51–69. Washington, D.C.: Smithsonian Institution Press, 1996.

Chatterjee, Partha. *The Nation and Its Fragments: Colonial and Postcolonial Histories.* In

The Partha Chatterjee Omnibus. New Delhi and New York: Oxford University Press, 1999.

Chatwin, Bruce. *The Songlines.* New York: Viking, 1987.

Clutton-Brock, Juliet. *Horse Power: A History of the Horse and the Donkey in Human Societies.* Cambridge, Mass.: Harvard University Press, 1992.

———. *A Natural History of Domesticated Mammals.* 2d ed. Cambridge, U.K.: Cambridge University Press, 1999.

Danielson, Virginia, Scott Marcus, and Dwight Reynolds. *The Garland Encyclopedia of World Music.* Vol. 6, *The Middle East.* New York: Routledge, 2002.

Dargie, David. "Umngqoolo: Xhosa overtone singing and the Song Nondel'ekhaya." *African Music* 7, no. 1 (1991): 33–47.

———. *Xhosa Music: Its Techniques and Instruments, with a Collection of Songs.* Cape Town and Johannesburg: David Philip, 1988.

Darwin, Charles. *The Descent of Man, and Selection in Relation to Sex.* New York: New York University Press, 1989.

Deleuze, Gilles, and Félix Guattari. *A Thousand Plateaus.* Trans. Brian Massumi. Minneapolis: University of Minnesota Press, 1987.

Desjacques, Alain. "La dimension orphique de la musique mongole." *Cahiers de Musiques Traditionnelles* 3 (1990): 97–107.

Devlet, Marianna. *Petroglify na dne Sayanskogo Morya* [Petroglyphs on the bottom of the Sayan Sea]. Moscow: Russian Academy of Sciences, Institute of Archaeology, 1998.

D'iakonova, V. P. "Lamaism and Its Influence on the Worldview and Religious Cults of the Tuvans." *Anthropology and Archeology of Eurasia* 39, no. 4 (2001): 53–75.

Diushaliev, Kamchybek, and Ekaterina Luzanova. *Kyrgyzskoe narodnoe muzykal'noe tvorchestvo* [Kyrgyz folk musical art]. Bishkek: Soros Fund-Kyrgyzstan, 1999.

Donahoe, Brian. "'Hey, You! Get Offa My Taiga!' Comparing the Sense of Property Rights Among the Tofa and Tozhu-Tyva." Halle/Saale, Germany: Max Planck Institute for Social Anthropology Working Paper, series no. 38, 2002.

Donald, Merlin. *A Mind So Rare: The Evolution of Human Consciousness.* New York: Norton, 2001.

———. *Origins of the Modern Mind: Three Stages in the Evolution of Culture and Cognition.* Cambridge, Mass.: Harvard University Press, 1991.

Dor, Rémy. "Les huchements du berger turc 1: Interpellatifs adressés aux animaux de la cour et de la demeure." *Journal Asiatique* 273, nos. 3–4 (1985): 371–424.

———. "Les huchements du berger turc [2]: Du huchement-aux-morts à l'appel des chevaux." In *Les Ottomans et la mort,* ed. G. Veinstein, 39–55. Leiden: Brill, 1996.

———. "Les huchements du berger turc 3: Interpellatifs adressés au gros bétail." *Turcica* 27 (1995): 199–222.

———. "À la recherche d'un proto-langage: analyse de quelques huchements turcs relatifs au petit bétail." *Bulletin de la Société de linguistique de Paris* 98 (2003): fasc. 1, 385–408.

Dulam, Sendenžavyn. "Conte, chant et instruments de musique: quelques légendes d'origine mongoles." *Etudes Mongoles* 18 (1987): 33–47.

During, Jean. *Musiques d'Asie Centrale: l'esprit d'une tradition.* Paris: Cité de la Musique/ Actes Sud, 1998.

———. "Rhythmes ovoïdes et quadrature du cycle." *Cahiers de Musiques Traditionnelles* 10 (1997): 17–36.

———. "The Symbolic Universe of Music in Islamic Societies." In Danielson et al., eds., *The Garland Encyclopedia of World Music*. Vol. 6, *The Middle East,* 177–188. New York: Routledge, 2002.

Edwards, Mike. "Masters of Gold." *National Geographic* 203, no. 6 (2003).

Eliade, Mircea. *Shamanism: Archaic Techniques of Ecstasy.* Trans. Willard R. Trask. Princeton: Princeton University Press, 1964. Originally published as *Le Chamanisme et les techniques archaïques de l'extase.* Paris: Librairie Payot, 1951.

Fales, Cornelia. "The Paradox of Timbre." *Ethnomusicology* 46, no. 1 (2002): 56–95.

Farkas, Ann. "Filippovka and the Art of the Steppes." In Aruz et al., eds., *The Golden Deer of Eurasia: Scythian and Sarmatian Treasures from the Russian Steppes,* 3–17. New York: Metropolitan Museum of Art and New Haven, Conn.: Yale University Press, 2000.

Feld, Steven. *Sound and Sentiment: Birds, Weeping, Poetics, and Song in Kaluli Expression.* Philadelphia: University of Pennsylvania Press, 1982.

———. "Waterfalls of Song: An Acoustemology of Place Resounding in Bosavi, Papua New Guinea." In *Senses of Place,* ed. Steven Feld and Keith H. Basso, 91–136. Santa Fe, N.M.: School of American Research Press, 1996.

Fernandez, James W., ed. *Beyond Metaphor: The Theory of Tropes in Anthropology.* Stanford: Stanford University Press, 1991.

Filatov, Sergei. "Altai Burkhanism: Faith or a Dream of Faith?" *Anthropology and Archeology of Eurasia* 39, no. 4 (2001): 76–91.

Frye, Northrop. *Fearful Symmetry: A Study of William Blake.* Princeton, N.J.: Princeton University Press, 1947.

Garrone, Patrick. *Chamanisme et islam en asie centrale.* Paris: Librairie d'Amérique et d'Orient/Jean Maisonneuve Successeur, 2000.

Godwin, Joscelyn. *Harmonies of Heaven and Earth: The Spiritual Dimension of Music from Antiquity to the Avant-Garde.* Rochester, Vt.: Inner Traditions International and New York: Harper and Row, 1987.

Grieg, John Andrew. "Rāgamālā Painting." In *The Garland Encyclopedia of World Music.* Vol. 5, *South Asia,* ed. Alison Arnold, 312–318. New York: Garland Publishing, 2000.

Grousset, René. *The Empire of the Steppes: A History of Central Asia.* Trans. Naomi Walford. New Brunswick, N.J.: Rutgers University Press, 1970.

Halemba, Agnieszka. "Contemporary Religious Life in the Republic of Altai: The Interaction of Buddhism and Shamanism." *Sibirica* 3, no. 2 (2003): 165–182.

Hallez, Xavier, and Saïra and Abdulkhamit Raïymbergenov. *Le chant des steppes: musique et chants du Kazakhstan.* Paris: Editions du Layeur, 2002.

Hallowell, A. Irving. "Bear Ceremonialism in the Western Hemisphere." *American Anthropologist* 28, no. 1 (1926): 1–175.

Hamayon, Roberte. "Des usages de 'jeu' dans le vocabulaire rituel du monde altaïques" [*Jeux rituels*]. *Études mongoles et sibériennes* 30–31 (1999–2000): 11–45.

———. *La chasse à l'âme: Esquisse d'une théorie du chamanisme Sibérien.* Nanterre: Société d'ethnologie, 1990.

———. "Shamanism in Siberia: From Partnership in Supernature to Counter-Power in Society." In *Shamanism, History, and the State,* ed. Nicholas Thomas and Caroline Humphrey, 76–90. Ann Arbor: University of Michigan Press, 1996.

Harrison, K. David. *Altai-Sayan Language and Ethnography Project.* Swarthmore, Penn., Swarthmore College. Online 2004. http://www.swarthmore.edu/SocSci/Linguistics/aslep/quickfacts.php.

———. "A Tuvan Hero Tale with Commentary, Morphemic Analysis and Translation." *Journal of the American Oriental Society* (forthcoming).

Hatto, Arthur T. *The Manas of Wilhelm Radloff.* Reedited, newly translated, and with a commentary by Arthur T. Hatto. Vol. 110 of *Asiatische Forschungen: Monographienreihe zur geschichte, kultur und sprache der völker ost-und zentralasiens.* Wiesbaden: Otto Harrassowitz, 1990.

Higgins, Andrew. "Tunes of War as Throat-Singers Go for the Jugular." *The Independent* (London), April 27, 1995.

Hoppál, Mihály. "Life and Works of Mongush B. Kenin-Lopsan." In Mongush B. Kenin-Lopsan, *Shamanic Songs and Myths of Tuva,* xix–xxiii. Budapest: Akadémiai Kiadó and Los Angeles: International Society for Trans-Oceanic Research, 1997.

Humphrey, Caroline. "Chiefly and Shamanist Landscapes in Mongolia." In *The Anthropology of Landscape: Perspectives on Place and Space,* ed. Eric Hirsch and Michael O'Hanlon. Oxford: Clarendon Press, 1995.

———. *Marx Went Away—But Karl Stayed Behind.* Ann Arbor: University of Michigan Press, 1998.

Humphrey, Caroline, and David Sneath. *The End of Nomadism?* Durham, N.C.: Duke University Press, and Cambridge, U.K.: White Horse Press, 1999.

———, eds. *Culture and Environment in Inner Asia.* Vol.. 2: *Society and Culture.* Cambridge, U.K.: White Horse Press, 1996.

Humphrey, Caroline, with Urgunge Onon. *Shamans and Elders: Experience, Knowledge and Power among the Daur Mongols.* Oxford and New York: Clarendon Press, 1996.

Huun-Huur-Tu. *The Orphan's Lament.* Compact disc. Shanachie Entertainment, 1994.

———. *Sixty Horses in My Herd.* Compact disc. Shanachie Entertainment, 1993.

Huun-Huur-Tu and Malerija. *Malerija.* Compact disc. Produced by Sayan Bapa. Green-Wave Records, 2003.

Hyde, Lewis. *Trickster Makes this World: Mischief, Myth, and Art.* New York: Farrar, Straus and Giroux, 1998.

Jacobson, Esther. "Early Nomadic Sources for Scythian Art." *Scythian Gold: Treasures from Ancient Ukraine,* ed. Ellen D. Reeder, 59–70. New York: Harry N. Abrams in association with the Walters Art Gallery and the San Antonio Museum of Art, 1999.

Jakobsen, Merete Demant. *Shamanism: Traditional and Contemporary Approaches to the Mastery of Spirits and Healing.* New York and Oxford: Berghahn Books, 1999.

Jargalant Altai: Xöömii and Other Vocal and Instrumental Music from Mongolia. Compact disc. Produced by Chris Johnston. Pan Records 2050, 1994.

Juliano, Annette L., and Judith A. Lerner, eds. *Monks and Merchants along the Silk Road.* New York: Harry N. Abrams with the Asia Society, 2001.

Kabzínska-Stawarz, Iwona. *Games of Mongolian Shepherds.* Warsaw: Institute of the History of Material Culture, Polish Academy of Sciences, 1991.

Kendall, Laura, "Korean Shamans and the Spirits of Capitalism." *American Anthropologist* 98, no. 3 (1996): 512–527.

Kenin-Lopsan, Mongush B. *Algyshi tuvinskikh shamanov* [*Algysh*s of Tuvan shamans]. Kyzyl: Novosti Tuvy, 1995.

———. *Chogaaldar chyyndyzy* [Collected works]. Kyzyl: Novosti Tuvy, 1993.

———. *Magiia tuvinskikh shamanov* [The magic of Tuvan shamans]. Kyzyl: Novosti Tuvy, 1993.

———. *Mify tuvinskikh shamanov* [Myths of Tuvan shamans]. Kyzyl: Novosti Tuvy, 2002.

———. *Obriadovaia praktika i fol'klor tuvinskogo shamanizma* [Ritual practice and folklore of Tuvan shamanism]. Novosibirsk: Nauka, 1987.

———. *Shamanic Songs and Myths of Tuva.* Budapest: Akadémiai Kiadó and Los Angeles: International Society for Trans-Oceanic Research, 1997.

———. "Tuvan Shamanic Folklore." In *Shamanic Worlds,* ed. Marjorie Mandelstam Balzer, 110–152. Armonk, N.Y.: North Castle Books, 1997.

———. *Tuvinskie shamany* [Tuvan shamans]. Moscow: Transpersonal Institute, 1999.

Khazanov, Anatoly M. *Nomads and the Outside World.* Trans. Julia Crookenden. Cambridge, U.K.: Cambridge University Press, 1984.

Kondratieva, Natalia M., and Vladimir V. Mazepus. "Cattle Incantations in the Culture of the Altaians." *Altaica* 3 (1993): 40–49.

Koreniako, V. A. "Nomadic Animalistic Art: Its Origins and Historical Destinies." *Anthropology and Archeology of Eurasia* 38, no. 1 (1999): 73–94.

Krader, Lawrence. "A Nativistic Movement in Western Siberia." *American Anthropologist* 58, no. 2 (1956): 282–292.

Kunanbaeva, Alma. "Kazakh Music." In Danielson et al., eds., *The Garland Encyclopedia of World Music.* Vol. 6, *The Middle East,* 956–958. New York: Routledge, 2002.

Kyrgys, Zoya K. "Pesennaia kul'tura tuvinskogo naroda" [The vocal culture of the Tuvan People]. Kyzyl: Tuvinskoe Knizhnoe Izdatel'stvo, 1992.

———. *Tuvinskoe gorlovoe penie* [Tuvan throat-singing]. Novosibirsk: Nauka, 2002.

Larionova, A. S. "Yakuty" [The Yakuts]. In vol. 1, book 1, *Traditsionnaia kul'tura korennykh narodov sibiri* [Traditional culture of the native peoples of Siberia] of *Muzykal'naia kul'tura sibiri* [The musical culture of Siberia], ed. B. A. Shindin, 185–208. Novosibirsk: Novosibirsk State Conservatory, 1997.

Lawergren, Bo. "The Ancient Harp from Pazyryk." *Beitrage zur allgemeinen und vergleichenden Archäologie* 9–10 (1990): 111–118.

———. "The Spread of Harps between the Near and Far East during the First Millennium A.D.: Evidence of Buddhist Musical Cultures on the Silk Road." *Silk Road Art and Archaeology* 4 (1995–96) [Journal of the Institute of Silk Road Studies, Kamakura]: 233–275.

Leroi-Gourhan, André. *Gesture and Speech.* Trans. Anna Bostock Berger. Cambridge, Mass.: MIT Press, 1993.

Levin, Theodore. *The Hundred Thousand Fools of God: Musical Travels in Central Asia (and Queens, New York).* Bloomington: Indiana University Press, 1996.

Levin, Theodore, and Michael Edgerton. "The Throat Singers of Tuva." *Scientific American* 281, no. 3 (September 1999): 70–77.

Levin, Theodore, and Razia Sultanova. "Classical Music of the Uzbeks and Tajiks." In Danielson et al., eds. *The Garland Encyclopedia of World Music.* Vol. 6, *The Middle East,* 909–920. New York: Routledge, 2002.

Lévi-Strauss, Claude. *The Raw and the Cooked.* Trans. John and Doreen Weightman. New York: Harper and Row, 1969.

Lindquist, Galina. *Shamanic Performances on the Urban Scene: Neoshamanism in Contemporary Sweden.* Stockholm: Stockholm University, Stockholm Studies in Social Anthropology 39, 1997.

Love, J. W., et al. "Musical Instruments." In *The Garland Encyclopedia of World Music.* Vol. 9, *Australia and the Pacific Islands,* ed. Adrienne L. Kaeppler and J. W. Love, 371–403. New York: Garland Publishing, 1998.

Mainogasheva, V. E. "O Khakasskom geroicheskom epose i alyptyx nymaxe 'Aï-Xuuchin' [On Xakas heroic epic and the heroic tale Ai-Xuuchyn]. In *Xakasskii geroicheskii epos Ai-Xuuchyn* [The Xakas heroic epic Ai-Xuuchyn], 11–47. Vol. 2 of *Pamiatniki fol'klora narodov sibiri i dal'nego vostoka* [Monuments of the folklore of Siberian and Far Eastern peoples]. Russian Academy of Sciences, Siberian Branch, Institute of Philology. Novosibirsk: Nauka, 1997.

Mänchen-Helfen, Otto. *Journey to Tuva*. Trans. Alan Leighton. Los Angeles: Ethnographics Press, 1992. Originally published as *Reise ins asiatische Tuwa*. Berlin: Der Bücherkreis, 1931.

Marsh, Peter. *The Horse-head Fiddle and the Cosmopolitan Reimagination of Tradition in Mongolia*. New York: Routledge, 2005.

McClary, Susan. *Feminine Endings: Music, Gender, and Sexuality*. Minneapolis: University of Minnesota Press, 1991.

Miller, Geoffrey. "Evolution of Human Music through Sexual Selection." In *The Origins of Music*, ed. Nils L. Wallin, Björn Merker, and Steven Brown, 329–360. Cambridge, Mass.: MIT Press, 2000.

Molino, Jean. "Toward an Evolutionary Theory of Music and Language." In *The Origins of Music*, ed. Nils L. Wallin, Björn Merker, and Steven Brown, 165–176. Cambridge, Mass.: MIT Press, 2000.

Mongush, Marina Vasil'evna. *Istoriia buddizma v Tuve (vtoraia polovina 6ogo–konets 20ogo v.)* [The history of Buddhism in Tuva (second half of the sixth–end of the twentieth centuries)]. Novosibirsk: Nauka, 2001.

———. "The Tuvinians in China: Aspects of Their History, Language, and Culture." In Humphrey and Sneath, eds., *Culture and Environment in Inner Asia*, vol. 2, 116–133. Cambridge, U.K.: White Horse Press, 1996.

Morgan, David. *The Mongols*. Oxford: Blackwell, 1990.

Moyle, Natalie Kononenko. *The Turkish Minstrel Tale Tradition*. New York: Garland Publishing, 1990.

Muxambetova, Asiya, ed. *Kurmangazy i traditsionnaia muzyka na rubezhe tysiacheletii* [Qurmanghazy and traditional music at the turn of the millennium: proceedings of an international conference dedicated to the 175th anniversary of Qurmanghazy's birth, Almaty, November 9–11, 1998]. Almaty: Daik-Press, 1998.

Myers, John. "Musical Genres in China: Instruments: *Pipa*." In *The Garland Encyclopedia of World Music*. Vol. 7, *East Asia: China, Japan, and Korea*, ed. Robert C. Provine, Yosihiko Tokumaru, and J. Lawrence Witzleben, 167–170. New York: Routledge, 2002.

Naipaul, V. S. "A Second Visit." In *The Writer and the World*. Introduced and ed. Pankaj Mishra. New York: Alfred A. Knopf, 2002.

Nattiez, Jean-Jacques. "The Contribution of Musical Semiotics to the Semiotic Discussion in General." In *A Perfusion of Signs*, ed. Thomas A. Sebeok, 121–142. Bloomington: Indiana University Press, 1977.

Neumann, Erich. *Art and the Creative Unconscious*. Princeton, N.J.: Princeton University Press, 1959.

Ondar. *Back Tuva Future*. Compact disc. Warner Brothers Records, 1999.

Panofsky, Erwin. *Gothic Architecture and Scholasticism*. New York: Meridian Books, 1957.

Pegg, Carole. *Mongolian Music, Dance, and Oral Narrative*. Seattle: University of Washington Press, 2001.

Picken, Laurence E. R. "The Origin of the Short Lute." *Galpin Society Journal* 8 (1966): 32–42.

Pika, Aleksandr, ed. *Neotraditionalism in the Russian North*. Edmonton: Canadian Circumpolar Institute Press and Seattle: University of Washington Press, 1999.

Plato. *The Republic of Plato*. Trans. Francis MacDonald Cornford. 1st American ed. New York: Oxford University Press, 1945.

Potapov, Leonid Pavlovich. *Altaiskii shamanizm* [Altai shamanism]. Leningrad: Nauka, 1991.

———. "The Shaman Drum as a Source of Ethnographical History." In *Shamanism in Siberia*, ed. Vilmos Diószegi and Mihály Hoppál, 169–181. Budapest: Akadémiai Kiadó, 1978.

Powers, Harold. "Illustrated Inventories of Indian Rāgamālā Painting." Review article. *Journal of the American Oriental Society* 100, no. 4 (1980): 473–493.

Reeder, Ellen D., ed. *Scythian Gold: Treasures from Ancient Ukraine*. New York: Harry N. Abrams in association with the Walters Art Gallery and the San Antonio Museum of Art, 1999.

Reichl, Karl. *Singing the Past: Turkic and Medieval Heroic Poetry*. Ithaca, N.Y.: Cornell University Press, 2000.

Roerich, Nicholas. *Altai-Himalaya: A Travel Diary*. New York: Frederick A. Stokes Company, 1929. Reprint. Brookfield, Conn.: Arun Press, 1983.

Roseman, Marina. *Healing Sounds from the Malaysian Rainforest: Temiar Music and Medicine*. Berkeley and Los Angeles: University of California Press, 1991.

Roux, Jean-Paul. "La Danse Chamanique de l'Asie Centrale. In *Les Danses Sacrées*. Paris: Éditions du Seuil, 1963.

———. *La religion des turcs et des mongols*. Paris: Payot, 1984.

Rudenko, Sergei I. *Frozen Tombs of Siberia*. Trans. M. W. Thompson. Berkeley and Los Angeles: University of California Press, 1970.

Sagalaev, A(ndrei) M(arkovich), and I. V. Oktiabr'skaia. *Traditsionnoe mirovozzrenie tiurkov Iuzhnoi Sibiri: Znak i ritual* [The traditional worldview of the Turks of South Siberia: Sign and ritual]. Novosibirsk: Nauka, 1990.

Samuels, David W. *Putting a Song on Top of It: Expression and Identity on the San Carlos Apache Reservation*. Tucson: University of Arizona Press, 2004.

Schafer, Edward H. *The Golden Peaches of Samarkand: A Study of T'ang Exotics*. Berkeley and Los Angeles: University of California Press, 1963.

Schorske, Carl. *Fin-de-Siècle Vienna*. New York: Vintage Books, 1981.

Sedgwick, Mark. *Against the Modern World: Traditionalism and the Secret Intellectual History of the Twentieth Century*. New York: Oxford University Press, 2004.

Sheikin, Y(uri) I. *Istoriia muzykal'noi kul'tury narodov Sibiri: sravnitel'no-istoricheskoe issledovanie* [History of the musical culture of Siberian peoples: comparative-historical research]. Moscow: Vostochnaia Literatura, 2002.

——— and V. S. Nikiforova. "Altaiskoe epicheskoe intonirovanie" [Altai epic intonation]. In *Altaiskie geroicheskie skazaniia Ochi-Bala [i] Kan-Altyn* [The Altai heroic tales Ochi-Bala and Kan-Altyn], 47–70. Vol. 15 of *Pamiatniki fol'klora narodov sibiri i dal'nego vostoka* [Monuments of the folklore of Siberian and Far Eastern peoples]. Russian Academy of Sciences, Siberian Branch, Institute of Philology. Novosibirsk: Nauka, 1997.

Shevtsov, V. N. "Okhotnich'e-skotovodcheskie zvukopodrazhaniia i vozglasy u khakasov" [Hunting and cattle-raising sound imitations and cries among the Khakas]. In *Muzykal'naia etnografiia severnoi azii* 10 [Musical ethnography of Northern Asia], ed. Yuri I. Sheikin, 108–129. Novosibirsk: Novosibirsk State Conservatory, 1988.

Shirokogoroff, Sergei. *Psychomental Complex of the Tungus.* London: Kegan Paul, 1935. Reprint. New York: AMS Press, 1982.

———. "The Shaman's Assistant." In *Shamans Through Time: 500 Years on the Path to Knowledge,* ed. Jeremy Narby and Francis Huxley, 90–93. New York: Jeremy Tarcher/ Putnam, 2001.

Smith, Huston, and Kenneth Stevens. "Unique Vocal Abilities of Certain Tibetan Lamas." *American Anthropologist* 69, no. 2 (1967): 209–212.

Smith, Huston, Kenneth N. Stevens, and Raymond S. Tomlinson. "On an Unusual Mode of Chanting by Certain Tibetan Lamas." *Journal of the Acoustical Society of America* 41, no. 5 (1967): 1262–1264.

Stanner, W.E.H. *On Aboriginal Religion.* Sydney: University of Sydney, 1989.

Stravinsky, Igor. *An Autobiography.* New York: Simon and Schuster, 1936. Reprint. W. W. Norton, 1962.

Strehlow, T.G.H. *Songs of Central Australia.* Sydney: Angus and Robertson, 1971.

Subanaliev, Sagynaly. *Traditsionnaia instrumental'naia muzyka i instrumentii* kyrgyzov [Traditional instrumental music and instruments of the Kyrgyz]. Bishkek: Uchkun, 2003.

Süzükei, Valentina. *Burdonno-obertonovaia osnova traditsionnogo instrumental'nogo muzit-sirovaniia tuvintsev* [The drone-overtone basis of traditional instrumental music-making of the Tuvans]. Kyzyl: Tuvinskii nauchno-issledovatel'skii institut iazyka, literatury, i istorii [Tuvan Research Institute of Language, Literature, and History], 1993.

———. *Tuvinskie traditsionnye muzykal'nye instrumenty* [Tuvan traditional musical instruments]. Kyzyl: Tuvinskii nauchno-issledovatel'skii institut iazyka, literatury, i istorii [Tuvan Research Institute of Language, Literature, and History], 1989.

———. *Muzykal'naia kul'tura Tuvy v dvadtsatom stoletii* [The musical culture of Tuva in the twentieth century]. Forthcoming.

———. "Tuvintsy" [The Tuvans]. In vol. 1, book 1, *Traditsionnaia kul'tura korennykh narodov sibiri* [Traditional culture of the native peoples of Siberia] of *Muzykal'naia kul'tura sibiri* [The musical culture of Siberia], ed. B. A. Shindin, 346–365. Novosibirsk: Novosibirsk State Conservatory, 1997.

Taruskin, Richard. *Stravinsky and the Russian Traditions: A Biography of the Works through Mavra.* Berkeley and Los Angeles: University of California Press, 1996.

Tasmagambetov, Imangali, and Zainolla Samashev. *Saraishyq/Saraichik.* Almaty: Berel, 2001.

Tatarintsev, Boris. *Tuvinskoe gorlovoe penie: problemy proiskhozhdeniia* [Problems of the origins of Tuvan throat-singing]. Kyzyl: Mezhdunarodnyi nauchnyi tsentr "Xöömei" [International scholarly center "Xöömei"], 1998.

Taube, Erika. *Skazki i predaniye altaiskikh tuvintsev* [Tales and legends of the Altai Tuvans]. Moscow: Vostochnoi Literatury, 1994.

———. *Sovremennoe sostoyanie traditsionnykh form byta i kul'tury tsengel'skikh tuvintsev* [The contemporary state of traditional forms of life and culture among the Tsengel Tuvans]. Warsaw: Etnografia Polska, 1981.

Taussig, Michael. *Mimesis and Alterity: A Particular History of the Senses.* New York: Routledge, 1993.

Tchoroev, Tyntchtykbek. "Historiography of Post-Soviet Kyrgyzstan." *International Journal of Middle East Studies* 34, no. 2 (2002): 351–374.

Tengir-Too: Mountain Music of Kyrgyzstan. Compact disc/DVD. Smithsonian Folkways Recordings SFW CD 40520, 2006.

Thomas, Nicholas, and Caroline Humphrey. *Shamanism, History, and the State.* Ann Arbor: University of Michigan Press, 1996.

Trân Quang Hai. "A la découverte du chant diphonique." In *Moyens d'investigation et pedagogie de la voix chantée: actes du colloque tenu les 8, 9, et 10 février 2001 au Conservatoire national de région de Lyon. . . .*, ed. Guy Cornut, 117–132. Lyon: Symétrie, 2002.

Turner, Terrence. "'We are parrots,' 'Twins are birds': Play of tropes as operational structure." In *Beyond Metaphor: The Theory of Tropes in Anthropology*, ed. James W. Fernandez, 121–158. Stanford: Stanford University Press, 1991.

Tuva, Among the Spirits: Sound, Music, and Nature in Sakha and Tuva. Produced by Theodore Levin and Joel Gordon. Compact disc. Smithsonian Folkways SFW 40452, 1999.

Tuva: Voices from the Center of Asia. Compact disc. Produced by Eduard Alekseev, Zoya Kyrgys, and Theodore Levin. Smithsonian Folkways SF 40017, 1990.

Tuva: Voices from the Land of the Eagles. Soloists of the Tuva Ensemble. Compact disc. Pan Records 2050, 1991.

Uspensky, Viktor Aleksandrovich, and Viktor Mikhailovich Beliaev. *Turkmenskaia muzyka* [Turkmen music]. Ed. Shakhym Gullyev. Almaty: Soros Fund—Kazakhstan, 2003. Originally published in Moscow: Muzgiz, 1928 (vol. 1) and Moscow: n.p., 1936 (vol. 2).

Uzbekistan: Music of Khorezm. Produced by Otanazar Matyakubov and Theodore Levin. Compact disc. UNESCO/Auvidis D 8269, 1996.

Vainshtein, Sevyan. "The Êrens in Tuvan Shamanism." In *Shamanism in Siberia*, ed. Vilmos Diószegi and Mihály Hoppál, 457–476. Budapest: Akadémiai Kiadó, 1978.

———. "A Musical Phenomenon Born in the Steppes." *Soviet Anthropology and Archaeology* 18, no. 3 (1979–80): 68–81. First published as "Fenomen muzykal'nogo iskusstva, rozhdennyi v stepiakh." *Sovietskaia etnografiia*, no. 1 (1980): 149–159.

———. *Nomads of South Siberia: The Pastoral Economies of Tuva.* Ed. and with an introduction by Caroline Humphrey. Trans. Michael Colenso. Cambridge: Cambridge University Press, 1980. First published as *Istoricheskaia etnografiia tuvintsev* [Historical ethnography of the Tuvans]. Moscow: Nauka, 1972.

———. *Tuvintsy-Todzhintsy* [The Tuvan-Todzhins]. Moscow: Vostochnoi Literatury, 1961.

Van Deusen, Kira. "The Shamanic Gift and the Performing Arts in Siberia." In *Shamanskii Dar* [The Shamanic Gift], ed. V. I. Kharitonova, 223–239. Moscow: Russian Academy of Sciences, Institute of Ethnology and Anthropology, 2000.

———. *Singing Story, Healing Drum: Shamans and Storytellers of Turkic Siberia.* Montreal: McGill-Queen's University Press and Seattle: University of Washington Press, 2004.

van Tongeren, Mark C. *Overtone Singing: Physics and Metaphysics of Harmonics in East and West.* Revised 2d ed. Amsterdam: Fusica, 2004.

Vertov, K., G. Blagodatov, and E. Iazovitskaia. *Atlas muzykal'nykh instrumentov narodov sssr* [Atlas of musical instruments of the peoples of the USSR]. Moscow: State Musical Press, 1963.

Vinogradov, Andrei. "Ak Jang in the Context of Altai Religious Tradition." Master's degree thesis, University of Saskatchewan, 2003.

Volkov, Solomon. *Testimony: The Memoirs of Dmitri Shostakovich.* Trans. Antonina W. Bouis. New York: Harper and Row, 1979.

Wade, Nicholas. "Early Voices: The Leap to Language." *New York Times,* July 15, 2003.

Wallin, Nils L., Björn Merker, and Steven Brown. *The Origins of Music.* Cambridge, Mass.: MIT Press, 2000.

Watt, James C. Y. "The Legacy of Nomadic Art in China and Eastern Central Asia." In Bunker, ed., *Nomadic Art of the Eastern Eurasian Steppes,* 198–209. New York: Metropolitan Museum of Art, 2002.

Westermarck, Edward. *Ritual and Belief in Morocco.* London: Macmillan, 1926.

Wills, Gary. "The Day the Enlightenment Went Out." *New York Times,* November 4, 2004, op-ed page.

Xakas Institute of Language, Literature and History. *Istoriia xakasii s drevneishikh vremen do 1917 goda* [The history of Xakasia from the earliest times until 1917]. Moscow: Nauka/Vostochnaia Literatura, 1993.

Yanagi, Sōetsu. *The Unknown Craftsman: A Japanese Insight into Beauty.* Tokyo/New York/London: Kodansha International, [1972] 1989.

Yenhu, Tsui. "A Comparative Study of the Attitudes of the Peoples of Pastoral Areas of Inner Asia Towards their Environments." In Humphrey and Sneath, eds., *Culture and Environment in Inner Asia,* vol. 2: 1–24. Cambridge, U.K.: White Horse Press, 1996.

Zataevich, Aleksandr Viktorovich. *250 kirgizskikh instrumental'nykh p'es i napevov* [250 Kyrgyz instrumental songs and tunes]. Moscow: n.p., 1934.

———. *500 kazakhskikh pesen i kuiev* [500 Kazakh songs and *kuis*]. Alma-Ata: n.p., 1931.

———. *1000 pesen kirgizskogo naroda* [1,000 songs of the Kyrgyz people]. Orenburg: n.p., 1925.

———. Kirgizskie instrumental'nye p'esy i napevy [Kyrgyz instrumental songs and tunes]. Comp. and ed. V. Vinogradov. Moscow: n.p., 1971.

Zemp, Hugo. *Voix de tête, voix de poitrine* [Head Voice, Chest Voice]. 16 mm film/VHS recording. Coproduced by Ateliers d'ethnomusicologie (Geneva) and CNRS Audiovisuel, 1987.

Zemp, Hugo, and Trân Quang Hai. "Recherches expérimentales sur le chant diphonique." *Cahiers de Musiques Traditionnelles* 4 (1991): 27–68.

Zhukovskaia, N. L. "Lamaism in Tuva." *Anthropology and Archeology of Eurasia* 39, no. 4 (2001): 48–49.

Znamenski, Andrei A. *Shamanism and Christianity: Native Encounters with Russian Orthodox Missions in Siberia and Alaska, 1820–1917.* Westport, Conn.: Greenwood Press, 1999.

———. *Shamanism in Siberia: Russian Records of Indigenous Spirituality.* Dordrecht, The Netherlands: Kluwer Academic Publishers, 2003.

Zuckerkandl, Victor. *Sound and Symbol.* Trans. Willard R. Trask. New York: Pantheon Books, 1956.

INDEX

ACCESSING
AUDIO FILES

Audio clips are available for this volume at https://media.dlib.indiana.edu /collections/sn00bg13s. A list of tracks follows.

Track No.	Duration	Description	Performer	Page
1	0:51	Evening Roundup in Chandman, Mongolia	***	40
2	1:03	Wind Harmonics on Stringed Instruments	***	39
3	1:01	Artyy-Saiyr	Vasili Chazyr	52
4	1:12	Alash	Mergen Mongush	53
5	0:53	*Kargyraa* in a Cave	Anatoli Kuular	36
6	0:51	*Kargyraa*	Eres-ool Mongush	54
7	0:56	*Xöömei*	Sundukai Mongush	55
8	2:22	Jew's Harp	Oleg Kuular	56
9	2:18	The River Herlen	Xongorzul	57
10	2:46	*Borbangnadyr* with Water	Anatoli Kuular	60
11	1:59	*Kai*: My Topshuur	Sarymai Orchimaev	63
12	1:04	Buyant Gol	Sengedorj	68
13	1:13	Gooj Nanaa	Sengedorj	68
14	0:35	*Amyrga*	Maar-ool Sat	79
15	0:33	Two Lovers on Horseback	Gombojav	83
16	0:34	Running Horse	Gombojav	83
17	0:23	Wounded Bear	Gombojav	83
18	0:39	Young Show-off	Gombojav	83
19	0:40	Camel Gait	Gombojav	83

Track No.	*Duration*	*Description*	*Performer*	*Page*
19	0:40	Camel Gait	Gombojav	83
20	1:14	Animal Sound Mimicry	Albert Saspyk-ool	85
21	1:32	Animal Sound Mimicry	Alexander Tülüsh	87
22	1:21	Mountain *Kargyraa*	Aldyn-ool Sevek	89
23	0:56	Steppe *Kargyraa*	Aldyn-ool Sevek	89
24	1:14	Contour of Altai Mountains	Gombojav	92
25	1:19	Contour of Hangai Mountains	Gombojav	92
26	1:09	The Sound of a Mountain Singing	Evgeni Ulugbashev	93
27	3:16	Mountain Voices	Evgeni Ulugbashev	94
28	0:55	Shanchyg	Anatoli Kuular	97
29	2:17	Gallop of Jonon Har	Bat-Erdene	111
30	1:36	Talking Jew's Harp	Sarymai Orchimaev	116
31	1:22	The River Eev	Deleg Bayansair	123
32	1:08	Black-Spotted Yak	Dari Bandi	136
33	4:01	Animal Signals	Dari Bandi	136
34	0:49	Sheep Domestication Song (Mongolia)	Gombosurengiin Begzjav	138
35	0:33	Sheep Domestication Song (Tuva)	Doluma Lopsanchap	138
36	0:56	Yak-Milking Melody	Tserenedimit	139
37	3:01	Chyraa-Xor	Huun-Huur-Tu	148
38	2:34	*Xöömei* on Horseback	Anatoli Kuular and Kaigal-ool Xovalyg	148
39	1:21	*Ezenggileer*	Marjymal Ondar	148
40	4:15	Ancestors	Huun-Huur-Tu	217

Total 60:00

ACCESSING
VIDEO FILES

Video clips are available for this volume at https://media.dlib.indiana.edu
/collections/sn00bg13s. A list of tracks follows.

THEODORE LEVIN

began his musical travels in Inner Asia in 1974, and has been traveling there ever since. He holds a Ph.D. in music from Princeton University and is Professor of Music at Dartmouth College. As an advocate for music and musicians from other cultures, he has produced recordings, curated concerts and festivals, and contributed to international arts initiatives. His first book, *The Hundred Thousand Fools of God: Musical Travels in Central Asia (and Queens, New York)*, was published by Indiana University Press.

VALENTINA SÜZÜKEI

received her *Kandidat* degree from the Russian Institute of the History of Art in Saint Petersburg and holds the position of senior academic officer of the Tuvan Institute for Humanities Research in Kyzyl, Tuva. She is author of three books on Tuvan music, including a forthcoming book on the musical culture of Tuva in the twentieth century.

CPSIA information can be obtained
at www.ICGtesting.com
Printed in the USA
LVHW081833120722
723326LV00004B/48